PERSPECTIVES IN
PHONOLOGY

CSLI
Lecture Notes
No. 51

PERSPECTIVES IN PHONOLOGY

edited by
Jennifer Cole and Charles Kisseberth

CSLI Publications
CENTER FOR THE STUDY OF
LANGUAGE AND INFORMATION
STANFORD, CALIFORNIA

Copyright ©1994
Center for the Study of Language and Information
Leland Stanford Junior University
Printed in the United States
99 98 97 96 95 94   5 4 3 2 1

Library of Congress Cataloging-in-Publication Data

Perspectives in phonology / edited by Jennifer Cole and Charles Kisseberth.
    p.   cm. – (CSLI lecture notes ; no. 51)
    Includes bibliographical references.
    ISBN 1-881526-55-0 – ISBN 1-881526-54-2 (pbk.)
    1. Grammar, Comparative and general—Phonology. I. Cole, Jennifer (Jennifer S.) II. Kisseberth, Charles W. III. Series.
    P217.P44 1994
    414—dc20   94-30497
                                            CIP

CSLI was founded early in 1983 by researchers from Stanford University, SRI International, and Xerox PARC to further research and development of integrated theories of language, information, and computation. CSLI headquarters and CSLI Publications are located on the campus of Stanford University.

CSLI Lecture Notes report new developments in the study of language, information, and computation. In addition to lecture notes, the series includes monographs, working papers, and conference proceedings. Our aim is to make new results, ideas, and approaches available as quickly as possible.

Contents

A Dynamic Computational Theory of Accent Systems   1
JOHN GOLDSMITH

The Russian Declension: An Illustration of the Theory of Distributed Morphology   29
MORRIS HALLE

Weight of CVC can be Determined by Context   61
BRUCE HAYES

Cyclic Phonology and Morphology in Cibemba   81
LARRY M. HYMAN

On Metrical Constituents: Unbalanced Trochees and Degenerate Feet   113
MICHAEL KENSTOWICZ

On Domains   133
CHARLES W. KISSEBERTH

Syntactic and Semantic Conditions in Kikongo Phrasal Phonology   167
DAVID ODDEN

Complex Onsets as Single Segments: The Mazateco Pattern   203
DONCA STERIADE

Isolated Uses of Prosodic Categories   293
MOIRA YIP

Preface

This collection of papers grew out of a conference held in May, 1991 at the University of Illinois at Urbana-Champaign, in celebration of the twenty-fifth anniversary of the Department of Linguistics. The goal of the conference was to provide a forum for the discussion of some of the leading ideas and innovations in phonology today. Over one hundred researchers and students participated in presentations and lively debate. The conference imposed no single theme under which all of the papers were organized, and the papers in this volume address a range of issues and problems in current phonological theory, examining many levels of phonological representation.

Segment Structure. At the level of segment structure, **Steriade** examines the representation of consonants in phonology, and proposes that the aperture positions of closure and release constitute nodes in feature structure which serve as anchors for other distinctive features. With this idea, she accounts for a wide range of properties of the complex consonant articulations in Mazateco, and other Amerindian languages.

Stress. Looking beyond segmental phonology to the domain of the suprasegmental, we have three papers that deal with the analysis of stress in phonological theory. **Hayes** presents arguments from the stress systems of Cahuilla, Latin, and Yupik that the weight assigned to a CVC syllable can vary, even within a single language. He argues that a CVC syllable may be heavy or light, according to the broader phonological context in which it occurs. **Kenstowicz** considers some of the important differences between two influential theories of stress: the Halle-Vergnaud theory of the bracketed grid, and the rhythmic theory developed by Hayes and by McCarthy & Prince. He examines the treatment of heavy-light sequences and orphan light syllables in a wide range of languages, including Latin, Manam, Swedish, Auca, Winnebago, Old English, and several Arabic dialects. Through his careful comparison, the reader gains a clear picture both of the range of data that both theories must account for, and the sort of empirical evidence which will render support for either theory. Still looking at stress, but from an entirely different perspective, **Goldsmith** considers how the properties of quantity-insensitive stress systems can arise out of a dynamic computational theory, without recourse to the symbolic representations of metrical constituent structure that form the basis of the standard approach. Within a strictly linear model of representation, Goldsmith treats stress prominence as a function of the inherent or positional weight of a syllable and the weight influence exerted by adjacent syllables. He adopts a dynamic computational network, a network consisting of units with an associated arithmetic for calculating their relative weight, as the formal device to model stress. His approach is intended to replace standard derivational analyses with their extrinsically ordered rules, and operates without explicit rules of stress assignment or parsing.

Metrical Structure and Domains. The papers by Hayes and Kenstowicz deal with stress as a manifestation of metrical constituent structure, and as such address more broadly the nature of metrical structure and its theoretical explanation. Along these lines, **Yip** examines the role of metrical structure in Chinese. She argues that despite the lack of any obvious cues, the metrical constituents of mora, syllable and foot play an important role in the phonology and morphology of some Chinese dialects. Although there is no independent evidence for the existence of metrical structure in Chinese phonology from syllable weight distinctions, resyllabification or alternating stress, her analysis shows that the mora, syllable, and iambic foot all play a role in determining well-formedness in loanword phonology, templatic morphology, and other prosodic phonological processes. She claims that her conclusions support a theory in which metrical constituents are part of the core vocabulary of universal grammar. Drawing on the theory of metrical constituents, or domains, **Kisseberth** demonstrates that the principles of foot construction used to parse feet in stress systems can be employed to create domains for the realization of high tones in Xitsonga. The domains-based analysis provides a principled account of a complex system of tone displacement and tone spread in that language.

Tone. In addition to Kisseberth's analysis of Xitsonga tone, the paper by **Odden** examines the tonal properties of Kikongo, focusing on the interaction of phonology, syntax and semantics. He considers the properties of phrase structure and quantifier structure that bear on the realization of tone, and argues that the phonological component needs direct access to information from other grammatical components. The tonal problems he considers involve deletion of a lexical high tone in a variety of complex environments.

Phonology Interfaces. Odden's paper provides an excellent demonstration of the interaction between phonology and other grammatical components in tonal phonology, and **Hyman** addresses the role of morphology in defining cyclic phonological domains in the segmental phonology of Cibemba. He discusses consonant mutations induced by suffixation that have apparent non-local applications. He proposes a cyclic analysis in which the morphological structure [[[Root] Caus] Appl] defines two cyclic domains for consonant mutation, but is restructured by infixation to produce the surface form Root-Appl-Caus. Hyman considers and rejects alternative non-cyclic and morphological explanations, and demonstrates how a two-level, non-derivational approach can account for the facts.

Morphology. Understanding the interaction between phonology and morphology is just part of the larger problem of understanding the role of morphology in grammar as a whole. A range of proposals exist, which treat morphology as an aspect of syntax, as an aspect of the lexicon, or as an independent module. **Halle** presents a model of Distributed Morphology, in which morphology is distributed among various grammatical components, including the syntax-semantics module, the vocabulary, and the word-synthesis and morpho-phonological modules. With this framework, he presents an analysis of Russian noun declension in which abstract morphemes, specified for syntactic and grammatical properties but unspecified in phonological form, are used to account for complex paradigms of morpho-phonological alternation.

Acknowledgements

We are grateful to the University of Illinois Department of Linguistics for their support of the conference on *The Organization of Phonology: Features and Domains*, in recognition of the twenty-fifth anniversary of the department. We thank the sponsors of the conference at the University of Illinois: Beckman Institute for Advanced Science and Technology, Cognitive Science/ Artificial Intelligence Steering Committee, College of Liberal Arts and Science, and the Department of Linguistics. A special thanks to all the people who presented papers at the conference, and for their patience in waiting for this volume to be published. We appreciate the assistance of Lynn Murphy, and the support of the University of Illinois Research Board grant which funded her work in preparing this manuscript for publication.

We are very appreciative of the talent and hard work supplied in large doses by Linda May in producing the final LaTex version of this document.

A Dynamic Computational Theory of Accent Systems

John Goldsmith
The University of Chicago

1 Introduction

The purpose of this paper is to describe the basic functioning of dynamic computational theories, and to show how this family of theories can be applied to provide a revealing typology of quantity-insensitive accentual systems.[1] To this end, we will discuss quantity-sensitive systems briefly—in part, to reveal the nature of the boundary between the two types of systems. We will illustrate how the mechanisms of this theory operate to provide linguistic accounts of systems that are familiar to phonologists working in this area, and for this reason, I have focused in the presentation on accentual systems which have been discussed at some length in the literature, and on generalizations for which considerable evidence has been amassed.

In a sense, this work is the study of an alternative account of linearity in phonology. There is a small irony to this observation: most of the important work in phonological theory over the last fifteen years or so, the work of the post-SPE period, has focused on developing an account of phonological representations that overcomes the limitations inherent in the assumption of complete linearity in phonological representations used in the classical period of generative phonology. To say that there is something more or something new to study in the structure of linear representations sounds off-beat, if not downright *rétro*.

But there is much to be done, in fact. Just as autosegmental phonology explored, and explores, the consequences of multi-linear representation for phonology and develops the ways in which this richer conception of phonological representation provides explanations for phenomena which flow structurally out of the architecture of the representational model, so too the present dynamic theory offers a new account for some of the fundamental properties of phonological systems – first and foremost, their rhythmicity – an account in which these properties derive from the basic representational architecture, rather than a system of rules distinct and separate from the representational base.

---

[1] I am grateful to Gary Larson, Caroline Wiltshire, and Jessie Pinkham for their assistance in the preparation of this paper. This material is based upon work supported by the National Science Foundation under Grant No. BNS 9009678.

Our view of linear representation has traditionally been that it is simply a matter of concatenation, the most simple and trivial relationship that can exist between the successive units that make up a linear sequence. The units simply *appear*, one after another, on such an account. Dynamic computational theories drop this assumption, and adopt what is, I would suggest, the next most simple assumption—though one which is, to be sure, more general than the simple concatenation assumption. Dynamic computational theories explore the premise that successive units in a phonological string enter into specific, quantitative relationships with their left- and right-hand neighbors, relationships that give rise automatically to the fundamental patterns of rhythmicity that we observe in most accentual systems.

The theory that I present may give the impression at first glance of being a computer implementation of a familiar theory—metrical theory, in the event. That is not at all the message I wish to convey. The fact that I have used a computer to perform the calculations and present the results graphically[2] is simply a matter of convenience, since the calculations that formulas such as (2) require would be wearisome and best left to a simple calculator. We are accustomed to thinking that our phonological rules, as we formulate them on paper, are well formalized, but rarely subject that assumption to test; generative phonologists, quite rightly, do take it for granted that a formal implementation of their rule system is a necessary, not a dispensable, part of the task. The computations offered below are not an implementation of traditional metrical phonology; they are intended to be a replacement of them. Put another way, if the present theory is correct, then familiar derivational metrical theory is a finite approximation to the actual theory of accent, much as the step by step procedure of long division that we learned in school is a particular implementation of the mathematics of division.

We explore problems of accentuation in this paper, for several reasons. First of all, it forms a well-studied subdiscipline in phonology, about which a good deal is known, and an established body of results exists which one can turn to. Second, in many languages, the principles of accentuation are arguably real from a psychological point of view, and do not have the questionable quasi- morphological status of many phonological rules. Thirdly, the present accounts of accent systems typically require complex derivational rule interactions, of the sort that dynamic computational theories

---

[2]The graphs and the calculations in this paper were produced by Quattro Pro 3.0, a spreadsheet program. Spreadsheet programs are excellent "blackboards" for working out the effects of various assumptions within a dynamic computational theory, as Gary Larson pointed out to me; in most cases, they have the additional advantage of producing useful graphical output at the same time as they perform the needed calculation. We are currently producing a set of programs for distribution to linguists interested in exploring this theory, so that they will not need to write their own programs.

disallow; they therefore serve as an instructive testing ground for the ambitions of the approach.

A few words of technical introduction. A dynamic computational theory consists of a linear string of k units, which we may refer to as units u_1, u_2,..., u_k; for our present purposes, these units may be thought of as syllables, and this linear string, or tier, as the metrical grid of familiar metrical theory.[3] Each unit u_i has an activation level at any given time t, which we will denote as u_i^t. That activation is the sum of three things: the positional activation of the unit; the internal activation of the unit; and the lateral activations passed from unit to neighboring unit. This is illustrated schematically in Figure 1. We discuss each factor in turn in a moment. But the main point to recognize is that when given certain elementary specification of its parameters, the system settles into (or calculates) a set of activation values for each unit (that is, each syllable). The calculation of these activation values is (so claims the theory) how the accentual pattern of the word or phrase is established in each natural language.

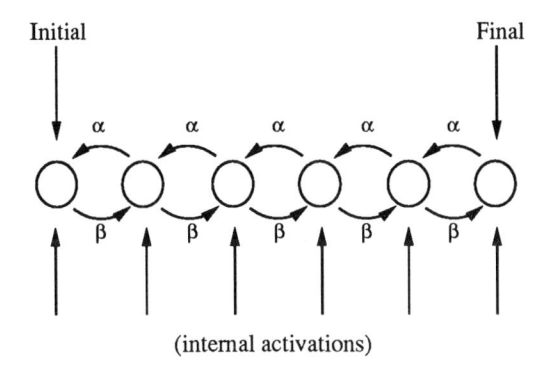

Figure 1: Dynamic computational network

In certain representational respects, this is not radically different from the familiar metrical grid of Liberman (1975), Liberman and Prince (1977), Prince (1983), and others. In metrical grid theory, we find a grid in which a column of x's – grid-marks – is placed over each syllable, in such a fashion that the number of grid marks corresponds to the accentual prominence of the syllable in question, as in (1).

---

[3]In other work, in collaboration with Gary Larson, we have explored a wide range of analyses of sonority and syllabification using precisely the same model.

(1)   x
     x   x
     x x x x
     A la ba ma

Each syllable in the traditional metrical grid is assigned a number, the height of its particular column; we might for the moment call that its "metrical height." In the present dynamic computational theory, each syllable is assigned a number, which differs from its metrical height in three ways: first, the metrical height can only be a positive number, while its activation level can be positive or negative; second, the metrical height can only be an integral value, and its activation level can be any rational number; third, what is phonologically relevant in traditional metrical theory is absolute height, while in dynamic computational models, it is the identification of peaks that is phonologically interpreted, not the absolute height.[4] The important difference, to which we return in a moment, is just how the metrical grid-marks, and the activation levels, are formally arrived at. Let us consider the three sources of activation within the dynamic computational system.

First, there is *positional* activation, which is specific to, and relevant to, only the first and last units of the sequence, units u_1 and u_k. They will be assigned a positional activation equal to I (for "initial") and F ("final"), respectively, in a language-particular fashion. These numbers, like all the numbers in the model, can be negative as well as positive.

The *internal* activation of a unit on the metrical grid is the measure of the syllable's weight, determined, as we know, in a language particular fashion. When all units on the metrical grid are assigned the same internal activation regardless of the internal structure of the syllable in question, we have a quantity-insensitive accentual system, the topic of our extended discussion below.[5] When the internal activation of the syllables varies from syllable to syllable, the result is a quantity-sensitive accentual system.

The *lateral* activations which pass from a unit to its left- and right-hand neighbors form the heart of the present system. Each unit u_i, whose activation is x_i, passes a quantity of activation (sometimes negative, sometimes

---

[4]This third difference is less significant than it may sound, since virtually all lengthy treatments of metrical theory appeal at one point or other to principles which raise or lower the absolute height of a column, or set of columns, for the convenience of the analyst.

[5]In the discussion that follows, we assume that the internal activation for all units is zero. This is not necessarily the case; the internal activation may be the same for all units, but different than zero. This assumption has a significant impact on the results, which we shall return to below in Section 3.

positive) to its left-and right-hand neighbors, a quantity which is a fixed proportion of its own total activation. In particular, we establish once and for all for a given language two important coefficients – fixed numbers – on each given network-tier; we call these coefficients α and β. α is the coefficient that expresses the strength of the activation signal that a given unit sends to its lefthand neighbor, and β is the coefficient that expresses the strength of the activation signal that a unit sends to its righthand neighbor. Thus a unit with an activation level of x_i^t at time t will send a signal of strength $\alpha \cdot x_i^t$ to its left hand neighbor (u_{i-1}) which that unit (u_{i-1}) will use in recomputing its own level of activation at the next instant, that is, at time $t+1$. Similarly, that same unit u_i^t will send a signal of strength $\beta \cdot u_i^t$ to its right hand neighbor (u_{i+1}) which is used in the recomputation of u_{i+1}'s activation level at time $t+1$. All of the units of the system continue to recompute their activation levels, simultaneously, until the system reaches a steady state, or equilibrium (this steady state may be approached asymptotically, to be sure).

Technically, then, each unit in a network composed of k units computes its activation value according to the following equation:

(2) $\quad x_i^{t+1} = P(i) + \alpha \cdot x_{i+1}^t + \beta \cdot x_{i-1}^t + N(i)$

where P(i) indicates positional activation:

$\quad P(1) = I,\ P(k)=F,\ \text{and}\ P(j) = 0\ \text{for all other j}.$[6]

and N(i) indicates internal activation; N(i)=0 for all i, in our initial discussions.

In sum, then, such a network is the basis of the behavior of the metrical grid that we have explored over the past fifteen years. No longer will we have or need, I would suggest, a derivational account of the behavior of the relative prominence of each member of the metrical grid, a derivational account in which structure is assigned step by step, in which rules exist in a fashion distinct from the representation, in which rules are

---

[6] Another way to think of this system is as the nth power of a matrix which is applied to the vector which specifies the initial state of the units. We may think of the initial state of the k units as the k-vector **V**, and we may construct a k by k matrix which represents a single recomputation of the system, that is, a single passage of activation from each unity to its two neighbors. Such a matrix will be all zeros excepts for the supradiagonal $(x_{i,i+1})$, which is everywhere α, and the subdiagonal $(x_{i,i-1})$, which is everywhere β. The system takes on the value $V + M^t$ (V) at time t, where M^t is the tth power of M. This matrix must reach – exactly, or asymptotically – a limit for the system to display the equilibrium state that is necessary for these dynamic computational models.

extrinsically ordered, and in which this extrinsic ordering is the means necessary to express the fact that generalizations (such as alternating stress and stress clash avoidance) can be in conflict, and the only apparent fact that one of the principles will necessarily appear to win out over the other. The goal of the dynamic computational theory is to retain what is valid about our representational theories, and to dispense with the weaknesses of derivational manipulations of those representations, without losing sight of the richnesses and complexities found in naturally occurring phonological systems.

These basic observations are summarized in the following table:

(3)

Network notions	Familiar concepts
Internal activation	syllable weight
Positional activation	End Rule effects
Contextual activation	rhythm/perfect grid; culminative accent

Let us consider a simple example, to illustrate the effects of these local connections. Let us suppose that $\alpha = -.8$ and $\beta = 0$, for simplicity's sake, and that the final unit has a positional activation of 1.0. No other activations are present at the initial state of the system: there is no initial activation (I) on the first unit, and no internal activation. The initial state (represented with the bar graph) and final state (represented by a line graph) are given in (4); the evolution of this system is illustrated in (5), iteration by iteration. We see that a wave of positive and negative activation passes leftward from the end to the beginning of the network; we see that, with a negative value of α, there is an essential rhythmicity built into the architecture of this system.

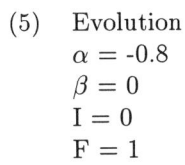

A Dynamic Computational Theory of Accent Systems

(4) Wave from Right to left, Final High:
$\alpha = -0.8$
$\beta = 0$
$I = 0$
$F = 1$

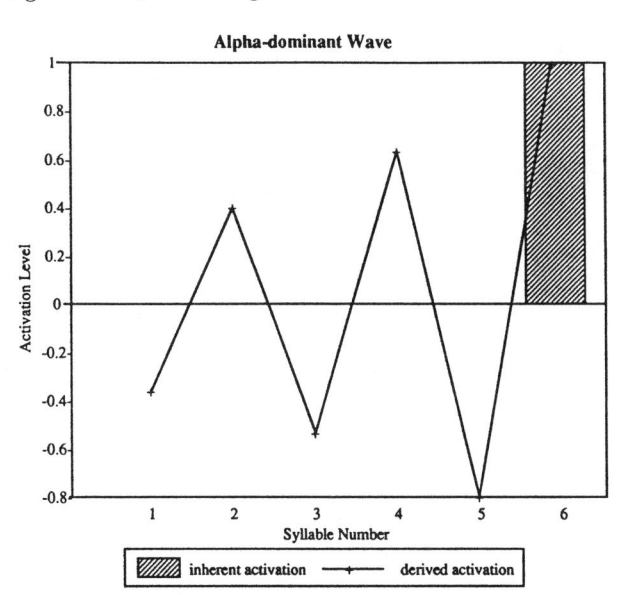

Alpha-dominant Wave

(5) Evolution
$\alpha = -0.8$
$\beta = 0$
$I = 0$
$F = 1$

Alpha-dominant Wave

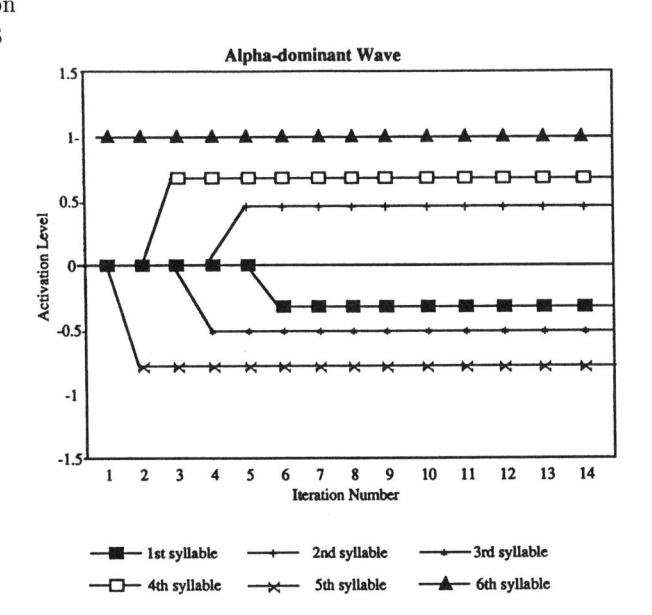

By the same token, we can also see that the rhythmic effects of the system are in large measure independent of the exact choices of the numbers involved. We have chosen in (4) to specify α as -0.8, but any value for α that is between -1.0 and 0.0 will give the same "qualitative" result—a wave with peaks on odd numbered syllables, counting from the end of the word, and troughs on the even numbered syllables. The qualitative character of the system will be an important characteristic of dynamic computational systems.

In this simple example, the rhythmic character seems to be the direct result of a pulse that begins at one end of the word, either the left or the right end. We should observe, however, that much the same rhythmic effect is achieved by assigning to each of the units the same degree of internal activation (1.0, say); we shall refer to this common activation as a *bias*. Such a system is still quantity-insensitive, in the sense that all units receive the same (here, non-zero) activation regardless of their internal structure. We shall return to this characteristic, important for our understanding of the system, in Section 3; for now, we shall assume that bias is zero.

Let us turn now to a consideration of quantity-insensitive accent systems from the point of view of this system.

2 Quantity Insensitive Accent Systems

We consider first a dynamic computational theory of accent for quantity insensitive systems. There are, for such systems, four essential parameters that can be independently varied: I, F, α, and β, as described above (assuming that the bias is zero, as we have noted). I and F represent the positional activation of the first and last syllable; α and β, the left and right coefficients described above. These parameters are fixed, once and for all, for each language; they define what the accentual pattern is for a given language.[7] The logic of this position is a familiar one in current linguistic thought, to be sure, though the particulars here are slightly different; just as one may specify a syntax as being the sum of the settings of the parameters specified by a Universal Grammar, and just as one may specify a metrical system as the sum of the parameter settings (End Rule (Initial, Row 1), for example, or QS [Quantity-sensitive]), so too dynamic computational models consist of a complete set of settings of parameters. The only differences in the present case is that, first of all, the settings need not be selected from a finite set (we have here a continuous set of values to draw from); and second, the parameters here are settings in the representations, not in a distinct set of rules.

---

[7]We will weaken this statement below to allow for I and F to vary across grammatical category. α and β are fixed, once and for all, for a given language's accent system.

The effects of increasing or decreasing the I or F variables is relatively straightforward: an increase in I or F will lead to a greater strength of the first or last syllable, respectively. "Increasing" or "decreasing" is, of course, a linguist's metaphor: the parameters are set once and for all for a given language, and learning a language amounts to discovering the appropriate setting of each parameter. The linguist, however, may wish to – in effect – play with the system, and see what results from varying each parameter's setting; each set of settings specifies a particular possible or existing accentual system.

However, if the effects of increasing I and F are straightforward, the effects of increasing or decreasing α and β are anything but transparent. It will be our goal in this section to explore the behavior of the accent systems that arise from various choices of α and β. A two-dimensional illustration of the space of all values of α and β is given in (6). The region bounded by the four hyperbolas represents the region within which the network will converge; outside of that region, the network will not converge—it will, to the contrary, explode, and not settle into an equilibrium state.[8]

(6) Chart of α versus β

Region of Convergence

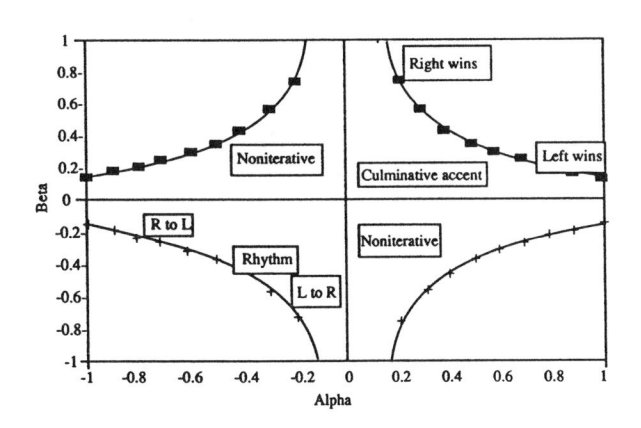

Regions of Convergent Behavior

---

[8]The shape suggests (accurately) that (as Henry Pinkam has pointed out to me) the discriminant of the matrix involved in the evolution of this function is a function of the product xy.

The region in which the dynamic computational theory converges consists of the range of all the possible (and only the possible) quantity-insensitive accentual systems. There are, that is, only four principal parameters to consider: α, β, I, and F, and the quality of the system is largely determined by the choice of α and β, that is, by the location of the system within the coordinates of (6).

We will explore the behavior of the subparts of the graph in (6), beginning with the lower left-hand quadrant, that in which α and β are both negative. As we shall see, the negative values of α and β give rise to rhythmic patterns; after that, we shall explore the other regions, in which positive values may emerge.

Let us review the basics of some metrical systems which have been made familiar to us from the works of Hayes, Halle and Vergnaud, and others. These simple examples represent the basic cases that are familiar to metrical phonologists, and serve for us the end of illustrating how cases whose treatment within the familiar framework of metrical phonology finds a simple account within the present framework.

Weri (Boxwell and Boxwell 1966, discussed in Hayes 1980[9] and Halle and Vergnaud 1987, among other places) presents a system in which the final syllable is accented, as are all odd numbered syllables, counting from the end of the word. This is illustrated in (7). This pattern is achieved by setting α equal to a value between -1.0 and 0: -0.8, in the example in (8); F is equal to a positive number (we may normalize this value to 1.0), and I = 0.0. β is zero, since apparently no activation is passed to the right; we leave it, therefore, at 0.0. The graphic illustration in (8), as with the parallel examples to follow, consists of two descriptions of the system's state: the state described by the bar graph, in which only the 10th unit has a non-zero bar over it, illustrates the initial state of the system, while line graph shows the equilibrium state that it settles into.

(7)   Weri:
      ŋ nt́ p   'bee'
      k̀ p̄ ́   'hair of arm'
      ̆ ̀ am t́   'mist'
      àk nètepál   'times'

The proposal, then, is that the wave of activations illustrated in (8) *is* the prosodic structure of this system; there are no rules other than those that we have discussed. The system directly settles into an equilibrium

---

[9]I am indebted (as are most workers on metrical theory) to the collection of prototypical examples established by Hayes in this work.

pattern whose maxima (peaks) specify where the phonological accents are located.

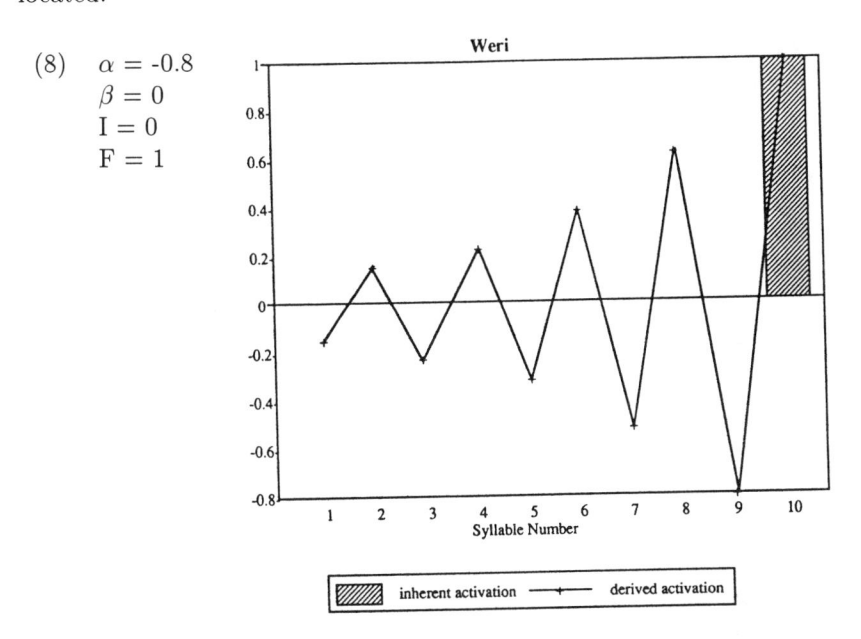

(8) $\alpha = -0.8$
$\beta = 0$
$I = 0$
$F = 1$

Weri

[Graph showing derived activation across syllables 1-10, with inherent activation shaded at syllable 10]

inherent activation ——+—— derived activation

The next familiar example is that of Warao (Osborn 1966, cited in Halle and Vergnaud 1987), which differs from Weri essentially only in that the penultimate syllable in Warao is stressed, rather than the final, as in Weri; see the forms in (9). In traditional metrical phonology, this is accounted for by marking the final syllable as extrametrical, in effect hidden from later metrical rules such as the End Rule. In the present theory, there are no external rules, and no rule ordering, and such an account is entirely unavailable. Penultimate accent is, in the present theory, accounted for by the interaction of a negative value of F, the positional activation on the final syllable, together with a negative value of α. This is illustrated in (10), which differs minimally from the illustration in (8); it differs only in the negative value of F. In each case, a dampened wave propagates from right to left across the word. These examples illustrate clearly the way in which a negative value of α, along with a zero setting (or near zero setting) of β, produces the effect of stress iterating from right to left across the word. There are, within this theory, however, no explicit rules which iterate, and the passage of information from right to left is due to the inherent architectural properties of the system, rather than a language-particular characteristic.

(9) Warao:
   yàpurùkitàneháse   'verily to climb'
   nàhoròahàkutái   'the one who ate'
   yiwàranáe   'he finished it'
   enàhoròahàkutái   'the one who caused him to eat'

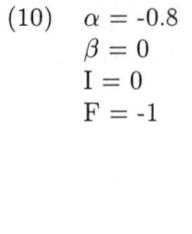

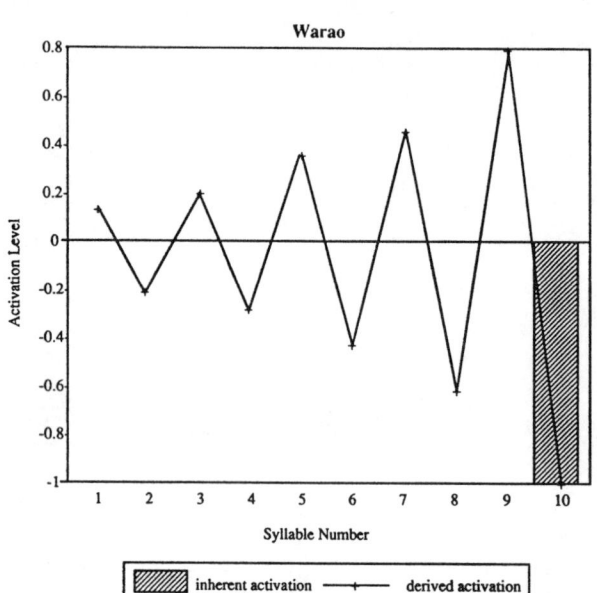

(10) $\alpha = -0.8$
      $\beta = 0$
      $I = 0$
      $F = -1$

The third example to consider is the mirror image of the Weri case, such as in Maranungku (Tryon 1970), in which the initial syllable is accented, and an iterative wave propagates from left to right across the word. The parametric settings for such a system are $I = 1$, $F = 0$, $\alpha = 0$, $\beta = -0.8$. Examples of Maranungku forms are given in (11), and a typical dynamic representation is given in (12).

(11) Maranungku:
   tíralk   'saliva'
   mérepèt   'beard'
   yángarmàta   'the Pleiades'
   lángkaràtetì   'prawn'

(12) $\alpha = 0$
$\beta = -0.8$
$I = 1$
$F = 0$

Maranungku

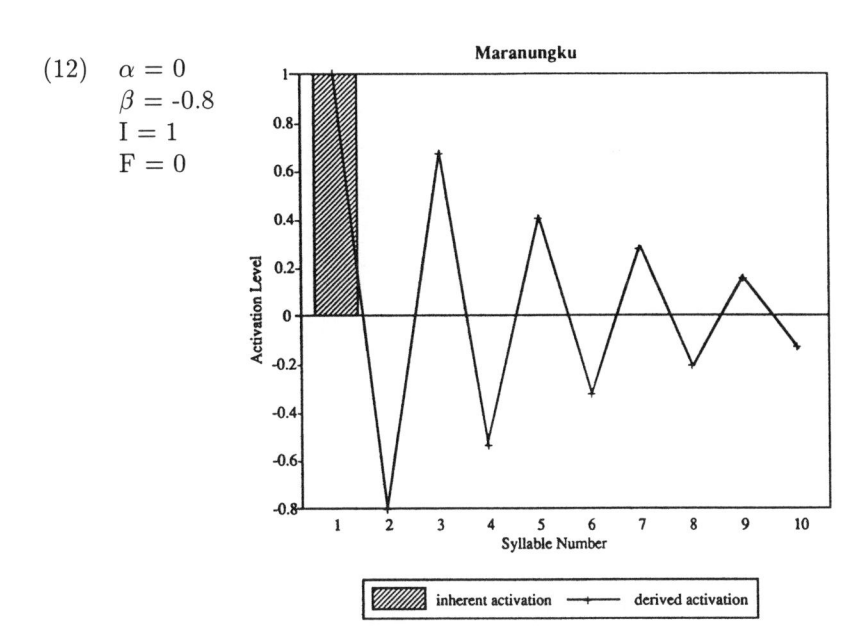

(graph showing activation level vs. syllable number 1–10, with inherent activation and derived activation)

In the three cases which we have considered so far, the choice of parameters that we have explored has been especially simple, in that there was only one positional activation—either I or F was zero in all three cases.[10] But the normal case that we find in accentual systems is that the positional activations are *not* zero; it is typical to find that I is positive (that is, the first syllable is accented), and that F is either positive or negative, but not zero (that is, either the final or the penultimate syllable is accented, though there is more to say about this, as we will see below). Let us consider first the common system in which I is positive, and F is negative. Again focusing on the case where α and β are negative, the negative positional activation on the final syllable gives rise to a positive activation on the penult (through an α-effect).

Garawa (Furby 1974) illustrates this quite common class: accent falls on both the initial syllable and on the penult, corresponding to a positive setting of I, a negative setting of F, and a negative value of α (in order that

---

[10]When only one positional activation is present, it is difficult to detect the presence of two lateral effects; that is, when there is positional activation on the first syllable (I > 0 or I < 0), the appearance of a rightward β-effect (that is, a rightward propagating wave as the result of a sufficiently large, negative β) will make it evident that β is, in fact, negative, and not zero or positive; on the other hand, in such a system, if there is no positional activation on the final syllable (if F = 0, that is), it will be difficult to detect whether α is zero or not. When there is no reason to think that the α is not zero, I have assumed that it is zero (similarly for β).

the negative value of F should translate into a positive value for the penultimate syllable). In such systems, we typically find either accent iterating from left to right, on odd- numbered syllables counting from the first, or else accent iterating from right to left, on every other syllable to the left of the penult, depending on the relative magnitudes of α and β. Garawa falls into the latter category, as illustrated in (13), and this pattern illustrates the result of a system in which the α-effect is stronger than the β-effect: in which, that is, $\alpha < \beta$ (though, more to the point, the absolute value of $|\alpha|$ is greater than that of $|\beta|$, since α is negative); see (14).

(13) Garawa:
 púnjala 'white'
 wátjimpàŋu 'armpit'
 nářiŋinmùkunjìnamìřa 'at your own many'

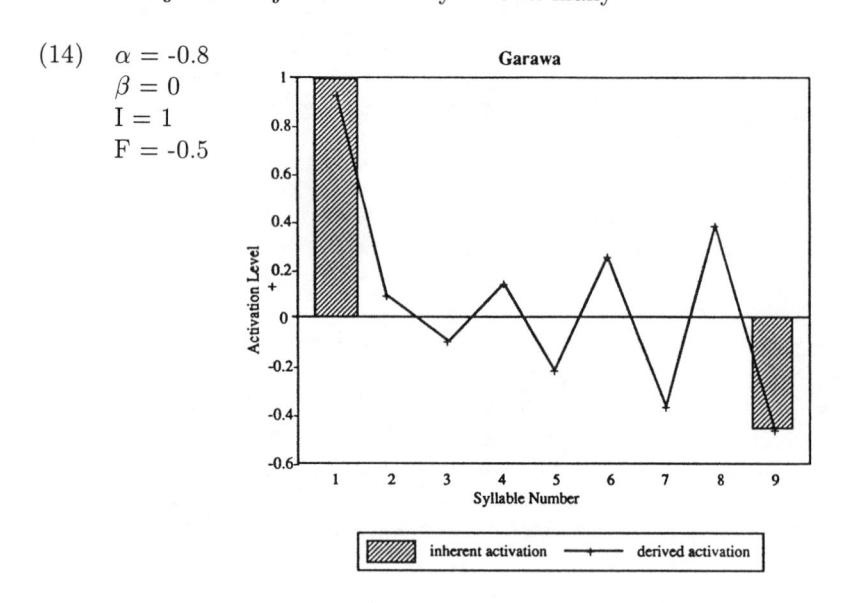

(14) $\alpha = -0.8$
 $\beta = 0$
 $I = 1$
 $F = -0.5$

In Garawa, despite the large α-effect – the large magnitude of the leftward moving wave – we observe a clash avoidance effect, whereby when a word has an odd number of syllables, we would expect the second syllable to be accented, because it is on the positive side of the wave propagated leftward from the final syllable. However, the second syllable is *not* stressed in Garawa, a familiar effect known as stress clash avoidance (Prince 1983).

Stress clash avoidance appears to be universal among quantity-insensitive systems, though it is far from universal among quantity-sensitive systems. The impossibility of accent on two successive syllables emerges directly from the interpretation of the equilibrium state of the network that we suggested earlier, that is, that a syllable is phonologically accented if and only if it is a peak, or local maximum; by definition, two successive syllables cannot both be peaks—if they were, each would be higher than the other, a logical impossibility. Hence, as long as we maintain this particular interpretation of phonological accent, stress clash avoidance will not be additionally specified, but will rather emerge directly out of the equilibrium state that is derived. We observe precisely this effect in Garawa; the second syllable may be positive, but it is less than that found on the first syllable, and hence it is not a peak—hence not phonologically accented.

We have so far explored systems that resemble traditional metrical systems in that they are apparently iterative either leftward or rightward.[11] The quantitative typology of the chart in (6) leads us to consider the significance of the intermediate zone, where neither α nor β are near zero, and both are negative. This is, in effect, the region in which both a leftward and a rightward propagation of a wave should be apparent, and, of course, the observation of such a system would be strong support for this wave-oriented conception of rhythmicity, as contrasted, in particular, with the constituency view of Halle and Vergnaud and others.

The well-known example of Lenakel is just such an example. As is well-known (cf. Lynch 1978, Hayes 1980, and others), accent in Lenakel is unusual in that stress is assigned according to principles that appear to be quite different in nouns when compared with the principles operative

---

[11] The notion of constituency, the reader will observe, has only a limited status within this theory. There is a natural way to define metrical constituents within the present framework; there are, in fact, two natural ways, since the wave that results from the approach discussed in the text invites two natural ways in which to make the cuts: one can make cuts at the local maxima (peaks) or at the local minima (troughs). Metrical theory has traditionally chosen the former, while syllabification theory, when faced with exactly the same problem, has chosen the latter. This difference reflects the traditional phonologist's intuition that stressed syllables are foot-peripheral, while the nuclear element of a syllable is typically syllable-internal, at least in the presence of a coda. The present theory invites a greater reconsideration of these questions, which we address in a longer work presently in progress. Suffice it to say, for our present purposes, that constituency plays a minor and derivative role in present framework.

in verbs and adjectives. Verbs and adjectives (see (15)) are stressed on the penultimate syllable, on the first syllable, and on every alternate (odd numbered) syllable as we count from left to right, starting with the beginning of the word, with the exception that the antepenult is never stressed. Nouns, on the other hand, bear penultimate stress, and show a pattern of accent assignment on alternate syllables counting from the *end* of the word, alternating leftward from the penultimate syllable. See (17).

(15) Lenakel verbs, adjectives
  ř̀ìmǫlgéygɛy   'he liked it'
  nìmařǫlgéygɛy   'you pl. liked it'
  nìmamàřǫlgéygɛy   'you pl. were liking it'
  tìnagàmařǫlgéygɛy 'you pl. were liking it'

(16) Lenakel verbs, adjectives,
  $\alpha = -0.4$
  $\beta = -0.6$
  $I = 0.5$
  $F = -1.0$

Lenakel Verbs and Adjectives

inherent activation —+— derived activation

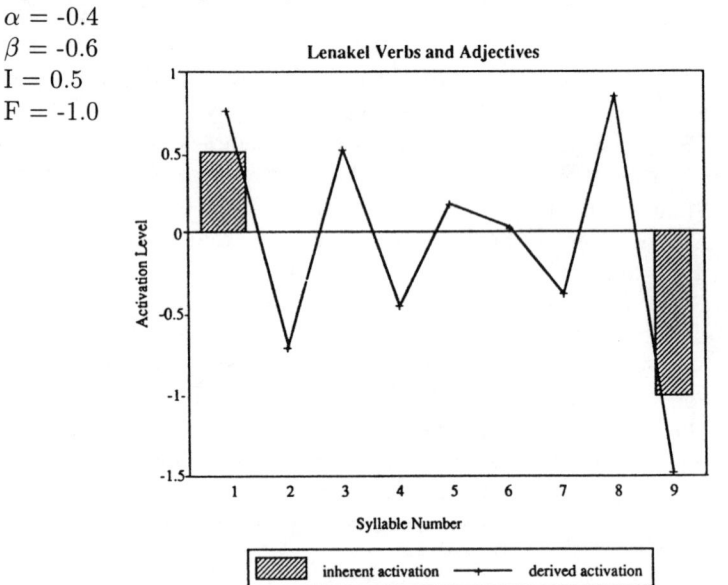

(17) Lenakel nouns
  kàmadóa   'k.o. taro'
  nim^{w}àg@lág@l 'beach'
  tub^{w}àlugál kh 'lungs'

A Dynamic Computational Theory of Accent Systems

(18) Lenakel nouns
$\alpha = -0.4$
$\beta = -0.6$
$I = 0$
$F = -1$

Lenakel Nouns

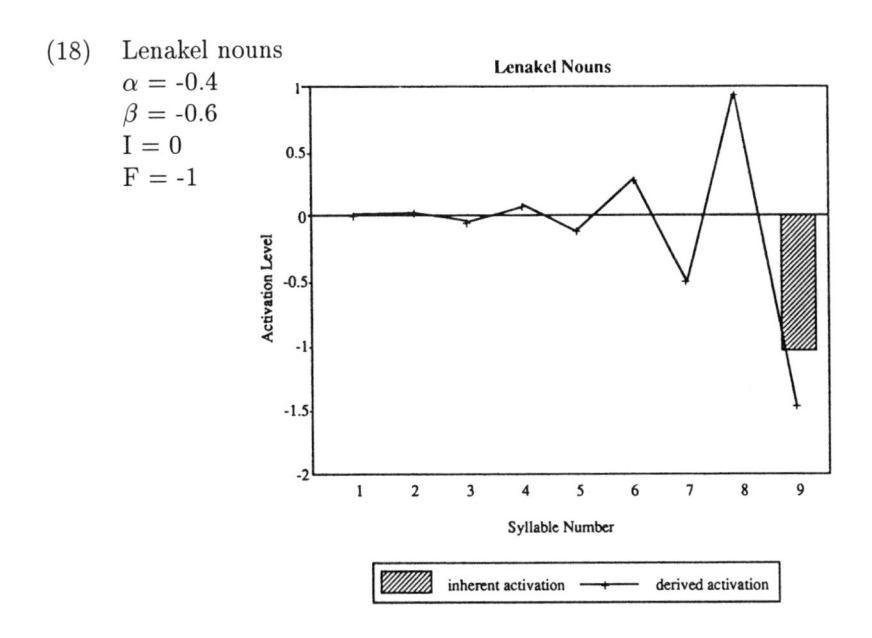

[Graph: Activation Level vs. Syllable Number, with legend showing inherent activation (hatched bar) and derived activation (line with crosses)]

This pattern is a peculiar embarrassment to traditional accounts of Lenakel, accounts which distinguish essentially between rules and representations. In nouns, not only is the initial stress of the verbs missing, but the direction of iteration of the rule that creates alternating stress must change depending on lexical category. In the present model, however, nothing of the kind is necessary; not only is this case not an embarrassment, it is precisely the kind of case that is predicted by the theoretical model. We need simply say that in the case of nouns, there is no Initial activation; crucially, however, the values of α and β remain fixed across the entire language. Because there is no Initial activation in the case of nouns, there is no rightward-spreading wave for the β-coefficient to pass on. There is, from a mathematical point of view, both a wave propagated leftward and a wave propagated rightward; the one which is stronger will, by and large, drown out the other from a purely quantitative point of view, but when the rightward moving wave is removed, by the non-occurrence of initial stress in the nominal system, the wave moving *sotto voce* leftward from the penult becomes entirely audible.

3 Quantity-insensitive Systems with Bias, and Some Observations on Quantity Sensitivity

We have so far considered only cases where the internal activations to all segments was zero, equally and across the board. By definition, quantity-insensitive systems assign equal internal activation to each unit, but that activation need not be zero; it may be a quantity (which we shall refer to as *bias*) which all the units uniformly receive. A non-zero bias will give rise to a rhythmic system as well, as illustrated in (19), where a negative bias is applied, and in (20), where a positive bias is assigned. Rhythmicity of much the sort that we have already explored is inherent to the system, whether activation comes in from one unit or from all of them.[12] In these two examples, the rhythm emerges in a β-dominant system, that is, one where β is significantly negative and α is zero or negligibly close to it. This is similar (though, as we shall clarify, not entirely equivalent to) the traditional conception of a rhythmic pattern assigned from left to right, just as an α-dominant system is similar to the notion of a rhythmic system assigned from right to left.

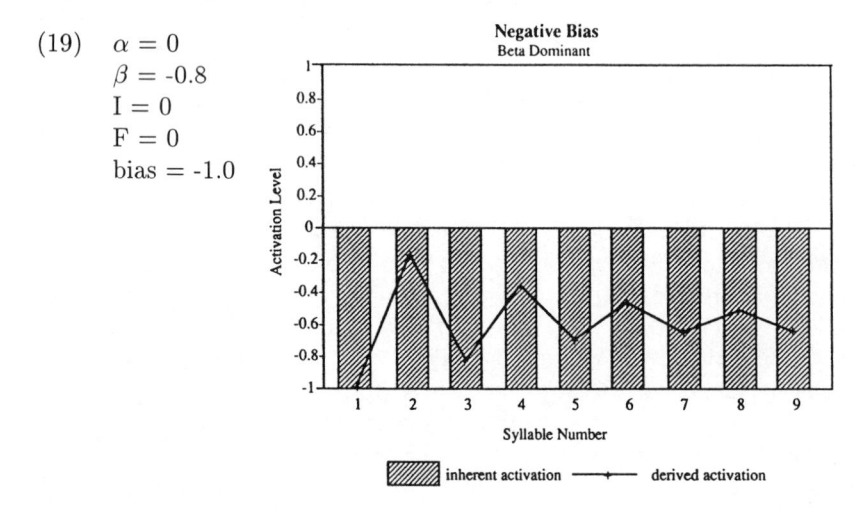

(19) $\alpha = 0$
$\beta = -0.8$
$I = 0$
$F = 0$
bias $= -1.0$

Negative Bias
Beta Dominant

---
[12]Since everything is linear, the final state D of initial state X + Y (D = f(X + Y)) is equal to the sum of the final state derived from initial X plus the final state derived from initial Y (that is, f(X + Y) = f(X) + f(Y)). Let us take X to be the state in which all segments have internal activation "1"; then we see that the shape of the curve derived from such an initial activation is independent of the strength of that activation—that is, varying the internal activation common to all the units will change only the scale (that is, the height) of the wave that is produced, but nothing else. In particular, the location of the peaks and troughs will be unaffected. We may therefore consider only three cases with no loss of generality—the case where the bias is 0, the case where the bias is 1, and the case where it is -1.

(20) $\alpha = 0$
$\beta = -0.8$
$I = 0$
$F = 0$
bias $= 1.0$

Positive Bias
Beta Dominant

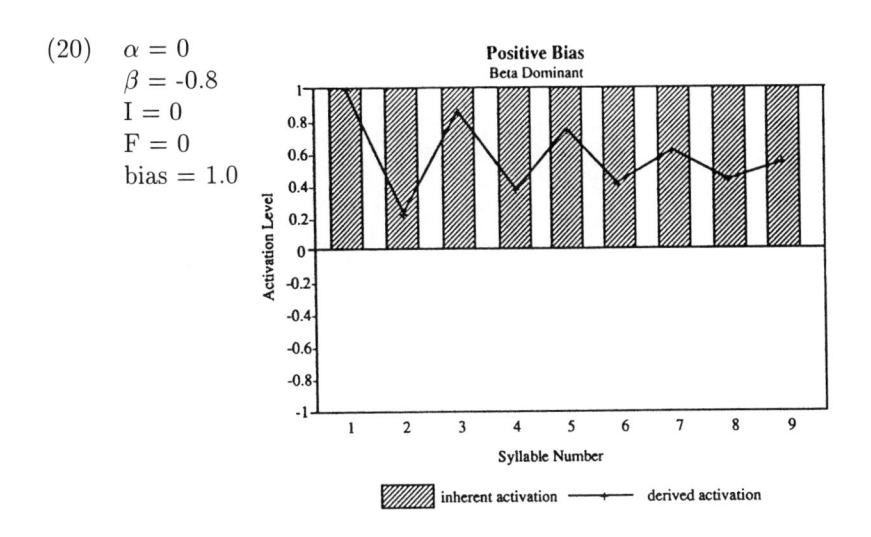

We may now notice an interesting result arising from the combination of the bias effect and the positional activations that we have explored to this point. In a β-dominant system such as that given in (20), if the Final parameter F is set to a negative value, such as -0.5, we will get a similar but distinct pattern, that given in (21). This pattern is precisely that which is described in metrical phonology as a left-to-right alternating stress pattern with final extrametricality, that is, where the final syllable is unable to bear stress. This example should make clearer the sense in which this dynamic computational theory is not an implementation of metrical theory, though it does contain subparts that correspond, in certain ways, to familiar subparts of metrical theory. We have just seen that certain effects that are associated with extrametricality correspond to a negative F coefficient in the present framework. Such a setting is not specially created *for* extrametricality, however, as we have already seen. There is, then, arguably a tighter theoretical fit among the entities at work in this model.

(21) $\alpha = 0$
      $\beta = -0.8$
      $I = 0$
      $F = -1.2$
      bias $= 1$

Positive Bias
Beta Dominant

x-axis: Syllable Number
y-axis: Activation Level

inherent activation ——+—— derived activation

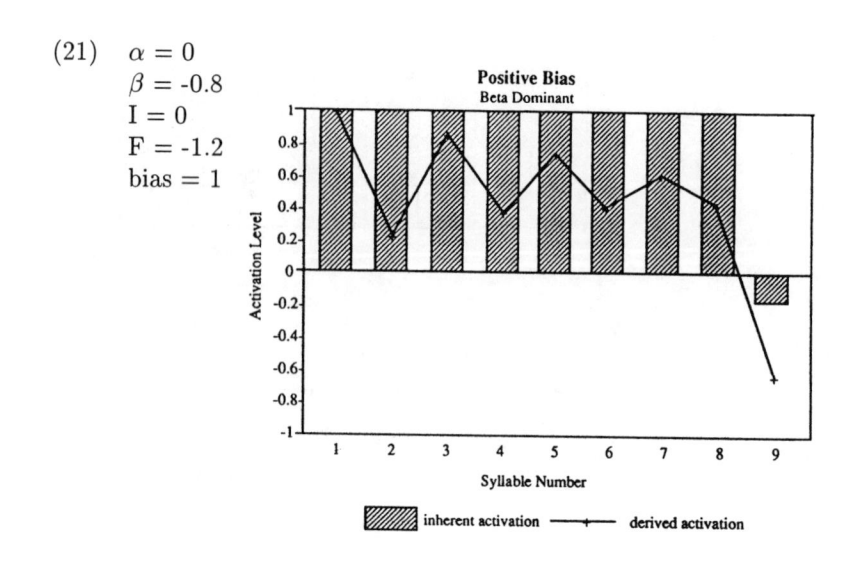

As we explore further, we see that the present theoretical model includes some of the equivalents of extrametricality of this sort, but in a qualitatively different fashion from that which we are accustomed to seeing in traditional metrical theory. In particular, the final syllable is not "invisible" in any sense of the term, though invisibility is the governing metaphor for extrametricality in metrical theory. This difference leads to an interesting prediction. In the present system, there is no way to use the equivalent of extrametricality in conjunction with a α-dominant, that is, a "right to left" pattern of rhythmicity. That is, we cannot directly generate a pattern of accent in which the accent regularly falls on the antepenult syllable, a result which is extremely easy to generate within traditional metrical phonology. Within a traditional metrical approach, one need simply mark the final syllable as extrametrical, and then assign a trochaic foot to the right-hand end of the word.

The only way to generate this pattern within the present system is within a quantity-sensitive system; within such a system, it is easy to generate antepenultimate accent, illustrated in (22). A quantity-sensitive system is, by definition, one for which the activation of each of the (non-peripheral) syllables is not uniform: some syllables have more internal activation than others. As the following diagrams illustrate, it is a simple matter to establish a system with a local maximum on the antepenult (and *not* the ultima) when there are differences in the internal activation of the penult and the antepenult.

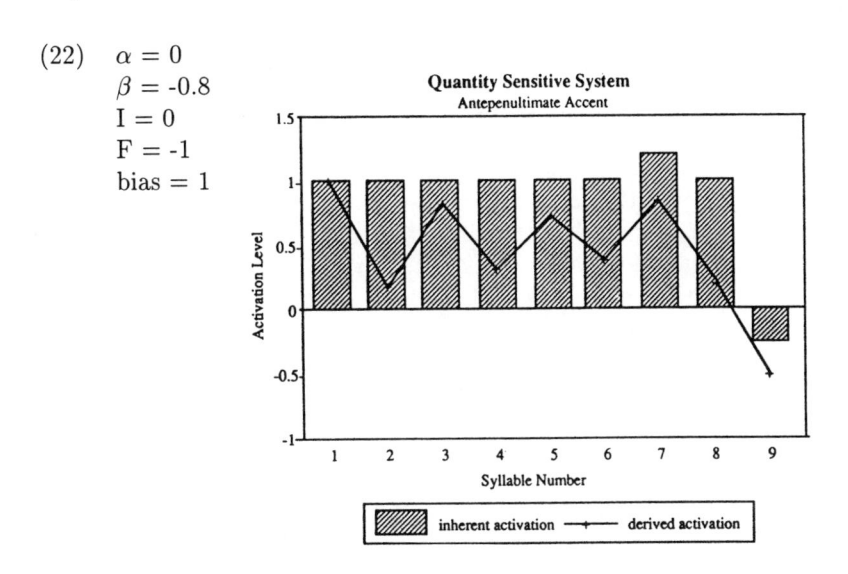

(22) $\alpha = 0$
      $\beta = -0.8$
      $I = 0$
      $F = -1$
      bias $= 1$

Quantity Sensitive System
Antepenultimate Accent

[Bar and line chart: Activation Level vs. Syllable Number (1–9), showing inherent activation (hatched bars) and derived activation (line with crosses).]

A deeper investigation of this system brings out an interesting and striking characteristic. Under most natural values of α and β (that is, when they are not trivially near zero) and under natural assumptions regarding the range of variation in syllable weight between heavy and light syllables, we find that there must be a peak on either the antepenult, the penult, or the ultima—that is, it is not possible to have three non-peak syllables in a row. This result is a familiar one, from the phonologist's point of view: the final three syllables of a word constitute a window inside of which a stress, that is, a local peak of activation, must appear. From the perspective of the present theory, this is not a condition on sound-structure, nor a condition on permissible constituents, but simply a mathematical result that follows from the nature of the arithmetic relations between adjacent elements.

A complete exploration of the various possibilities that can be produced with this system would take us beyond the scope of this short paper. But this brief discussion will help us nonetheless to see what the dynamic computational theory does when it determines that stress is assigned, for example, to the penultimate or the antepenultimate syllable. This determination is made on the basis of a simultaneous weighing of a number of distinct factors: in the cases considered so far, these factors are largely determined by the fixed bias applied to each unit, plus the lateral effects coming in from either side, and a unit which is more highly activated than its neighbor, then, is phonologically accented. Other factors, based on syllable-internal structure (or, in the odd case, on idiosyncratic information), can also be taken into account in just the same computation. The entire phonological system becomes, on this account, a large weigher of alternative configurations quantitatively expressed, and when alternatives come into conflict, the conflicts are resolved quantitatively. Categorical (that is, yes/no) effects are created, in the cases we have seen, on the basis of selecting which units are local maxima, that is, more active than their neighbors.

We may briefly review the effect of adding the effects of quantity sensitivity. This consists, as we have indicated, of an internal activation to some syllables which not all syllables receive. Let us assume, for simplicity's sake, that some syllables – in familiar terms, the heavy ones – receive an additional amount of activation, H; the others, the light ones, do not. The factors that we have discussed up to now allow us to accurately model the kinds of metrical systems that have motivated in the traditional metrical literature a burgeoning of theoretical devices, such as obligatory branching foot structure of various types. Consider the contrast between two similar metrical systems (I follow here a discussion in van der Hulst (ms.) which provides a helpful discussion of the problems for current metrical theory; the point is a general one, of course): both Rotuman (Churchward 1940) and Yapese (Jensen 1977) are quantity-sensitive systems in which stress falls on the ultima or the penult, depending on syllable weight. If, in that final window of two syllables, there is only one heavy syllable, then that syllable is the stressed syllable. If there are two heavy syllables (that is, if both the penult and the ultima are heavy), then the final syllable is stressed. The systems differ, however, with respect to where stress falls when both the ultima and the penult are light: in Rotuman, the stress falls on the penult, and in Yapese, the stress falls on the ultima.

(23) (after van der Hulst) Final Two Syllables' Weight: Light, Heavy

Language	H L]	L H]	L L]	H H]
Rotuman	*	*	*	*
Yapese	*	*	*	*

The complexities of such systems do not require derivational complexities, as the computations of the dynamic computational theories demonstrate. The results given in (23) are given by a dynamic grammar in which

A Dynamic Computational Theory of Accent Systems

$\alpha = -0.8$,[13] and heavy syllables receive an internal activation of 2.0 (that is, 2.0 more than the other syllables, the light syllables). The difference between the two systems results from the character of the bias applied to the system, as the discussion just above suggests. When the bias is positive (+1.0), then the resulting system is that seen in Yapese, that is, when all the syllables are light, the ultima has the highest activation level (1.0, in fact). When the bias is negative (-1.0), the penult has the highest activation (-0.20), as in Rotuman. These are the only cases that behave differently; when there are heavy syllables, the two systems work the same qualitatively, as (24) illustrates.

(24) Final Two Syllables' Weight: Light, Heavy

bias	Language	H L]	L H]	L L]	H H]
neg	Rotuman	1.8 -1.0	-1.8 1.0	-.2 -1.0	.2 1.0
pos	Yapese	2.2 1.0	-1.4 3.0	.2 1.0	0.6 3.0

More generally, problems of quantity-sensitive accent assignment can be accounted for thoroughly within the present theory, without the use of ordered renderings of constituent structure, as this example illustrates.

4 Other Quadrants

We have so far investigated the properties of only one of the four quadrants of the graph of α,β given in (6), that in the lower left-hand corner, where α and β are both negative. In this section, we will briefly consider two qualitatively distinct types of behavior found in the other quadrants.

Consider, first, the quadrant in which α is negative and β is positive (the upper left-hand quadrant), and the quadrant in which α is positive and β is negative (the lower right-hand quadrant). When the only inherent activation comes from I or F, the result is much like that given in (25). The phonological interpretation of this system is straightforward; these systems contain only one peak. When α is positive, the right-hand end of the word will be non-rhythmic in general, and when β is positive, the left-hand end of the word will be non-rhythmic. We find here, therefore, the case of words with non-rhythmic stress.

---

[13] Though the specific value, of course, of this and most of the other values does not matter; the properties of the dynamical system that we are interested in here are qualitative, and we care about the entire subspace of the phase space within which the same qualitative effects are found.

(25) $\alpha = -0.2$
$\beta = 0.6$
$I = -1.0$
$F = -1.0$

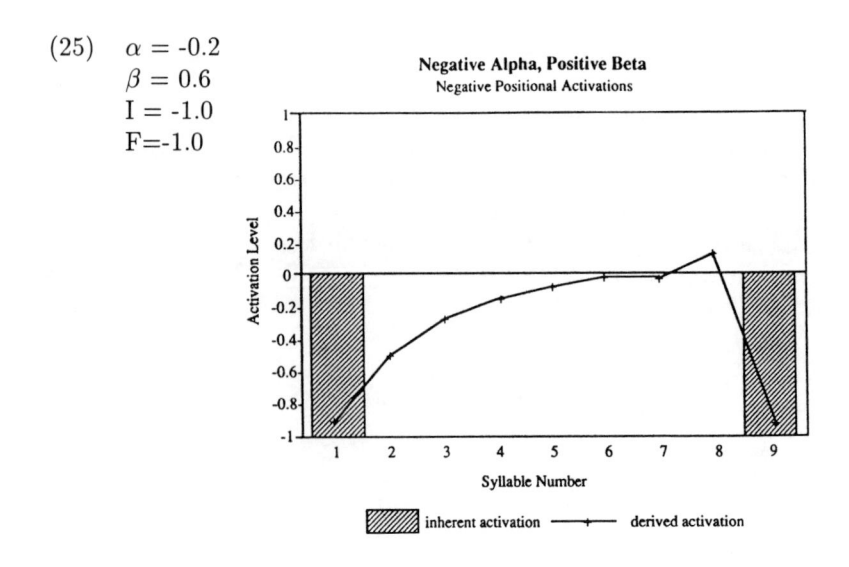

Negative Alpha, Positive Beta
Negative Positional Activations

[Graph: Activation Level vs Syllable Number (1-9), showing inherent activation (hatched) at syllables 1 and 9, and derived activation curve. Legend: inherent activation, derived activation.]

The other case to consider is that where both α and β are positive. This region of the α-β phase space is of some interest when we consider the treatment of non-rhythmic, quantity-sensitive languages, systems in which certain syllables are specified as heavy (and which have an inherent activation for that reason). Consider the derived activation of a system in which α is positive (β is zero), and in which a sequence of three syllables is accented, that is, has an inherent activation of 1.0. We assume in this example that I=F=0. This is illustrated in (26), where we see the effect that has been discussed in the literature under the rubric of "Meeussen's Rule" (Goldsmith 1984): in a sequence of accented elements, only the leftmost "wins," that is, in the present terms, only the leftmost is a local peak of activation.

(26) Meeussen's Rule
$\alpha = 0.5$
$\beta = 0$
$I = 0$
$F = 0$

Positive Alpha
Meeussen's Rule Effects

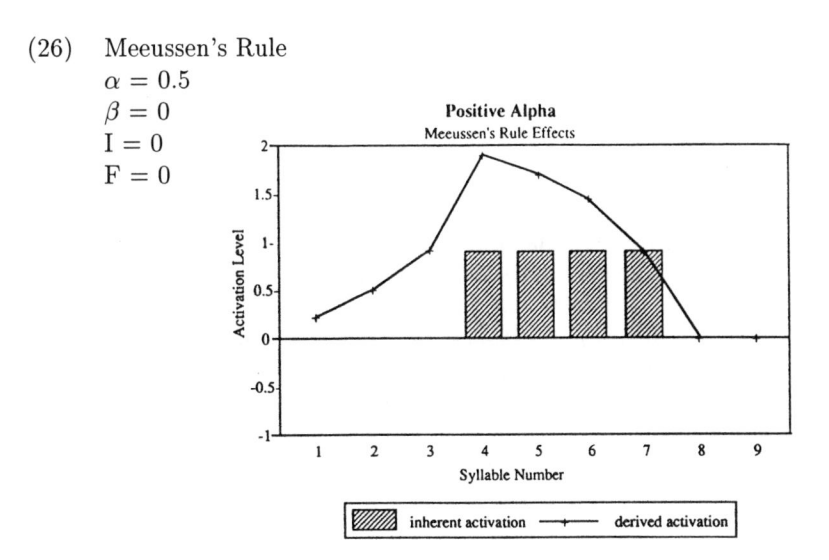

[Graph: Activation Level vs Syllable Number, with inherent activation (hatched bars) and derived activation (line with crosses)]

Qualitatively distinct behaviors can thus emerge out of the interaction of the limited continuous parameters that define the dynamic computational theory. Larson and I explore these models in considerably greater depth in a work now in progress.

5 Concluding Observations

It is helpful to draw a distinction in phonological theory between the theories of representations, of levels, and of rules. It may appear that the major proposal of the theory of dynamic computational systems is as a revision of our theory of phonological representations: the proposal entails, for example, a representation in which the positive and negative real numbers play a role, thus enriching our representation. This apparent focus on the theory of representations would be entirely in line with the trends in phonological theory since the mid-1970s.

Such a view would be inaccurate, however. The primary motivation and the primary goal of the work described here concerns the theory of phonological rules, and to a lesser degree the theory of phonological levels, and it is only marginally and in passing a modification of the theory of representations. In fact, the theory of the metrical grid as developed over the last ten years has been qualitatively integrated directly into this theoretical model. By contrast, the goal of this work is to explore the possibility of shifting the line between our traditional conception of rules and of representation: to shift the burden of dealing with dynamic modifications of representations from the rules back to the representations themselves.[14] I have explored the motivation and importance of this in other places (Goldsmith 1990, Chapter 6.4-6.6; Goldsmith 1991, in press).

Our larger goal is a theory of formal grammar in which the central consideration is the quantitative resolution of conflict. This perspective is close in many respects to the autolexical view of Sadock (1991), and close as well to views of cognition that have been influenced by connectionist thinking, and to the broad class of computational treatments of soft constraint resolution. The treatment of accentual systems which we have explored in this paper is illustrative of a wide variety of traditional problems in linguistic analysis for which an arguably deeper account can be obtained without recourse to those aspects of more familiar linguistic theory which have served to place the greatest gulf between linguistic theory and the other cognitive sciences.

The present work has been heavily informed by current work on neural networks and connectionism, though its point of theoretical orientation is perhaps radically different from much of the work presented within that general perspective. A seeming gulf separates most of the theoretical work on language done within the traditions of generative grammar, and those informed by formal and mathematical traditions allied with the study of connectionist networks and dynamical systems.[15] This gulf serves only to isolate workers on either side from the benefits that can be achieved from a more open-minded perspective; I believe the present paper illustrates the ways in which additional theoretical tools can provide new and more compelling theoretical models for the phonologist.

---

[14] A number of observers of the phonological scene have made similar remarks over the past ten years, and on this score there seems to be virtual unanimity.

[15] Notable exceptions to this include the recent work of Legendre and Smolensky (1990) and Prince (1991). My own understanding of the potential of connectionist modeling is heavily influenced by Smolensky (1988).

References

Boxwell, H. and M. Boxwell. 1966. Weri phonemes. In S. A. Wurm (ed.), *Papers in New Guinea Linguistics* No. 5, pp. 77-93. Canberra: Australian National University.

Churchward, C. M. 1940. *Rotuman grammar and dictionary.* Australian Medical Publishing Company.

Furby, C. 1974. Garawa phonology. *Pacific Linguistics* Series A, No. 37. Canberra: Australian National University.

Goldsmith, John. 1984. Meeussen's Rule. In Mark Aronoff and Richard Oehrle (eds.), *Language sound structure: Studies in phonology presented to Morris Halle by his teacher and students.* Cambridge, MA: MIT Press.

Goldsmith, John. 1990. *Autosegmental and Metrical Phonology.* Oxford: Basil Blackwell.

Goldsmith, John. 1991. Phonology as an intelligent system. In Donna Jo Napoli and Judy Kegl (eds.), *Bridges between psychology and linguistics: A Swarthmore Festschrift for Lila Gleitman.* Lawrence Erlbaum.

Goldsmith, John. In press. Local modeling in phonology. In Steven Davis (ed.), *Connectionism: Theory and practice.* Oxford: Oxford University Press.

Goldsmith, John and Gary Larson. 1990. Local modeling and syllabification. In Karen Deaton, Manuela Noske, and Michael Ziolkowski (eds.), *Papers from the 26th Annual Regional Meeting of the Chicago Linguistic Society: Parasession on the Syllable in Phonetics and Phonology.*

Goldsmith, John and Gary Larson. In preparation. Dynamic computational models in phonology.

Halle, Morris and Jean-Roger Vergnaud. 1987. *An essay on stress.* Cambridge, MA: MIT Press.

Hayes, Bruce. 1980. *A metrical theory of stress rules.* Ph.D. dissertation, Massachusetts Institute of Technology. Circulated by the Indiana University Linguistics Club, 1981.

Hulst, Harry van der. 1991. *Notes on the representation of stress.* ms., University of Leiden.

Jensen, J. 1977. *Yapese reference grammar.* Honolulu: University Press of Hawaii.

Larson, Gary. 1990. Local computational networks and the distribution of segments in the Spanish syllable. In Karen Deaton, Manuela Noske, and Michael Ziolkowski (eds.), *Papers from the 26th Annual Regional Meeting of the Chicago Linguistic Society: Parasession on the Syllable in Phonetics and Phonology.*

Larson, Gary. In preparation. *Dynamic computational networks.* Ph.D. dissertation, University of Chicago.

Legendre, Géraldine and Paul Smolensky. 1990. Can connectionism contribute to syntax? Harmonic Grammar, with an application. In Karen Deaton, Manuela Noske, and Michael Ziolkowski (eds.), *Proceedings of the 26th Meeting of the Chicago Linguistic Society.*

Liberman, Mark. 1975. *The intonational system of English.* Ph.D. dissertation, Massachusetts Institute of Technology. Published by Garland Press, New York, 1979.

Liberman, Mark and Alan Prince. 1977. On stress and linguistic rhythm. *Linguistic Inquiry* 8:249-336.

Lynch, John. 1978. A grammar of Lenakel. *Pacific Linguistics* Series B No. 55. Canberra: Australian National University.

Osborn, H. 1966. Warao I: Phonology and morphophonemics. *International Journal of American Linguistics* 32:108-123.

Prince, Alan S. 1983. Relating to the grid. *Linguistic Inquiry* 14:19-100.

Prince, Alan. 1991. *Quantitative consequences of rhythmic organization.* ms., Brandeis University.

Sadock, Jerrold. 1991. *Autolexical grammar.* Chicago: University of Chicago Press.

Smolensky, Paul. 1988. On the proper treatment of connectionism. *Behavioral and Brain Science* 11:1-74.

Tryon, D. T. 1970. An introduction to Maranungku. *Pacific Linguistics* Series B, Number 14. Canberra: Australian National University.

The Russian Declension
An Illustration of the Theory of Distributed Morphology[1]

Morris Halle
Massachusetts Institute of Technology

1 Sketch of the Theory of Distributed Morphology

The formation of words by means of derivation, compounding and inflection has traditionally been regarded as the main subject matter of morphology. This characterization of morphology leaves open the relationship that exists between morphology and other major components of a grammar such as the Syntax, the Phonology and the Vocabulary/Lexicon. As a result, radically different views on this relationship have been espoused by different linguists. Thus, Lieber (1991) has argued – as did Lees (1960) – that morphology belongs in the syntax. Jensen (1990) by contrast believes that word formation belongs in the Vocabulary/Lexicon, whereas proponents of Lexical Phonology (for example, Kiparsky (1982)) have assumed that affixation processes, which constitute a large fraction of all morphological operations, must be interleaved with the rules of the phonology and are, therefore, part of the phonology.

These three approaches are in contrast with the more traditionalist view that the morphology constitutes a module of the grammar that is separate and distinct from the rest. A variant of this view is championed in the just published book *Autolexical Syntax* by J. Sadock (1991:101), who writes: "In answer to Stephen Anderson's (1982) question 'Where's Morphology?' I would not respond . . . that it is in the lexicon but rather 'It's in the morphological component, where it belongs'."

The work presented below does not assume that all morphological phenomena are accounted for in a single component of the grammar. Like Anderson (1992), we take it that "word structure can only be understood as the product of interacting principles from many parts of the grammar." We assume therefore that some morphological phenomena are accounted for in the Vocabulary module, others in the Syntax-Semantics module, and yet others in special modules, which have been dubbed here *Word Synthesis* and *Morphophonology*. On this view, then, morphology is distributed among the different components of a grammar, and it is this fact that has

---

[1] I am grateful to M. Kenstowicz, H. G. Lunt and A. Marantz for help in the preparation of this paper.

led us to suggest the phrase *distributed morphology* as the label for the theoretical framework about to be described.[2]

The five main modules of a grammar are the Vocabulary, Syntax-Semantics, Word Synthesis, Morphophonology and Phonology, and they are assumed to have the organization shown in (1).

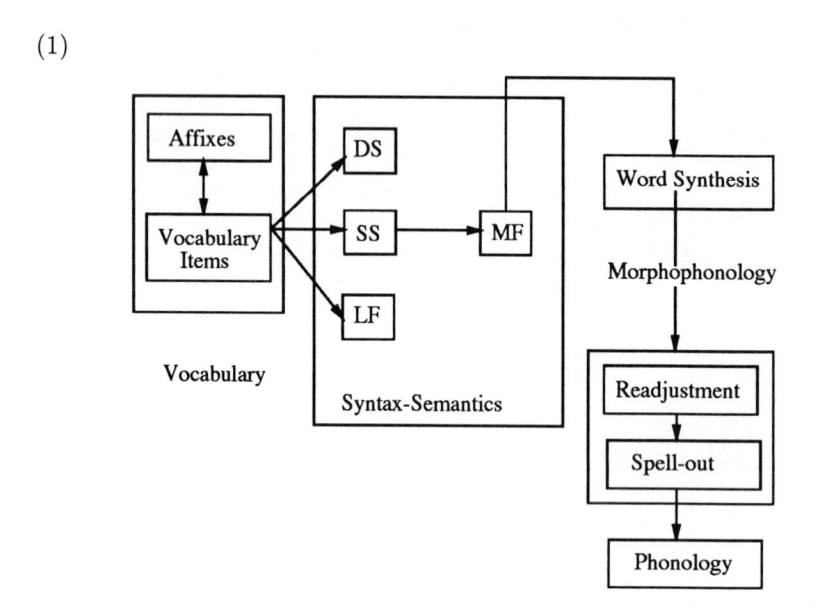

(1)

[Diagram showing: Vocabulary module containing Affixes and Vocabulary Items; Syntax-Semantics module containing DS, SS, MF, LF; Word Synthesis; Morphophonology containing Readjustment and Spell-out; Phonology]

The four blocks inside the Syntax-Semantics module in (1) express graphically the fact that this module is concerned with four distinct representations of a sentence. Three of these are the familiar: SS, DS, and LF. The fourth representation – Morphological Form (MF) – is the one that serves as input to the rules of the *Word Synthesis* module.

It is assumed here that for a given sentence the same Vocabulary items figure simultaneously in all four of these representations. Items selected from the Vocabulary are arranged in each of the four representations subject to various constraints and conditions. Thus, the relation that holds between the SS representation of a sentence and both its DS and LF counterparts is mediated by the "move alpha" or "affect alpha" transformation.

---

[2] An earlier version of the framework was presented in Halle 1990. The version of the theory presented below reflects my understanding of the issues as of May, 1991. Work done since that time in close collaboration with Alec Marantz has resulted in a number of modifications, of which the most important concerns the insertion of vocabulary items into sentences. For details see Marantz and Halle, 1993.

The relation SS:DS differs from the relation SS:LF with regard to the elements that are affected by "move alpha": in the relation SS:LF the affected elements are operators, whereas in the relation SS:DS they may be both operators and non-operators. The relation SS:MF is mediated by special principles to which we now turn.

In all four representations the formatives in the terminal sequence are organized into hierarchical constituents. Linear – left-to-right – order is imposed only on MF representations, but not on the other three. This left-to-right order is imposed primarily by placing the head of a constituent either at its beginning or at its end. Additional principles govern other aspects specific to MF representations. Among the principles that are responsible for the most important differences between SS and MF representations are the two given in (2), which have been adapted from Marantz 1988:

(2) a. A relation holding at SS between two elements X and Y may be expressed in the MF representation by the affixation of the lexical head of X to the lexical head of Y.

b. The relation of left- resp. right-adjacency between elements in a sequence is associative; that is, $X*(Y*Z) = (X*Y)*Z$, where $A*B$ stands for "A is left-adjacent to B."

Head-to-head movement (2a) is the primary device responsible for the "mirror principle" that Baker (1988) has shown to hold between the order of certain morphemes in a word and the underlying syntactic structure of the clause in which the word figures. The associativity principle (2b), on the other hand, accounts for disparities between syntactic and morphological constituent structure (bracketing) such as in the English sentence *John's working*, where the auxiliary verb is phonetically attached to the subject although syntactically it is part of the Verb complex.[3]

It is to be noted that while the elements in the terminal strings of MF representations are linearly ordered and may differ more or less radically from those found in the Surface Structure, they do not necessarily form words. In particular, words often differ to various degrees from the units that appear in terminal strings of the representations in the Syntax-Semantics module and they may contain elements not present in MF. In the model represented in (1) words are formed in a special component labelled *Word Synthesis*.

---

[3]Principles quite similar to those in (2) are central in Sadock's *Autolexical Syntax* (1991). In particular, Sadock's Incorporation Principle (IP) corresponds roughly to (2a) while his Cliticization Principle (CP) is the counterpart of (2b).

A simple example of the introduction of a formative by the Word Synthesis component is provided by the Present/Past tense forms of the English verb in (3a,b).

(3) a. They worked in Boston
     b. They do not work in Boston

Following Pollock 1989 and Chomsky 1991 we assume that the Tense formative is generated under the INFL node of the top-most clause as illustrated in (3c).

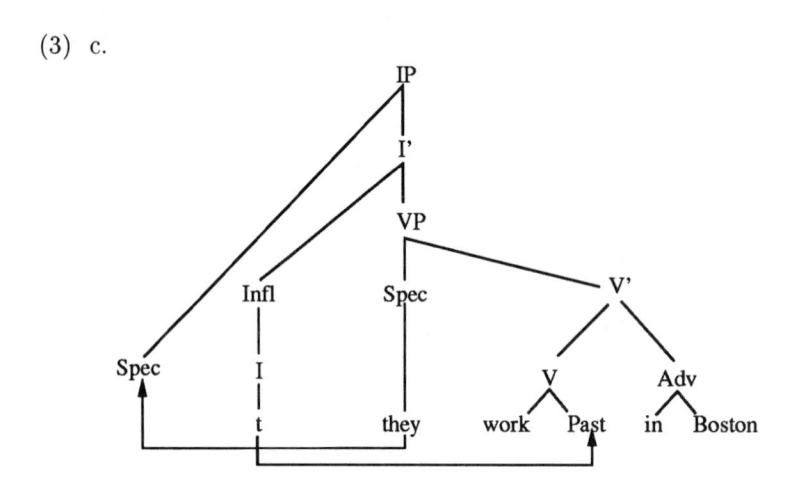

(3) c.

[tree diagram: IP dominating Spec and I'; I' dominating Infl and VP; Infl dominating I and t; VP dominating Spec (they) and V'; V' dominating V (work Past) and Adv (in Boston); arrows showing movement of t to Spec position and Past to V]

Absent certain blocking conditions such as the presence of negation, the Tense formative is moved down next to the main verb with which it is merged into a single word in the Word Synthesis Component, (cf. (3a)). When the movement of the Verb into position next to Tense is blocked – for example, by the presence of negation in (3b) – the bare Verb surfaces by itself.

A further consequence of blocked Verb movement is that it prevents suffixation of the Tense formative to the verb stem. Since Tense in English is morphologically a suffix, it cannot surface without its stem. Therefore, when the Tense formative in MF has no Verb stem to which it may be suffixed – as for example in (3b) – a special rule of the Word Synthesis component inserts the auxiliary verb *do* next to the Tense formative. As the example (3b) shows insertion of the auxiliary *do* occurs even when the Tense formative is phonetically null; that is, *do* insertion is triggered by the presence of the Tense formative without regard to the latter's phonetic actualization: even a suffix that is phonetically zero is paired with a stem in the output.[4]

In English, in most instances Vocabulary items representing lexical categories – that is, nouns, verbs, adjectives and adverbs – may function as words in utterances. English Vocabulary items may thus directly serve as input to the Phonology without undergoing any modification by either Word Synthesis or the Morphophonology. By contrast, in many languages the bare stem is rarely the correct form to be used in the surface form of a sentence.

For example, the thematic affixes – also known as word or inflection class marker (Harris 1991) or verbalizing suffix (Halle 1973) – play a major role in the Morphophonology and Phonology of words, but are absent in the four levels of representations of the Syntax-Semantics. In the lapidary formulation of Harris (1991:59): "The class-marking suffixes have no meaning or function; they obey no higher semantic or syntactic authority. They are simply pieces of form that must be at the right place at the right time, by their own rules." As documented in detail by Harris, Spanish nouns, adjectives and adverbs do not surface without a thematic suffix. He writes (1991:56): "...*all* Spanish roots, stems, and affixes that belong to the major categories noun, adjective and adverb are in fact bound morphemes: such stems and affixes must always undergo (further) affixation in order to form a complete prosodic word... The only unaffixed words in Spanish, then, are *si* 'yes', *no* 'no', prepositions and other 'small change' items, mostly clitics."

Spanish is by no means unusual in not allowing bare, unadorned Vocabulary items to figure as words in utterances. This is all but self-evident in IE languages with rich inflectional systems such as Latin, Russian, or Latvian.[5]

---

[4] In a paper presented at the 1991 WCCFL meeting Pullum and Zwicky take issue with many of the proposals in Halle (1990). A special section of their criticism is aimed at the admission of zero morphemes like that of the English present tense illustrated in (3). They state (1991:5) that "a zero-inflected form is nothing more than the stem unaffected by any rule; *work* in *they work* will have no affixes at any level of analysis." If *work* in *they work* has "no affixes at any level of analysis," then there is no explanation for the fact that *do* support is triggered in *they do not work*, but not in *they had John not work today*. On the account presented above, the tense affix is present in *they do not work*, but not in *they had John not work today*, where *work* indeed appears without any affixes. Pullum and Zwicky do not discuss this obvious consequence of their proposal. It goes almost without saying that unless and until explained away the facts reviewed above undermine essential aspects of Zwicky and Pullum's case. For additional comments on Pullum and Zwicky (1991), see notes 6, 11 and 18 below.

[5] Carstens (1991) has argued that the word prefixes in Swahili and some other Bantu languages reflect the number – singular/plural – of the head noun and that the different classes represent an elaborate system of noun genders. On Carstens' view then the

It is obvious that formal account must be taken of this fundamental difference between languages. Like Harris, I propose to do this by postulating that in Russian, words – that is, the special units that are dealt with by the Morphophonology and Phonology – must conform to the template in (4).

(4) $[[[\text{VOCABULARY ITEM} + \text{Theme}] + (\left\{\begin{array}{c}\text{Tense}\\ \text{Gerund}\\ \text{Part.}\\ \text{Inf.}\end{array}\right\})\,]\,(\text{Inflection})]$

In part, this structure is already present in the MF representation and thus due to the operation of the Syntax-Semantics, but other parts, for example, the insertion of the Theme, the fusion of syntactically independent morphemes such as case and number into a single inflectional affix, or the establishment of noun-adjective concord, are implemented by special rules that together constitute the Word Synthesis component.

In addition to inserting syntactically inert morphemes such as the Thematic suffixes (=inflection class markers) of Spanish and Russian words or the English supporting verb *do*, the rules of the Word Synthesis component establish linear order and nesting among the morphemes. Moreover, Word Synthesis rules are responsible for various concord phenomena such as the Number-(Case-)Gender agreement between the head noun in a Russian or Spanish NP and the specifiers and adjectives that the noun governs (see, for example, (11), (12)). As noted below there is reason to suppose that the rules of the Word Synthesis component differ from those of the Morphophonology in that the Word Synthesis rules are pure redundancy rules in that they cannot change any of the features already present in the string, they can only add new elements to those already there.

The template (4) expresses the fact that in Russian, every word representing a major lexical category must be supplied with a Theme formative. The parenthesized material in (4) appears in verbs, adjectives and nouns, but not in adverbs. All three of these classes of words require an inflection. Finite forms of the verb include in addition the Tense formative, whereas infinitives, gerunds and participles – of which the former two are deverbal adverbs and the third, deverbal adjectives – have special suffixes of their own.[6]

Swahili prefix system is in essence a gender/number agreement system not unlike that found in the IE languages. The word in Swahili must always include this agreement marker: unlike the word in English, the Swahili word thus cannot be a bare Vocabulary item by itself.

[6]It is worthy of special note that as indicated in the passage quoted above, Harris (1991) has shown that Spanish words conform to the template (4) in spite of the fact

Turning to the Vocabulary module at the left side of (1), we observe that it is made up of two components. One of these is a list of items that in English – though, as just noted, not in all languages – are largely identical with the words that appear in sentences. The second list contains the affixes and the "bound" roots of the language. We need the latter list to account for the fact – among others – that speakers are able to analyze previously unheard words like those in (5a) into their component affixes and to reject as ill-formed words such as those in (5b). Since unimpeachable morpheme collocations such as those in (5c) do not constitute actual words of the language we need a formal device for ruling these out. The component in (1) labelled Vocabulary Items performs this function: it lists the items that are word stems in the language. As has often been noted in the past, another function of the list is to serve as the repository for the noncompositional semantics of words such as those in (5d).

(5)a. un+poison+ous+ness weather+li+ness organ+iz+at+ion+al+ize
   b. *eat+ness *grammar+ness *usurp+ly *standard+ize+ly
   c. *London+ian cf. Boston+ian *Shakespear+ic cf. Homer+ic
   d. homi+cide vs. insecti+cide

Following an old tradition reflected, for example, in Saussure's treatment of the word as a sign consisting of a *signifiant* and a *signifie*, I assume that a morpheme is represented by a *complex symbol* consisting of two separate parts: an identifying index and a set of grammatical markers. Information about the morpheme's meaning and its syntactic and grammatical idiosyncrasies is conveyed by these markers. For the large majority of formatives the identifying index is a sequence of phonemes. This formally reflects the proposition that a morpheme's identifying index is directly related to its phonetic form. For a minority of morphemes this is not the case. The distinguishing feature of these morphemes is that their contextual variants are phonetically unrelated. Such morphemes are supplied with a special identifying index – represented here by the capital letter Q – whose phonetic reflexes are spelled out by a special block of rules in the Morphophonology.

---

that at least Spanish nouns and adjectives have only very rudimentary inflections.
  In their criticism of Halle (1990), Pullum and Zwicky (1991) ask "which of the possible order of the morphemes in Latin *amo* 'I love' is the right one? LOVE + Ind + Act + Pres + 1P + Sg is one possibility; there are 6! - 1 = 719 others." As I have just tried to show, the linear order and nesting of morphemes such as Tense, Person, Number is determined in part by the syntax, in part by the rules of the Word Synthesis component. While much about this subject remains to be discovered, it is misleading of Pullum and Zwicky to suggest that so little is known about the problem that all combinatorially possible arrangements of morphemes need to be considered.

I refer to morphemes with identifying indices composed of sequences of phonemes as *concrete morphemes* and distinguish them from *abstract morphemes*, whose identifying index is the capital letter Q. Most abstract morphemes are inflectional morphemes, such as Plural, Past, Possessive, but there also exist inflectional morphemes that are concrete, as well as noninflectional morphemes that are abstract. An example of a concrete inflectional morpheme is the English progressive aspect marker *+ing*, which has a unique phonological shape, whereas an example of an abstract noninflectional morpheme is the verb *be*, which both in English and in many other languages has surface reflexes of great variety that cannot be correlated by means of phonologically plausible rules.

In (6a) I illustrate the complex symbol of a noun recently added to the English Vocabulary and in (6b) the complex symbol of the English Past morpheme.

(6) Identifying Index: a. /skʌd/   b. Q
    Grammatical Markers:
    Lexical Category   ___]$_N$]$_V$___]$_V$
    Meaning   'a surface-to-surface missile'   Past
    Morphological properties   stem etc.   suffix

In (7a) I have illustrated some of the phonetic realizations of the English Past formative. I have given in (7b) the Spell-out rules of the Past morpheme that account for the different actualizations of the Past tense morpheme illustrated in (7a).

(7)   a.   i.   mean+t, kep+t, bough+t
             ii.   hit, drove, began
             iii.   play+ed, pass+ed, wait+ed

       b.   i.   Q → [t]   in env. X′ + ___, Past
                             where X′ = mean, keep, ...
             ii.   Q → 0   in env. X″ + ___, Past
                             where X″ = hit, drive ...
             iii.   Q → [d]   /___, Past

Spell-out rules like those in (7b) rewrite the abstract symbol Q as a sequence of one or more phonemes, or delete the symbol Q. Since Spell-out rules are also ordered, the application of a given Spell-out rule bleeds all Spell-out rules ordered below it for lack of a triggering Q. As a result the application of the first rule in (7b), which rewrites Q as /t/, bleeds the third Spell-out rule in (7b), which rewrites Q as /d/.[7] This bleeding property of the Spell-out rules accounts for the fact that in English doubly marked past forms such as *bough+t+ed, wrote+ed* are ungrammatical.[8]

The ordering of rule (7biii) after rules (7bi, ii) reflects the fact that Spell-out rules are ordered by the principle – traditionally attributed to Paṇini – that a less general rule takes precedence over a rule that is more general. This will be illustrated in greater detail in the discussion of the Readjustment and Spell-out rules of Russian in the second part of this paper.[9]

It is not unusual for affixation to be accompanied by modifications in the stem. I have illustrated in (8) two simple instances of such stem modification in the English Plural. The examples in (8a) illustrate stem final continuant voicing in the Plural, whereas the examples in (8b) illustrate vowel ablaut in verb stems.

(8) a. house+s shelve+s wive+s bath+s mouth+s
[+cont] → [+voice] in env. [X'__] + Q, Plural
where [X' [+cont]] = house, shelf, mouth, etc.

b. swam, ate, sang
[-cons] → [+low] in env. [Y __ Z] + Q, Past
where [Y [-cons] Z] = swim, eat, sing, etc.

Voicing by rule (8a) takes place only in a small number of English nouns. For instance, *house* is the only noun ending in /s/ that is subject to stem-final voicing (there is no voicing in, for example, *blous+es, spous+es,*

---

[7]It also bleeds the second Spell-out rule in (7b), but this is vacuous since the list of items to which the second rule applies is distinct from the list of those that are subject to the first rule.

[8]In languages such as Yiddish (Perlmutter 1988) and Breton (Stump 1989), where doubly marked plurals are grammatical, this is achieved with the help of a Readjustment rule that reduplicates the abstract Plural morpheme. For some discussion, see Bromberger and Halle 1989 and Halle 1989.

[9]Since the bleeding property of ordered rules can account for many instances where rules apply disjunctively I conjectured in Halle 1992b that there may be no need or role for a special principle of disjunctive rule order of the kind proposed by Chomsky and Halle (1968) (SPE), Kiparsky (1973), and Anderson (1986). I now think that this guess was incorrect. There are a number of examples arguing for a special principle of disjunctivity; specifically, the block of rules governing vowel quantity in English (the so-called Trisyllabic Shortening, Civ Lengthening, and Prevocalic Lengthening) (see Myers 1987, Halle and Vergnaud 1987); and the treatment of /r/ in Eastern Massachusetts English and vowel deletion/epenthesis in Lardil discussed by McCarthy (1991) under the heading of "rule inversion."

plac+es, buss+es, etc.); noun-final [f, θ] voice in the plural of a handful of nouns but remain voiceless in the plural of most nouns; for example, *coughs, cuffs, fourths, myths*.

Similarly, only a small number of verbs undergo vowel ablaut in the past tense by rule (8b). It might be noted that ablaut is not limited to verbs with a zero Past formative as shown by examples such as *flee fle+d, buy bough+t*; nor is every verb form with a zero Past formative subject to ablaut, as shown by Past forms such as *rid, beat, spread*.

The changes in the stem illustrated in (8) are implemented by the *Readjustment rules* that are part of the Morphophonology. Like the Spell-out rules Readjustment rules may be restricted to apply to particular lists of morphemes.

The Readjustment rules affect not only phonological properties of stems; they may also affect the grammatical information in the complex symbol. An example of this type of Readjustment rule is the rule that underlies some of the case syncretisms, widely attested in Indo-European noun and adjective declensions. A typical instance is the case syncretism of the Russian Accusative stated in (9).

(9) In the Plural and in the Singular of Declension Class II[10]
the Accusative is identical with the Genitive if the stem
is animate and with the Nominative, otherwise

As discussed in Sections 2.3.1 and 2.3.2, Russian nouns have several Nominative and Genitive Plural suffixes whose distribution is of considerable complexity. In view of this complexity it is essential not to have to state these distributions more than once in the grammar. A straightforward way of avoiding the nonfunctional repetition of the distribution of the different case suffixes is by postulating that under the conditions given in (9) Accusative is replaced by Genitive or Nominative. Formally we implement this by means of a Readjustment rule (cf. (30)) that rewrites Accusative as Genitive if the stem is animate, and as Nominative elsewhere. I illustrate the effects of applying this rule in (10).

(10) /car'/ [+anim, Class II] + /o/ Theme + Q [Sing, Acc]
'tsar' ↓
Gen

/dolot/ [-anim, Class II] + /o/ Theme + Q [Plural, Acc]
'chisel' ↓
Nom

---

[10]The role of declension class is further explained below.

Like the nouns in Spanish, Latin, Latvian and other Indo-European languages, the nouns of Russian belong to different declension classes. Class membership determines both the Theme vowel and the spell-out of the Number-Case suffix for a given word. In Russian declension class is correlated in large measure, but not totally, with gender. Class I nouns are mainly feminine, but include a fair number of masculine nouns. Class II nouns are exclusively nonfeminine, whereas class III nouns are feminine with the single exception of the noun *put'* 'path', which is masculine. In addition there is a large fourth class of indeclinable nouns, all of which are borrowings from various languages and are unrestricted as to gender. Thus, *kofe* 'coffee' is masculine, but *kafe* 'coffee-house' is neuter, and *miss* 'Miss' is feminine but *boa* 'boa' is masculine. In sum, declension class is largely predictable from gender in the case of nouns belonging to classes I and II. Nouns of class III are all feminine with the exception of *put'*—that is, for nouns of this class, gender is predictable from declension class. For indeclinable nouns, gender is predictable for nouns with animate referents, but not predictable for the rest. (For some additional comments, see Halle 1990, notes 8, 9, 11.)

To formally capture these redundancies we postulate the rules in (11).

(11)   a.   [+fem] → Class I
        b.   [-fem] → Class II
        c.   Class III → [+fem]

The rules (11) are typical redundancy rules in that they supply features only in contexts where these are missing; they cannot replace a feature already present. They differ in this respect from the Readjustment rules illustrated in (8), (9) and (10), which typically change previously assigned features. This difference between what Kiparsky has called the "structure-building" and "structure-changing" effects of rules correlates with the difference between rules of Word Synthesis vs. those of the Morphophonology. All rules of Word Synthesis are "structure-building": they invariably add information, but leave previously specified features intact. By contrast, Readjustment and Spell-out rules are "structure-changing."

The fact that the rules in (11) are not structure-changing is exploited in the manner in which information about gender and declension class is supplied to Vocabulary items. In Russian, nouns of the indeclinable class are entered in the Vocabulary with both declension class and gender specified. Hence none of the rules in (11) will affect them. Nouns of declension class III will be specified for declension class but not for gender; they receive gender from (11c). The noun *put'*, which is the sole exception to rule (11c), will have both gender and declension class supplied in its Vocabulary entry.

Finally, rules (11a,b) will apply to nouns unspecified for declension class, whose gender is given. Exceptions to rule (11b) such as *mužčina* 'man' or *maxaradža* 'maharajah', which are masculine in gender yet belong to declension class I, are supplied with both gender and declension class in the Vocabulary and are therefore unaffected by rule (11).

Unlike nouns, adjectives are – universally – unspecified for gender and obtain their gender feature from the noun that they modify. Noun-adjective concord is formally implemented by special rules of Word Synthesis. The concord rules assign not only gender but also animacy, case and number to adjectives and also to other noun modifiers including numerals. Since like the rules in (11) concord rules are part of the Word Synthesis module, they cannot change previously assigned features. This fact plays an important role in the notoriously complex distribution of these grammatical markers in Russian numeral phrases, which I discussed in Halle 1990.[11]

I have stated the concord rules of Russian informally in (12).

(12) In an NP the gender, animacy, number and case of the head noun are copied onto the specifiers and adjectives that are in the head noun's domain.

Since the concord rule (12) copies gender from the head noun, it is necessary that the redundancy rule (11c) apply before (12). On the other hand, since rules (11a,b) apply to adjectives as well as to nouns it is necessary to order (11a,b) after (12). The rule of case syncretism (9) must obviously apply after both the concord rule (12) and the redundancy rules (11). Since the rule of case syncretism (9) is a Readjustment rule, this order is an automatic consequence of the organization of the different modules in (1).[12]

---

[11] Since theories are to be judged above all by their empirical consequences it is a serious shortcoming of Pullum and Zwicky's (1991) criticisms of the theory of Halle (1990) that no notice is taken of the main empirical result of that study: the distribution of Case in Russian numeral phrases.

[12] As we have seen above both declension class and gender are among the grammatical markers of nouns. It was observed by Aronoff (1992) that a fundamental difference between declension class and gender is that only gender, but never declension class is copied by concord rules such as (12). The inferences to be drawn from this observation remain to be elaborated.

2 The Declension of Russian Adjectives and Nouns

In the section below the theoretical framework that has been sketched in Section 1 is subjected to empirical test by utilizing it in the description of the declension of Russian adjectives and nouns.

2.1 Information about Russian Phonology

Russian has the vowel system shown in (13).

(13)

	i	y	u	e	o	a	E	O
back	−	+	+	−	+	+	−	+
round	−	−	+	−	+	−	−	+
high	+	+	+	−	−	−	−	−

The vowels E/O are the "abstract" vowels (Yers) of the Slavic languages, first introduced into the analysis of the modern Slavic languages by the late Theodore Lightner (1972). There have been several proposals as to how these vowels are to be represented in underlying representations, of which the most attractive one – to my mind – is that advanced by Kenstowicz and Rubach (1987). Since the issue is tangential to the main subject matter of this paper I assume without further discussion Kenstowicz and Rubach's proposal that the Slavic "abstract" vowels are represented as feature complexes without associated timing slot. It is the absence of a timing slot that distinguishes [E,O] from the "concrete" [e,o] with which they share all distinctive features.[13]

I have given in (14) an informal statement of the surface distribution of the abstract vowels.

(14) The abstract vowels /E/ /O/ merge with /e/ /o/ if they are followed in the next syllable by an abstract vowel, elsewhere they are deleted.

In view of (14) word final Yers are always deleted. For various reasons, many of them noted already by Lightner (1972), it is necessary to postulate that in their underlying representation (almost) all Russian words end in a vowel including in many instances a Yer. I adopt this proposal and assume below that words that phonetically end with a consonant have in

---

[13] This decision assumes that it will be possible to solve in a satisfactory manner the formal problems the Kenstowicz-Rubach proposal raises for the treatment of stress in the Slavic languages. The ultimate disposition of this problem is unlikely to impact crucially on the issues under discussion here.

their underlying representation a word final Yer. For example, the Sg-Nom masculine adjective pronounced in the standard literary pronunciation [prastój] is represented underlyingly as /prost+o+j+O/. The word final /O/ is deleted by rule (14) while the stem vowel /o/ is actualized as [a] by virtue of the neutralization process discussed directly below.[14]

The concrete vowels are pronounced as indicated in (13) only when bearing word stress. When unstressed they are subject to neutralization processes of various kinds, which differ from dialect to dialect. The effects of these processes, which are referred to in the literature as *akan'e, okan'e, ikan'e*, etc., are systematically omitted from consideration below.

I have given in (15) a chart of the Russian consonants. Consonants enclosed in parentheses do not appear in underlying representations.

(15) labials   p p' b b' f f'   (v v')   m m'   (w)
     dorsals   k (k') g (g') x (x')
     coronals
     [+ant]   t t' d d' s s' z z' c n n' l l' r r'
     [−ant]   š (š') ž (ž') č'   j

The basic fact to be noted about the consonants is that they come in pairs traditionally designated as "hard vs. soft." The phonetic correlate of this distinction is that all consonants in Russian are pronounced with a raised tongue body: "hard" consonants are [+high, +back], "soft" consonants [+high, −back].

In representing the glide with the IPA symbol /j/ I am side-stepping the question as to the proper representation of glides and their role in the structure of the Russian syllable, which is in need of further investigation. My present guess is that in Russian the glide /j/ has the same feature composition as the vowel /i/ and like the latter is supplied with a single timing slot. (Mutatis mutandis, the same is true of the glide /w/ and the vowel /u/.) The difference between glides and vowels is therefore reflected by their different position in the syllable: vowels are found exclusively in the head of the rime, glides are to be found elsewhere. This is not necessarily true of glides everywhere. For example, I believe that in Semitic the glides /j,w/ are [−consonantal] segments whose major articulator is coronal, respectively labial. The Semitic glides thus differ from those of Russian and other IE languages, whose major articulator is dorsal. All four types of glides appear in the African language Fula. This is manifested in Fula con-

---

[14]Szpyra (1992) has argued that the correct way to account for the effects of the Yers described in (14) is by special treatment of the Yers in the syllabification rules. Since the matter is peripheral to the issues under discussion, I do not deal with Szpyra's proposals here beyond remarking that they seem to me to be on the right track.

sonant gradation, where certain [y,w] alternate with the dorsal consonants [Ng,g], whereas other [y,w] alternate with labials [mb,b] and coronals [nj,j], respectively. Following Sagey (1986), I assume that in the former glides the major articulator is dorsal, while in the latter glides the major articulator is labial and coronal, respectively. For some additional discussion see Halle (1992a).

The only other facts to be noted about Russian phonology here are the rules in (16).[15]

(16) a. Before front vowels consonants are automatically "softened," that is, they become [-back].
 b. After [-back] consonants the vowel /y/ surfaces as /i/.
 c. The glides /j,w/ are deleted when followed by a consonant (syllable onset).
 d. Vowels are deleted when followed by a vowel.

Rule (16a) accounts for the "softening" of /m/ in the Pl-Instr in (17) and elsewhere.

Rules (16c,d) are modernized versions of the truncation rules central to Jakobson's (1948) analysis of the Russian conjugation, which profoundly influenced the evolution of generative phonology in the 1960s.

Rules (16a,b) belong in the noncyclic (or post-cyclic) rule block of the phonology and are therefore not subject to the "strict cycle" condition (see Kiparsky 1982). Rules (16c,d) are cyclic rules of the language and are therefore subject to the "strict cycle" condition.[16]

---

[15] Rule (16c) might be written more formally as

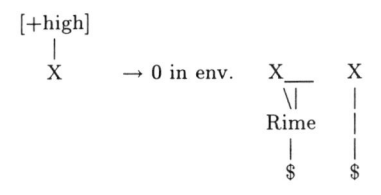

$$\begin{array}{c} [+\text{high}] \\ | \\ X \end{array} \rightarrow 0 \text{ in env.} \quad \begin{array}{cc} X\_\_ & X \\ \backslash| & | \\ \text{Rime} & | \\ | & | \\ \$ & \$ \end{array}$$

[16] Since cyclic rules do not apply to the innermost constituent of a word, glide-consonant and vowel-vowel sequences are found in stems; for example, /ajv/ 'quince', /tajg/ 'taiga', and /pauk/ 'spider', /aist/ 'stork'.

2.2 The Adjective Declension

An example paradigm of the adjective declension is given in (17). The noun declensions are exemplified in (23).

(17)

Singular	I	II	
	'simple' f.	'simple' m.	'simple' n.
nom	prost+a+j+a	prost+o+j	prost+o+j+o
acc	prost+u+j+u	like nom. or gen. (see (9) and Sect. 2.4)	
gen	prost+o+j	prost+o+v+o	
dat	prost+o+j	prost+o+m+u	
prep	prost+o+j	prost+o+m	
instr	prost+o+j(+u)	prost+y+m	

Plural		
nom		prost+y+j+e
acc		prost+y+j+e/y+x
gen		prost+y+x
dat		prost+y+m
prep		prost+y+x
inst		prost+y+m,+i

2.2.1 The Spell-out of the Theme Morpheme

In Russian, like in many other languages, adjectives do not have inherent gender but obtain it by a special Word Synthesis rule from the noun that is the syntactic head of the phrase.

As noted in part I and as discussed in greater detail in Halle (1990) declension class rather than gender determines the inflections that a given word takes. In the adjectives this distinction plays only an indirect role, since all adjectives of feminine gender belong to class I whereas all adjectives of nonfeminine (that is, masculine or neuter) gender are class II. As can readily be seen in the paradigms in (17) the distinction between masculine and neuter adjectives is neutralized everywhere except in the Sg-Nom and Sg-Acc. Moreover, in the plural there is only a single paradigm: distinctions among different inflection classes are neutralized in the Plural.

The Russian Declension

Like the nouns and adjectives of Latvian Russian adjectives and nouns have the constituent structure (18).

(18)   [[[Stem] + Q,Theme]$_{A,N}$ + Q,Number-Case]$_{A,N}$

I shall assume the identifying index Q of the adjective Theme is spelled out as /oj/, whereas the identifying index of the noun Theme is /o/.

(19)   a.   Q → /o+j/ in env. __,Theme]$_A$
        b.   Q → /o/ in env. __,Theme]$_N$

The adjective Theme mirrors the historical evolution of the adjective inflection quite directly. The inflected forms of the modern adjective derive from forms in which the inflected adjective was followed by the inflected form of the 3. pers. pronoun /j/. The historical evolution is fairly transparent in such modern forms as the Class I Sg-Nom /prost+a+j+a/ or Sg-Acc /prost+u+j+u/, where the Number-Case endings appear twice: once after the adjective stem and again after the pronominal clitic. Historical processes have obscured the traces of this development in most of the other forms.

As is readily seen in (17), the Theme vowel does not always surface as /o/. It appears as /a/ in the Sg-Nom of class I adjectives, and as /u/ in the Sg-Acc of Class I adjectives, whereas the Theme vowel is /y/ in the Sg-Instr of Class II adjectives and throughout the Plural. These facts are captured by the Readjustment rules in (20).

(20)

$$/o/ \rightarrow \begin{cases} \text{[-round] (/a/) in env. [I]} \_\_ \text{+j]}_A + \text{Q,Sg-Nom} \\ \text{[+high] (/u/) in env. [I]} \_\_ \text{+j]}_A + \text{Q,Sg-Acc} \\ \text{[-round, +high] (/y/) in env. [II]} \begin{cases} \_\_ \text{+j]}_A + \text{Q,Sg-Inst} \\ \_\_ \text{+j]}_A + \text{Q, Pl} \end{cases} \end{cases}$$

Fundamental to the treatment proposed here is the assumption that both Readjustment and Spell-out rules apply cyclically and that all Readjustment rules are ordered before the Spell-out rules. The Spell-out rule for the Theme vowel must therefore be context-free, because the rule applies at a stage in the derivation where the Number-Case morpheme is still invisible (cf. (18)). As a consequence, the different manifestations of the Theme vowel must be accounted for by means of the Readjustment rules (20) that apply on the second pass through the rules of the Morphophonology.

It might be noted that the change which the Theme vowel undergoes in the last two contexts in (20) is the joint product of its changes in the first two contexts. More importantly, since both Readjustment and Spell-out rules apply cyclically the Readjustment rules (20) apply on the second pass through the cyclic rules as they require reference to the Number-Case information which is available only at that stage in the derivation (cf. (18)). Finally, the rules in (20), like all rules in the Morphophonology, have been ordered in conformity with the Paṇini-an principle mentioned above so that the more restricted rules precede those that are less restricted. It is by virtue of this principle that in (20) the vowel change in the Plural is ordered last, for unlike the other three rules in the block, this rule requires mention of neither declension class nor Case for its correct application, since in the Plural the Theme vowel is/y/ in all Cases.

2.2.2 Realization of the Number-case Morpheme

As an inspection of the forms in (17) readily shows, the Theme vowel is followed everywhere by a consonant, which in most cases is followed by a vowel in turn. It was remarked above that in their underlying representation – i.e., the representation that serves as input to the rules of the phonology – all Russian words end in a vowel, it will therefore be assumed that in the forms where no vowel surfaces after the consonant, the form ends with the abstract Yer vowel, which is deleted word finally by rule (14). The question that needs to be answered at this point is whether these post-Theme Consonant-Vowel sequences are spell-outs of the different Number-Case morphemes or whether they require a different treatment.

As noted by Jakobson (1958) "of the 33 non-syllabic phonemes of the Moscow norm of the Russian literary language, only four – /j/, /v/, /m/, and /x/ – occur in case endings." In order to capture this restriction formally it is necessary to assume that the spell out rules for the Number-Case morphemes of Russian adjectives and nouns supply vowels only and that the post-Theme consonants are inserted by a set of Readjustment rules (see (21) and (25) below) that are separate and distinct from the rules spelling out the Number-Case morpheme (see (22) and (26)). If we had assumed that the Number-Case suffixes are spelled as Consonant-Vowel sequences we should have had no way to capture the fact that the variety of consonants appearing in post-Theme position is severely restricted.

The Theme vowel is followed by [v] only in the Sg-Gen of class II adjectives. In Russian as well as in other Slavic languages [v] is a surface reflex of the glide /w/. It was noted by Flier (1972) that alternations between /j/ and /w/ are pervasive in Russian. I assume that all of these alternations including those in the Sg-Gen are handled by a single Readjustment rule that turns /j/ into /w/ in a variety of morphological contexts. The rule will

The Russian Declension

be referred to as the j>w rule below, but because of its marginal relevance to the subject of primary interest here it will not be further discussed.

The Readjustment rules (21) and the Spell-out rules (22) together thus generate the Number-Case endings of the adjectives. The Readjustment rules insert /m/ or /x/ between the Adjective stem and the Number-case morpheme.

(21)

$$O \rightarrow \begin{cases} /m/ \begin{cases} \text{in env. } [\text{II}]\ldots]_A + \underline{\quad} \text{ Q, Sg-Prep} \\ \text{in env. } [\text{II}]\ldots]_A + \underline{\quad} \text{ Q, Sg} \\ \text{in env. } \quad\quad]_A + \underline{\quad} \text{ Q, Pl} \end{cases} \text{-Dat/Inst} \\ /x/ \quad \text{in env. } \quad\quad]_A + \underline{\quad} \text{ Q, Pl-Gen/Prep} \end{cases}$$

By virtue of (16c) the glide /j/ is deleted when the Number-Case morpheme begins with a consonant; i.e., wherever rule (21) applies. The process of glide deletion was noticed as central in the Russian verbal inflection in Jakobson (1948); its role in the adjective inflection was obscured by failure to understand the special role of /j/.

In view of the analysis that has been proposed here the Number-case suffixes are all vowels and they are spelled out by the rules in (22).[17]

(22)

$$Q \rightarrow \begin{cases} /o/ \text{ in env.} \begin{cases} [\text{II, Neut}]_A \ldots \underline{\quad}, \text{Sg-Nom} \\ [\text{II}]_A \ldots \underline{\quad}, \text{Sg-Gen} \end{cases} \\ /a/ \text{ in env.} \quad\quad [\text{I}]_A \ldots \underline{\quad}, \text{Sg-Nom} \\ \quad\quad\quad\quad\quad\quad [\text{II}]_A \ldots \underline{\quad}, \text{Sg-Dat} \\ /u/ \text{ in env.} \begin{cases} [\text{I}]_A \ldots \underline{\quad}, \text{Sg-Acc} \\ [\text{I}]_A \ldots \underline{\quad}, \text{Sg-Inst(opt)} \end{cases} \\ /e/ \text{ in env.} \quad\quad]_A \ldots \underline{\quad}, \text{Pl-Nom} \\ /i/ \text{ in env.} \quad\quad]_A \ldots \underline{\quad}, \text{Pl-Inst} \\ /O/ \text{ in env.} \quad\quad]_A \ldots \underline{\quad} \end{cases}$$

---

[17] The rules (22) leave unaccounted for all accusative forms, except those of the singular of class I adjectives. This special problem of the Russian nominal inflection is taken up in sec. 2.4.

Since the Spell-out rules replace the abstract marker Q with a string of phonemes, the application of a given rule in (22) bleeds every later rule. As elsewhere in the Morphophonology, the rules in (22) are ordered by decreasing complexity, reflecting the Paṇini-an principle of rule precedence.

It is a consequence of ordering rules in this manner that the actual instances to which all but the earliest rule applies will be a subset of the complement of the earlier rules. The instances to which such a rule applies may therefore lack a common denominator. We see this with special clarity in the default rule, the rule ordered last in a set like (22). This rule, which spells out the Case-Number morpheme as Yer, applies where none of the earlier rules could apply; i.e., in an environment that has no positive defining features. In sum, in a grammar in which the Paṇini-an principle holds and rules are ordered by decreasing complexity, we should expect to find rules that apply in contexts for which there can in principle be no common denominator. Collins (1991) has made interesting use of this insight in his treatment of the instrumental case in Ewe, Russian and some other languages.

A second consequence of this property of ordered rules is that wherever an earlier optional rule fails to apply the default rule must be invoked. The prediction is borne out by the Spell-out rules (21), where the Sg-Instr suffix of Class I adjectives is spelled out as /O/ by the default rule, when the optional Spell-out rule failed to spell it out as /u/.[18]

---

[18] Pullum and Zwicky (1991) express strong reservations about extrinsic rule ordering. They state that from "a metatheoretical point of view, this is decidedly a retrograde move." It is difficult to extrapolate from their discussion how without recourse to rule ordering they propose to treat the phenomena captured by the default rule in (22) and elsewhere. Nor do Pullum and Zwicky inform the reader how they would deal with the rather different type of evidence for rule ordering reviewed in Bromberger and Halle (1989). Since "metatheoretical" considerations must not prevent us from dealing correctly with empirical issues, Pullum and Zwicky's reservations cannot be taken as compelling in light of these unanswered questions.

2.3 The Noun Declension

The paradigms of the Russian noun declension are illustrated in (23).

(23)

	I 'lip'	'reason'	II 'tsar'	'chisel'
Sg nom	gub+a	um	car,	dolot+o
acc	gub+u	um	car,+a	dolot+o
gen	gub+y	um+a	car,+a	dolot+a
dat	gub,+e	um+u	car,+u	dolot+u
prep	gub,+e	um,+e	car,+e	dolot,+e
inst	gub+o+j+(u)	um+o+m	car,+o+m	dolot+o+m
Pl nom	gub+y	um+y	car,+i	dolot+a
acc	gub+y	um+y	car,+e+j	dolot+a
gen	gub	um+o+v	car,+e+j	dolot
dat	gub+a+m	um+a+m	car,+a+m	dolot+a+m
prep	gub+a+x	um+a+x	car,+a+x	dolot+a+x
inst	gub+a+m,+i	um+a+m,+i	car,+a+m,+i	dolot+a+m,+i

	III 'square'
Sg nom	ploščad,
acc	ploščad,
gen	ploščad,+i
dat	ploščad,+i
prep	ploščad,+i
inst	ploščad,+j+u
Pl nom	ploščad,+i
acc	ploščad,+i
gen	ploščad,+e+j
dat	ploščad,+a+m
prep	ploščad,+a+x
inst	ploščad,+am,+i

2.3.1 The Theme Vowel of Nouns

Nouns have exactly the same constituent structure as the adjectives; i.e., (18). Nouns differ from adjectives in that their Theme spell-out rule is (19b), rather than (19a). They also are subject to different Readjustment rules for the Theme and to different spell-out rules for the Number-Case morphemes.[19] Like the Adjective Theme, the Noun Theme, which is spelled out as /o/ by rule (19b), is subject to the Readjustment rules (24).

(24)

$$/o/ \rightarrow \begin{cases} /e/ & \text{in env.} \quad \begin{bmatrix} \text{-back} \\ \text{+cons} \end{bmatrix} + \underline{\quad}]_N + \quad \text{Q,Pl-Gen (cond)} \\ /O/ & \text{in env.} \quad [\text{III}] \qquad\qquad +\underline{\quad}]_N + \quad \begin{cases} \text{Q,Sg-Inst,} \\ \text{Q,Pl-Inst (list)} \end{cases} \\ /a/ & \text{in env.} \qquad\qquad\qquad\quad \underline{\quad}]_N + \quad \text{Q,Pl- Inst} \begin{cases} \text{Dat} \\ \text{Prep} \end{cases} \end{cases}$$

The Theme vowel becomes /e/ in the Pl-Gen of nouns whose stem ends in a "soft" consonant.[20] It becomes Yer in class III nouns: this occurs regularly in the Sg, in the Pl we get Yer only in the five Class III nouns: /lošad,+O+m,+i/ 'horses', /dver,+O+m,+i/ 'doors', /dočer,+O+m,+i/ 'daughters', /l,ud,+O+m,+i/ 'people', /det,+O+m,+i/ 'children'. The Theme vowel becomes /a/ in the Plural-Dative, Instrumental and Prepositional.

2.3.2 The Spell-out and Readjustment Rules of the Number-Case Morphemes in Nouns

Russian possesses a large number of indeclinable nouns. I assume that these nouns belong to a separate declension class designated by the feature [-D], whereas the other three declension classes are designated as [+D]. One of the peculiarities of the indeclinable nouns is that they are not subject to any of the insertion rules (25). This fact is reflected in (25) by the feature [+D] in certain rules.

(25)

$$0 \rightarrow \begin{cases} /j/ & \text{in env.} \quad \begin{cases} [\text{I}] \\ [\text{III}] \end{cases} \ldots]_N + \underline{\quad} + \text{Q,Sg-Inst} \\ & \qquad\qquad\quad [+D] \ldots]_N + \underline{\quad} + \text{Q,Pl-Gen (cond)} \\ /m/ & \text{in env.} \quad \begin{matrix} [\text{II}] & \ldots]_N + \underline{\quad} + \text{Q,Sg-Inst} \\ [+D] & \ldots]_N + \underline{\quad} + \text{Q,Pl-Dat/Inst} \end{matrix} \\ /x/ & \text{in env.} \quad [+D] \ldots]_N + \underline{\quad} + \text{Q,Pl-Prep} \end{cases}$$

---

[19] A special exception is constituted by the ten neuter nouns *bremja* 'burden,' *vremja* 'time,' *vymja* 'udder,' *znamja* 'banner,' *imja* 'name,' *plamja* 'flame,' *plemja* 'tribe,' *semja* 'seed,' *stremja* 'stirrup,' *temja* 'top of the head.' In the Sg-Nom these nouns are subject to neither of the two Spell-out rules (24) and (26) and surface with their bare stem. Because of the marginal character of this phenomenon I have not taken formal account of these exceptional forms below.

[20] Details on the fronting of /o/ to /e/ in the Plural Genitive as well as on the other rules applying in this Case are discussed separately in Section 2.3.1 below.

The Russian Declension

Like in the adjectives, a consonant (or glide) is inserted before certain Number-Case endings in the regularly declinable nouns as indicated in (25). As in the adjectives, the motivation for not treating these consonants as integral parts of the Number-Case suffix is that this is the only means of capturing formally the generalization that only /j/, /m/, or /x/ can figure in this position and that several different Number-Case suffixes begin with the same consonant or glide.

The rules (25) inserting /m/ and /x/ apply in a subset of the cases where these consonants are inserted in the adjective declension by the rules in (21). The main difference between (21) and (25) is the rule inserting the glide /j/. In the adjectives /j/ is part of the Theme. There is therefore no /j/ insertion rule in (21). In the nouns the glide is inserted in the Sg-Inst after all class I and III stems. The glide is inserted also in the Pl-Gen under special conditions that are discussed in Section 2.3.1 below.

The Number-Case morphemes of nouns are spelled out by the rules in (26). I have marked with an asterisk the rules that are identical with those for adjectives.

(26)

$$Q \rightarrow \begin{cases} /o/\text{in env.} & [\text{II,Neut}]_N + \ldots \_\_, \text{Sg-Nom}* \\ /a/\text{in env.} & \begin{cases} [\text{II}]_N + \ldots \_\_, \text{Pl-Nom (cond)} \\ [\text{II}]_N + \ldots \_\_, \text{Sg-Gen} \\ [\text{I}]_N + \ldots \_\_, \text{Sg-Nom} \end{cases} \\ /u/\text{in env.} & \begin{cases} [\text{I}]_N + \ldots \_\_, \text{Sg-Acc}* \\ [\text{I}]_N + \ldots \_\_, \text{Sg-Instr (opt)}* \\ [\text{III}]_N + \ldots \_\_, \text{Sg-Instr} \\ [\text{II}]_N + \ldots \_\_, \text{Sg-Dat}* \end{cases} \\ /i/\text{in env.} & \begin{cases} [\text{II}]_N + \ldots \_\_, \text{Pl-Nom (cond)} \\ [\text{III}]_N + \ldots \_\_, \text{Sg-Gen/Dat/Prep} \\ [+D]_N + \ldots \_\_, \text{Pl-Inst}* \end{cases} \\ /e/\text{in env.} & \begin{cases} [\text{II}]_N + \ldots \_\_, \text{Pl-Nom (cond)}* \\ [\text{I}]_N + \ldots \_\_, \text{Sg-Dat} \\ [+D]_N + \ldots \_\_, \text{Sg-Prep} \end{cases} \\ /y/\text{in env.} & \begin{cases} [\text{I}]_N + \ldots \_\_, \text{Sg-Gen} \\ [+D]_N + \ldots \_\_, \text{Pl-Nom} \end{cases} \\ /O/\text{in env.}]_N + \ldots \_\_* \end{cases}$$

Like in the adjectives, the default Spell-out for the noun case endings is the abstract Yer vowel /O/. It should be noted that the final rule in the block (26) is not restricted to applying only after declinable nouns, but applies freely also to indeclinable nouns.

As readily seen by comparing (26) with (22), all six vowels figuring in (22) appear also in (26). In addition, the vowel /y/ figures in (26) but not in (22). Moreover, the Spell-out rules for the Pl-Nom realize this morpheme as /a, e, i, y/ depending mainly on the gender and declensional category of the noun, but include also a significant component of lexical idiosyncrasy. The details are discussed in Section 2.3.2.

It will be recalled that the phonological rule (16d) deletes vowels in position before vowels. As a consequence the Theme vowel will appear in the output only in those forms where a consonant or glide has been inserted by rule (25). Since (25) fails to insert a glide or consonant in a fair number of Cases, the Theme vowel does not surface in a great many Number-Case forms.

The Theme vowel however does not cause the deletion of a stem final vowel in indeclinable nouns. I assume that like all nouns and adjectives, indeclinable nouns are subject to the Theme spell-out rule (18). Since some indeclinable noun stems end in a vowel, we might expect the Theme vowel to trigger rule (16d) and thus cause deletion of the vowel ending the indeclinable noun stem. For example, the indeclinable noun /kofe/ undergoes Theme vowel spell-out, yielding the string /kofe+o/. This string could be subject to (16d) which would result in the incorrect deletion to the stem-final /e/. We prevent this from happening by postulating that the Theme is not a cyclic morpheme and therefore does not trigger the cyclic rule (16d). The Theme vowel itself is deleted by rule (16d) when followed by a vowel-initial Number-Case suffix. Since, as noted, all indeclinable nouns are subject to the default Spell-out rule for Number-Case the form under discussion enters the phonology as [[kofe+o]+O]. Since the Theme is not a cyclic suffix, the cyclic rule (16d) will apply to our form first on the second cycle; that is, to the string /kofe+o+O/. Here the Yer will trigger deletion of [o] by rule (16d), subsequent to which the Yer will itself be deleted by rule (14). This is illustrated in (27) where I have given examples of the derivation of a few Number-Case forms of nouns.

(27)

	gub+o (I, Pl-Inst)	um+o (II, Sg-Gen)	ploščad̞+o (III, Sg-Inst)
(24)	gub+a		ploščad̞+O
(25)	gub+a+m		ploščad̞+O+j
(26)	gub+a+m+i	um+o+a	ploščad̞+O+j+u
(14, 16)	gub+a+m̞+i	um+a	ploščad̞+j+u

	dolot+o (II, Sg-Inst)	car̞+o (II, Pl-Nom)	kofe+o (indecl., Sg-Instr)
(24)		car̞+a	
(25)	dolot+o+m		
(26)	dolot+o+m+O	car̞+a+y	kofe+o+O
(14, 16)	dolot+o+m	car̞+i	kofe

2.2.3.1 The Pl-Gen Forms of Nouns

As shown in (23) all Pl-Gen forms of nouns end with a consonant or glide (j/w>v). This implies that the Pl-Gen morpheme is spelled out everywhere with the abstract vowel /O/.

The central distinction among the Pl-Gen forms is whether in the output they terminate in their stem consonant, as in [gub, dolot], or whether they end with a glide that is part of the material added to the stem as in /um+o+v, car̞+e+j, ploščad̞+e+j/.[21]

In nouns of the first type, the Pl-Gen morpheme is added directly after the Theme vowel. The Theme vowel is then deleted by rule (16d). Subsequent application of the Yer rule (13) deletes the Yer resulting in a consonant final word. (Cf. (28).)

---

[21] Many of the ideas of the treatment below derive from Jakobson 1957. For additional details see Jakobson 1958, and Garde 1980, secs. 239-246.

In nouns of the second type, the Theme vowel surfaces in the Pl-Gen as either /o/ or /e/; for example, /um+o+v/ 'reason', /car,+e+j/ 'tsar', /ploščad,+e+j/ 'square'. The Theme vowel surfaces because of the insertion of the glide after the Theme vowel by rule (25). (Cf. (28).)

The main complexity of the Pl-Gen actualization lies in the conditions, detailed below, under which glide insertion takes place.

The glide is inserted after all class III stems.

After class I stems the glide is inserted after stems ending in clusters consisting of a consonant followed by a "soft" liquid /r, l,/ or by /č š ž/. It is inserted also after an arbitrary list of class I stems that – by and large – have desinential stress in the Plural.

After class II stems the glide is generally inserted only after masculine, but not after neuter stems. There are, however, exceptions in both directions. Thus, a small number of masculine nouns fail to insert the glide. Among these are measure words such as *gramm* 'gram', *amper* 'ampere', *vol't* 'volt'; names of nationalities such as *baškir* 'Bashkir', *rumyn* 'Romanian'; paired objects such as *glaz* 'eye' and *pogon* 'epaulette' as well as a set of listed items such as *raz* 'time', *volos* 'hair', and so forth. Neuter nouns after which the glide is inserted are *mor,e* 'sea', *pol,e* 'field', *oblako* 'cloud', plus a number of words formed with the suffixes /Oj/ and /Ec/ such as *plat'e* 'dress', and *okonce* 'window' (diminutive). There are a fair number of stems where native usage vacillates as regards glide insertion.

Glide insertion, which is implemented by rule (25), is, of course, separate and independent of Theme vowel fronting, which is implemented by rule (24). In contrast to glide insertion, the conditions under which the Theme vowel is fronted by rule (24) are quite simple. As observed by Jakobson (1957), rule (24) applies if the stem ends with a "soft" – that is, [-back] – consonant or with one of the palatal consonants, /č š ž/. It is plausible to assume that in Russian palatal consonants are underlyingly [-back]. It is therefore possible to restrict fronting by rule (24) to the position after [+cons, -back].

The glide inserted by rule (25) is /j/, and it is turned into /w/ after back vowels by the operation of the j>w rule; that is, in all instances where rule (24) did not turn /o/ into /e/.

Two consequences of the account above are worth noting especially: i. Theme vowel fronting by rule (24) never takes place after stems ending with the glide /j/. This follows directly from the fact that /j/ is not [+cons] but [-cons], whereas fronting of the Theme vowel /o/ to /e/ takes place only after [+cons, -back] segments. ii. Since vowels are deleted before vowels (cf. rule (16d)), the effects of the fronting rule are observable only in forms that undergo glide insertion by (25). In forms that do not undergo glide insertion, the Theme vowel will be invariably deleted by rule (16d).

We illustrate the derivations of Pl-Gen forms in (28) below. In examining these it should be recalled that the Plural-Genitive desinence is spelled out everywhere as the back Yer (by the default rule in (26)).

(28)

	gub+o	um+o	car,+o
(24)			car,+e
(25)		um+o+j	car,+e+j
j > w		um+o+w	
(26)	gub+o+O	umo+ow+O	car,+e+j+O
(16b, 14)	gub	um+o+w	car,+e+j

	dolot+o	ploščad,+o
(24)		ploščad,+e
(25)		ploščad,+e+j
j > w		
(26)	dolot+o+O	ploščad,+e+j+O
(16b, 14)	dolot	ploščad,+e+j

2.2.3.2 The Pl-Nom of Nouns

The Pl-Nom morpheme has a single Spell-out rule for nouns of Classes I and III, in both contexts Pl-Nom is spelled out as /y/. If the stem ends with a "soft" [-back] consonant, rule (16b) applies and fronts the /y/ to /i/. By contrast Pl-Nom has four different spell-outs for class II nouns. For Class II nouns the basic rule is that they take the suffix /a/ if they are neuter, whereas they take /y/ if they are masculine. There are however numerous exceptions. In sketching these below I follow mainly the account in Jakobson 1957 and Garde 1980 (Sections 236-7, 243).

Nouns formed with the suffix /+in/ lose this suffix and take /e/ in the Pl-Nom. These nouns systematically delete the /+in/ suffix in the plural. For example, /angl,iCan,+in - angl,ičan,+e/ 'Englishman' (Sg/Pl-Nom). The only exception to this is /s,em,jan,+in - s,emjan,+in+y/ 'family man', which takes the regular /y/ ending and also fails to delete the /in/ suffix.[22]

A small number of neuter nouns take /i/ in the Pl-Nom; for example, /kol,en+o - kol,en,+i/ 'knee', /pl,eč+o - pl,eč+i/ 'shoulder', /ok+o - oč+i/ 'eye'. Other neuters take /y/; for example, /jablok+o - jablok+y > jablok,+i/ 'apple'. The distinction between /i/ and /y/ is reflected in the fact that /i/ triggers the /k-č/ alternation in /ok+o - oč+i/ 'eye', whereas /y/ does not, as in /jablok+y > jablok,+i/ 'apples'.

Masculine stems that in the plural are subject to a special rule "softening" their final consonant take the regular /y/ suffix, which is actualized as [i] by rule (16b); for example /čert - čert,+i/ 'devil', /sos,ed - sos,ed,+i/ 'neighbor'.

Numerous masculine stems take the /a/ ending in the Pl-Nom; for example, /l,es+a/ 'forests', /glaz+a/ 'eyes'. Nouns formed with the suffixes /or/ and /tor/, always take /a/; for example, /prof,es+or+a, konduk+tor+a/.

2.4 The Accusative Case

As noted in Part I the Russian Accusative Case has a distinct suffix only for class I stems in the Singular, everywhere else the Accusative is indistinguishable from either the Genitive or Nominative. This is true of nouns as well as of adjectives. We review the different instances of Case syncretism in order.

In Class III nouns the Accusative coincides with the Nominative. Both Case morphemes are actualized by the abstract vowel /O/. Since this vowel represents the default Case, it suffices not to include Class III nouns in any of the other Spell-out rules for the Sg. Acc. Case morpheme (cf. (26)).

This simple move is not available in the remaining instances. In the Plural, for both adjectives and nouns the Accusative is identical with the Genitive, if the stem is animate, and with the Nominative otherwise. And the same principle holds for class II nouns and adjectives in the Singular.

As we have seen in Sections 2.3.1 and 2.3.2 the rules governing the actualization of the Pl-Nom and Pl-Gen morphemes are of considerable

---

[22]Since none of these nouns has stress on the Pl-Nom suffix it is in principle impossible to determine whether the suffix is /e/ or /i/ in the literary standard pronunciation, since these two vowels merge phonetically when unstressed. I have maintained the distinction here because it surfaces in certain other dialects. Nothing of any importance here hinges on this decision.

complexity. In view of this it clearly would be undesirable to express the fact that the Accusative is identical with the Nominative, respectively Genitive, by adding new environments to the Readjustment and Spell-out rules. In fact, the attempt to do so is fraught with so many technical problems that anyone undertaking it is likely to become discouraged almost at once.

The most straightforward account of the Plural facts is to postulate a Readjustment rule that changes the Accusative to Genitive or Nominative in the relevant instances. The rule would have the form (29a).

(29a)

$$\text{Acc} \to \left\{ \begin{array}{l} \text{Gen in env. [+animate]}_{A,N} \cdots \\ \text{Nom in env} \qquad \qquad \cdots \end{array} \right\} \text{Q, Pl} \_\_$$

Essentially the same rule applies to class II adjectives and nouns in the Singular as well. We need therefore in addition to (29a) a rule that has the effects of (29b).

(29b)

$$\text{Acc} \to \left\{ \begin{array}{l} \text{Gen in env. [+animate]}_{A,N} \cdots \\ \qquad \qquad \text{[Class II]} \\ \text{Nom in env. [Class II]} \quad \cdots \end{array} \right\} \text{Q,} \_\_$$

It is an open question at this time how two rules such as (29a) and (29b) are to be formally combined so as to express the fact that they are largely identical. What is beyond dispute is that the fact of their partial identity must be taken account of in the form of the rules. Utilizing the familiar notation employed in SPE these partial identities among the rules would be taken into account by rewriting the two rules above as in (30).

(30)

$$\text{Acc} \to \left\{ \begin{array}{l} \text{Gen in env. [+animate]}_{A,N} \; \cdots \\ \qquad \quad < \text{[Class II]} >_a \\ \text{Nom in env.} < \text{[Class II]} >_a \; \cdots \\ \qquad \text{Cond: if a, not b} \end{array} \right\} \text{Q,} < \text{Pl} >_b \_\_$$

References

Anderson, Stephen R. 1982. Where's morphology? *Linguistic Inquiry* 13:571-612.

Anderson, Stephen R. 1986. Disjunctive order in inflectional morphology. *Natural Language and Linguistic Theory* 4:1-31.

Anderson, Stephen R. 1990. *A-morphous morphology.* Cambridge: Cambridge University Press.

Aronoff, Mark. 1992. Noun classes in Arapesh. *Morphology yearbook* (pp. 21–31). Dordrecht: Kluwer.

Baker, Mark C. 1988. *Incorporation: A theory of grammatical function changing.* Chicago: University of Chicago Press.

Bromberger, Sylvain and Morris Halle. 1989. Conceptual issues in morphology. Lecture presented at Stanford University.

Carstens, Vicki M. 1991. *The morphology and syntax of determiner phrases in Kiswahili.* Ph.D. dissertation, University of California, Los Angeles.

Chomsky, Noam. 1991. Some notes on economy of derivation and representation. In R. Freidin (ed.), *Principles and parameters in comparative grammar*, pp. 417-454. Cambridge, MA: MIT Press.

Chomsky, Noam and Morris Halle. 1968. *The sound pattern of English.* New York: Harper and Row. Reprinted 1991, Cambridge, MA: MIT Press.

Collins, Christopher. 1991. *Default case in Ewe and elsewhere.* ms., Department of Linguistics, Massachusetts Institute of Technology.

Flier, Michael. 1972. On the source of derived imperfectives in Russian. In D. Worth (ed.), *The Slavic word*, pp. 236-260. The Hague: Mouton.

Garde, Paul. 1980. *Grammaire russe I.* Paris: Institut d'Etudes Slaves.

Halle, Morris. 1973. The accentuation of Russian words. *Language* 49:312-348.

Halle, Morris. 1989. On abstract morphemes and their treatment. Lecture presented at the University of Arizona.

Halle, Morris. 1990. An approach to morphology. *Proceedings of NELS* 20:1.150-184.

Halle, Morris. 1992a. Phonological features. In W. Bright (ed.), *International encyclopedia of linguistics*, pp. 207-212. New York: Oxford University Press.

Halle, Morris. 1992b. The Latvian declension. *Morphology yearbook* (pp. 32–47). Dordrecht: Kluwer.

Halle, Morris and Jean-Roger Vergnaud. 1987. *An essay on stress.* Cambridge, MA: MIT Press.

Harris, James W. 1991. The exponence of gender in Spanish. *Linguistic Inquiry* 22:27-62.

Jakobson, Roman. 1948. Russian conjugation. *Word* 4:155-167.

Jakobson, Roman. 1957. The relationship between genitive and plural in the declension of Russian nouns. *Scando-Slavica* 3:181-186.

Jakobson, Roman. 1958. Morfologičeskie nabljudenija nad slavjanskim skloneniem (Sostav russkix padežnyx form). In *American Contributions to the Fourth International Congress of Slavists*, pp. 127-156. The Hague: Mouton. Quoted here from the English translation in Jakobson 1984.

Jakobson, Roman. 1984. *Russian and Slavic grammar.* Berlin: Mouton.

Jensen, John T. 1990. *Morphology: Word structure in generative grammar.* Amsterdam: John Benjamins.

Kenstowicz, Michael and Jerzy Rubach. 1987. The phonology of syllabic nuclei in Slovak. *Language* 63:463-497.

Kiparsky, Paul. 1973. 'Elsewhere' in phonology. In Stephen R. Anderson and Paul Kiparsky (eds.), *A Festschrift for Morris Halle*, pp. 93-106. New York: Holt, Rinehart and Winston.

Kiparsky, Paul. 1982. Lexical morphology and phonology. In I-S. Yang (ed.), *Linguistics in the morning calm.* Seoul: Hanshin.

Lees, Robert B. 1960. *The grammar of English nominalizations.* The Hague: Mouton.

Lieber, Rochelle. 1992. *Deconstructing morphology: Word formation in syntactic theory.* Chicago: University of Chicago Press.

Lightner, Theodore. 1972. *Problems in the theory of phonology.* Edmonton/Champaign: Linguistic Research, Inc.

Marantz, Alec. 1988a. Clitics, morphological merger and the mapping to phonological structure. In *Theoretical morphology*, pp. 253-270. San Diego: Academic Press.

Marantz, Alec. 1988b. Apparent exceptions to the Projection Principle. In *Morphology and modularity: In honour of Henk Schultnik*, pp. 217-232. Dordrecht: Foris.

Marantz, Alec and Morris Halle. 1993. Distributed morphology and the pieces of inflection. ms., Department of Linguistics, Massachusetts Institute of Technology.

McCarthy John. 1991. Synchronic rule inversion. ms., Department of Linguistics, University of Massachusetts, Amherst.

Myers, Scott. 1987. Vowel shortening in English. *Natural Language and Linguistic Theory* 5:485-518.

Perlmutter, David M. 1988. The split morphology hypothesis: Evidence from Yiddish. In M. Hammond and M. Noonan (eds.), *Theoretical morphology*, pp. 79-100. San Diego: Academic Press.

Pollock, J-Y. 1989. Verb movement, universal grammar, and the structure of IP. *Linguistic Inquiry*, 20:365–424.

Pullum, Geoffrey K. and Arnold M. Zwicky. 1991. A misconceived approach to morphology. *Proceedings of the Tenth West Coast Conference on Formal Linguistics*.

Sadock, Jerrold M. 1991. *Autolexical syntax: A theory of parallel grammatical representations*. Chicago: University of Chicago Press.

Sagey, Elizabeth C. 1986. *The representation of features and relations in non-linear phonology*. Ph.D. dissertation, Department of Linguistics, Massachusetts Institute of Technology.

Stump, Gregory T. 1989. A note on Breton pluralization and the elsewhere condition. *Natural Language and Linguistic Theory* 7:261-275.

Szpyra, Jolanta. 1992. Ghost segments in nonlinear phonology: Polish Yers. *Language* 68:277–312.

Weight of CVC can be Determined by Context

Bruce Hayes
University of California, Los Angeles

1 Introduction

The contrast of heavy vs. light syllables is central to the phonology of many languages. Typologically, we observe two patterns. In Latin and other languages, both long-voweled (CVV) and closed (CVC) syllables count as heavy, with CV syllables light. In Cahuilla (Seiler 1977) and various other languages, only CVV is heavy, with both CVC and CV light.

Moraic theory (Hyman 1985, McCarthy and Prince 1986, Hayes 1989, Ito 1989, Zec 1988) adapts and formalizes the traditional notion of mora to account for this. Heavy syllables in Latin contain two moras (formalized /μ/ below), light syllables one:

(1) **Latin: CV Light; CVC, CVV, CVVC Heavy**

```
    σ           σ         σ          σ
    |          /\        /\         /\
    μ         μ μ        μ μ        μ μ
   /|         /| |       /|/        /|/\
   t a   vs.  t a t      t a        t a t

  ([ta])     ([tat])    ([ta:])    ([ta:t])
```

In a language like Cahuilla, the structures are the same, except that CVC is assigned only one mora:

(2) **Cahuilla: CV, CVC Light; CVV, CVVC Heavy**

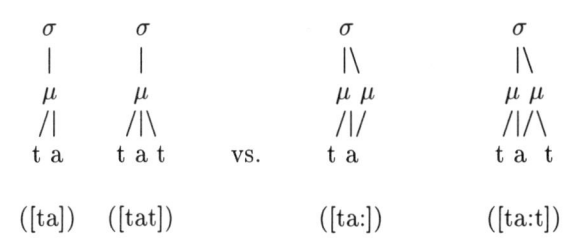

```
    σ       σ            σ          σ
    |       |           /\         /\
    μ       μ           μ μ        μ μ
   /|      /|\          /|/        /|/\
   t a     t a t   vs.  t a        t a t

  ([ta])  ([tat])      ([ta:])    ([ta:t])
```

For rules that can create these structures in various languages, see Hayes (1989).

This article addresses a possibility inherent within moraic theory: that the representation for CVC can differ by context within a single language. By this I mean that there can be language-specific rules of the form: "Assign second mora to CVC in context X" or "Remove second mora from CVC in context Y." Such a move has been suggested by Kager (1989) for English; Kager's view is that certain stressless CVC syllables in English and Dutch are light. This results phonetically in vowel reduction and (at least for English) in the formation of syllabic resonants.

Letting CVC vary in weight by context of course increases the expressive power (and thus lessens the predictive power) of phonological theory. I suggest that this is compensated for in two ways: it provides increased insight into prosodic phenomena in various languages, and it allows significant restrictions to be placed on the metrical theory of stress.

I propose that while heavy and light CVC may on occasion form a derived contrast, they never contrast in underlying representation. In this respect, syllable weight resembles syllable division: while a language may syllabify (for example) /VplV/ as /Vp.lV/ in some morphological or phonological contexts and as /V.plV/ in others (cf. English *uplift* vs. *apply*), there appear to be no cases of underlying /Vp.lV/ ~ /V.plV/ contrasts.

While moraic theory provides a straightforward way of describing the distinction of heavy vs. light CVC, it is not the only means of doing so; the theory of syllable constituency proposed by Levin (1985) and similar work could easily be modified in the same direction. This could be done, for example, by placing weight-bearing coda consonants in the syllable nucleus and weightless consonants outside it (cf. Anderson 1984).

2   Metrical Preliminaries

I assume here a theory of foot structure developed by Hayes (1985, 1987) and McCarthy and Prince (1986) and presented more fully in Hayes (forthcoming). The central idea is that the "atoms" of metrical representation, that is, the basic templates for metrical feet, form a very small set: namely moraic trochees, syllabic trochees, and iambs, defined as follows. In the diagrams below, /˘/ stands for a light syllable, /–/ for a heavy.

(3) a. **Moraic Trochee:**
two light syllables, first strong: (x .)
⌣ ⌣

or one strong heavy: (x)
—

b. **Syllabic Trochee:**
two syllables of any weight, first strong: (x .)
σ σ

c. **Iamb:**
two syllables with first light and second strong: (. x)
⌣ σ

or one strong heavy: (x)
—

This seemingly arbitrary set of templates has a basis in an extralinguistic principle, stated below:

(4) **Iambic/Trochaic Law**

i. Elements contrasting in intensity naturally form groupings with initial prominence.

ii. Elements contrasting in duration naturally form groupings with final prominence.

This principle has widespread effects in rhythmic phenomena, for example, perceptual experiments, music and metrics (for discussion see Hayes, forthcoming). The foot templates of (3) are the ones that most clearly satisfy the Iambic/Trochaic Law, while also allowing most syllables in any given string to be parsed into feet.

The inventory of (3) lacks foot templates of the shortest possible type, that is, /⌣/ in languages that refer to syllable weight and /σ/ in languages where stress is computed solely by syllable count. The role, if any, that such "degenerate" feet should play in metrical theory is a difficult question (for discussion, see Kager 1989 and Hayes, forthcoming). For present purposes, we need only assume that languages tend to avoid creating such degenerate feet, and indeed appear to avoid them entirely in certain contexts.

The ban on degenerate feet allows us to make more sense of the rather disparate-seeming recipe for the iamb: the *canonical form* of the iamb is

/˘ ´/; also allowed is anything shorter, but not degenerate. The Iambic/Trochaic Law is most clearly applicable to the canonical form.

From McCarthy and Prince (1986), Prince (1991) and other work, I assume that foot construction is not just a mode of assigning stress, but an organizing principle of the phonology. For example, in various languages the phonological rules appear to have a conspiratorial effect in creating optimal foot structure, for example, by "repairing" feet that have been damaged by segmental rules, or by converting a foot from suboptimum to optimum form. The latter phenomenon is found in iambic feet: conversion of a /˘ ˘́/ iamb to the canonical /˘ ´/ shape optimizes it.

With this background, I can now consider three examples of variable-weight CVC.

3 Cahuilla

Cahuilla, a Uto-Aztecan language of Southern California, has been investigated in detail in the work of Seiler (1957, 1965, 1977). Stress in Cahuilla is normally stem-initial, with trains of alternating secondary stresses going outward from the main stress in either direction. The alternation is "quantity-sensitive," in that heavy syllables attract stress and reset the alternating count for strings of light syllables.

Two expository simplifications are adopted here. First, I ignore the cases of stress on prefixes, which are straightforward and do not affect the point at issue. Second, I allow here the creation of degenerate feet of the form /˘́/ on final syllables when only one syllable is left over in the left-to-right parse. In fact, there are reasons both theoretical and empirical not to do this (Hayes, forthcoming), but the issue is not relevant to present concerns.

With these simplifications assumed, here are the Cahuilla stress rules:

(5) **Cahuilla Stress**

    a. Form moraic trochees (cf. (3)) from left to right.
    b. Form a higher metrical layer assigning main stress to the leftmost foot.

Since moraic trochees refer to syllable weight, we must define the heavy syllable: in Cahuilla this is normally CVV(C), where VV is a long vowel or diphthong. Consider the forms below. In (6a), the two moraic trochees that are constructed are both of the form /˘́˘/; whereas in (6b), left-to-right foot parsing creates first /´/, then /˘́˘/. In either case, the leftmost foot attracts main stress through construction of a higher "word layer."

(6) a.　　(x .)(x .)　　　b.　　(x) (x .)　　　　foot construction
　　　　　ᵕ ᵕ　ᵕ ᵕ　　　　　　　　—　ᵕ ᵕ
　　　　　táka lìčem　　　　　　　qá:nkìčem

　　　　　(x　　　)　　　　　　　(x　　　)　　　word layer
　　　　　(x .)(x .)　　　　　　　(x)(x .)　　　construction
　　　　　ᵕ ᵕ　ᵕ ᵕ　　　　　　　　—　ᵕ ᵕ
　　　　　táka lìčem　　　　　　　qá:nkìčem

　　　　　'one-eyed ones'　　　　'palo verde, plur.'　　(Seiler 1977:27)

It is easy to show that in ordinary circumstances, CVC counts as a light syllable. For example, if CVC were heavy, the word *táxmuʔàt* 'song' (Seiler 1965:57) would be counted as /– ᵕ ᵕ/ and be stressed **táxmùʔat*. The observed stressing follows if *táxmuʔàt* is /ᵕ ᵕ ᵕ/.

The phenomenon of interest to this article is a morphological process of "intensification" (Seiler 1977:58), which applies to stems beginning CVCV or CVCCV. In either case, the second C receives greater length, transcribed by Seiler with consonant doubling.

(7) a.　čéxiwèn　　'it is clear'　　b.　wélnet　　'mean one'
　　　　čé**xx**ìwen　'it is very clear'　　　wéll**n**èt　'very mean one'

Note that *čéxxiwen* is stressed like *qá:nkìčem*, suggesting that it is quantitatively /ᵕ ᵕ ᵕ/. Noting this, Seiler (1977:58) characterizes the lengthening as a prosodic (as opposed to purely segmental) phenomenon: "as an invariant we find that the initial syllable receives an extra mora, thus a total value of two morae. As a consequence, the second vowel of the sequence will bear secondary stress." The crucial point is that Intensification is a *weight*-changing phenomenon; it is this that results in shifts in secondary stress. (This also argues against the view that Intensification is somehow extraphonological or paralinguistic.)

Moraic theory provides a straightforward formalization of Seiler's suggestion. I express Intensification as the insertion of an additional mora into the stem-initial syllable. Where the amplified syllable already contains a final consonant, it is this consonant that receives the mora (cf. (8b)). Where there is no final consonant, the inserted mora is linked to the onset of the following syllable, as in (8a).

(8) a.
```
        σ         σ         σ        b.    σ         σ           input form,
        |         |         |              |         |           syllabification
        μ         μ         μ              μ         μ           (without
       /|        /|        /|\            /|\       /|\          Intensification,
       č e       x i       w e n          w e l     n e t        → čéxiwèn,
                                                                 wélnet)

        σ         σ         σ              σ         σ           Intensification
       |\         |         |             |\         |
       μ μ        μ         μ             μ μ        μ
       /|        ../|       /|\           /| :      /|\
       č e       x i        w e n         w e l     n e t
```

The stress pattern of intensified forms follows straightforwardly from the syllable weights that have been assigned, shown in (9).

(9) a.
```
        (x          )        b.   (x          )       stress assignment
        (x ) (x  .)                (x ) (x )
        σ    σ   σ                 σ     σ            (= čéxxiwen, wéllnèt)
       |\    |   |                |\     |
       μ μ   μ   μ                μ μ    μ
       /| \ /|  /|\               /| |  /|\
       č e   x i w e n            w e l  n e t
```

That is, čéxxiwen is stressed as /– ˘ ˘/, while wéllnèt is stressed like ordinary /– ˘/ words.

Two loose ends must be cleared up. First, I state in (10) the principles that link up the inserted moras in the right places.

(10) **Stray Mora Association (Cahuilla)**

Stray moras associate with
(a) non-moraic syllable-final consonants, if present; else
(b) the onset of the following syllable.

I will not speculate on to what extent such principles can be made universal. A cautionary fact in this respect is that the linkings appear to vary across dialects of Cahuilla. The rules stated above hold for the Desert dialect described by Seiler; in contrast, in the Mountain dialect, intensification takes the form of vowel lengthening. For example, the intensified forms analogous to those of (7) are čé:xiwe and wé:lnet (data from Pamela Munro (p.c.), to whom many thanks). It appears that in Mountain Cahuilla, the inserted mora is always linked to the vowel.

The other issue concerns the phonetic interpretation of the output forms in (9)—are we entitled to transcribe the moraic /l/ of (9b) as [ll], despite the fact that it is only singly linked? The suggestion here is that linkage of a segment to its own mora implies greater phonetic length. This is intuitively plausible, since the mora is a timing unit, and a consonant without its own mora must share with the preceding vowel.

Summing up, Cahuilla shows a fairly clear derived contrast between heavy and light CVC syllables. In particular, the regular vs. intensive forms of *welnet* form a minimal pair in this respect, as in (11).

(11) a.
$$\begin{array}{ccc} \sigma & \sigma & \\ | & | & \\ \mu & \mu & = \text{[welnet]} \\ /|\backslash & /|\backslash & \\ \text{w e l} & \text{n e t} & \end{array}$$
b.
$$\begin{array}{ccc} \sigma & \sigma & \\ |\backslash & | & \\ \mu\ \mu & \mu & = \text{[wellnet]} \\ /|\ | & /|\backslash & \\ \text{w e l} & \text{n e t} & \end{array}$$

The evidence for contextually weighted CVC in Cahuilla is twofold: the extra mora induces an audibly distinct durational pattern, and the heavy CVC syllables behave just like heavy CVV for purposes of stress assignment.

4 Latin

As I have analyzed it (Hayes 1987, forthcoming), the normal metrical foot of Latin is the moraic trochee, that is, $/\smile\smile/$ or $/-/$. This foot is assigned at the right edge of the stress domain, after an earlier rule that marks final syllables as extrametrical (in the sense of Hayes 1982). This gives the typical pattern of antepenultimate stress where the penult is light and penultimate stress where the penult is heavy. The data below are from Allen 1973:155). Angle brackets surround extrametrical syllables.

(12) a.
$$\begin{array}{c} (\text{x .}) \\ -\ \smile\smile\ \text{<->} \\ \text{ko:nfíki unt} \end{array}$$
b.
$$\begin{array}{c} (\text{x}) \\ \smile\ -\ \text{<->} \\ \text{pe pér ki:} \end{array}$$

c.
$$\begin{array}{c} (\text{x}) \\ \smile\smile\ -\ \text{<->} \\ \text{ini mí: kus} \end{array}$$
d.
$$\begin{array}{c} (\text{x}) \\ -\ -\ \smile\ \text{<->} \\ \text{eksí:sti mo:} \end{array}$$

This proposal in fact follows a very early foot-based analysis of Allen (1973:177), a work from which much of the following account is taken.

A curious corner of the Latin stress system is the treatment of words that had the quantitative shape /˘ –/. In the terminology of Hayes (forthcoming), these exhibit the "unstressable word syndrome." That is, the final syllable is extrametrical and cannot be stressed, and the preceding light syllable is too short to constitute a well-formed foot. In general, languages appear to adopt a wide variety of strategies to resolve "unstressable words." The strategies that Latin uses are the following. (a) Revoke extrametricality, so that the final heavy syllable can serve as a foot, as in (13a). It is likely that this option was taken in Latin when a /˘ –/ word occupied phrase-final position (Allen 1973:186-188). (b) A process of "incorporation" applies, whereby the final /–/ syllable is made a weak member of a foot whose head is the preceding light, as in (13b).

(13) a. **Revocation of Extrametricality**

$$\begin{array}{ccccc} & & & & (x) \\ \smile <-> & & \smile - & & \smile - \\ e\ go{:} & \to & ego{:} & \to & e\ gó{:} \end{array}$$

b. **Incorporation**

$$\begin{array}{ccccc} & & (x) & & (x\ .) \\ \smile <-> & & \smile <-> & & \smile - \\ e\ go{:} & \to & e\ go{:} & \to & é\ go{:} \end{array}$$

The incorporation strategy creates feet that, although outside the permitted forms for moraic trochees, are at least not degenerate. It is the incorporation strategy that I will focus on here.

The output of incorporation was often subsequently "repaired" by the application of an optional segmental rule. This is the so-called "Iambic Shortening" of the early Classical period (Allen 1973:179-185), which had precisely the effect of converting /˘́–/ words into /˘́˘/, a canonical moraic trochee. For example, *égo:* 'I' became *égo*, with the /˘́˘/ output pattern; similarly *béne:, dúo:* became *béne, dúo*. I express the rule in moraic terms in (14a), with an example of its application in (14b).

(14) a. **Latin Iambic Shortening** b.

$$\begin{array}{ccc} (x\ .) & & (x\ .) \\ \sigma\ \sigma & \to & \sigma\ \sigma \\ |\ |\backslash & & |\ | \\ \mu\ \mu\ \mu & & \mu\ \mu \end{array}$$

$$\begin{array}{ccc} (x\ .) & & (x\ .) \\ \sigma\ \sigma & & \sigma\ \sigma \\ |\ |\backslash & \to & |\ | \\ \mu\ \mu\ \mu & & \mu\ \mu \\ |\ /|/ & & |\ /| \\ e\ g\ o & & e\ g\ o \end{array}$$

Note that words whose feet were *already* canonical did not undergo shortening.

(15) a. (x) b. (x) c. (x .)
     —   —   ˘ ˘
     ám <bo:> lon <ge:> simu <la:>

/CVCV:/ was not the only possible segmental configuration that would give rise to /˘ −/ quantity in Latin; the same would be expected of /CVCVC/. What is of interest here is evidence suggesting that Iambic Shortening applied to these words as well. This of course cannot be detected in the orthographic record, but is supported by evidence from Latin metrics.

Latin verse was quantitative, in that a well-formed line consisted of a particular sequence of heavy and light syllables. From verse of the period, it can be determined that CVC syllables in the Iambic Shortening environment were frequently scanned as light, as in the following cases from Allen (1973:182–183).

(16) a. ˘ ˘ − − −   b. ˘ ˘ − −   metrical scansion
        úter wostró:rum   dédit dó:no: verse text

In fact, such scansions follow from the analysis as stated so far, virtually without alteration. Iambic Shortening would remove the second mora from the final syllable of a CVCVC word, as in (17b). I assume further that a consonant stranded in this way is reaffiliated within its own syllable, as shown in (17c).

(17) a. (x .)   b. (x .)   c. (x .)
        σ σ   σ σ   σ σ
        | |\   → | | → | |
        μ μ μ   μ μ   μ μ
        | /| | | /| | /|··
        u t e r   u t e r   u t e r

I conclude that Latin had surface minimal pairs for the weight of CVC. CVC not affected by Iambic Shortening was heavy, whereas CVC to which the rule had applied was light. Latin being dead, we cannot know what phonetic correlates this weight distinction had, but from the analogy of living languages (English, Dutch, and Cahuilla, above; and Yupik, below) we can surmise that light CVC was phonetically shorter.

5 Yupik

The prosodic systems found in the Yupik Eskimo languages have attracted a great deal of interest from metrical phonologists, thanks to the absorbing descriptions and analyses published by Woodbury (1981, 1987), Jacobson (1985), Miyaoka (1985), Leer (1985), and other scholars of Yupik. Here, I only skim over a small part of the topic, focusing on the evidence for light vs. heavy CVC. The reader may find these claims integrated into a fuller analysis in Hayes, forthcoming.

To a very rough approximation, it may be said that most Yupik languages stress all heavy syllables, and every even numbered member of a string of light syllables, counting from left to right. This is a rather common type of stress pattern (for numerous parallels see Hayes, forthcoming, Chap. 6). Formally, I treat the pattern as the result of parsing the word from left to right into iambs (cf. (3c)). This analysis will be illustrated below.

The criterion of syllable weight used in Yupik is unusual, and varies across dialects. In the Norton Sound dialect of Central Alaskan Yupik, I assume that *word-initial* CVC is heavy, whereas elsewhere CVC is light. In terms of the proposal here, we would say that CVC syllables are syllabified as bimoraic initially, monomoraic elsewhere. CVV is heavy across the board.

Given this, the stress pattern of many words follows straightforwardly, as in the following example.

(18) a. $\mu\mu$ μ μ μ syllabification (initial CVC heavy)
           aŋ yaχ pa ka   'my big boat' (Krauss 1985:21)

      b.   (x)(.   x)   construction of iambs from left to right
           $\mu\mu$ μ μ μ
           aŋ yaχ pa ka

That is, since /–́/ and /⌣ ⌣́/ are legal iambs (and /⌣́/ is not), we get stress on the first and third syllables.

The output form in (18b) is in fact not a surface form. A rule that is found throughout Yupik lengthens vowels when they occur in the stressed position of a disyllabic foot. I state this rule as in (19).

(19) **Iambic Lengthening**:
$$\emptyset \to \mu \;/\; \begin{array}{c}(.\;\;x)\\ \sigma\;\sigma\\ |\;\;|\backslash\\ \mu\;\;\mu\;\mu\end{array}\;\_\_$$

Iambic Lengthening completes the derivation of (18), as shown in (20).

(20) $\begin{array}{cccc}(x\;)&(.&x\;)\\ \mu\mu\;\;\mu&&\mu\mu\;\;\mu\\ \text{áŋ}\;\;\text{yaχ}&\text{pá:}&\text{ka}\end{array}$ Iambic Lengthening

Iambic Lengthening is of interest as an example of a segmental rule that enforces canonical foot structure: the /˘ ´/ feet that result from it obey the Iambic/Trochaic Law.

The syllable quantity pattern of Norton Sound Yupik is a simple example of the quantity of CVC varying by position, that is, heavy initially vs. light non-initially. In fact, it is not a fully convincing example, since one might just as well add a special rule that *stresses* initial CVC rather than weighting it (cf. Woodbury 1987:695). Further examples, perhaps more persuasive, follow.

Some background will be needed: all of the Yupik languages have Iambic Lengthening, and all have a pervasive phonemic vowel length contrast, found in both initial and non-initial syllables. It can be noted from examples like (21) below that vowel length is often involved in minimal pairs, which realize crucial grammatical contrasts. One wonders, then, what the effect of a length neutralization rule like Iambic Lengthening would be on the intelligibility of utterances. *A priori*, it would be expected to wipe out crucial contrasts when a short vowel in even position contrasts with a long vowel.

In fact, such neutralizations are almost always avoided. The various dialects all show some means of keeping underlying /V:/ distinct from iambically-lengthened [V:]. For example, older speakers of Siberian Yupik (Krauss 1975) lengthen underlying /V:/ to [V::] (an overlong vowel) whenever it occurs on the right side of a foot. This maintains the distinction: the underlying distinction /V/ vs. /V:/ is realized phonetically either as [V́:] vs. [V́::] or as [V] vs. [V́:], depending on the odd-even count established by foot structure.

In Central Alaskan Yupik, a rather different solution to the neutralization problem is taken, namely: (a) the syllable *preceding* the underlying long vowel is given a stress; and (b) where this syllable is underlyingly light, it is made heavy by gemination of the following consonant. I will refer to this process as "Pre-Long Strengthening." Examples of it (from Jacobson 1985:30-31) are given below.

(21) a. /qaya**pix**kani/ → qayápixkáni
→ qayá:**pix**ká:ni
'his own future authentic kayak'

b. /qaya**pix**ka:ni/ → qayá:**píx**ká:ni
'in his(another's) future authentic kayak'

c. /**qa**yani/ → qayá:ni
'his own kayak'

d. /**qa**ya:ni/ → **qá**yyá:ni
'in his (another's) kayak'

The boldface syllables precede an underlying long vowel in (21b,d), and so undergo Pre-Long Strengthening. Examples (21a,c) are given for contrast; the boldface syllables do not precede an underlying long vowel and thus surface unchanged.

To formalize Pre-Long Strengthening, we must consider two problems. First, it can be shown that Pre-Long Strengthening cannot apply before stress assignment. The reason is that it respects the same left-to-right alternating count that governs the stress rule. In (22) the boldface syllable is an *even*-numbered member of a light-syllable string. It does not undergo Pre-Long Strengthening (which would yield *maqíkká:txun); rather, it undergoes Iambic Lengthening instead.

(22)
(. x)(x)   (.   x) (x)   'with their (other's)
μ μ μμ   μ   μ   μμ μμ   μ   future steambath material'
ma **qi** ka:t xun →   ma qí: ká:t xun   Jacobson (1985:37)

In contrast, for the examples of (21b,d), the boldface syllable is an *odd*-numbered member of a light-syllable string, and it undergoes Pre-Long Strengthening.

Since Pre-Long Strengthening makes use of the same left-to-right alternating count of light syllables as the stress rule, it would make sense to order Pre-Long Strengthening after stress. But this seems problematic, since Pre-Long Strengthening itself is stress-assigning, as was seen in (21b,d).

A second difficulty with Pre-Long Strengthening is its apparently heterogeneous structural change: it adds both a stress and, where necessary, gemination. Given the general goal of constraining the class of possible phonological rules, it would seem unfortunate to adopt a rule that includes two separate structural changes.

The currently standard approach in treating these two problems is one developed in work by Leer (1985), Woodbury (1987), Weeda (1989, 1990), and Halle (1990). These analyses differ in various important respects, but deal with the Pre-Long Strengthening problem in a similar way. The basic idea is to implement a new type of iambic foot for Yupik, whose possible structures are outlined in (23).

$$(23) \quad \text{a. Possible feet:} \quad \begin{matrix}(x) & (.\ x) & (x) \\ - & \smile\smile & \smile\end{matrix} \quad \text{b. Impossible:} \quad \begin{matrix}(.\ x) \\ *\smile -\end{matrix}$$

Because /⌣ ⌢/ is not a foot, a /⌣ –/ sequence encountered in a parse is made into two feet instead of one, as in (24b) (note that /⌣̆/ feet are allowed). This gives the stressing effect of Pre-Long Strengthening. Where a CV syllable is made into a foot by this process, it is then bulked by a later rule to /–/, as shown in (24c).

$$(24) \text{a.} \quad \begin{matrix}\smile & - & \smile \\ \text{qa} & \text{ya:ni}\end{matrix} \quad \xrightarrow{\textbf{Foot Parsing}} \quad \text{b.} \quad \begin{matrix}(x) & (x) \\ \smile & - & \smile \\ \text{qa} & \text{ya:ni}\end{matrix} \quad \xrightarrow{\textbf{Bulking of CV}} \quad \text{c.} \quad \begin{matrix}(x) & (x) \\ - & - & \smile \\ \text{qayya:ni}\end{matrix}$$

This ingenious account solves the ordering paradox noted above, since the effects of Pre-Long Strengthening emerge from the stress rule itself. Moreover, we need not posit that a single rule can do two separate things, since the bulking of stressed CV syllables is done by a separate rule.

Nonetheless, there are serious objections to this account. First, it requires use of a foot construction algorithm ((23)) that plays no role in other languages, as far as I am aware. This means that the general theory of foot structure must be weakened solely to cover the Yupik facts. Second, under this theory it is puzzling that the segmental phonology (i.e., Iambic Lengthening, (19)), should conspire to create precisely the /⌣ ⌢/ feet that the basic foot inventory excludes, as in (25).

$$(25) \quad \begin{matrix}(.\ x) \\ \smile\smile\smile \\ \text{qayani}\end{matrix} \quad \rightarrow \quad \begin{matrix}(.\ x) \\ \smile - \smile \\ \textbf{qaya:ni}\end{matrix} \quad = (21\text{c})$$

Moreover, the /ˇ/ feet, which are assumed to be well-formed at the underlying level, all get repaired; because of the rule of Syllable Bulking illustrated in (24c), none of them actually reach the surface.

Summing up, the standard analysis has negative implications for the theory of foot typology (or at least for the one advocated here) and requires us to suppose that the basic metrical system and the segmental system work at cross-purposes.

The alternative account of Pre-Long Strengthening I argue for here is based on two ingredients. First, I assume as before that CVC may vary in its weight according to context. Second, I assume (cf. Hayes forthcoming, Myers 1991) that in some languages foot construction is "persistent," in the sense that the parsing algorithm continually reapplies to insure well-formedness whenever syllable count or quantities are altered by segmental rules.

In the proposed analysis, I assume that Yupik uses the same iambs found in many other languages of the world (cf. (3c)); in particular, /˘ ´/ is allowed as an iambic foot. Pre-Long Strengthening is construed as affecting syllable weight, rather than metrical structure. In particular, whenever a syllable precedes a long vowel within the same foot, it is made heavy by the addition of a mora.

(26) **Pre-Long Strengthening**

$$\emptyset \rightarrow \mu \;/\; \begin{matrix} (\,. & & x\,) \\ \sigma & & \sigma \\ |\cdot\cdot & & |\backslash \\ \mu & \underline{\quad} & \mu\;\mu \\ & & |/ \\ & & \text{[-cons]} \end{matrix}$$

This is illustrated in the derivations in (27).

Weight of CVC can be Determined by Context 75

(27)

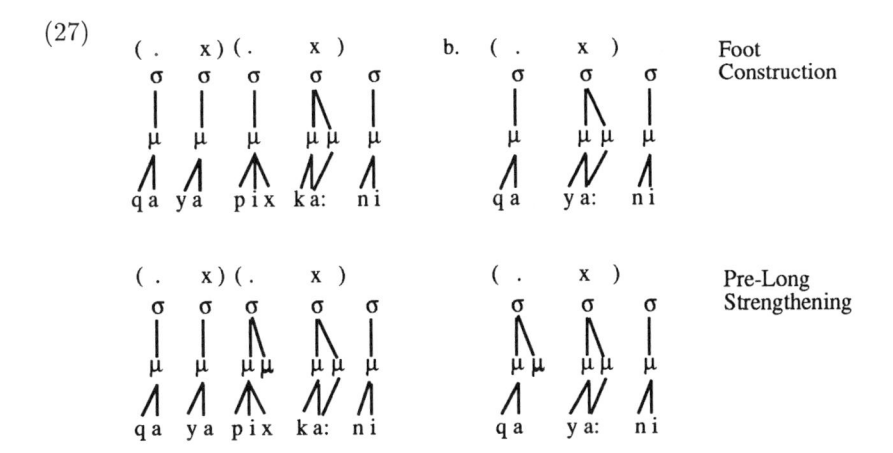

```
     ( .    x ) ( .     x   )         b.    ( .    x    )         Foot
       σ   σ   σ    σ    σ                    σ    σ    σ         Construction
       |   |   |    ∧    |                    |    ∧    |
       μ   μ   μ   μ μ   μ                    μ   μ μ   μ
       ∧   ∧   ∧   N    ∧                    ∧   N    ∧
       qa  ya  pix ka:  ni                   qa  ya:   ni
```

```
     ( .    x ) ( .     x   )               ( .    x    )         Pre-Long
       σ   σ   σ    σ    σ                    σ    σ    σ         Strengthening
       |   |   ∧    ∧    |                    ∧    ∧    |
       μ   μ  μ μ  μ μ   μ                   μ μ  μ μ   μ
       ∧   ∧   ∧   N    ∧                    ∧   N    ∧
       qa  ya  pix ka:  ni                   qa  ya:   ni
```

The algorithm for filling a stray mora is similar to that stated for Cahuilla above: stray moras associate with (a) non-moraic syllable final consonants, if present; else (b) stressed vowels (this is needed for Iambic Lengthening); else (c) the onset of the following syllable. Provision (a) applies to (28a) below, provision (c) to (28b).

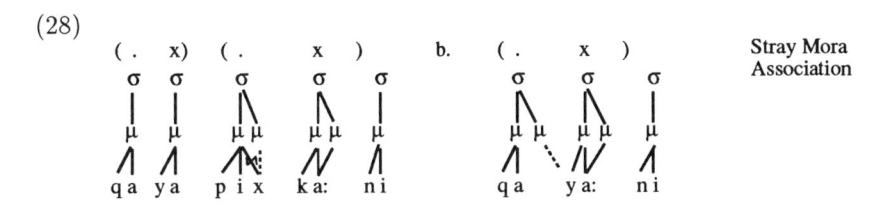

(28)

```
     ( .   x) ( .      x   )        b.    ( .    x    )           Stray Mora
       σ   σ   σ    σ    σ                   σ    σ    σ          Association
       |   |   ∧    ∧    |                   ∧    ∧    |
       μ   μ  μ μ  μ μ   μ                  μ μ  μ μ   μ
       ∧   ∧   ∧:  N    ∧                   ∧   N    ∧
       qa  ya  pix ka:  ni                  qa  ya:   ni
```

Pre-Long Strengthening creates ill-formed feet of the shape /- ́-/. Since these are disallowed as possible iambs, and since footing is hypothesized to be persistent, the /- -/ sequence is reparsed as two /-/ feet.

(29)

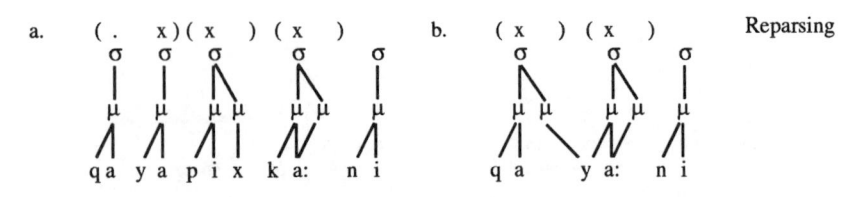

a.
```
( .  x )( x    ) ( x    )       b.   ( x    ) ( x    )        Reparsing
  σ  σ  σ    σ    σ              σ      σ    σ
  |  |  /\   /\   |               /\     /\   |
  μ  μ  μ μ  μ μ  μ               μ μ    μ μ  μ
  /\ /\ /\ | /\/  /\              /\  \/\/  /\
  qa ya pi x k a:  n i             q a  y a:  n i
```

It is this reparsing that gives rise to the stressing effects of Pre-Long Strengthening; stressing is not part of the rule itself.

The final outcomes are then determined by Iambic Lengthening.

(30)

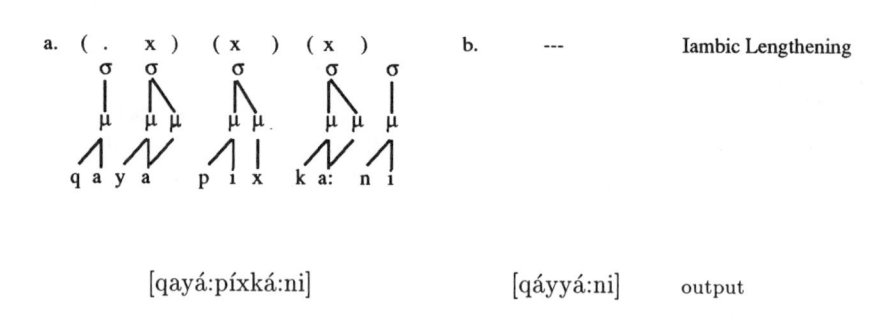

a.
```
( .  x  ) ( x   ) ( x   )        b.    ---         Iambic Lengthening
  σ  σ    σ    σ   σ
  |  /\   /\   /\  |
  μ  μ μ  μ μ  μ μ μ
  /\ /\/  /\ | /\/ /\
  q a y a  p i x k a:  n i
```

    [qayá:píxká:ni]   [qáyyá:ni]   output

Note that this analysis crucially depends on the distinction between heavy and light CVC. For example, the second syllable of (20) and the third syllable of (30a) are light and heavy respectively, though both are CVC. In fact, this claim appears to be supported by phonetic evidence. Woodbury (1981:46) observes that for the Chevak dialect, the coda consonant of the CVC syllables that I have analyzed as bimoraic is phonetically longer; and Woodbury (p.c.) notes that this pattern in fact holds for the rest of Alaskan Yupik. Note that the phonetic facts agree with those of Cahuilla, where coda consonants are likewise phonetically longer when they bear their own mora.

The distinction between mora-bearing and mora-sharing coda consonants has other phonetic consequences as well. In particular, Woodbury (1981:46-49) observes that when a continuant consonant is in the coda and (in my terms) has its own mora, it is realized as extra strident; for example, /y/ with its own mora is realized as [z].

Note finally that heavy CVC syllables derive from other sources as well, for instance, from the rule illustrated under (18) that creates heavy initial CVC, or indeed from Iambic Lengthening.

(31) (. x)   (. x)   (. x)   (. x)
      μ μ   μ μ μ   →   μ μμ   μ μμ μ
      qa yaχ   paŋ yux tuq   qa yáχ   paŋ yúx tuq
      'he wants to get a big kayak' (Jacobson 1985:30)

Given my formulation of Iambic Lengthening in (19), it is predicted to apply to CVC syllables as well, producing the characteristic phonetic outcomes for heavy CVC.

To sum up this section: I have taken a new approach to the problem of Pre-Long Strengthening in Yupik, suggesting that it is basically a quantitative rather than a metrical process, with additional stress effects attributed to persistent footing. The benefits of doing this are as follows. First, we can assume that the iambic feet of Yupik are just like those found in the rest of the world's iambic systems. Second, under the new analysis, segmental phonology respects foot structure; indeed, through Iambic Lengthening the segmental rules enforce canonical ($/\smile \acute{-}/$) iambic form.

6 Conclusion

The argument made here for variable weight in CVC syllables is based on three things. First, variable weight is audible, with straightforward durational correlates in living languages. Second, variable CVC weight lets us make sense of phonological patterns that would otherwise seem puzzling. Third, variable CVC provides alternative analyses for cases which would otherwise require weakening of metrical stress theory.

References

Allen, W. Sidney. 1973. *Accent and rhythm.* Cambridge: Cambridge University Press.

Anderson, Stephen R. 1984. A metrical interpretation of some traditional claims about quantity and stress. In Mark Aronoff and Richard T. Oehrle (eds.), *Language sound structure: Essays presented to Morris Halle by his teacher and students.* Cambridge, MA: MIT Press.

Halle, Morris. 1990. Respecting metrical structure. *Natural Language and Linguistic Theory* 8:149-176.

Hayes, Bruce. 1982. Extrametricality and English stress. *Linguistic Inquiry* 13:227-276.

Hayes, Bruce. 1985. Iambic and trochaic rhythm in stress rules. In M. Niepokuj, et al. (eds.), *Proceedings of the Thirteenth Meeting of the Berkeley Linguistics Society*, pp. 429-46.

Hayes, Bruce. 1987. A revised parametric metrical theory. *Proceedings of the Northeastern Linguistic Society* 17.

Hayes, Bruce. 1989. Compensatory lengthening in moraic phonology. *Linguistic Inquiry* 20:253-306.

Hayes, Bruce. forthcoming. *Metrical stress theory: Principles and case studies.* Chicago: University of Chicago Press.

Hyman, Larry. 1985. *A theory of phonological weight.* Dordrecht:Foris.

Ito, Junko. 1989. A prosodic theory of epenthesis. *Natural Language and Linguistic Theory* 7:217-259.

Jacobson, Steven A. 1985. Siberian Yupik and Central Yupik prosody. In Michael Krauss (ed.) *Yupik Eskimo prosodic systems: Descriptive and comparative studies.* Fairbanks, AK: Alaska Native Language Center.

Kager, René. 1989. *A metrical theory of stress and destressing in English and Dutch.* Dordrecht: Foris.

Krauss, Michael. 1975. St. Lawrence Island Eskimo phonology and orthography. *Linguistics* 152:39-72.

Krauss, Michael. 1985. A history of the study of Yupik prosody. In Krauss (1985a), pp. 7-23.

Leer, Jeff. 1985. Toward a metrical interpretation of Yupik prosody. In Krauss (1985a), pp. 159-172.

Levin, Juliette. 1985. *A metrical theory of syllabicity.* Ph.D. dissertation, Massachusetts Institute of Technology, Cambridge, MA.

McCarthy, John and Alan Prince. 1986. *Prosodic morphology,* ms., University of Massachusetts and Brandeis University.

Miyaoka, Oshito. 1985. Accentuation in Central Alaskan Yupik. In Krauss (1985a), pp. 57-75.

Myers, Scott. 1991. Persistent rules. *Linguistic Inquiry* 22:315-344.

Prince, Alan. 1991. Quantitative consequences of rhythmic organization. *Proceedings of the 27th Meeting of the Chicago Linguistic Society.*

Seiler, Hansjakob. 1957. Die Phonetischen Grundlagen der Vokalphoneme des Cahuilla. *Zeitschrift für Phonetik und Allgemeine Sprachwissenschaft* 10:204-223.

Seiler, Hansjakob. 1965. Accent and morphophonemics in Cahuilla and Uto-Aztecan. *International Journal of American Linguistics* 31:50-59.

Seiler, Hansjakob. 1977. *Cahuilla grammar.* Banning, CA: Malki Museum Press.

Weeda, Don. 1989. Trimoraicity in Central Alaskan Yupik and elsewhere. ms., University of Texas, Austin.

Weeda, Don. 1990. Foot extrametricality in Central Alaskan Yupik. ms., University of Texas, Austin.

Woodbury, Anthony. 1981. *Study of the Chevak dialect of Central Yupik Eskimo.* Ph.D. dissertation, University of California, Berkeley.

Woodbury, Anthony. 1987. Meaningful phonological processes: A study of Central Alaskan Yupik Eskimo prosody. *Language* 63:685-740.

Zec, Draga. 1988. *Sonority constraints on prosodic structure.* Ph.D. dissertation, Stanford University, Stanford, CA.

Cyclic Phonology and Morphology in Cibemba

Larry M. Hyman
University of California, Berkeley

1 Introduction[1]

Several recent studies have either proposed modifying our conception of cyclicity or have questioned the generality or viability of cyclic rule application, particularly in the area of stress. Concerning English stress, the cornerstone of cyclic phonology, Sainz (1988) has renewed the call for a non-cyclic account, while Chen (1991) carefully weighs the evidence and casts doubts about the generality of "cyclic effects." Looking at stress systems in general, Halle and Kenstowicz (1991) allow for cyclicity (often as a diacritic property of specific affixes), but deny the view of lexical phonology (Kiparsky 1982, etc.) that cyclicity results from the interleaving of morphology and phonology. The crucial question ultimately to be answered is: Under what circumstances must a phonological rule be interpreted as applying in cyclic fashion? The literature has plenty of suggestions, although the actual cases where cyclicity is totally unavoidable – particularly in non-stress phonology – do not seem to be as unambiguous as one might think.[2] Still, cyclic effects are undeniable in a number of cases and must be accounted for.

In this paper, I take a close look at some rather striking cyclic effects that arise in the verb stem phonology of a number of Bantu languages. In order to achieve a reasonable level of observational adequacy, I restrict my

---

[1]This paper was presented at the conference on "The Organization of Phonology: Features and Domains," at the University of Illinois at Urbana-Champaign on 3 May 1991, as well as at a workshop at the University of California at Berkeley. I am very grateful for the helpful questions and comments that I received at each presentation – especially from Sharon Inkelas, who did more than her share of listening and responding as this paper was originally conceptualized and subsequently developed.

[2]Several recent claims of cyclic rule application are at least open to other interpretations. For example, Pulleyblank's (1985) cyclic analysis of tone in Tiv seems to be restateable with (most or all of) the suffixal tones coming in at one stratum and the prefixal tones coming in at a later stratum (possibly even postlexically, i.e., as if proclitic to the verb). As another example, a major argument of Kenstowicz and Rubach (1987) for cyclicity in Slovak seems to be that cyclic rule application automatically yields the left-to-right rule application required by this largely suffixing language. Since directionality of rule application has to by stipulated in other languages, one can legitimately question whether the Slovak data presented unambiguously establish the claimed cyclicity, or whether they are simply compatible with a cyclic interpretation.

comments to one language, Cibemba, spoken in Zambia, which I have been able to investigate over the past eight months at Berkeley and for which extensive documentation is available.[3,4] In the following, I present the data that support a cyclic interpretation, strengthen the argument as best I can, and then consider alternatives.

2 Preliminaries

First, a few preliminaries concerning Cibemba phonology in general. As seen in (1a), Cibemba has a rather simple underlying consonant system.[5]

(1) a. p   t   (c) k   b. i   u   ii   uu
        B   D   (j) G   e   o   ee   oo
        (f) s   a   aa
        w   y
        m   n   ń   (ŋ)   Also: į and ų [see below]

Consonants in parentheses are of marginal underlying status. The voiced consonants /B, D, G/ have the realizations in (2a), i.e. they are realized as voiced stops after a homorganic nasal, but have weaker articulations in other positions, including zero in the case of G.

(2) a. B → b / m __ ; otherwise = [β]
        D → d / n __ ; otherwise = [l]
        G → g / ŋ__ ; otherwise = [w], [y], or ∅ (depends on V's)

    b. k → č / [__ {i, e}
        g → ǰ / [__ {i, e}   (i.e. ŋg → nǰ)

    c. s → š / __ i (and 'į')

---

[3]Research into the structure of Cibemba began in my undergraduate field methods course in the Fall semester of 1990 with Dr. Lawrence Mukuka serving as informant. I would especially like to thank Dr. Mukuka for his insightful participation in that course and for his contributions and patience with me during the months of careful study that ensued.

[4]The available documentation includes a 1500-page dictionary (White Fathers 1947) that provides considerable information on the phonological and morphological structure of the Cibemba verb, as well as two grammars (van Sambeek 1955 and Sims 1959), a doctoral dissertation (Sharman 1963), and several articles that were also quite helpful. There appears to be considerable dialect variation in the Cibemba cluster. In this paper, I limit myself to the central dialect, as spoken by Lawrence Mukuka, a native speaker from Citumukulu in the Kasama District.

[5]For further examples and a slightly different interpretation, see Kashoki (1968).

As seen in (2b), morpheme-initially velars palatalize before high and mid front vowels (see Hyman 1992), and as seen in (2c), /s/ palatalizes before a high front vowel. Following Cibemba orthography, the voiced labial obstruent is written as 'b', while the derived alveopalatals are transcribed as 'c', 'j' and 'sh', respectively.

Turning to the vowel system, in (1b) we note first that Cibemba has a basic system of five vowels which occur short and long. For present purposes, we can assume that these vowels are underspecified as in (3), with the redundancy rules in (4) filling in the blanks.

(3) Underspecified V features:

	i	u	e	o	a	i̥	u̥
High		-	-			+	+
Low					+		
Back		+		+			+

(4) Default spelling rules:

    a. [+low] → [-high] ; otherwise: [o high] → [+high]
    b. [o low] → [-low]
    c. [+low] → [+back] ; otherwise: [o back] → [-back]

As observed in (3) and (4), the high vowels /i/ and /u/ are underspecified for height, while the mid vowels /e/ and /o/ are prespecified as [-high]. The basic motivation for this move, which has been also recognized by Rugemalira (1990) for Runyambo, Archangeli and Pulleyblank (1991) for Haya, and others, is that prespecification of [-high] can account for the widespread Bantu height harmony that causes alternations such as in (5).

(5) Vowel harmony affecting /i/ in verb suffixes,
    e.g., applicative -il- vs. -el-:[6]

    a. -sit-   'buy'   →   -sit-il-   'buy for/at'
        -fúl-   'forge' →   -fúl-il-   'forge for/at'
        -kak-   'tie'   →   -kak-il-   'tie for/at'

---

[6]Throughout this paper, verb forms will be cited with hyphens separating the different morphemes. These forms do not surface as such, but rather require an inflectional "final vowel" (FV) morpheme, usually -a, to complete the construction of a verb stem. Also not transcribed is the predictable s-palatalization in (2c). Hence, the verb root -sit- 'buy' in (5a) is actually realized -shit- (or -shit-a with an -a FV).

b. -sek- 'laugh (at)' → -sek-el- 'laugh (at) for/at'
    -sos- 'speak'   → -sos-el- 'speak for/at'

In (5a), we see that the applicative suffix is realized as *-il-* after a high or low vowel, but as *-el-* after a mid vowel. The rule in (6) shows the spreading of this prespecified [-high] onto a following vowel:[7]

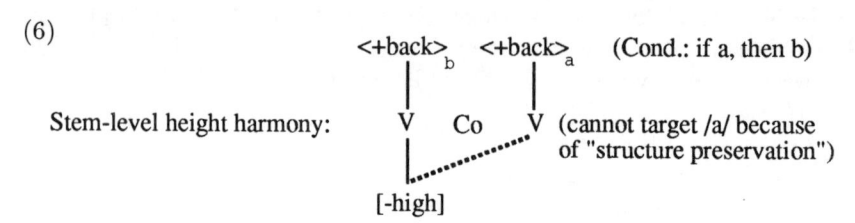

(6)

Stem-level height harmony: <+back>_b <+back>_a   (Cond.: if a, then b)
                                   | |
                                   V   Co   V   (cannot target /a/ because
                                   |........./   of "structure preservation")
                                [-high]

It will have been noticed both in (1b) and in (3) that I include two additional high vowels marked by a diacritic. These are the reflexes of the historical "superclosed" vowels of Proto-Bantu which, though phonetically identical to their non-diacritic counterparts in present-day Cibemba, must be distinguished from them for two important reasons. First, as seen in (7), the superclosed vowels do not undergo height harmony.

(7) First motivation for /i̧/ and /u̧/: exemption from height harmony, e.g., causative *-i̧-*:

a. -end-   'walk [intr]' → -ens-i̧-   'to walk [tr]'
                                        (cf. -ens-i̧-w- 'be walked')
    -sel-   'move [intr]' → -ses-i̧-   'move [tr]'
                                        (cf. -ses-i̧-w- 'be moved')

b. -kos-   'be strong'   → -kos-i̧-   'strengthen'
                                        (cf. -kos-i̧-w-
                                         'be strengthened')
    -ónd-   'be slim'   → -óns-i̧-   'to slim'
                                        (cf. -óns-i̧-w- 'be slimmed')

I account for this by marking them in (3) as exceptionally prespecified as [+high], and hence not able to acquire a [-high] specification from the spreading rule in (6). Recall that the forms to the right of the arrow in

---

[7] The angled brackets in this rule are designed to capture the fact that /u/ lowers to [o] only after /o/, not after /e/, e.g., *-kont-ok-* 'be broken' vs. *lép-uk-* 'be torn'. There thus is an asymmetry in the way height harmony affects /i/ vs. /u/, something which probably can be traced back to Proto-Bantu.

(7) undergo s-palatalization, thus becoming -ensh-i̧-, -sesh-i̧- etc. When followed by a vowel such as the FV -a, -i̧- glides to [y], which is then "absorbed" into the preceding alveopalatal fricative, yielding -ensh-a, -sesh-a, etc. In order to show that -i̧- does in fact escape height harmony, the corresponding passives are given in parentheses. With the FV -a, these become -ensh-i̧-w-a, -sesh-i̧-w-a, and so forth, i.e., without height harmony. The height harmony rule in (6) thus cannot affect an underlying [+high] vowel (cf. also section 3 below).

This prespecified [+high] also allows us to account for the fact that /i̧/ and /u̧/ alone trigger the consonant mutations summarized in (8).

(8) Consonant mutation (CM) before causative -i̧-,
i.e., before prespecified [+high]:

    a. p, b   →   f
    b. t, d, l, k, g →   s

All oral consonants mutate before these vowels: labials become [f], linguals become [s]. Examples are given in (9) showing the mutation of these consonants before the causative suffix -i̧-. Though not transcribed in most cases in this paper, recall that every s, whether underlying or derived from CM, palatalizes to sh before both i vowels.

(9) a. -leep-   'be long'   → -leef-i̧-   'lengthen'
        -up-   'marry'   → -uf-i̧-   'marry off'
        -lub-   'be lost'   → -luf-i̧-   'lose'
        -lob-   'be extinct'   → -lof-i̧-   'exterminate'

    b. -fiit-   'be dark'   → -fiis-i̧-   'darken'
        -ónd-   'be slim'   → -óns-i̧-   'make slim'
        -lil-   'cry'   → -lis-i̧-   'make cry'
        -buuk-   'get up [intr]'   → -buus-i̧-   'get [s.o.] up'
        -lúng-   'hunt'   → -lúns-i̧-   'make hunt'

    Recall: s → sh / __ {i, i̧}
    Hence: -fiish-i̧-, -ónsh-i̧-, -lish-i̧-, -buush-i̧-, -lúnsh-i̧-, etc.

To summarize, there are two phonological arguments for recognizing two sets of high vowels in Cibemba: (a) /i/ and /u/ undergo height harmony to become [e] and [o], respectively, while "diacritic" /i̧/ and /u̧/ do not; (b) diacritic /i̧/ and /u̧/ trigger CM, while /i/ and /u/ do not. Both of these differences are accounted for by prespecifying "exceptional" /i̧/ and /u̧/ as [+high].

3 The Problem

With these preliminaries out of the way, we are now in a good position to appreciate the basic problem posed by data such as in (10).

(10)
a. -leep-el-   'be long for/at'   vs. -leef-es-i̧-   'lengthen for/at'
    -up-il-   'marry for/at'   vs. -uf-is-i̧-   'marry off for/at'
    -lub-il-   'be lost for/at'   vs. -luf-is-i̧-   'lose for/at'
    -lob-el-   'be extinct for/at' vs. -lof-es-i̧-   'exterminate for/at'

b. -fiit-il-   'be dark for/at'   vs. -fiis-is-i̧- 'darken for/at'
    -ónd-el-   'be slim for/at'   vs. -óns-es-i̧-   'make slim for/at'
    -lil-il-   'cry for/at'   vs. -lis-is-i̧-   'make cry for/at'
    -buuk-il-   'get up for/at'   vs. -buus-is-i̧- 'get [s.o.] up for/at'
    -lúng-il-   'hunt for/at'   vs. -lúns-is-i̧- 'make hunt for/at'

Recall: s → sh / __ {i, i̧}
Hence: -fiish-ish-i̧-, -óns-esh-i̧-, -lish-ish-i̧-, -buush-ish-i̧-, -lúnsh-ish-i̧-

In (10) I have added the applicative suffix -il- or -el- to the verbs in (9), adding the meaning 'for' [some person or some reason] or 'at' [some place]. In the left hand column, there are no surprises. On the other hand, the forms in the right hand column are quite puzzling. These involve the causativized verbs of (9) to which an applicative -il- or -el- has been added. What is observed in these forms is that *both* the root-final consonant has been mutated as has been the [l] of the applicative suffix itself (yielding -is- and -es-). The question is how?[8]

To account for these data, the argument will now be made that causativization precedes applicativization. That is, we have the morphological bracketing indicated in (11a), where two kinds of evidence are also cited. First, as seen in (11b), because of unpredictable semantics, there are many cases where the causative suffix -i̧- must be listed with its verb root. More dramatically, as shown in (11c), there are many cases where the verb root does not even exist without the lexicalized causative -i̧- suffix.

---

[8]Forms such as -sos-el- 'speak for/at', -lás-il- 'wound for/at' (→ lásh-il-) with root-final underlying /s/ show that there cannot be a rule that mutates -il-/-el- to -is-/-es- when preceded by an [s]. Kisseberth and Abasheik (1975) suggest such an analysis of Chimwi:ni, where perfective -il-/-el- comes out as -iz-/-ez- when preceded by a strident consonant (or the palatal nasal). It is likely that an -i̧- is involved here too.

(11)a. Causativization "precedes" applicativization,
i.e., [[[verb] CAUS] APP]. Evidence from (a)
unpredictable semantics; (b) frozen causatives (no base verb)

   b.

-pól-	'be well'	-pós-i̧	'greet' (lit. 'cause to be well; heal')
-láb-	'forget'	-láf-i̧-	'delay' (lit. 'cause to forget')
-tamb-	'stare, watch'	-tamf-i̧-	'drive off'
-túm-	'send, order'	-túm-i̧-	'organize a work party'

   c.

-pamp-,-pamb-	-pamf-i̧-	'press, urge'
*-pán-	-pán-i̧-	'miss, fail to catch'
*-búuC-	-búusi̧-	'enquire'
*-en-	-en-i̧-	'be hard to please'
*-ap-, *-ab-	-af-i̧-	'cause trouble, be troublesome'

However, as shown in (12), even in these cases the applicative suffix appears between the verb root and the -i̧- suffix.

(12) a.

-pós-i̧-	→	-pós-es-i̧-	'greet for/at' (<-pós-el-i̧-, etc.)
-láf-i̧-	→	-láf-is-i̧-	'delay for/at'
-tamf-i̧-	→	-tamf-is-i̧-	'drive off for/at'
-túm-i̧-	→	-túm-is-i̧-	'organize a work party for/at'

   b.

-pamf-i̧-	→	-pamf-is-i̧-	'press, urge for/at'
-pán-i̧-	→	-pán-is-i̧-	'miss, fail to catch for/at'
-búus-i̧-	→	-búus-is-i̧-	'enquire for/at'
-en-i̧-	→	-en-es-i̧-	'be hard to please for/at'
-af-i̧-	→	-af-is-i̧-	'cause trouble, be troublesome for/at'

The same "interfixing" is observed in (13), where the inflectional perfective suffix *-il-/-el-* is also inserted between the verb root and the causative *-i̧-* suffix. Again, two applications of CM are required: one on the root-final consonant, one on the suffix *-il-* or *-el-*:

(13) Inflectional -il-/-el- of 'perfective' -il-e/-el-e ending is also "interfixed" before -i̧-:

a. -leef-i̧-   'lengthen'   →   -leef-es-i̧-e   'lengthened'
                                                  (<-leef-el-i̧-e, etc.)
    -uf-i̧-   'marry off'   →   -uf-is-i̧-e   'married off'
    -luf-i̧-   'lose'   →   -luf-is-i̧-e   'lost'
    -lof-i̧-   'exterminate'   →   -lof-es-i̧-e   'exterminated'

b. -fiis-i̧-   'darken'   →   -fiis-is-i̧-e 'darkened'
    -óns-i̧-   'make slim'   →   -óns-es-i̧-e   'made slim'
    -lis-i̧-   'make cry'   →   -lis-is-i̧-e   'made cry'
    -buus-i̧-   'get [s.o.] up' →   -buus-is-i̧-e 'got [s.o.] up'
    -lúns-i̧-   'make hunt'   →   -lúns-is-i̧-e 'made hunt'

With s-palatalization and y-absorption:
-leef-esh-e, -uf-ish-e, -luf-ish-e, -lof-esh-e, -fiish-ish-e, -óns-esh-e, -lish-ish-e, -buush-ish-e, -lúnsh-ish-e

The most straightforward way to account for these facts is to propose cyclic derivations such as those in (14).

(14)   UR   MORPH   PHON   MORPH   PHON
a.   -lub- →   -lub-i̧- → -luf-i̧- → -luf-il-i̧- → -luf-is-i̧-
        'be lost' 'lose'   'lose for/at' (-luf-ish-i̧-)

b.   -lil- →   -lil-i̧- → -lis-i̧- → -lis-il-i̧- → -lis-is-i̧-
        'cry'   'make cry'   'make cry for/at' (-lish-ish-i̧-)

To the bare verb roots, we first add the causative -i̧- suffix and then apply CM. We then add the applicative suffix -il-, inserting it between the verb root and the causative -i̧-. This interfixing creates a new derived environment, allowing for the reapplication of CM, as shown. A similar account would be proposed for the perfective suffix.[9]

What (14) represents is not only the cyclic application of a phonological rule, but an interpretation that crucially relies on the interleaving of morphology and phonology to produce the cyclicity. For different reasons, Halle and Kenstowicz (1991), Goldsmith (1991) and others have recently questioned this basic assumption of lexical phonology and would like a less

---

[9] This suffix actually has a much more interesting fuller story that I treat in Hyman (in press).

morphological and/or less derivational interpretation of cyclic effects, where they are found. Since this analysis does rely on the interleaving of morphology and phonology, let us consider the possibility in (15) that CM applies non-cyclically from right to left:[10]

(15) Alternative non-cyclic right-to-left iterative mutation
[not affecting root-initial C]:

a. -lub-il-į- → -lub-is-į- → -luf-is-į- 'lose for/at' (-luf-ish-į-)
b. -lil-il-į- → -lil-is-į- → -lis-is-į- 'make cry for/at' (-lish-ish-į-)

In (15), all the morphology is present from the beginning, with the causative suffix first conditioning CM on the applicative suffix -il- and then on the roots -lub- and -lil-, as shown. Can this iterative solution work?

For the non-cyclic alternative in (15) to work, there are some problems to be overcome. First, in (16) we note that CM does not apply morpheme-internally (which also explains why it never affects the *initial* consonant of a -CVC- verb root):

(16) Consonant mutation does not apply morpheme-internally:

-kálip-   →   -kálif-į-   (*-kásif-į-)
'be painful'   'cause pain'
-polopook-   →   -polopoos-į-   (*-posofoos-į-)
'crackle'   'make crackle'
-pemekees-   →   -pemekees-į-   (*-pemesees-į-)
'pant'   'make pant'

We therefore restrict CM to applying only at the ends of morphemes.[11]

Second, in (17) we see that CM cannot apply across the reciprocal suffix -*an*-.

---

[10]This analysis is suggested also by the palatalization of labials in Southern Bantu (see Louw 1975 for a survey of this phenomenon and Khumalo 1987 for a recent autosegmental statement of Zulu showing that an affected labial need not be segment-adjacent to the passive -w- suffix that causes mutations).

[11]This is of course different from saying that CM must apply only in a derived environment. Most interpretations of the strict cycle, e.g., would not block the propagation of CM onto the internal, underlined consonants in the starred forms provided in parentheses in (16). As mentioned in the preceding footnote, this is exactly the way long-distance palatalization of labials applies in much of Southern Bantu.

(17) Consonant mutation does not apply across reciprocal (REC) -an-:

    a.   -pál-   →   -pál-an-   →   -pál-an-i̧-   (*-pás̱-an-i̧-)
            'resemble'   'resemble e.o.'   'cause to resemble e.o.'

    b.   -pu̧nk-   →   -pu̧nk-an-   →   -pu̧nk-an-i̧-   (*-pu̧ns̱-an-i̧-)
            'bump into'   'bump into e.o.'   'cause to bump into e.o.'

    c.   -pet-   →   -pet-an-   →   -pet-an-i̧-   (*-pes̱-an-i̧-)
            'coil'   'be coiled together'   'coil together'

The explanation that would be necessary here is that because nasals do not themselves undergo CM, the /n/ of -an- blocks the propagation of mutation to its left. Or perhaps we can attribute the blocking of CM to the vowel /a/, if /i̧/ represents a [+ATR] vowel, as it actually surfaces in Kinande, for instance. In this case, we would say that mutation cannot apply across /a/ because of the mutual antipathy between [+ATR] and [+low].[12]

Neither of these accounts can be extended, however, to the data in (18).

(18) Consonant mutation does not apply across intransitive reversive -uk-:

    a.   -kak-   →   -kak-uk-   →   -kak-us-i̧-   (*-kas̱-us-i̧-)
            'tie'   'become untied'   'cause to become untied'

    b.   -ang-   →   -ang-uk-   →   -ang-us-i̧-   (*-ans̱-us-i̧-)
            'feel light'   'be light'   make light

    c.   -sup-   →   -sup-uk-   →   -sup-us-i̧-   (*-suf̱-us-i̧-)
            'be lively'   'be quick'   'quicken'

Here we see that CM affects only the intransitive reversive suffix -uk- and not the verb root that precedes it. Note that the cyclic account automatically makes the right prediction for both data sets in (17) and (18), since in these forms there is no stage in the derivation where the suffix -i̧- is adjacent to the verb root. Finally, note in (19) that some verbs cannot take the -i̧- causative suffix directly, but rather require what I refer to as

---

[12]This "grounded" antipathy is documented by Archangeli and Pulleyblank (1991). However, even if Kinande suggests [+ATR], note that the vowel /a/ is transparent rather than opaque with respect to right-to-left ATR spreading in that language (Mutaka 1986; Schlindwein 1987; Hyman 1989a).

Cyclic Phonology and Morphology in CiBemba

an -*is*-/-*es*- "intermorph" that can itself be separated from the causative -*i̧*- by the applicative -*il*-.[13]

(19) CM does not apply across -*is*-/-*es*- "intermorph":

a. -pump-   →   -pump-is-i̧   (*-pumf̱-is-i̧)
    'depart hurriedly'   'cause to depart'
    -imb-   →   -imb-is-i̧-   (*-imf̱-is-i̧-)
    'dig'   'cause to dig'
    -ib-   →   -ib-is-i̧-   (*-if̱-is-i̧-)
    'steal'   'cause to steal'

b. -sek-   →   -sek-es-i̧-   (*-ses̱-es-i̧-)
    'laugh (at)'   'make laugh (at)'
    -lipil-   →   -lipil-is-i̧-   (*-lipis̱-is-i̧-)
    'pay'   'make pay'
    -sit-   →   -sit-is-i̧-   (*-sis̱-is-i̧-)
    'buy'   'make buy, sell'

What is important is that unlike Luganda, for instance, Cibemba does not allow the -*i̧*- of the -*is-i̧*- sequence to mutate the final consonant of the preceding verb root.[14] Assuming that the suffixes -*is*- and -*i̧*- are spelled out in that order, cyclicity again correctly predicts that the final consonant of the verb root will not undergo CM.

To summarize, it does not appear possible to restate the cyclic application of CM in (14) as a right-to-left iterative application as in (15). I will also assume that it is not desirable to restate CM as in (20), where C' = a mutated consonant:

$$(20) \quad \begin{matrix}[-\text{nasal}]\\ C \end{matrix} \rightarrow C' \; / \; \underline{\quad} \; (\text{-}il\text{-}) \; \text{i̧}$$

The rule in (20) states that an oral consonant will undergo CM if it is either immediately followed by /i̧/, or if it is only separated from /i̧/ by an (applicative or perfective) -*il*- suffix, which itself undergoes the shorter expansion of the rule. Even ignoring the question of how to get the two subparts of (20) to apply conjunctively (a problem since they are in an "elsewhere" relationship), it would be unfortunate if we had to incorporate

---
[13]Thereby deriving -*pump-is-is-i̧* 'cause to depart for/at', *imb-is-is-i̧* 'cause to dig for/at', etc.

[14]In Luganda, both -*i̧*- and -*is-i̧*- regularly occur as causative suffixes, producing forms such as *lóot*- 'dream', *lóos-i̧*- or -*lóos-es-i̧*- 'cause to dream', the last form showing double mutation caused by -*es-i̧*- (Ashton et al. 1954:342).

mention of specific affixes or such an obvious violation of locality as in rule (20). I will therefore assume that (20) is not a viable alternative to the cyclic application of CM in (14).

4 More Cyclic Effects

The case for cyclicity is thus rather appealing and, in fact, can be strengthened somewhat. Consider the data in (21).

(21) (Non-causative) verbs marked by intensive (INT) -is-i̩-/-es-i̩-:

    a. -leep-   'be long' → -leep-es-i̩- 'be very long'
        -kálip- 'be painful' → -kálip-is-i̩- 'be very painful'
        -lub-   'be lost' → -lub-is-i̩- 'be very lost'

    b. -lil-   'cry' → -lil-is-i̩- 'cry a lot'
        -fiit-   'be dark' → -fiit-is-i̩- 'be very dark'
        -ónd-   'be slim' → -ónd-is-i̩- 'be very slim'

Here we see the same intermorph + causative sequence -is-i̩- being used as an intensive, and again the preceding verb root is not mutated.[15] Now consider the corresponding intensivized causative verbs in (22).

(22) Causative verbs marked by intensive -is-i̩-/-es-i̩- :

    a. -leef-i̩- 'lengthen' → -leef-es-i̩- 'make very long'
        -kálif-i̩- 'cause pain' → -kálif-is-i̩- 'cause a lot of pain'
        -luf-i̩-   'lose' → -luf-is-i̩- 'make very lost'

    b. -lis-i̩-   'make cry' → -lis-is-i̩- 'make cry a lot'
        -fiis-i̩- 'darken' → -fiis-is-i̩- 'make very dark'
        -óns-i̩- 'make slim' → -óns-es-i̩- 'make very slim'

In the above examples the final consonant of the verb root *is* mutated. The proposed cyclic spell-outs in (23) will account for these data as well:

---

[15] Because the intensive "intermorph" -is-/-es- always occurs with an invariant s (which however can undergo s-palatalization), it is not possible to determine whether it is from morphophonemic /s/ or whether -is-i̩-/-es-i̩ can be derived, say, from -il-i̩-/-el-i̩ (i.e., from the applicative -il-/-el- followed by "causative" -i̩-).

(23)
   a. [[verb] INT] →   [verb -is-i̧-]
   b. [[verb] CAUS] INT] → [[verb -i̧-] INT] → [verb -is-i̧-][16]

In (23a), the intensive is spelled out at once or successively as -is- plus -i̧-. In (23b), we first spell-out the causative as -i̧- (and apply CM), and then spell out the intensive, with the intermorph -is- going inside.

The alternative to (23b) would be that the intensive is spelled out after the causative -i̧-, creating sequences such as *-óns-i̧-es-i̧- 'make very slim'. If there could be two -i̧- suffixes, then each application of CM would be conditioned by a separate -i̧- vowel. As stated in (24), there are three reasons why this analysis cannot be correct:

(24)   -óns-esh-i̧- 'make very slim' cannot be from *óns-i̧-es-i̧-
      for three reasons:

    a. -i̧-es- sequence should result in long vowel (by gliding + CL);
    b. -i̧- should block vowel height harmony;
    c. -i̧- should condition s-palatalization.

First, as stated in (24a), an -i̧-es- sequence should result in a long vowel by gliding and compensatory lengthening, but it doesn't. Second, as stated in (24b), the -i̧- before -es- should block vowel height harmony, but doesn't. Finally, as stated in (24c), the -i̧- before -es- should condition s-palatalization, but doesn't. As a result, if *óns-i̧-es-i̧- were the correct analysis, this form would incorrectly surface as *-ónsh-iish-i̧- rather than the correct -óns-esh-i̧-. The cyclic interpretation in (23b) appears thus to be unavoidable.

Now consider the data in (25).

---

[16]Equally possible is that the last stage of this derivation is [VERB-is-i̧-i̧], i.e., with two -i̧- suffixes. While the -i̧-i̧ sequence would simplify anyway, and hence cause no phonological difficulties for us, it will be pointed out in section 6 that the "repeated morph constraint" of Menn and MacWhinney (1984) is pervasively respected in Cibemba (and in Bantu in general), and hence -i̧-i̧ should not be expected.

(25) Additional argument based on repetitive
[REP] /-aG-/ suffix (G → Ø):

a. -mát-ik-   'mud a wall'   -mát-a-ik-   'rep. mud a wall'   (*-mát-)
    -món-ek-   'be seen'   -món-a-ik-   'be rep. seen'   (-mán- 'see')
    -kont-ek- 'be broken'   -kont-a-ik- 'be rep. broken'   (-kont- 'hit')
    -ón-ek-   'be destroyed'   -ón-a-ik-   'be rep. destroyed' (-ón- 'destroy')

b. -sum-in-   'agree'   -sum-a-il-   'rep. agree'   (*-sum-)
    -pees-el- 'breathe   -pees-a-il- 'rep. breathe'   (*-pees-)
               with difficulty'   with difficulty'

As indicated, an additional argument for cyclicity can be made based on the repetitive suffix -aG- (whose /G/ is deleted on the surface). In these examples we see what appears to be the "interfixing" of the repetitive suffix -aG- before another suffix.[17]

To show that -aG- is interfixed in the same sense as the applicative -il- suffix seen above, consider the sequences -aG-uk- and -aG-ul- in (26).

(26) -aG-uk- [intr] and -aG-ul- [tr] added to specified verb roots mark repeated action:

a. -end-   'go'   →   -end-a-uk-   'go rep.'   (*end-uk-)
    -fúm-   'come out'   →   -fúm-a-uk-   'come out rep.'   (*-fúm-uk-)
    -lil-   'cry'   →   -lil-a-uk-   'cry rep.'   (*-lil-uk-)

b. -cít-   'do'   →   -cít-a-ul-   'do rep.'   (*-cit-ul-)
    -eb-   'tell'   →   -eb-a-ul-   'tell rep.'   (*-eb-ul-)
    -min-   'swallow'   →   -min-a-ul-   'swallow rep.'   (*-min-un-)

In Cibemba, -uk- is an intransitive suffix and -ul- its transitive counterpart. Note that the starred forms without -aG- do not exist. Given this fact, there appear to be at least three possible scenarios to derive the above forms, as indicated in (27).

---

[17]This suffix is labeled "distributive" by Sims 1959 and "frequentative" by van Sambeek (1955).

(27) At least three possible scenarios to derive the verb forms in (26):

a. [[verb]intr REP] → [verb - aG - uk] or [[verb] [aG - uk]]
   [[verb]tr REP] → [verb - aG - ul] or [[verb] [aG - ul]]

b. [[verb]intr REP] → [verb - aG]intr → [verb - aG - uk]
   [[verb]tr REP] → [verb - aG]tr → [verb - aG - ul]

c. [[verb]intr REP] → [verb - uk] → [verb - aG - uk]
   [[verb]tr REP] → [verb - ul] → [verb - aG - ul]

In (27a) we add the two suffixes simultaneously to the verb root; in (27b) -aG- is added first, followed by -uk- or -ul-; and in (27c), -uk- or -ul- is spelled out first, followed by the interfixing of -aG-. I will now provide support for the derivation in (27c).

A first argument concerns verbs such as in (28).

(28) a. -fimb-   'cover'   →
         -fimb-uk-   'be uncovered' → -fimb-a-uk- 'be rep. uncovered'
         -fimb-ul-   'uncover'   → -fimb-a-ul- 'rep. uncover'

   b. -kont-   'hit sharply'   →
         -kont-ok-   'be broken'   → -kont-a-uk- 'be broken in pieces'
         -kont-ol-   'break'   → -kont-a-ul- 'break up into pieces'

Here we see that the -uk- and -ul- suffixes have a "reversive" meaning ('to un-VERB'), and that the -aG- suffix clearly takes the reversive meaning rather than the non-reversive one. As a result, the outputs in (28) cannot mean 'be repeatedly covered', 'repeatedly cover', and so forth. According to (27c), then, we first derive the -uk- and -ul- forms (with their reversive meaning), and then interfix -aG-.

A second argument is suggested by the forms in (29).

(29) a. -lép-uk- 'be torn' → -lép-a-uk- 'be torn in pieces' (*-lép-)
         -lép-ul- 'tear'   → -lép-a-ul- 'tear into pieces'

   b. -put-uk- 'be cut'   → -put-a-uk- 'be cut in pieces'   (*-put-)
         -put-ul- 'cut'   → -put-a-ul- 'cut in pieces'

Here the argument is that starred verb roots such as *-lép- and *-put- do not exist. The most straightforward way to derive the outputs in (29) is thus to interfix -aG- before the lexically specified -uk- or -ul- that must co-occur with these roots.

The suggestion, then, is that all of the forms in (27)-(29) are derived as in (30).

(30) a. [[[verb]intr REV] REP] → [[verb - uk] REP] → [verb - aG - uk]
     b. [[[verb]tr REV] REP] → [[verb - ul] REP] → [verb - aG - ul]

First the reversive suffix is spelled out respectively as -uk- or -ul-, followed by the spelling out of -aG- as an interfix. This derivation thus closely parallels the interfixed spelling of the applicative -il- suffix seen above in (14).

The third argument for interfixing of -aG- comes from CM, particularly as it affects labials. Consider in (31) the status of phonetic [f] in Cibemba:

(31) Status of [f] in Cibemba

  a. Historically, all [f]s derive from CM before *i̥ and *u̥.
  b. As a result, the vast majority of [f]s occur before [i] and [u], e.g. noun class 8 prefix fi- (< *bi̥-); -fú- 'die' (< *-kú̥-), etc.
  c. Although there are some sporadic [fe] and [fo] sequences, there is no *[fa] except (crucially) from the source shown in (32b,c).
  d. Thus, there are no -CVf- verb roots.

Historically, all [f]s derive from CM before the Proto-Bantu superclosed vowels *i̥ and *u̥.[18] As a result, the vast majority of [f]s in present-day Cibemba occur before phonetic [i] and [u]. Although there are some sporadic [fe] and [fo] sequences, crucially there is no *[fa],[19] and no verb root of the shape -CVf-.

Now note the surface [f]s in (32). These [f]s can be accounted for by recognizing sporadic underlying superclosed -u̥C- suffixes where, recall, the diacritic vowel /u̥/ is prespecified as [+high].

---

[18]Though not synchronically determinable in all cases in Cibemba, Guthrie (1971:57) indicates that the labials *p and *b mutate to [f] before both *i̥ and *u̥, while the linguals *t, *d, *k, *g mutate to [f] only before u̥ (mutating instead to [s] before *i̥, as was indicated in (8b)).

[19]I have found one exception, sééfà, 'sieve', clearly a loanword.

(32) Derived [f] from sporadic underlying -ʉC- suffixes
      (/ʉ/ is prespecified [+high]):

a.	-bomf-ʉm-	'be soft'	-koof-ʉm-	'bend over from weight'
	-pámf-ʉk-	'be enormous'	-cémf-ʉl-	'sip'
b.	-pof-ʉk-	'be pierced'	-pof-a-ʉk-	'be rep. pierced'
	-pof-ʉl-	'pierce'	-pof-a-ʉl-	'pierce rep.'
c.	-tíf-ʉk-	'crack [intr]'	-tíf-a-ʉk-	'crack [intr] rep.'
	-tíf-ʉl-	'crack [tr]'	-tíf-a-ʉl-	'crack [tr] rep.'

This [+high] prespecification not only derives the [f]s in question, but also accounts for the disharmony of forms such as -bomf-ʉm- 'be soft' and -pof-ʉk- 'be pierced', where the underlying diacritic /ʉ/ fails to undergo height harmony to become phonetic [o].

Accepting this account of [f], now consider the repetitive forms in (32b,c). A surface [f] is derived, even though the conditioning superclosed /ʉ/ does not directly follow it. In (33) I provide an appropriate cyclic derivation of these forms:

(33) Proposed cyclic derivation of (32b,c), assuming sporadic -ʉC- suffixes:

a. [[[poC] REV] REP] → [[pof-ʉk] REP] → [pof-a-ʉk]
b. [[[tíC] REV] REP] → [[tíf-ʉk] REP] → [tíf-a-ʉk]

First we spell out the reversive suffix as a superclosed -ʉk-, conditioning CM. Then we spell out the repetitive suffix as -aG-, which interfixes before the -ʉk-. This, then, is the final support for cyclicity in the Cibemba verb stem.[20]

5 Alternative Approaches to CM

At this point it is necessary to consider an alternative that has not yet been mentioned. Perhaps CM is not a phonological rule at all, but rather is

---

[20]Because of examples to be cited in section 6, where the applicative -il- is interfixed between the reciprocal -an- and the causative -i suffixes, I have not attempted to account for the interfixing by relying on Aronoff's (1988) notion of affixation-to-head. In Cibemba not all interfixing involves suffixation directly to the verb root. The exact mechanism by which interfixing is to be done is of course an interesting issue in its own right, though not one I'll be able to resolve here. (See, however, Hyman (in press) for discussion of this issue as it pertains to "imbrication" of the perfective -il-/-el- suffix.)

morphological in nature. The following three observations seem to support this conclusion:

First, it will have been noticed that I have refrained from indicating how CM might be expressed in formal terms. Somehow a so-called superclosed high vowel transfers its relative constriction onto a preceding non-nasal, i.e., onto a consonant that can accept a [+strident] specification. At this stage of the language, the process seems to be only vaguely motivated from a "natural" or phonetic point of view (but see Zoll 1994).

Second, since there are no alternations, the evidence for superclosed /ʉ/ is essentially distributional, as we just saw in predicting surface [f], and hence slight. Since there is an underlying /s/ in the language, the distributional evidence for underlying superclosed /i̧/ is somewhat obscured.

Finally, it should be noted that CM alternations are triggered only by two morphemes in the language: the causative -i̧- suffix of which we have seen many examples, and the deverbal agentive suffix -i̧ which is exemplified in (34).

(34) CM alternations are triggered only by two morphemes, causative -i̧- and agentive -i̧:

    a. -bamb- 'succeed in killing' → mu-bamf-i̧ 'successful hunter'
    b. -fúl- 'forge' → mu-fús-i̧ 'blacksmith'
    c. -loG- 'bewitch' → mu-los-i̧ 'wizard'
    d. -lind- 'protect' → mu-lins-i̧ 'guardian'
    e. -lúng- 'hunt' → mu-lúns-i̧ 'hunter'

The nominalization process indicated in (34) is restricted only to certain verbs. Alongside it is an alternative agentive noun formation process which involves the prefixation of *ka-* and the derivational FV *-a*: *ka-fúl-a* 'blacksmith', *ka-lúng-a* 'hunter', and so forth. Since the agentive derivation in (34) is in the process of being replaced by another one that does not involve an -i̧ suffix, we can predict that Cibemba will some day have CM only before the causative -i̧- suffix and may subsequently lose CM altogether.[21]

It is thus appropriate to consider the alternative of viewing CM as allomorphy: morphemes may have a causative allomorph whose final (oral) consonant is mutated. Whether right or wrong, a solution in terms of allomorphy does not make the cyclicity go away. As summarized in (35), we still have the problem of predicting the environment in which the mutated allomorph is chosen.

---

[21] As has already happened in certain other Bantu languages (e.g., Chichewa, Xhosa/Zulu), where there are only remnants of an *i̧* causative (and of CM).

(35) CM as allomorphy, with the mutated allomorph chosen:

   a. When under the scope of causative -i̯- [overgenerates:
      cf. (17), (18), (19); undergenerates: cf. (10), (12), (13) etc.]
   b. When underlyingly adjacent to -i̯- [undergenerates: cf. (10) etc.]
   c. When derivatively adjacent to -i̯- [undergenerates: cf. (10) etc.]
   d. When either underlyingly or derivatively adjacent to -i̯-
      (i.e., cyclic analysis)

If chosen whenever under the scope of causative -i̯-, the mutated allomorph will be wrongly selected in some cases. If chosen only whenever underlyingly adjacent to -i̯-, or if chosen only whenever derivatively adjacent to -i̯-, the mutated allomorph will fail to be selected in some cases when it should be. The only thing that would work is (35d): choose the mutated allomorph whenever immediately followed by causative -i̯- in either underlying *or* derived structure.

This brings us to the major weakness of the cyclic analysis. We have thus far seen the need for CM to apply on two separate cycles. What we have not seen is any case where CM must apply *three* times, or more than three times. Given other properties of the language, it simply is not possible to get the input we need for CM to unambiguously apply more than twice within a single verb stem.[22] Is this an accident, or is this restriction principled? Either way, (36) shows how a two-level approach can easily handle the facts of CM, whether construed as allomorphy or as phonology:

---

[22] What we need for a triple cycle is a derivation such as the following (where C' = a mutated consonant):

CVC-i̯- → CVC'-i̯- → CVC'-il-i̯- → CVC'-is-i̯- → CVC'-is-il-i̯- → CVC'-is-is-i̯-

As seen, we first add the causative suffix -i̯- and mutate the final consonant of the verb root. We then, in two separate suffixations, interfix a first -il-, mutate it, and then interfix a second -il- and mutate it. The problem is how to establish that there have been two successive -il- interfixings. First, note that we cannot use the causative or intensive sequences -is-i̯-/-es-i̯- as evidence, since I have found no way to establish unambiguously that either one is from underlying -il-i̯-. Second, it so happens that whenever the perfective -il-/-el- is added to an applicativized verb, instead of getting two suffixes in sequence, the two "imbricate" (Bastin 1983) to form a long vowel -iil-/-eel- suffix, e.g., -lub- 'be lost', -lub-il- 'be lost for/at', -lub-iil-e 'was lost for/at', etc. In the causative, we obtain -luf-i̯- 'lose', -luf-is-i̯- 'lose for/at', -luf-iis-i̯- 'lost for/at', i.e., no evidence for two -il- suffixes, both of which mutate to -is-. For a full description of imbrication, see Hyman (in press).

(36) A two-level approach to CM either as allomorphy or as phonology (C' = mutated):

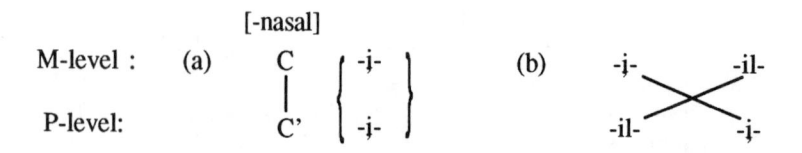

$$\begin{array}{lll} & & \text{[-nasal]} \\ \text{M-level:} & \text{(a)} & \text{C} \quad \left\{ \begin{array}{l} \text{-i̧-} \\ \text{-i̧-} \end{array} \right. \\ \text{P-level:} & & \text{C'} \end{array} \qquad \text{(b)} \quad \begin{array}{c} \text{-i̧-} \quad \text{-il-} \\ \times \\ \text{-il-} \quad \text{-i̧-} \end{array}$$

i.e., (a) a P-level mutated C' is required when followed by -i̧- at either M or P level; (b) the M level suffix order -i̧-il- occurs in the order -il-i̧- t P level.

In the above illustration, I have utilized the formalism of Lakoff (1993) and some non-derivational concepts developed by Lakoff having parallels in the work of Goldsmith (1993), Karttunen (1991), and others. In (36) the morphological or M-level can be seen as identical to the underlying representations of lexical phonology, while the phonological or P-level can be identified with the lexical (roughly, phonemic) level of lexical phonology. Thus, (36a) says that an M-level (oral) C corresponds to the mutated P-level consonant (C') whenever it is followed by a superclosed -i̧- vowel at either the M-level or the P-level. According to (36b), an M-level sequence of causative -i̧- followed by applicative -il- corresponds to a reversed P-level sequence of applicative -il- followed by causative -i̧-. By unifying these two correspondence statements, a case of double mutation comes out looking like (37).

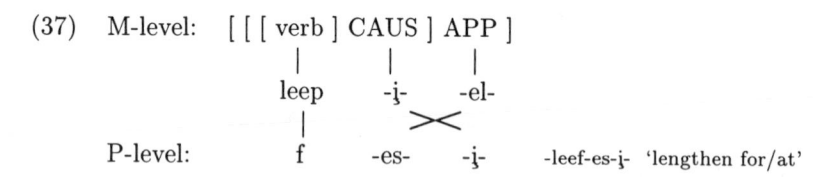

(37) M-level: [[[verb] CAUS] APP]
             | | |
             leep   -i̧-   -el-
             | ><
P-level: f   -es-   -i̧-   -leef-es-i̧- 'lengthen for/at'

As in Lakoff's reanalysis of Kiparsky's cyclic analysis of Icelandic u-umlauting, cyclicity here translates into a dual environment, i.e., an environment being met at two different linguistically significant levels.[23] Is the price of

---

[23] An alternative that I assume would be less attractive to phonologists would be to say that CM is triggered either by "morphosyntactic [semantic?] adjacency" or phonological adjacency. Thus, in the example in (37), the morphosyntactic representation [[[leep] CAUS] APP] would be responsible for the mutation of -leep- to -leef-, while the phonological representation [[[leep] el] i̧] would be responsible for the mutation of

avoiding cyclicity, then, to be the abandonment of a derivational approach to phonology?

6 Levels or Cycles?

This last move might seem a little dramatic, given this one example.[24] Given that a two-level analysis works as simply as it does, let us ask the basic question of what the relation is between levels vs. cycles? Since CM applies at most twice per form, one could propose a derivational rule of CM that applies both at stratum 1 and stratum 2. The two strata would have to differ as in (36b). One could reluctantly accept two different suffix orders (perhaps also the power to metathesize them) or, one might attempt to view the -i- suffix as non-concatenative (or "simultaneous" with -il-) at stratum 1, but linearized at stratum 2, or some variation of this.

As clarified in (38), neither of these proposals is consistent with the traditional view of Bantu verb phonology or with recent attempts to translate this in accordance with current views of lexical phonology.

(38) a. Traditional view of Bantu verb phonology:
  i. stem domain includes verb root + suffixes
     [= cyclic stratum 1?]
  ii. word domain includes verb stem + prefixes
     [= non-cyclic stratum 2?]

  b. Problem: some stem-domain phonology is non-cyclic:
  i. vowel harmony (recall stem-level height harmony in (6))
  ii. l-nasalization (l → n / N V __)

While Bantuists are used to distinguishing between stem-level vs. word-level phonology, the two representations that are needed in (36) and (37) both concern the stem. In addition, not all stem-domain phonology is cyclic in Cibemba. As seen in (39) and (40), the stem-level rule of vowel height harmony must apply non-cyclically or the starred outputs result.

---

applicative -el- to -es-. The difference between this statement and the account in (36a) is that the latter allows us to generalize a phonological condition, viz. /i/, for all applications of CM. In other words, the fact that CAUS is spelled out as -i- is irrelevant to the morphosyntactic condition. While I generally favor parallel representations, needed throughout the grammar (cf. Sadock 1990), further research would be needed to explore the implications of having a split allomorphy/morphophonemic analysis.

[24] See, however, Hyman (1993a) for discussion of rule ordering problems in Haya tonology and Chimwi:ni consonant mutation, the latter based on Kisseberth and Abasheik (1975).

(39)
  a.   [mon] 'see' →   [[mon]ik] 'be seen' →   [[mon]ek]
          | | \ /
        [-high]   [-high]   [-high]

  b.   [[mon - ek]REP] →   *[mon - aG - ek]   (cf. -mon-a-ik-)
                                                                                         'be repeatedly
                                                                                         seen'

(40)
  a.   [[kont]$_{intr}$ REV] →   [[kont]uk] 'be broken' →   [[kont]ok]
            | | \ /
        [-high]   [-high]   [high]

  b.   [[kont - ok]REP] →   *[kont - aG - ok]

    (cf. -kont-a-uk- → kont-a-uk-) 'be broken into pieces'

In (39) and (40) we first add the suffixes -ik- and -uk-, respectively. If we then apply height harmony followed by -aG- interfixing, we arrive at incorrect outputs. The correct way to derive -mon-a-ik- 'be repeatedly seen' and -kont-a-ul- 'be broken into pieces' is for -aG- interfixing to precede height harmony, which therefore cannot be a cyclic rule.[25]

As a second example, consider the rule of l-nasalization exemplified in (41).

(41)
  a.   APP and PERF -il-/-el- → -in-/-en- after a nasal consonant:
      -lim- cultivate   -lim-in- 'cultivate for/at'   -lim-in-e 'cultivated'
      -túm- 'send'   -túm-in- 'send for/at'   -túm-in-e 'sent'
      -min- 'swallow'   -min-in- 'swallow for/at'   -min-in-e 'swallowed'

  b.   REV [trans] -ul-/-ol- → -un-/-on- after a nasal consonant:
      [[tóm] REV] →   -tóm-on-   'smack lips, kiss'   (<-tóm-> 'taste')
      [[ím] REV] →   -ím-un-   'uproot'   (-ím- 'stand up')
      [[pin] REV] →   -pin-un-   'turn over'   (*-pin-)

---

[25] Note that we cannot first harmonize -mon-ik- to -mon-ek-, then interfix -aG- to derive intermediate -mon-aG-ek- and reapply height harmony to produce -mon-a-ik-. The reason is that the harmony rule, as formulated in (6), does not have a provision for spreading [+high], i.e., to convert [e] back to [i].

Cyclic Phonology and Morphology in CiBemba

As seen in (41a), the applicative and perfective morphs -il- and -el- are realized as -in- and -en- when directly following a nasal consonant. In (41b) we observe that the transitive reverse suffix -ul-/-ol- is realized -un-/-on- after a nasal consonant. Crucially, as seen in (42), nasalization must not apply before the interfixing of the repetitive -aG- suffix:

(42) REP forms of (40b) surface as -a-ul-, not *-a-un- (< -aG-ul-):

[[tóm - ul] REP]   →   -tóm-a-ul-   'smack lips repeatedly'
[[ím - ul] REP]   →   -ím-a-ul-   'uproot repeatedly'
[[pin - ul] REP]   →   -pin-a-ul-   'turn over and over'

As demonstrated in (43), a cyclic application of *l*-nasalization produces an incorrect output.

(43)
a. [[pin]REV] →   [[pin]ul] →   [[pin - ul]REP] → -pin-a-ul-

b. [[pin]REV] →   [[pin]ul] →   [[pin]un] 'turn over' →
        | | \ /
    [+nasal]   [+nasal]   [+nasal]

[[pin-un]REP] → *-pin-a-un- 'turn over and over' (-pin-a-ul-)

Instead, what is needed is for *l*-nasalization to wait to apply until after -aG- has been interfixed; i.e., *l*-nasalization is a non-cyclic rule (just like height harmony).

If the above is correct, cyclicity cannot be a property of a stratum in Cibemba, but instead must be either a property of an arbitrary rule (CM) or of arbitrary morphemes, such as the causative -i̯-. Note in (44) that (cyclic) CM definitely precedes (non-cyclic) *l*- nasalization. In (44a) we see the nasal allomorphs of the perfective ending -in-e/-en-e. When -il-e/-el-e is added to a causative base, as in (44b), CM applies, bleeding *l*-nasalization.

(44) CM precedes l-nasalization:

    a. -fúm- 'go out' -fúm-in-e 'went out'
        -pón- 'drop (intr.)' -pón-en-e 'dropped'
        -pen- 'become crazy' -pen-en-e 'became crazy'

    b. -fúm-i̧- 'take out' -fúm-is-i̧-e 'took out'
        -pón-i̧- 'drop (tr.)' -pón-es-i̧-e 'dropped'
        -pen-i̧- 'make crazy' -pen-es-i̧-e 'made crazy'

A correct derivation is given in (45a), an incorrect one in (45b).

(45) a. -fúm-i̧- 'take out' → -fúm-il-i̧- → -fúm-is-i̧- 'took out'
      b. -fúm-i̧- 'take out' → -fúm-il-i̧- → *-fúm-in-i̧-

Separating cyclic CM from non-cyclic vowel harmony and *l*-nasalization is possible since CM appears to be the *first* phonological rule, preceding all others. In this sense, Cibemba appears to be compatible with Halle and Kenstowicz's (1991) distinction between earlier cyclic vs. later post-cyclic rule blocks. It is hard to see though how we can avoid the morphology-phonology interleaving that they reject at the same time.

7 Cyclic Morphology Proper?

The last bit of evidence I would like to present concerns the morphology itself. The phonological evidence for cyclicity has been presented and evaluated. There are some undeniable cyclic effects in Cibemba, though it has been difficult to justify the need for more than two phonological cycles. As a consequence, the facts can be captured quite elegantly by a two-level (non-derivational) approach, as we saw in (36). In the derivational approach in (14) there is a need for "interfixing," while in the non-derivational approach in (36) there is suffix-metathesis. Depending on one's approach to phonology, CM is either a cyclic rule or is a rule (or declaration) conditioned by adjacency to an /i̧/ at either of two distinct levels of representation.

While we have not been able to find a third cycle, as it were, there are some strictly morphological facts that also look cyclic in nature, and which therefore give us a second chance. As an example, consider the interaction between the reciprocal suffix -*an*- and the causative suffix -*i̧*-. As indicated in (46a), when the causative is bracketed outside the reciprocal, each feature is spelled out in a one-to-one fashion:

Cyclic Phonology and Morphology in CiBemba 105

(46) a. [[[verb] REC] CAUS] → VERB-an-i̧- (cf. (17))

b. [[[verb] CAUS] REC] → VERB-i̧-an-i̧ (cf. (47))

Relevant examples such as *-punk-an-i̧-* 'cause to bump into each other' were seen above in (17). In (46b), however, where the reciprocal is bracketed outside the causative, we see that *-i̧-* is spelled out both before and after *-an-*. Examples of this suffix doubling are given in (47).

(47) a. -fúm- →   -fúm-i̧- →   -fúm-i̧-an-i̧-   [-fúm-y-aan-y-]
       'go out'   'take out'   'take e.o. out'
       -kóm- →   -kóm-i̧- →   -kóm-i̧-an-i̧-   [-kóm-y-aan-y-]
       'reach'   'touch'   'touch e.o.'

b. -lub- →   -luf-i̧- →   -luf-i̧-an-i̧-   [-luf-y-aan-y-]
       'be lost'   'lose'   'lose e.o.'
       -lil- →   -lis-i̧- →   -lis-i̧-an-i̧-   [-liš-(y)-aan-y-]
       'cry'   'make cry'   'make e.o. cry'

When we take the output of (46) and introduce an applicative *-il-*, we get the results in (48).

(48) [[[[verb] CAUS] REC] APP] →
      VERB-i̧-an-is-(is)-an-i̧- (-is- < -il-)

a. -fúm-i̧-an-i̧- →   *-fúm-i̧-an-is-i̧-   ("expected")
   'take e.o. out'   <-fúm-i̧-an-is-i̧-an-i̧->   <White Fathers 1947>
                        -fúm-i̧-an-is-is-i̧-an-i̧-   'take e.o. out for/at'

b. -luf-i̧-an-i̧- →   *-luf-i̧-an-is-i̧-   ("expected")
   'lose e.o.'   <-luf-i̧-an-is-i̧-an-i̧->   <White Fathers 1947>
                        -luf-i̧-an-is-is-i̧-an-i̧-   'lose e.o. for/at'

Our expectation is that *-il-* will be interfixed before the final causative *-i̧-*. As indicated, this expected output is ungrammatical. In angled brackets I have placed the most frequent realization of such forms in the White Fathers' (1947) dictionary. Here we see the mutated applicative appearing as *-is-*, followed by a second occurrence of causative *-i̧-*. However, this *-is-i̧-* sequence is in turn followed by a second occurrence of the reciprocal suffix *-an-*, which in turn is followed by a *third occurrence* of the causative *-i̧-* suffix. My own informant systematically rejects this in favor of the third line of (48a,b); an intermorph -is- is required before the -is-i̧-an-i̧- sequence of the previous line.[26]

As exemplified in (49), the White Fathers' dictionary is full of "persistent" spelling of suffixes and seemingly unnecessary overuse of the intensive -is-i̧- sequence.[27] The second and third lines of both (49a) and (49b) are synonymous, though only certain verbs show such doublets.[28] The last line of the examples in (49a,b) have three reciprocal -an-, three -is- formatives, and three causative -i̧- suffixes.

(49) Rampant "persistent" spelling of suffixes, use of "intensive" -is-i̧-, hence:

a. -amb- 'slander'
    -amb-an- 'slander e.o.'
    -amb-an-is-i̧-an-i̧-
    -amb-an-is-i̧-an-is-is-i̧-an-i̧-
    'slander e.o. for/at'

b. -tamb- 'stare (at)'
    -tamb-an- 'stare at e.o.'
    -tamb-an-is-i̧-an-i̧-
    -tamb-an-is-i̧-an-is-is-i̧-an-i̧-
    'stare at e.o. for/at'

---

[26] Identifying the extra -is- is an interesting issue in itself. There are at least three possible sources of this -is-: 1) the intensive -is-i̧- sequence; 2) the identical (long) causative sequence -is-i̧-; 3) a second applicative -il-. If it is a second applicative -il-, we would have to interfix one -il-, mutate it, then interfix another -il- and mutate it. An undoubtedly related situation concerns the extra -is- that is found whenever one passivizes a verb stem that ends in an -an-i̧- sequence; e.g., punk-an-i̧- 'cause to bump into each other' passivizes not as *punk-an-i̧-u-, but as punk-an-is-i̧-u- 'be caused to bump into each other'. The generalization appears to be that -an-i̧- is "converted" to -an-is-i̧- whenever another suffix is added.

[27] The forms in (49) were among the best I could get accepted by Dr. Mukuka. In addition to dialect variation, I suspect there may be individual variation as well. All of the forms I cite in this paper without an asterisk were accepted as "grammatical" by my informant (and were also allowed by the dictionary and other sources consulted), though at times they were felt to be awkward or overloaded. Crucially, they were judged as grammatical vs. other elicited forms which were rejected outright.

[28] Much more common are doublets such as the following:

    -amb-an- / -amb-is-i̧-an-i̧-   'slander e.o.'
    -fumb-an- / -fumb-is-i̧-an-i̧-   'give e.o. generously'
    -íkat-an- / -íkat-is-i̧-an-i̧-   'hold/catch e.o.'

To form a reciprocal of these verbs, one can either add -an- to the verb root directly, or one can first add the "intensive" sequence -is-i̧-. When reciprocal -an- is then added, the causative morph -i̧- is spelled out again after -an-. Note, however, that the intensive meaning is not available in the is-i̧-an-i̧- forms, which are exactly synonymous with the -an- forms (as repeatedly acknowledged also by the White Fathers' dictionary). In other cases too, the intensive sequence -is-i̧- is accessible only if it is last in the verb stem, suggesting that its meaning does not percolate up to the verb stem level unless it is the rightmost affix.

Could these suffixal doublings and triplings be seen as a cyclic reapplication of morphological spelling rules?

Let us return to the contrast between (46a) vs. (46b). As I have suggested for other Bantu languages (Hyman 1993b), I believe there is a conflict in (46b). On the one hand, I assume a default spelling of morphological features that is cyclic, i.e., that respects the scope relations (represented by the brackets). On the other hand, languages may impose linear precedence requirements on specific morphs. In Cibemba, we need a way to build into the causative morph -i̧- that it should follow the reciprocal morph -an-, independent of cyclicity or scope. In (46a) this is no problem: the cyclic spell-out is -an-i̧-. In (46b), however, the cyclic spell-out is -i̧-an-, which must be "repaired" as -i̧-an-i̧-.

Adapting for this purpose Anderson's (1986) rule-ordering approach to position classes ("slots"), I propose in (50) that the reciprocal spell-out rule precedes the causative spell-out rule, as indicated. However, unlike the cases Anderson discussed, these spell-outs are effected in a cyclic fashion, as shown in (51).

(50) Rule ordering: REC(IPROCAL) → -an-
                     CAUS → -i̧-

(51)a. [[[punk] REC] CAUS] 'cause to bump into e.o.'(17b)
                                   Cycle 1:
            -an-   REC → -an-
             —   CAUS → -i̧-

                                     Cycle 2:
             —   REC → -an-
            -i̧-   CAUS → -i̧-

   b. [[[fúm] CAUS] REC] 'take e.o. out'(46a)
                                   Cycle 1:
             —   REC → -an-
            -i̧-   CAUS → -i̧-

                                   Cycle 2:
            -an-   REC → -an-
            -i̧-   CAUS → -i̧-

In (51a) the reciprocal is spelled out as -an- on the first cycle, which is all that can happen on this cycle. On the second cycle the base still has a REC feature, but we cannot spell out a suffix twice in a row (in accordance with the "repeated morph constraint" in (52a)). We thus move on to the second rule, which spells out the causative feature. In (51b) we cannot spell out the reciprocal on the first cycle, but do spell out the causative. We then move on to the second cycle and spell out the reciprocal. At this point, the causative spell-out rule reapplies on Cycle 2 and we get the observed doubling.

In order for this to work, we have to recognize the variant of the repeated morph constraint given in (52a).

(52) "Repeated morph constraint" (Menn and MacWhinney 1984)

a. *[+F]   [+F]   b. [+F]   [+G]   c. [+F]
     | | | | /\
     il   il   il   il   il il

As pointed out by Menn and MacWhinney (1984), Stemberger (1981), and others, morphology is frequently subject to a haplology effect whose shape may vary from case to case. Quite generally in Bantu, one does not spell out the same morphological feature, say [+F], twice in a row. Consider, for example, the suffixal properties of the Cibemba verb -léet- 'bring' in (53).

(53) a. -léet-el-   'bring to/for/at'
      b. -léet-an-   'bring each other'
      c. -léet-el-an-   'bring to/for each other'
      d. -léet-an-in-   'bring each other to/for/at'
      e. -léet-el-an-in-   'bring for each other for/at'
      f. *-léet-el-el-   'bring to/for [s.o.] for [sth.]'

As seen, the applicative suffix in (53a) and the reciprocal suffix in (53b) may combine in either order (with scope differences) in (53c) and (53d). In (53e) we see that the same verb stem can have two applicative suffixes: one before reciprocal -an-, one after. However, in (53f) we see that it is not possible to get two applicative suffixes spelled out in a row.

The constraint in Cibemba is restricted to the case in (52a). As seen in (54), Cibemba allows surface -il-il- sequences in several other cases:

(54) a. -lípil-   'pay'   -lípil-il-   'enter for/at'
      b. -lí-il-   'eat for/at'   -lí-il-iil-e   'ate for/at'
      c. -shaal-   'remain behind'   -shaal-ilil-   'remain behind for good'
          -bol-   'be rotten'   -bol-elel-   'be completely rotten'
      d. -pú-   'finish'   -pú-ililil-   'finish completely'
          -no-   'drink'   -no-enenen-   'drink up completely'

In (54a) we see that applicative *-il-* can be added to a verb that ends in an [il] sequence, since this does not produce two APP suffixes in a row. In (54b), the applicativized form *-li-il-* 'eat for/at' is followed by an allomorph of the *-il-* perfective suffix. Since the *-il-'s* are realizations of different morphological features, as schematized in (52b), there is no haplology. The schema in (52c) is illustrated in (54c), where the completive suffix *-ilil-* looks like two *-il-'s*, but in fact spells out one morphological feature not obviously related to the applicative. Finally, (54d) shows that this same suffix appears as *-ililil-*, i.e., triple, when following a -CV- verb root.

What I am suggesting, then, is that this double spelling of causative *-i̧-* and reciprocal *-an-* may be a "cyclic effect" in an analogous way to the double application of CM that we have seen in earlier examples. If correct, then forms such as in the last line of (49), with three *-an-*, three *-i̧-* and three *-is-* could be argued to instantiate the third cycle that the phonology failed to provide. In order to establish this last point, it would be necessary to present a complete statement of the verb stem morphology, particularly one that correctly generates all the suffixes in the right order and with the right doublings (ultimately, triplings). It is clear from the data presented in this paper that not every suffix doubles in an A-B-A fashion. The two suffixes that do double are causative *-i̧-* and reciprocal *-an-*.[29] As seen in examples such as (53c), applicative *-il-* does not double in this way. One possibility is that individual suffixes may be diacritically marked as to whether they produce cyclic spell-outs or not. Unfortunately, it has been hard to get a general statement that covers all the data without additional stipulations beyond the cyclic/non-cyclic distinction. For example, *-an-* causes cyclic respelling of *-i̧-*, but *-i̧-* does not cause cyclic respelling of *-an-*; similarly, *-is-i̧-* causes cyclic respelling of *-an-*, but *-an-* does not cause cyclic respelling of *-is-i̧-*. Separate from these asymmetries, applicative *-il-* never causes cyclic respelling (although, as we saw, it is responsible for the most transparent cyclic phonology in the language). The challenge to work all of this out is a demanding one whose significance clearly extends beyond Cibemba and comparative Bantu. Concerning the observed cyclic effects that we have seen in the Cibemba verb stem, suffice it to say that their interpretation may ultimately depend more on how we do the morphology, than on how we do the phonology.

---

[29] As mentioned in note 26, a cyclic interpretation of the extra *-is-* in (49) is not at all clear.

References

Anderson, Stephen R. 1986. Disjunctive ordering in inflectional morphology. *Natural Language and Linguistic Theory* 4:1-32.

Archangeli, Diana and Douglas Pulleyblank. 1991. The content and structure of phonological representations, chapter 2. ms. University of Arizona and University of Ottawa. To appear, MIT Press.

Aronoff, Mark. 1988. Head operations and strata in reduplication: A linear treatment. *Morphology Yearbook* 1-15.

Ashton, E. O., E. M. K. Mulira, E. G. M. Ndaluwa and A. N. Tucker. 1954. *A Luganda grammar.* London: Longmans, Green and Co.

Chen, Matthew. 1991. The English stress cycle and interlexical relations. In C. Georgopoulos and R. Ishihara (eds.), *Interdisciplinary approaches to language: Essays in honor of S.-Y. Kuroda*, pp. 51-73. Dordrecht: Kluwer Academic Publishers.

Bastin, Y. 1983. *La finale -ide et l'imbrication en bantou.* Tervuren: Musée Royal de l'Afrique Centrale.

Goldsmith, John. 1993. Harmonic phonology. In John Goldsmith (ed.), *The last phonological rule.* (pp. 21-60). Chicago: University of Chicago Press.

Goldsmith, John. 1991. Talk at Institute of Cognitive Science, University of California, Berkeley.

Guthrie, Malcolm. 1971. *Comparative Bantu, vol. 2.* Gregg Publishers.

Halle, Morris and Michael Kenstowicz. 1991. The free element condition and cyclic vs. noncylic stress. *Linguistic Inquiry* 22:457-501.

Hyman, Larry M. 1989a. Advanced tongue root in Kinande. ms., University of California, Berkeley.

Hyman, Larry M. 1992. Velar palatalization in Cibemba: A "non-duplication" problem. *Linguistique Africaine* 8:55-71.

Hyman, Larry M. 1993a. Problems in rule ordering in phonology: two Bantu test cases. In John Goldsmith (ed.), *The last phonological rule* (pp. 195-222). Chicago: University of Chicago Press.

Hyman, Larry M. 1993b. Conceptual issues in the comparative study of the Bantu verb stem. In Salikoko S. Mufwene and Lioba Moshi (eds.), *Topics in African Linguistics* (pp. 3–34). Amsterdam: John Benjamins.

Hyman, Larry M. In press. Imbrication in Cibemba. *Journal of African Languages and Linguistics*.

Hyman, Larry M. and Sam Mchombo. 1992. Morphotactic constraints in the Chichewa verb stem. Paper presented at the 18th Annual Meeting of the Berkeley Linguistic Society. To appear in proceedings.

Karttunen, Lauri. 1991. Finite-state phonology. ms., Xerox.

Karttunen, Lauri. 1993. Finite state constraints. In John Goldsmith (ed.), *The last phonological rule* (pp. 173–194). Chicago: Univeristy of Chicago Press.

Kashoki, Mubanga E. 1968. A phonemic analysis of Bemba. *Zambian Papers* No. 3. Institute for Social Research, University of Zambia.

Kenstowicz, Michael and Jerzy Rubach. 1987. The phonology of syllabic nuclei in Slovak. *Language* 63:463-497.

Khumalo, James Steven Mzilikazi. 1987. *An autosegmental account of Zulu phonology*. Ph.D. dissertation, University of Witwatersrand, Johannesburg.

Kiparsky, Paul. 1982. Lexical morphology and phonology. *Linguistics in the Morning Calm*, pp. 3-93. Seoul: Hanshin.

Kisseberth, Charles W. and Mohamed Imam Abasheik. 1975. The perfect stem in Chi-Mwi:ni and global rules. *Studies in African Linguistics* 6:249-266.

Lakoff, George. 1993. Cognitive phonology. In John Goldsmith (ed.), *The last phonological rule* (pp. 117–145). Chicago: University of Chicago Press.

Louw, J.A. 1975. Palatalization of bilabials in the passive, diminutive and locative in Xhosa and Tsonga. *Afrika und Übersee* 54:241-278.

Menn, Lise and Brian MacWhinney. 1984. The repeated morph constraint. *Language* 60:519-541.

Mutaka, Ngessimo. 1986. Vowel harmony in Kinande. ms., University of Southern California.

Pulleyblank, Douglas. 1985. A lexical treatment of tone in Tiv. In D.L. Goyvaerts (ed.), *African Linguistics* (pp. 421–476). Amsterdam: Benjamins.

Rugemalira, Josephat. 1990. Vowel harmony in Lunyambo. ms., University of California, Berkeley.

Sadock, Jerrold M. 1990. *Autolexical syntax*. University of Chicago Press.

Sainz, Susana. 1988. A noncyclic analysis of English word stress. *Working Papers of the Cornell Phonetics Laboratory*, No. 3.

Sambeek, J. van. 1955. *A Bemba grammar*. London: Longmans, Green and Co.

Schlindwein, Deborah. 1987. P-bearing units: A study of Kinande vowel harmony. *Proceedings of NELS 17*.

Sharman, John Campton. 1963. *Morphology, morphophonology and meaning in the single-word verb-forms in Bemba*. Ph.D. dissertation, University of South Africa.

Sims, G.W. 1959. *An elementary grammar of Cibemba*. Basutoland: Morija Printing Works.

Stemberger, Joseph P. 1981. Morphological haplology. *Language* 57:791-817.

The White Fathers. 1947. *Bemba-English dictionary*. Cilubula, Zambia.

Zoll, Cheryl. 1993. Consonant mutations in Bantu: Implications for feature geometry. Ms., University of California, Berkley.

On Metrical Constituents: Unbalanced Trochees and Degenerate Feet

Michael Kenstowicz
Massachusetts Institute of Technology

1 Introduction

A significant development within the phonological theory of the past ten years has been the expanded role of metrical constituents in phonological description and explanation. The phonetically elusive property of stress is now commonly regarded as the superficial reflection of a metrical grouping and hence not a genuine distinctive feature. In two influential studies, Borowsky (1983) and Myers (1987) showed that several rules of English phonology refer to the location of segments with respect to a sequence of stressed plus unstressed syllables—the trochaic foot. Equally significant has been the discovery by McCarthy and Prince (1986, 1990) of affixational and other morphological operations whose scope of application can be insightfully delimited by reference to metrical structure. Since these metrical groupings have no uniform or direct phonetic correlates, one presumes on acquisition grounds that the range of possible structures is severely circumscribed and essentially known in advance. The learning task then amounts to deciding which particular grouping is operative in the language at hand. The identification of the correct inventory of metrical constituents and the principles underlying their formation and deployment has thus become a principal research objective of contemporary linguistic theory.

In the study of this topic over the past five years or so, two competing theories have emerged—the Halle-Vergnaud theory (Halle and Vergnaud 1987, Halle 1990, and Halle and Kenstowicz 1991) and the theory developed independently by Bruce Hayes (1985, 1987, 1991) and by John McCarthy and Alan Prince (1986, 1990; Prince 1991) which, for lack of a better term, I refer to as the rhythmic theory. In this paper, I attempt to clarify some of the major differences between the two approaches and how they play out in particular cases, concentrating on two analytic questions: the treatment of heavy-light sequences and orphan light syllables. My purpose here is as much to provoke discussion as it is to try to adjudicate between the two. Both have proven to be productive frameworks in which previously unknown generalizations have emerged.

2 Two Views of Metrical Constituents

First, guiding intuitions and then more specific formalisms. For Halle and Vergnaud, organization into headed constituents is a phenomenon that takes place at various levels of linguistic structure. In phonology, it is a general counting device which can be employed not only for stress but other rules as well—any phonological process or phenomenon which requires locating a segment by counting from the beginning or end of the word or phrase. The metrical parsing is carried out on an abstract plane or grid projected from the line of phonemes and associated skeletal slots. There can be several simultaneous projections and their parameters need not coincide. The parsing is directional and delivers principally binary or unbounded constituents. It is also exhaustive, forcing the construction of degenerate, unary elements. The string can be premarked by stressing long vowels independent of context. A more recent development allows bracketing to be inserted prior to the parse to mark metrical junctures associated with affixation (Halle 1990, Halle and Kenstowicz 1991, Idsardi 1991). These premarkings are then respected by the parse as it sweeps from one edge of the word to the other.

Although grouping is postulated at higher levels of structure, most of the independent evidence corroborating metrical constituency (for example, stress shifts under vocalic elision and insertion) comes from processes that affect the bottom line of the grid. It is thus at this level that the two approaches compete with one another.[1] The guiding intuition underlying the alternative model is that metrical grouping is primarily a rhythmic phenomenon (Liberman and Prince 1977, Prince 1983). This position received an empirical boost from Hayes' (1985, 1987) discovery of a statistical skewing in the distribution of grouping types relative to the presence or absence of quantity. Stated in the most general terms, quantity-sensitive systems tend to be iambic or right-headed while quantity-insensitive systems are optimally left-headed or trochaic. More specifically, while some trochaic systems that group Strong+Weak can tolerate a long vowel in weak position (essentially ignoring quantity, for example, Finnish), iambic systems must respect quantity and cannot place a long vowel in weak position. The explanation for this surprising asymmetry is a law of rhythmic perception that is called into play in experiments (see discussion in Bell 1977) where a series of alternating pulses are differentiated by enhancing every other one: if the enhancement involves increasing the length of the stimulus, a

---

[1] It is worth observing, however, that in the Halle and Vergnaud theory rules of stress shift operating at higher levels of the grid are formulated in terms of a notation that crucially relies on constituency. With the possible exception of tone, stress is the only phonological feature which so readily mirrors syntactic bracketing. This affinity makes sense if stress is defined in terms of constituents.

weak position groups with a following strong; but when the enhancement involves intensity, the weak position groups with the preceding strong.

If grouping is primarily a rhythmic phenomenon, then it makes sense to build this asymmetry into the theory. Accordingly, rhythmic theorists have revamped the earlier symmetric parametrised systems of Hayes (1981) and Halle-Vergnaud (1987) into several distinct metrical parses (1).

(1) syllabic trochee: group σ σ → (σ σ)
                                    *

   iambic: group σ̆ σ as (σ̆ σ) and σ̄ as (σ̄)
                          *   *

   moraic trochee: group σ̆ σ̆ as (σ̆ σ̆) and σ̄ as (σ̄)
                                 *   *

This move has been encouraged by certain quantitative changes that are seen as reinforcing the iambic-trochaic opposition, much the way in which lip rounding enhances the front-back vocalic opposition. The most secure is the ubiquitous iambic lengthening phenomenon whereby (LĹ) is augmented to (LH́) (L = light, H = heavy). This process tends to be a "low-level" one: I know of no cases where a rule must be ordered after it, and it often preserves a short-long contrast as long-overlong. But in its sensitivity to level-ordering (Muskogean) and failure to affect schwa (Yupik), it appears to be genuinely phonological. More controversial are the quantity-sensitive trochaic systems such as Latin, English, and Arabic, where two lights group as strong-weak but a heavy syllable is always stressed and thus never occupies a recessive position as in Finnish. In these systems, a major question concerns the treatment of the heavy-light sequence. Given their commitment to the law of rhythmic perception, rhythmic theorists see a (HL) grouping as relatively mal-formed. Hayes (1991) does not allow his moraic trochee parse (1) to build such unbalanced trochees at all, while Prince (1991) treats them as relatively marked and subject to elimination. The vowel shortening via resyllabification originally proposed by Stampe (1972) for SPE's trisyllabic laxing in *divīne, divĭnity* and generalized by Myers (1987) to *tōne, tŏn-ic* vs. *tōnal* has been reinterpreted as movement from the relatively marked (HL) grouping to a less marked (LL). Trochaic shortening is not nearly as wide-spread as iambic lengthening, but this might reflect the relative complexity of the (HL) grouping to begin with. However, in view of the fact that English also has rules lengthening vowels in precisely the same trochaic context (cf. *algebra, algebrā-ic*; *Canada, Canādian*), it is unclear how robust the putative (HL) vs. (LL) asymmetry really is.[2]

---

[2]Analogous cases arise in iambic systems. For example, in Yupik a light syllable is

The familiar paradigm from Cairene Arabic in (2a) also spurns unbalanced trochees (HL). In this case, left-to-right parsing groups the first two lights; but when a heavy syllable is encountered, the parse begins over again on a following light. This result follows directly if (HL) is not a possible metrical grouping; and Hayes' (1987, 1991) moraic trochee parse is designed with this case in mind.

(2) a. LLL → (ĹL)L   kátabit
    HLL → (H́)(ĹL)   qaahíra, madrása
    LHL → L(H́)L   katábna

b. katabit   madrasa   katabna
    | | | | | | | | | | |
    * * *   (* * * *   * (** *

In the Halle-Vergnaud framework, the metrical equivalence of H and LL is achieved by allowing heavy syllables to project two metrical positions (an idea also exploited in Prince 1983). However, to account for the fact that

---

bulked before a long vowel in many dialects: underlying [qaya:ni] surfaces as *qáyyáni*. Hayes (1991) postulates a derivation in which the LH sequence parses as an iamb (LH); the light syllable then increments a mora creating (HH). Foot structure in Yupik is "persistant" and so evaluates this structure as malformed, inducing a reparsing to (H)(H). Halle (1990) treats this case by a rule that supplies bimoraic long-vowelled syllables with an opening bracket; a subsequent iambic parsing rule respects this boundary, thus guaranteeing that long-vowelled syllables initiate and (given their bipositional representation) close a metrical foot.

qayaani   qa yaa ni   qa yaa ni
| | | | | | | | | | | |
* ** *   →   * (* * *   →   (*)(**)(*)
                                 * * *

Hayes objects to this analysis on the grounds that it artificially blocks the parse from constructing the optimal (LH) iamb. But if (LH) is optimal, then why does the system allow another rule to lengthen the first syllable and derive (HH)? Hayes might respond by saying that structure preservation is overruled by a more dominant constraint that seeks to keep underlying LL and LH sequences distinct. (Recall that the former undergoes iambic lengthening and thus appears as (LH) in Yupik.) This example brings out another important difference between the two models. Because Halle-Vergnaud allow a prebracketing of the string, it makes sense for them to lump together the metrification of long vowels and unpredictable stresses in languages such as Aklan or Tubatulabal: in both cases a vowel is stressed independent of its odd-even location in the string. Since the rhythmic theory is premised on the different responses of iambic and trochaic grouping to syllable weight, heavy syllables acquire their stress along with light syllables in the course of the rhythmic parse. On this view, there is no motivation to treat heavy syllables and idiosyncratic stresses in the same fashion. So far the rhythmic theorists have been silent on how they propose to treat lexical stresses and pre/postaccenting morphemes.

the metrical parse begins anew after a heavy, Halle (1990) must premark bimoraic heavy syllables with a line-0 bracket (2b). This move is necessary because in the Halle-Vergnaud framework syllabification and metrical projection are two separate planes that intersect the skeletal tier. Metrical parsing that cuts across syllables is thus possible, though presumably a marked phenomenon. In addition to Winnebago (Halle 1990), Arabic broken plurals (McCarthy and Prince 1990) and Japanese loanword truncation (Ito 1991) are the best known examples of this syllable cross-cutting.

Rhythmic theorists have traded in the skeletal tier for a prosodic hierarchy in which phonological words are composed of feet, feet are built from syllables, and syllables contain moras. On this layered view of prosodic organization, the mora plays a central role expressing at least four different distinctions of traditional grammar: weight for stress rules (light vs. heavy syllables), gemination in consonants and vowels (long vs. short segments), conservation of prosodic position under deletion (compensatory lengthening), and internal constituency in the syllable (principally nuclear vs. nonnuclear position). For the rhythmic theorists, a metrical parse is built out of syllables and hence can never interrupt a syllable, though it must peek inside the syllable to check for weight. The opening bracket on the heavy syllable in *katábna* thus comes for free; but they must tell a different story for Winnebago, Arabic broken plurals, and Japanese truncation.

Another major difference between the two models concerns the treatment of single light syllables. With its commitment to exhaustive parsing, the Halle-Vergnaud model groups a single unmatched element into a degenerate constituent containing the obligatory head but lacking a dependent. The initial and final light syllables in Cairene *katábna* must either be shielded from parsing by extrametricality or else be stressed and then destressed by conflation or clash removal. For rhythmic theorists, stress reflects the grouping of two elements into an iamb or trochee. Stress on unpaired syllables is thus relatively unexpected. Hayes (1991) hypothesizes that stress on such runt constituents can only arise directly under the main word stress. On this view, the light syllables of LHL *katábna* remain unparsed essentially without stipulation.

3   Unbalanced HL Trochees

With this background to frame the discussion, let us now look at some particular cases. One system where the issues of unbalanced trochees and light syllables are particularly relevant is Latin, which has received considerable attention (see Mester 1993). In Latin, final extrametricality allows a right-to-left trochaic parse to plant a stress on the antepenult. The antepenult is unreachable when the penult is heavy; otherwise, the parse would yield a (LH) iamb, which cannot co-exist with a (ĹL) trochee. The important analytic question concerns HL sequences such as found in HHL<H> *exīstimō*. The quantitative trochaic parse in (1) should stop on the penult light since it cannot group (HL). But this incorrectly predicts penultimate stress (a possibility that as far as I know never arises in Latin or elsewhere). To allow the parse to proceed on to the antepenult, we may impose a system-wide ban on footing a single light syllable. As argued by Allen (1973), this seems to produce right results in Latin. In particular, it explains well the phenomenon of iambic shortening where disyllabic words of the structure L<H> such as *egō* 'I' shorten their final vowel. This change can be understood as a kind of last resort the system makes in order to assign a stress: the initial light coaxes the final heavy to remove its extrametricality so they can join together to produce a stress. But since Latin is a trochaic system that bars a light-heavy grouping, the final syllable sheds a mora and thus turns up short.

However, Allen notes (1973:181) that early Latin verse suggests that iambic shortening operated in pretonic position too: cf. ămīcus, but iamĭcítiam. Here a secondary stress appears on the word-initial light syllable, inducing a shortening on the following [mī], just as in *egō > egŏ. But if iambic shortening occurs outside of bisyllables and not just as a last resort, then the argument against (HL) grouping is jeopardized and might be reversed to imply that a light penult does in fact group with a preceding heavy in the unbalanced trochee. This is evident from the paradigms in (3), where a final heavy shortens after the single light in *capīs → capĭs* but not when preceded by the heavy-light sequence in *ímpedīs*.

(3)　căpĕre　　capis　　LH
　　 audīre　　 audīs　　HH
　　 dormīre　　dormīs　　HH
　　 aperīre　　aperīs　　LLH
　　 impedīre　ímpedīs　HLH

If ămĭcítia (cf. amīcus) tells as that a light plus heavy can group together shortening a heavy, then we must explain why this does not happen in HL<H> *ímpedīs*. The most natural explanation may be that the light has already grouped with the preceding heavy as (impe)<dīs> and hence is not free to join with the following heavy to induce iambic shortening. We might still try to preserve Allen's analysis if we say that extrametricality is only removed under compulsion to assign a word stress. L<H> *egō then becomes LH and eventually (L̊L) while HL<H> *impedīs* can retain the (H)L<H> analysis. Complicating all of this further is the phenomenon of cretic shortening in which H́LH scans as H́LL, indicating that L does not parse with preceding H and hence is free to participate in iambic shortening.

But then the final syllable cannot lose its extrametricality just in order to satisfy culmination. The shortening data thus seem in the end to be rather inconclusive.[3]

Another more direct argument for the unbalanced (HL) trochee comes from the enclitic stress shifts in (4) discussed by Steriade (1988) and later by Halle and Kenstowicz (1991).

(4) úbi   'where'   límina   'thresholds'
    ubí#libet 'wherever'   līminá#que   'and thresholds'
    (L)L#LL   (HL)L#L

The alternation in *úbi - ubí#libet* suggests that enclitic stress can reach back to the antepenult. But it systematically fails to do so when the base has antepenultimate stress and the clitic is monosyllabic: we have *līminá#que* not *līmína#que*. If the enclitic stress arises from reapplication of the antepenult stress rule, then we can explain its failure to land on [mi] if [mi] is already grouped with [lī] as heavy-light (līmi)na#que. The only free landing site for the enclitic accent is then the [na]. Stress shifts under enclisis thus furnish us with an additional tool to probe metrical constituency and in particular a possible asymmetry between LL and HL sequences.

Halle and Kenstowicz (1991) demonstrate that the Austronesian language Manam shifts stress under enclisis essentially parallel to Latin, the only difference being that extrametricality is a lexically determined feature of certain suffixes in Manam. Antepenultimately stressed *ʔú-doʔ-i* 'you took it' (LL)<L> has its accent dislodged by the enclitic in *ʔu-doʔ-í#be* 'you took it or' while penultimately stressed *ʔu-dóʔ-i* 'you took them'

---

[3]Mester (1993) sees cretic shortening as a response to the "prosodic trapping" of a light syllable under strict binarity: HLH# parses as (H)L<H> in contrast to LL<H>. If footing is persistent, then the system gets another chance to group the unfooted L with the <H>. Under the Hayesian inventory in (1), this refooting is basically paradoxical in that it must be allowed to group material that is made for an iamb (LH) and then somehow transform it into a trochee by the language-particular rule of shortening. These transformations make sense under the markedness approach of Prince (1991) which groups binarily and then evaluates the result with respect to the particular rhythmic pattern that is being imposed. Trochaic rhythm ranks the feet (LL), (H) > (HL) > (L) and allows readjustments so long as they advance the representation to a more highly valued form. As Mester observes, this view is compatible with either an original (H)L<H> or a (HL)<H> parse. The transformation of (H)L<H> to (H)(LH) improves the representation by imposing an exhaustive parsing while (H)(LH) → (H)(LL) yields the canonical trochee. But the regrouping of (HL)<H> to (H)(LH) trades (HL) for the more highly valued (H) as well as parses the extrametrical syllable and thus can step to (H)(LL) by the same logic. Reparsing of (LL)<H> to (L)(LH) is highly disfavored because it surrenders the best trochee for the worst. Under either of these views of cretic shortening as a (re)metrification, however, a stress clash is created. Whether this clash must be eliminated or is allowed to stand is unclear.

does not in ʔu-dóʔ-i#be 'you took them or'. This contrast follows if the inputs to the reapplication of the trochaic stress rule under enclisis are (LL)L#<L> vs. L(LL)#<L>. Closed syllables count as heavy in Manam, forcing final stress in malabóŋ 'flying fox' (cf. waríge 'rope') and blocking antepenultimate stress in u-rapún-di 'I waited for them' (cf. u-bázi-di 'I carried them'). In his discussion of enclitic stress, Lichtenberk (1983) does not describe bases terminating in a HL sequence as shifting stress under enclisis. Furthermore, a brief search of his grammar turned up the following cases consistent with this interpretation: ʔulémwa#be 'ten and' (p. 339) and toánda#be 'long ago' foc. (p. 387). These might reflect a (HL) metrical grouping of the base in which case no free syllables are available to seat a stress when the extrametrical enclitic is added: (HL)#<L>. However, this argument is not conclusive. Nouns of the structure HLL systematically stress the antepenult: émbeʔi 'sacred flute'. Halle and Kenstowicz (1991) metrify these cases as (H)(LL) and posit a rule of stress clash removal to generate (H)LL. An opponent of unbalanced trochees might argue that a base such as ʔulémwa parses as L(H)L. Addition of the clitic then allows a binary constituent to be built: L(H)(L#L). But the latter is subsequently cancelled by the independently needed clash rule. The Manam data are thus not conclusive with respect to the issue of unbalanced HL trochees.

Some additional evidence for the unbalanced trochee comes from differences among the Arabic dialects. In his study of the Bani-Hassan, Irshied (1984) shows that this dialect has the elision rule found in many other Bedouin dialects that deletes a short low vowel [a] when initial in a binary metrical constituent. We state this rule in (5a) and see its operation in the paradigms of (5b). The elision rule was a significant discovery in the development of metrical theory, since the deletion triggers shift of stress to the remaining element in the foot in order to preserve metrical constituency. The fact that stress shifts to the right (rather than deleting entirely or shifting to the left) provided an independent argument for the postulated constituency (see Al-Mozainy et al. 1985 and discussion in Halle and Vergnaud 1987).

(5)
a. [a] → ∅ / __
          |
        (* *)

b. [CaCaC]   sáḥab   (L)<L>   'he pulled'
   [CaCaC+aC]   sḥáb-at   (LL)<L>   'she pulled'
   [CaCaC+aC+V] sḥàb-át-uh   (LL)(L)<L>   'she pulled him'

c. saḥabat-uh → s ḥab at uh → ṣhab at uh
   | | | | | | | | | |
   (* *)(*)<*>   (. *) (*)<*>   (*) (*)<*>
    *   *   *   *   *   *

In Bani-Hassan final syllables are extrametrical and the parse proceeds trochaically from left to right. Final extrametricality explains the lack of elision in [sáḥab] and the left-to-right directionality assigns a stress to the penult in underlying four-syllable [sḥabátuh], as shown by the derivation in (5c).

When the first syllable is heavy in Bani-Hassan, the stress shifts to the penult upon the addition of a suffix: cf. HLĹL ʕàllam-át-uh.

(6) [CaCCaC]   ʕállam   (H)<L>   'he taught'
    [CaCCaC-aC]   ʕállam-at   (HL)<L>   'she taught'
    [CaCCaC-aC+V] ʕàllam-át-uh (HL)(L)<L>   'she taught him'

This follows straightforwardly if BHA forms (HL) trochees. If the parse stopped on the heavy syllable and started over again on the following two lights, we should have expected an elision in ʕàllam-át-uh. Interestingly, this is precisely what is found in other Bedouin dialects. For example, Irshied and Kenstowicz's (1984) Riyadh consultant has the paradigms in (7).

(7) sáḥab   ʕállam   (L)<L>   (H)<L>
    sháb-at   ʕállim-at   (LL)<L>   (H)L<L>
    shább-it-ah ʕallm-ít-ah   (LL)L<L>   (H)(LL)<L>

It has the same surface distribution of stress as the Bani-Hassan dialect except for the four-syllable forms. Here, Riyadh has increased the scope of elision to include the second syllable in HLLL sequences. This difference follows if Riyadh follows Cairene in allowing heavy syllables to project two metrical positions. Underlying [ʕallamatah] then parses (H)(LL)<L> and receives the derivation in (8). Later rules raising the low vowel in short open syllables and suppressing secondary accents yield the final derived forms.

(8) ʕal la mat-ak   ʕal l mat–ak
     ‖ | | | →   ‖ | |
     (**)(* *)<*>   (**)   (*)<*>
      *   *   *   *

A parallel contrast between metrically single and double-barrelled syllables in the Levantine Arabic dialects furnishes an additional argument for the existence of unbalanced (HL) trochees. We recall that these dialects have the well-known *fihím#na* vs. *fhím-na* contrast discovered by Brame (1973) that is nicely explained if the stress rule reapplies upon the addition of a clitic. Abu-Salim (1982) systematically investigated the scope of this phenomenon in his Palestinian dialect. The paradigm in (9) shows that initial heavy syllables shift stress just one syllable to the right under enclisis in Palestinian. This contrasts minimally with the situation in the Damascus dialect studied by McCarthy (1980), where stress shifts to the penult in *ʕallam-ə́t#o*.

(9) Palestinian (Abu-Salim 1982)
     ʕállam
     ʕállam-at
     ʕallámat#o

     Damascus (McCarthy 1980)
     ʕállam
     ʕállam-et
     ʕallam-ə́t#o

This systematic difference between the two dialects comes without stipulation if Damascus follows Bani-Hassan in projecting just a single slot per syllable (10a) while Palestinian follows Riyadh in projecting two from a heavy syllable (10b).

(10) a. ʕallam-ət   b. ʕal lam-at
         | | | ‖ | |
         (* *)<*>   (**)(*)<*>
          *   *   *

Addition of the clitic to (10a) frees the final -ət to host the enclitic accent. It cannot recede to the [la] since that syllable is grouped with the preceding heavy in the unbalanced trochee. For (ĹL)<L> bases, we predict a stress shift to the penult under enclisis for the Palestinian dialect: (ĹL)(Ĺ)#<L>. This would then be a case where enclitic accent could support the ban on (HL) grouping that is implied by the left-to-right "moraic" parse of Palestinian. Unfortunately this prediction cannot be (dis)confirmed because an early rule contracts CaCaC stems to CaCC in the relevant contexts (see Kenstowicz and Abdul-Karim 1980 for discussion).

To briefly summarize, the metrical constituency required by the low-vowel elision rule and stress shift under enclisis co-varies with projection of one vs. two stress-bearing units per syllable. Each phenomenon suggests that, at least in Arabic, the trochaic parse groups a heavy and light syllable when it is defined at the syllable level, that is, when there is just one stress-bearing unit per syllable.

4 Orphan Light Syllables

Let us now return to the question of the light syllables. In the description of Palestinian ʕállamat, adherence to exhaustive parsing forces degenerate footing of (L) even though it surfaces as unstressed: (H)(L)<L>. A rule removing a stress clash from a final degenerate must thus be postulated to distinguish this case from Cairene ʕallámit. If we give up exhaustive parsing and allow strict binarity as a parametric option, then the difference between the two dialects could be simply the presence versus absence of extrametricality: Palestinian (H)L<L> vs. Cairene (H)(LL). This difference in the treatment of single light syllables arises constantly when one compares the Halle-Vergnaud model of metrical grouping with its rhythmic competitors. Adapting to our own purposes a term from the printing trade for leftover pages in the gathering of a book, we refer to such unmatched syllables as "orphans." In this section we briefly survey some of the responses that are made to orphans from the perspectives of the two theories.

First, let's show that stressed orphans do indeed exist as an option, ruling out strict binarity universally (unless phonetically null syllables are invoked: see Burzio 1988). Pike's (1964) stress trains in the Peruvian language Auca furnishes a good example. Auca is well-known to students of metrical phonology as the first documented case of bidirectional parsing: the stem metrifies trochaically from left to right and then the string of suffixes parses from right to left. The Auca stress trains have recently been discussed independently by Halle and Kenstowicz (1991) and Hayes (1991) from the perspective of the two theories. Although differing in detail, the two analyses are essentially equivalent in their treatment of the stressed orphan in Auca. In the former analysis, the final syllable of the stem is extrametrical; upon suffixation, its extrametricality is lost and joins the left end of the stratum-2 suffixal train. When it occupies an even position in the right-to-left parse, it forms the head of a trochaic foot (11a). But when it occupies an odd position, it is an unmatched orphan and turns up stressed in Auca (11b). A UG ban on degenerate constituents would have trouble with this case.

(11) a. ápǽné#kãndápa   'he speaks'
        123#456 → (12)<3>#456 → (12)3#456 → (12)(3#4)(56)

    b. yíwǽmó#ŋámba   'he carves'
        123#45 → (12)<3>#45 → (12)(3)#(45)

In Hayes' analysis, the final syllable of the stem is not extrametrical; in an odd-syllabled stem, the final syllable forms an orphan. Although Pike's transcriptions and discussion do not distinguish primary from secondary stress, Hayes assembles circumstantial evidence that the final stress of the stem is stronger than the others and thus that the Auca data are consistent with his hypothesis that stressed orphans are licensed by the major word stress.

Granted that stressed orphans occur in Auca, we might still question their legitimacy in situations like Palestinian ʕállamat. Since no stress appears on the medial light syllable, wouldn't it be better not to have to plant a stress there only to remove it later? This issue arises constantly in phonological analysis of course and is not peculiar to stress. We feel more justified in taking this analytic step if we can demonstrate that at least in some cases the postulated intermediate stage can be detected. The best known case where this can be established is Winnebago (Miner 1979, Hale and White Eagle 1980, Halle and Vergnaud 1987, Hayes 1991). In words composed of light syllables, the first is skipped as extrametrical and then odd-numbered ones are stressed.

(12) wijúk   'cat'
     hipirák   'belt'
     hočičínik   'boy'
     hokiwárokè   'swing'

Exhaustive iambic parsing from left to right with initial extrametricality lays a stress on the final syllable of a word such as *hočičínik*: <L>(LĹ)(Ĺ). This stressed orphan must then be destressed under clash. Since the initial stress is primary in Winnebago, no stress would be permitted on the orphan under Hayes' hypothesis that licenses this move only under the major word stress.

There is some evidence that commitment to exhaustivity is correct in this case. Winnebago has a rule (Dorsey's Law) that inserts a copy of the nuclear vowel between a preceding voiceless stop and sonorant. This rule must apply after stress is assigned. In cases where Dorsey's Law disrupts a foot, the binary constituent is deformed and the stress rule applies over again from the spot of the foul to remetrify the rest of the string (Halle and Vergnaud's "domino condition"). In (13) we cite a case from Hale and White Eagle (1980) where Dorsey's Law does not interrupt a constituent and so the original stress is retained. Note that stress on the orphan emerges phonetically in this case. We can maintain this stress if a degenerate foot is formed and deletion under clash is ordered to apply after Dorsey's Law epenthesis.

(13) ha rakíšrujìkšnà   ha rakí šu rujìk ša nà   'pull taut' 2 d.
      | | | || | → | | | | || | | |
      <*>(* *)(* *) (*)   <*>(* *) * (* *) * (*)
           *   *   *   *   *   *

This example is thus comparable to other cases in phonology where an epenthetic vowel allows normally hidden structure to emerge (for example, the Yawelmani long vowels in [CVVCC] stems). (See Hayes 1991 for an alternative interpretation of Winnebago accent which, if true, would nullify the force of this example.)

The discussion of Old English metrical structure by Dresher and Lahiri (1991) brings out another feature of light syllables. In order to account for the syncope of open-syllable high vowels after a single heavy or two light syllables (14), Dresher and Lahiri propose to augment the UG inventory of metrical constituents with an internally structured foot in which the head must branch into two moras—a single heavy syllable or two lights.

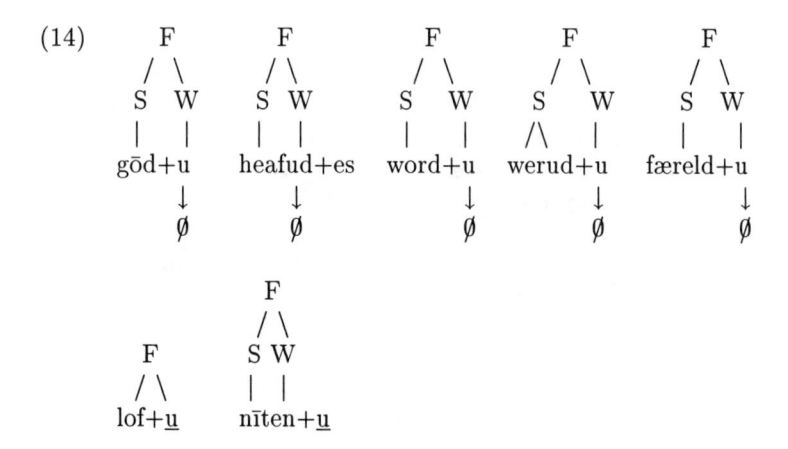

(14)
```
      F           F             F            F            F
     / \         / \           / \          / \          / \
    S   W       S   W         S   W        S   W        S   W
    |   |       |   |         |   |       /\   |        |   |
   gōd+u     heafud+es       word+u      werud+u      færeld+u
    ↓           ↓             ↓            ↓            ↓
    ∅           ∅             ∅            ∅            ∅


                    F
                   / \
      F           S   W
     / \          |   |
   lof+u̱       nīten+u̱
```

The optional light syllable dependent then locates the syncopating syllable. This analysis seems to be predicated on the tacit assumption that a weak sister position is the appropriate location for syncope. But from our current perspective, an orphan light syllable (either parsed or unparsed) would be an equally natural syncope site. Moreover, there would then be no necessity to expand the UG foot inventory. In (15) we show the structures assigned under the Halle-Vergnaud left-headed "moraic" parse and the rhythmic theorists' quantitative trochee. Since the major stress occurs word-initially in Germanic, the degenerate (L) is legitimate under Hayes' hypothesis on the distribution of unary constituents.

(15)
```
     good-u     heafud-es      word-u      werud-u      færeld-u
      ‖  |      ‖  |  ‖         ‖  |        |  |  |      |  ‖  |
     (**)(*)   (**)(*)(**)     (**)(*)    (* *)(*)    (*)(**)(*)

     (H) L     (H) L (H)       (H) L      (L L) L    (L)(H) L

     lof-u     niiten-u
      |  |     ‖  |  |
     (* *)    (**)(* *)

     (L L)    (H) (L L)
```

Either analysis successfully delimits the range of syncope in Old English.

Dresher and Lahiri state that secondary stress is retained on a heavy syllable following a heavy (ōþèrne) or two lights (ǽþelìnges) but is lost from a heavy following a light (cýninges, wésende) as well as word finally.

Under the Halle and Vergnaud analysis in which a heavy syllable projects two metrical positions, this contrast between initial lights and heavies in causing stress clash removal has a natural representational difference of the kind observed in Prince (1983): the stress-bearing units are adjacent in the (L)(H) sequence but not in the (H)(H) case, whose grid structure parallels a (LL)(LL) sequence.

(16) a. we sen de   b.   oo θ er ne
         | || | || || |
         (*)(**)(*)   (**)(**)(*)
          *   * *   *   * *

Given that the syllable is the only stress-bearing unit in the prosodic hierarchy, it is unclear if rhythmic theorists' can avail themselves of a comparable rationale for the asymmetry in (16).

At the outset we mentioned Finnish as a trochaic language which places long vowels in weak position and hence ignores quantity. Royal Skousen (1975) discussed this point in connection with his concern to demonstrate the productivity of phonological rules through their effects in loanword adaptation. He mentions that in the Swedish word *likör* 'liquor', the accented second syllable is realized with a long vowel. Since length is phonemic in Finnish, this word has been borrowed with a long vowel but adapted to the native stress pattern which, according to Skousen, accents the first syllable and odd-numbered nonfinal syllables (with an option of skipping a third-syllable light if the following syllable is heavy). Accordingly, Swedish *likör* is borrowed as *likööri*. Skousen also mentions a rule from the Savo dialects which he formulates as (17) that geminates a consonant after a stressed vowel followed by either a long vowel or diphthong. In these dialects Swedish *polis* is realized as *pólliisi* in contrast to Standard Finnish *póliisi*. A rhythmic theorist might interpret this innovation as the substitution of a moraic parse for the syllable trochee, with rejection of the presumably marked degenerate foot option.

(17)   C → C: / V́ __ VV

The system appears to reason as follows. To justify the initial stress, the foot must dominate two moras. A sequence of two lights is consistent with such an interpretation, but a LH sequence is not. There are two ways open to the stressed syllable to achieve metrification: steal the mora of the following syllable (Latin's iambic shortening) or sprout one of its own. Savo Finnish takes the latter path, realizing the incremented mora as gemination.

(18)

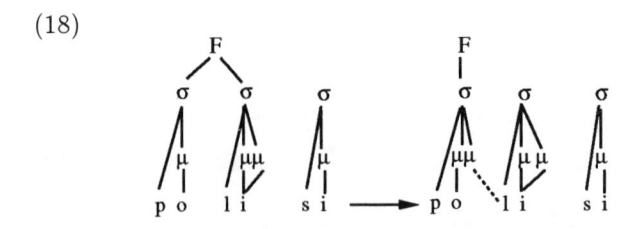

```
    F              F
   ╱╲             │
  σ  σ   σ      σ    σ   σ
  ╱╲ ╱╲  ╱╲         ╱╲  ╱╲  ╱╲
  μ μμ μ         μμ   μμ   μ
  │  ╲╱ │         ╲╱   ╲╱  │
  p o l i  s i  →  p o  l i  s i
```

This analysis implies that in Savo *pólliisi* the second syllable carries a stress as well, a point on which Skousen is silent.

A similar phenomenon is found in the iambic parsing Yupik dialects (Leer 1985) where underlying (LL) is realized as (LH) by iambic lengthening ([qayani] → *qayá:ni*) while a LH sequence appears as (H)(H) through gemination: [qaya:ni] → *qáyyá:ni*. As in the analysis of Cairene (2), the fact that heavy syllables always initiate a foot is achieved by prebracketing in Halle (1990).

(19) qayani   qayaa ni
      │ │ │   │ ‖ │
      * * *   *(** *

The metrical parse then respects the preassigned boundary. Hayes (this volume) objects to this kind of analysis on the grounds that the parse is prevented from building the "best" iamb (LH́). This objection is of course premised on the idea that iambic vs. trochaic parsing is a fundamental typological distinction that proliferates through the system, encouraging such rhythmic supports as iambic lengthening. In the Halle-Vergnaud model, prebracketing is an independent variable that may be called into play regardless of whether metrical feet are right or left-headed. Thus, the fact that bulking of a LH sequence to HH can be found in both iambic parsing Yupik and trochaic parsing Finnish comes as no surprise. Hayes' alternative analysis groups underlying [qaya:ni] as (LH)L and then postulates a rule of "prelong strengthening" to geminate the dependent L. The resultant (HH) is rhythmically ill-formed and reparses as (H)(H). Like the trochaic lengthening in *algebra, algebrā-ic*, the (LH) → (HH) transformation runs directly counter to the rhythmic requirements. One who is not favorably disposed to the iambic - trochaic distinction might see this as an internal contradiction. The rhythmic theorist could respond that the Yupik prelong strengthening pushes underlying (LH) off the metrical scale in order to maintain a contrast with the iambically lengthening (LL) → (LH), pointing to the fact that other dialects produce an equally marked overlengthening of (LH) to (LH$^+$).

We conclude that unbalanced trochees and orphaned light syllables will continue to receive close scrutiny as the two theories compete for empirical advantage.

References

Abu-Salim, Issam. 1982. *A reanalysis of some aspects of Arabic phonology: A metrical approach.* Ph.D. dissertation, University of Illinois at Urbana-Champaign.

Allen, W. Sidney. 1973. *Accent and rhythm.* Cambridge: Cambridge University Press.

Al-Mozainy, H., R. Bley-Vroman, and J. McCarthy. 1985. Stress shift and metrical structure. *Linguistic Inquiry* 16:135-144.

Bell, Alan. 1977. Accent placement and perception of prominence in rhythmic structures. In Larry Hyman 1977, pp. 1–14.

Borowsky, Toni. 1984. On resyllabification in English. *West Coast Conference on Formal Linguistics* 3:1-15.

Brame, Michael. 1973. On stress assignment in two Arabic dialects. In S. Anderson and P. Kiparsky (eds.), *A Festschrift for Morris Halle*, pp. 14-25. New York: Holt.

Burzio, Luigi. 1988. English stress. In P-M. Bertinetto and M. Loporcaro (eds.), *Papers from the 1987 Cortona Phonology Meeting*, pp. 153-176.

Dresher, Elan and Aditi Lahiri. 1991. The Germanic foot: Metrical coherence in Old English. *Linguistic Inquiry* 22:2.251-286.

Hale, Kenneth and Jose White Eagle. 1980. A preliminary metrical account for Winnebago accent. *International Journal of American Linguistics* 46:117-132.

Halle, Morris. 1990. Respecting metrical structure. *Natural Language and Linguistic Theory* 8:2.149-176.

Halle, Morris and Michael Kenstowicz. 1991. The free element condition and cyclic vs. noncyclic stress. *Linguistic Inquiry* 22:3.

Halle, Morris and J-R. Vergnaud. 1987. *An essay on stress.* Cambridge, MA: MIT Press.

Hayes, Bruce. 1985. Iambic and trochaic rhythm in stress rules. *Proceedings of the Berkeley Linguistics Society* 13:429-446.

Hayes, Bruce. 1987. A revised parametric metrical theory. In *Northeastern Linguistics Society*, pp. 274-289.

Hayes, Bruce. 1991. *Metrical stress theory: Principles and case studies*. ms., University of California, Los Angeles.

Hyman, Larry. 1977. Studies in stress and accent. *Southern California Occasional Papers in Linguistics* 4.

Idsardi, William. 1991. Stress in interior Salish. *Proceedings of the Chicago Linguistics Society* 27:1.

Irshied, Omar. 1984. *The phonology of Arabic: Bani-Hassan — a Bedouin Jordanian dialect*. Ph.D. dissertation, University of Illinois at Urbana-Champaign.

Irshied, Omar and Michael Kenstowicz. 1984. Some phonological rules of Bani-Hassan Arabic: A Bedouin dialect. *Studies in the Linguistic Sciences* 14:1.109-148.

Ito, Junko. 1991. Prosodic minimality in Japanese. *Proceedings of the Chicago Linguistics Society* 26:2.

Kenstowicz, Michael and Kamal Abdul-Karim. 1980. Cyclic stress in Levantine Arabic. *Studies in the Linguistic Sciences* 10:2.55-76.

Leer, Jeff. 1985. Evolution of prosody in the Yupik languages. In M. Krauss (ed.), *Yupik Eskimo prosodic systems: Descriptive and comparative studies*. Fairbanks: Alaska Native Language Center.

Liberman, Mark and Alan Prince. 1977. On stress and linguistic rhythm. *Linguistic Inquiry* 8:249-336.

Lichtenberk, F. 1983. *A grammar of Manam*. University of Hawaii Press.

McCarthy, John. 1980. A note on the accentuation of Damascene Arabic. *Studies in the Linguistic Sciences* 10:2.77-98.

McCarthy, John and Alan Prince. 1986. *Prosodic morphology*. ms.

McCarthy, John and Alan Prince. 1990. Foot and word in prosodic morphology: The Arabic broken plural. *Natural Language and Linguistic Theory* 8:2.209-284.

Mester, Armin. 1993. The quantitative trochee in Latin. *Natural Language and Linguistic Theory*, 12:1–62.

Miner, Kenneth. 1979. Dorsey's law in Winnebago-Chiwere and Winnebago accent. *International Journal of American Linguistics* 45:25-33.

Pike, Kenneth. 1964. Stress trains in Auca. In D. Abercrombie et al. (eds.), *In Honour of Daniel Jones*. London: Longmans.

Prince, Alan. 1983. Relating to the grid. *Linguistic Inquiry* 14:19-100.

Prince, Alan. 1991. Quantitative consequences of rhythmic organization. *Proceedings of the Chicago Linguistics Society* 26:2.

Skousen, Royal. 1975. *Substantive evidence in phonology*. The Hague: Mouton.

Stampe, David. 1972. *How I spent my summer vacation*. Ph.D. dissertation, University of Chicago.

Steriade, Donca. 1988. Greek accent: A case for preserving structure. *Linguistic Inquiry* 19:2.271-314.

On Domains
Charles W. Kisseberth
University of Illinois

1 Introduction

For more than a decade, the basic thrust of phonological research has been to emphasize the role of the *geometry* of phonological representations (often in conjunction with the notion of *underspecification* of phonological features) in accounting for the phonological patterns a language exhibits. While we believe that the success of this enterprise is not without question, it is not our purpose here to argue *against* this program of research. Rather we wish to suggest that another line of research (let us refer to this as "domain-based" research) may also offer significant insights into phonological patterns. We shall do this by presenting a fairly detailed account of certain aspects of the tonal structure of Xitsonga, a Bantu language spoken in Mozambique and South Africa.

We begin by presenting in section 2 an overview of the domain-based approach to phonology that we follow in this paper. This overview is sketchy and programmatic. It is intended merely to indicate the direction in which we are going. Then in section 3 we embark on a fairly detailed examination of a significant fragment of the tonal grammar of Xitsonga. Section 4 summarizes the main lines of our analysis.

2 A Domain-based Approach to Phonology

The domain-based view of phonology that we wish to develop here assumes (a) the existence of phonological representations (for present purposes, we may assume these representations to conform to the prevailing views), and (b) the existence of phonological rules. However, it assumes that prior to the application of a rule to a representation, there is an assignment of domain-structure ("D-structure") to the representation. A "domain" is a sequence of phonological material enclosed by a left and right bracket. Domains are of different *types*; consequently, the paired left and right brackets must be labelled. Thus a domain of category n consists of phonological material xyz enclosed by a left and a right bracket both labelled n $(....._n[\text{xyz}]_n...)$. For convenience we will label just the right bracket in all cases where no confusion can arise.

For any given domain category n, a representation is parsed into one or more n-domains. We do not assume that representations are *exhaustively* parsed for a given domain n; in other words, we allow domain structures such as:

$$...\text{v } [\text{w }]_n \text{ x } [\text{y}]_n \text{ z}...$$

where unparsed phonological material may appear before, after, or in between parsed phonological material. For an analysis which critically utilizes this view of domain structure, see Cassimjee and Kisseberth (1992). We *do* assume that domains of a given type do not overlap. Thus the following D-structure is ill-formed:

$$... \,_{ni}[\text{x }\,_{nj}[\text{y}]_{ni} \text{ z}]_{nj} ...$$

We leave it open as to whether n-domains may be nested inside other n-domains:

$$... \,_{ni}[\text{x }\,_{nj}[\text{y}]_{nj} \text{ z}]_{ni} ...$$

Xitsonga does not seem to us to require any sort of "cyclical" application of rules, and we generally accept the position of Cole and Coleman (1992) that finds cyclical analyses generally insufficiently motivated. But this matter is not directly pertinent to the present paper.

As mentioned above, a given representation may be parsed into domains of different types. One of the major claims that has been made in the literature is that domains conform to the Strict Layer Hypothesis (the hypothesis that claims that domains $x_i, x_j, ...x_n$ are hierarchically structured such that a higher domain x_i consists of a sequence of one or more instances of the next highest domain x_j and a domain x_j can contain within it neither other instances of x_j nor instances of any domain higher than itself). In other words, domain structures such as the following:

$$... \,_o [\text{x }_p [\text{y}]_o \text{ z}]_p ...$$

are considered ill-formed. In this paper we will demonstrate that there is a critical domain that we refer to as a P(rosodic)-domain, and this P-domain is not in a "strictly layered" relationship with morphological or syntactic domains such as the "word" or the "maximal projection" (noun phrase, verb phrase, main clause). Specifically, a P-domain may contain material smaller than a word, but it may also span two words; a P-domain may be internal to a maximal projection, but at the same time it may span adjacent maximal projections.

What are the domain types? We adopt the view that domains may be *direct* reflexes of phonological, morphological, and syntactic structure. For example, the *syllable* is a domain that is a direct function of the phonological representation. The *stem* is a domain that is a direct function of the morphological representation. A *noun phrase* is a domain that is a direct function of the syntactic representation.

We also assume, however, that D-structure is in part constructed, *derived* from the phonological, morphological and syntactic structure. That is to say, there are rules that build D-structure. This idea is of course the central idea of the theory of "prosodic domains" developed in Selkirk (1986) and much research derived from this seminal paper. Specifically, the hypothesis is that domains are constructed by placing brackets at the edges of particular types of syntactic constituents. The present paper relies heavily on this type of domain building rule.

For examples where D-structure is derived from the morphology, see Cole (1992). The idea here is simply that in some cases phonological rules may have as their domain of application some subpart of a word, where this subpart is not correlated with an actual morphological constituent but derives from the morphological constituency.

The aspect of the construction of D-structure that is of most importance to our view of domains involves the construction of domains *on the basis of the phonology*. Let us illustrate this concept. In our analysis of Xitsonga, we claim that High tones spread rightwards inside a P(rosodic)-domain. Spreading of High tones does not cross P-domains. We claim that phonological considerations play a significant role in the construction of P-domains. Specifically, a *High-toned syllable* projects a Left P-domain bracket to its Left. In other words, a High-toned mora is always at the Left edge of a P-domain. We call this the High Projection rule. We furthermore claim that a toneless syllable at the Right edge of non-verbal lexical categories projects a P-domain bracket to its Left (whether this is a Right or Left bracket is immaterial; for convenience, we will assume a Left bracket). As a result of this rule, a final toneless syllable in a non-verbal lexical item can never be gathered together into a domain with a preceding High tone. We call this the Final Projection rule.[1] We also propose that a toneless syllable followed immediately by a High tone in the same word projects a P-domain bracket to its Left (it is again immaterial whether this is a Right or Left bracket; we assume a Left bracket). This rule guarantees that a toneless syllable followed by a High in the same word will not be included in the same P-domain as the *preceding* High. The ultimate effect of this

---

[1] We have phrased the Final Projection rule in terms of a *toneless* word-final syllable. This restriction is not strictly necessary, since a High-toned syllable in this position would in any case project a Left bracket by the High Projection rule. Thus generalizing Final Projection to all syllables in final position would not make any incorrect predictions. For expository purposes, however, we continue to refer to the toneless nature of this syllable.

rule is to keep High tones from spreading into the syllable in front of High tones. We call this the Pre-High Projection rule. Lastly, we claim that a final toneless syllable in a maximal projection triggers a P-domain bracket to its Left (again, whether it is a Right or Left bracket is immaterial; we uniformly assume that it is a Left bracket). We call this rule Syntactic Projection. What this analysis claims is that while High Tone Spread is restricted to a P-domain, there are several rules involved in the construction of P-domains, and these rules refer to phonological entities (a High-toned syllable, a toneless syllable).

The idea that domains may be derived from the phonological representation is not of course new. Theories of metrical structure are obvious cases in point. The approach of Halle and Idsardi (1992) and Idsardi (1992) to the construction of metrical domains has obviously influenced our formulation of the rules constructing P-domains in Xitsogna. We simply believe that this idea – i.e., that phonological considerations may determine the construction of domains, and these domains in turn delimit the application of phonological rules – needs to be explored more fully. The present paper is a modest attempt to do so.

Now, if syntactic, morphological, and phonological configurations may all indirectly *project* D-structure (i.e., trigger the assignment of domain edges), it is clear that the brackets that they project must be indexed. We assume that more than one rule may yield a bracket with the same index (in other words, there may be fewer domain categories than rules that construct domains, since more than one rule may yield a given category). This notion will play a central role in our analysis of Xitsonga, where we claim that the rules of High Projection, Final Projection, Pre-High Projection, and Syntactic Projection all serve to define the same sort of domain (a Prosodic-Domain).

Let us assume then that rules assigning D-structure project indexed brackets. Next we must raise the question of what sort of role these indexed domains play in relation to the phonological rules. We assume that phonological rules may be restricted so that they apply only internally to a domain of type n. We leave open many issues—e.g., the question of whether rules apply internal to a *single* domain or to a *set* of domains. Phonological rules may also be triggered by the presence of a domain bracket (Left or Right) or the juncture of domain brackets ("$]_n$ $_n[$"). Again, we leave open various issues—e.g. should a single rule be permitted to refer to two different domain categories?

Given the above brief overview of the approach, let us turn our attention to the facts of Xitsonga.

3 Xitsonga Tonology and the Syntax-phonology Interface

Xitsonga is a Bantu language spoken in southern Mozambique and in the Republic of South Africa. We use the term "Xitsonga" to refer to the group of dialects known collectively as Xitsonga as well as to Ronga and Xitshwa. The tone pattern of these variations of Xitsonga is fundamentally the same, though there are interesting minor differences pertinent to the topic of this paper (some of which will be noted in the course of this study).

In this paper we will make certain fundamental but not particularly controversial assumptions. Specifically, we assume that only High tones are specified in the underlying structure of Xitsonga, and that Low tones are assigned by default to any syllables that are left unassociated following the application of tone rules such as the High Tone Spread rule under discussion. We also assume that the syllable is the tone-bearing unit (Xitsonga does not have an underlying vowel-length contrast), although this assumption is not particularly relevant for the present paper.

This paper focuses on the phonology-syntax interface in Xitsonga, particularly as it relates to a single rule in the Xitsonga tonal system; namely, the rule of High Tone Spread that extends a High tone iteratively onto a following toneless syllable. In order to account for the facts concerning High Tone Spread (both internal to the word and across words), we develop an analysis where the phonological representation of a sentence is factored into domains.

3.1 High Tone Spread in Xitsonga

Let us first of all establish the existence of the rule of High Tone Spread in Xitsonga. We will use the verbal word as our initial source of data. Like most Bantu languages, verbal roots in Xitsonga either have an underlying High tone (which links to the first syllable of the stem) or are toneless. In (1) we provide examples of toneless verb stems in the infinitive and in (2) we provide examples of High-toned verbs in the infinitive. (Penultimate syllables are lengthened in Xitsonga, but this Lengthening rule must operate in a specific domain. We do not address this issue in any detail here, but where pertinent, we will make note of the phenomenon. We indicate Lengthening with a colon after the penultimate vowel.)

(1) ku:-lwa 'to fight', ku:-ta 'to come',
    ku-hle:ka 'to laugh', ku-ri:ma 'to plough, cultivate',
    ku-ti:rha 'to work', ku-xavi:sa 'to sell',
    ku-hudu:la 'to pull', ku-riva:la 'to forget',
    ku-tlomute:la 'to fish', ku-rivate:ka 'to waste time',
    ku-hlanganye:ta 'to push firewood into the fire',
    ku-tsutsumela:na 'to run to one another'

(2) ku:-nwá 'to drink', ku:-fá 'to die',
    ku-fá:mbá 'to walk, go', ku-své:ká[2] 'to cook'
    ku-vó:ná 'to see', ku-kómbé:lá 'to ask for',
    ku-háké:lá 'to pay', ku-lángú:tá 'to look at',
    ku-phákámí:sa 'to lift up', ku-vúlávú:la 'to speak'
    ku-cúmbúlúká:nya 'to break in two',
    ku-tsémákányí:sa 'to divide in two'

It is clear from (1) that in the infinitive of toneless verbs there are no High-toned syllables on the surface. This suggests that the infinitive prefix /ku/ does not have a High tone underlyingly and neither do these verb stems. In (2), the verb stem does have a High tone underlyingly. Following the standard analysis of Bantu languages, we assume that this High tone is underlying unassociated and links by a general principle to the first syllable of the stem (the notion "stem" includes the obligatory final vowel /a/ at the end of many verbal forms). It will be noted that the High tone on the first stem syllable spreads rightward. The pattern observed is that if the stem is one to three syllables, then all the stem syllables are High. If the stem has four or more syllables, then the High associates as far as the penultimate syllable. However, when these verbs are phrase-medial, then all of the syllables of the stem receive the High tone. This tone pattern is the same one found in Tshivenḓá (cf. Cassimjee 1992). We will not in this paper be concerned with specifying how this difference between shorter and longer High-toned verb stems is to be accounted for, since it does not impact directly on the main concerns of this paper. It seems obvious, however, that the spreading of a High tone in the High verb stems is ultimately related to the rule of High Tone Spread that we will be discussing immediately below.

---

[2]The orthographic representation of the verb 'cook' would be with /sw/ in South Africa, but /sv/ in Mozambique. Much of this paper was written with the assistance of Bento Sitoe of Eduardo Mondlane University in Maputo, Mozambique. Bento is a speaker of the Xidzonga variety of Xitsonga, and the great preponderance of original material cited in this paper comes from his speech.

On Domains

When we examine the Xitsonga verb in the present tense, we find immediate evidence that there is a rule which spreads a High tone rightwards. To see this rule in operation, we need only to compare the first person (singular or plural) forms with the third person plural forms of toneless verb stems.

(3) ndz-a-ti:rha, v-á-tí:rha (work)
     ndz-a-hle:ka, v-á-hlé:ka (laugh)
     ndz-a-ti:sa, v-á-tí:sa (bring)
     ndz-a-ri:la, v-á-rí:la (cry)
     ndz-a-ri:ma, v-á-rí:ma (cultivate)
     ndz-a-dza:ha, v-á-dzá:ha (smoke)

     ndz-a-hudu:la, v-á-húdú:la (pull)
     ndz-a-tsutsu:ma, v-á-tsútsú:ma (run)
     ndz-a-tirhi:sa, v-á-tírhí:sa (use)
     ndz-a-hlaku:la, v-á-hlákú:la (weed)
     ndz-a-riva:la, v-á-rívá:la (forget)

     ndz-a-tlomute:la, v-á-tlómúté:la (fish)
     ndz-a-lulami:sa, v-á-lúlámí:sa (repair)
     ndz-a-tsutsume:la, v-á-tsútsúmé:la (run to)

     h-a-lulamisela:na, v-á-lúlámísélá:na (fix for e.o.)
     h-a-xavisela:na, v-á-xávísélá:na (sell for e.o.)
     h-a-tsutsumela:na, v-á-tsútsúmélá:na (run to e.o.)

     ndz-a:-ya, v-á:-yá (go)
     ndz-a:-lwa, v-á:-lwá (fight)

The present tense form of the verb (in its "long form", a form used when the verb is sentence-final, for example) consists of a subject prefix followed by the vowel /a/ followed by the verb stem. The underlying forms of the subject prefixes shown in (3) are /ndzi/ (1 sg.), /hi/ (1 pl.), and /vá/ (3 pl.) There is a contraction of these prefixes with the vowel /a/, and this contraction produces /ndza/, /ha/, and /vá/. From the data in (3), we see that the prefixes /ndzi/, /hi/, and /a/ must all be toneless. The third person plural subject prefix, however, contributes a H tone to the representation and this High tone spreads rightward as far as the penultimate syllable.

In our view, the extent of spreading is a direct indication of the domain structure of a form (since High tone spreads throughout a domain). If so, then we know that the final syllable of the above words must be outside the P-domain initiated by the High-toned third person subject prefix. We have not examined sufficient data to determine what the precise principle is that sets the last syllable in (3) off into a separate P-domain. We suggest, however, that it has something to do with the position of the word in the sentence, and we will refer to the phenomenon as Syntactic Projection. Syntactic Projection will assign a Left bracket to the Left of the Rightmost (toneless) syllable in some syntactically-defined domain.

Given Syntactic Projection, then the data in (3) can be analyzed in a very straightforward fashion. We take High-toned syllables to initiate P-domains in Xitsonga, and we accomplish this by hypothesizing that a High-toned syllable projects a Left P-domain bracket to its Left (henceforth: High Projection). Given representations such as /ndzalulami:sa/ and /válulami:sa/, the application of Syntactic Projection and High Projection will yield: *ndzalulami:* [*sa* and [*válulami:* [*sa*. We follow Halle and Idsardi (1992) in assuming a Bracket Matching Convention [=BMC] which, following the assignment of opening brackets, provides closing brackets by constructing maximally large domains that do not violate the well-formedness principles governing domains. The BMC will yield *ndzalulami:*[*sa*] and [*válulami:*] [*sa*]. (Recall that we do not assume that parsing has to be exhaustive, and therefore there is no automatic assignment of domain structure to the initial syllables in *ndzalulami:*[*sa*]. This point is not however critical to the present discussion.) Given [*válulami:*] [*sa*], the rule of High Tone Spread will simply spread the High tone associated to the initial syllable throughout the domain.[3]

The analysis we have sketched does face one complication from the data in (3). It appears that monosyllabic verb stems at the end of the sentence cannot trigger Syntactic Projection since in *v-á:-yá* and *v-á:-lwá* the High from the subject prefix spreads *onto the final syllable*. If we understand that Syntactic Projection is a kind of extraprosodicity effect, then *v-á:-yá* and *v-á:-lwá* appear to reflect a fairly natural limitation on extraprosodicity: namely, extraprosodicity may fail to apply when it would have the effect of making the entire root invisible to prosodic rules.

---

[3] We are not actually committed to the autosegmental characterization of the phenomenon whereby there is a High tone on one tier which is linked to the first syllable and a rule of spreading adds linkages between this High tone and the following syllables. All that is critical here is that the High tone at the Left edge of the domain is realized on all of the syllables of the domain. It is not our intention here to explore all of the possible ways in which this insight could be expressed. For that reason, we will use the autosegmental terminology of "spreading".

On Domains   141

So far we have seen that a High tone from a subject prefix will spread into a following toneless verb stem and that when the verb is at the end of the sentence, the final syllable of the verb is excluded from the spreading domain. In the next section we examine the case where a verb is followed by a complement.

3.2 The Tonal Pattern Where a Complement Follows the Verb

In this section we will examine the interaction of verbal tone with a following noun complement. We need to make a few introductory remarks concerning nominal tone in Xitsonga. Nouns consist of a class prefix (sometimes phonologically null) plus a stem. All of the noun class prefixes used here are toneless. Noun stem may be entirely toneless: *nyama* 'meat', *ti-n-guvu* 'clothes', *xi-komu* 'hoe', *xi-hlambetwana* 'cooking pot', *xi-hontlovila* 'giant', *svi-phukuphuku* 'fools'. They may also have a High tone in their representation: *ma-tandzá* 'eggs', *homú* 'cow', *xi-fáki* 'maize', *ma-kóti* 'vultures'. When there is a succession of High-toned syllables, we take the sequence to involve a single High tone multiply linked: *m-bútí* 'goat', *nyóká* 'snake', *húkú* 'chicken'.

There is one point that perhaps we should make concerning the tone of the noun considered in isolation. Notice that in nouns such as *xi-fáki* and *ma-kóti*, the penultimate High tone does not spread onto the final syllable (this is true not just of the isolation pronunciation, but also in other environments as well; thus Syntactic Projection is not an explanation for these facts). There are different ways that one might approach this problem; for example, one might propose that the High Tone Spread rule operates only in derived environments (i.e., a High tone may spread onto a following syllable only if these syllables arise across morpheme boundaries). Such a proposal will not however account for the full range of data in Xitsonga. We adopt a rather different treatment. We propose that the final toneless syllable of a noun (and other non-verbal word classes as well) projects *at the lexical level* a Left P-domain bracket to its Left. This will place the last syllable of a noun in a different P-domain from the rest of the noun stem. Consequently, in *xi-fáki*, the last syllable will be outside the scope of High Tone Spread since it will not be in the same P-domain as the High toned syllable. We will refer to the rule involved as Final Projection.

We will begin our examination of the case where a complement follows the verb by considering toneless nouns. In (4) we compare two types of verbs: in the first example, the verb ends in a High tone; in the second example, the verb ends in a toneless syllable. Notice that when the verb ends in a High, this High extends throughout the noun as far as the penultimate syllable. (Notice, incidentally, that when the present tense verb is followed by an object, no /a/ vowel occurs between the subject prefix and the verb stem.)

(4) vá-xává nyá:ma 'they are buying meat'
ndzi-xava nya:ma 'I am buying meat'

vá-xává tí-n-gú:vu 'they are buying clothes'
ndzi-xava ti-n-gu:vu 'I am buying clothes'

vá-xává xí-kó:mu 'they are buying a hoe'
ndzi-xava xi-ko:mu 'I am buying a hoe'

vá-kúmá xí-hlámbétwá:na 'they are getting a cooking pot'
ndzi-kuma xi-hlambetwa:na 'I am getting a cooking pot'

vá-tísá xí-hóntlóví:la 'they are bringing a giant'
hi-tisa xi-hontlovi:la 'we are bringing a giant'

vá-ríválélá sví-phúkúphú:ku 'they forgive fools'
ndzi-rivalela svi-phukuphu:ku 'I forgive fools'

It is clear from these data that the final syllable of the verb does not trigger Syntactic Projection, whereas the final syllable of the noun complement does. Given just this much data, Syntactic Projection could conceivably affect only the last syllable in an *utterance*. But we shall see below that "utterance" is too large a unit; Syntactic Projection applies to some subpart of the entire utterance. We shall consider what this subpart is as we proceed.

It should be noted that in the case of a High verb stem, the High of the verb stem also spreads into a following toneless noun in the same manner.

(5) ndzi-lává nyá:ma 'I want meat'
ndzi-lává xí-kó:mu 'I want a hoe'
ndzi-vóná xí-hlámbétwá:na 'I see a cooking pot'
ndzi-vóná xí-hóntlóví:la 'I see a giant'
ndzi-jóndzísá[4] xí-phúkúphú:ku 'I am teaching a fool'

So far we have only examined the case where the complement noun is toneless. Let us examine nouns of other tonal shapes. We begin with nouns that have an initial toneless syllable followed by a High tone.

---

[4] The verb 'teach' in the South African orthography would be written /dyondzisa/, whereas in Mozambique it is written /jondzisa/.

(6) <u>Noun has the structure 0HX</u>

ndzi-já ta:ndz!á 'I am eating an egg'
vá-xává ta:ndz!á 'they are buying an egg'
ndzi-lává ho:m!ú 'I want a cow'
vá-xává ho:m!ú 'they are buying a cow'
ndzi-lává xi-f!á:ki 'I want maize'
ndzi-vóná ma-k!ó:ti 'I see vultures'

Notice that while the H of the verb extends as far as the final syllable of the verb, it does not go onto the initial syllable of the noun. Furthermore, note that the High tone of the noun is downstepped. There is one point about the pronunciation of the first four examples that should be noted: a toneless (lengthened) penult syllable displays a phonetic falling pitch after a High-toned antepenult, provided that the onset of the penultimate syllable does not have one of a group of consonants that is known as *depressor consonants* in the literature. The syllable *ta* in *ndzi-já ta:ndz!á* 'I am eating an egg' does not have a depressor onset, thus the phonetic realization is [ndzi-já tândzá]; the syllable *ho* on the other hand does have a depressor onset, and thus does not show a falling pitch in *ndzi-lává ho:m!ú* 'I want a cow'. We do not enter into any discussion of the depressor consonants due to the fact that they have no role to play in the construction of domains in Xitsonga (unlike in the Nguni language family, where their role is considerable). It should be stressed that they *do* have a notable phonetic effect on the realization of High-toned syllables, an effect that we are not indicating in our transcriptions.

The crucial point about the data in (6) is that the initial toneless syllable in the noun must be excluded from being in the same P-domain as the verb. We accomplish this by proposing a *lexical* rule that says that any toneless syllable in front of a High-toned syllable projects a Left P-domain bracket to its Left. It will become apparent shortly why this must be a lexical rule and not a rule that affects any toneless syllable in front of a High-toned syllable. We call this rule Pre-High Projection.

Let us now review how our analysis works. Consider *vá-xává ho:m!ú* 'they are buying a cow'. Lexically there are two words: *vá-xava* and *homú*. We take High-Projection, Final Projection, and Pre-High Projection to all be lexical rules. They will assign the domain structures [*vá-xava* and [*ho* [*mú*. When these words are then combined syntactically into a sentence, the post-lexical rule of Syntactic Projection will not alter the domain-structure (there is no final toneless syllable at the end of the syntactic configuration that will project additional domain structure beyond what is already present as a result of the lexical rules). Thus we will have the representation [vá-xava [ho [mú, to which the Bracket Matching Convention will apply to yield the representation: [vá-xava] [ho] [mú]. The rule of High Tone Spread will then apply to yield [vá-xává] [ho] [mú].

There are of course alternatives to our Pre-High Projection rule. For example, we could allow the toneless syllable to be gathered together into the same domain as the preceding High tone, but prevent that High from spreading onto the toneless syllable by claiming that the Obligatory Contour Principle constrains spreading. In other words, vá-xává hom!ú does not become *vá-xává hómú because this would be a violation of the constraint that two High tones cannot be adjacent. Placing such a constraint on High Tone Spread makes two claims. First, it predicts that High Tone Spread will never extend a High onto a toneless syllable in front of a High. Data immediately below shows that this is an incorrect prediction. Second, accounting for the absence of spreading onto ho in vá-xává hom!ú has nothing to do with the absence of spreading onto the final syllable in vá-tísá xí-hóntlóví:la 'they are bringing a giant'. At first glance this claim seems to be a reasonable one. However, we shall ultimately provide evidence that the two phenomenon *must be related*, and we propose that domain structure permits us to capture this relationship.

We have not remarked yet on the downstepping of the H in the noun in examples such as *ndzi-vóná ma-k!ó:ti*. In the data so far considered, this downstepping can be treated as a very superficial matter whereby any High tone separated from a preceding High by a toneless syllable is downstepped. We shall have more to say concerning downstep shortly.

Let us now turn to nouns that have more than one toneless syllable before a High tone.

(7) <u>Noun has the structure 0*0HX</u>

   ndzi-já má-ta:ndz!á 'I am eating eggs'
   vá-xává má-ta:ndz!á 'they are buying eggs'
   ndzi-já xí-do:h!é 'I am eating a peanut'
   ndzi-lává tí-ho:m!ú 'I want cattle'
   vá-xává tí-ho:m!ú 'they are buying cattle'
   ndzi-vóná vá-la:l!á 'I see enemies'
   ndzi-vóná sví-gal!á:na 'I see a tick'

Notice that here High Tone Spread does extend the High into the noun, but leaves the syllable immediately in front of the H in the noun unaffected. Our analysis, of course, accounts nicely for these data. Our lexical rules of domain-construction take *vá-xava* and *ti-homú* and yield [vá-xava and *ti* [*ho* [*mú*. When these two words are combined into a sentence, the Syntactic Projection rule will be irrelevant and the Bracket Matching Convention yields [*vá-xava ti*] [*ho*] [*mú*]. High Tone Spread internal to a domain (along with Downstepping) will result in the correct *vá-xává tí-hom!ú*.

If a noun begins with a H tone, we find some extremely interesting data:

(8) Noun has the structure HX

ndzi-vóná ny!ó:ká 'I see a snake'
ndzi-vóná h!ú:kú 'I see a fowl'
ndzi-já v!ú:svá 'I am eating porridge'
ndzi-bá n'w-!á:ná 'I am beating a child'
ndzi-vóná k!ó:ti 'I see a vulture'
ndzi-lává m-b!ú:tí 'I want a goat'

vá-xává mb!ú:tí 'they are buying a goat'
vá-xávélá n'w!á:ná 'they are buying s.t. for the child'
vá-xávélá ns!á:tí 'they are buying s.t. for the wife'

Notice that the (multiply-linked) H of the noun is always downstepped in relationship to the High at the end of the verb. Notice furthermore that the High inside the verb (both the lexical High of the verb stem and a High-toned subject prefix) spreads onto the last syllable of the verb.

These data are very critical in terms of our analysis. Consider the example *vá-xávélá n'w!á:ná* 'they are buying s.t. for the child'. Notice that the H tone from the verb stem spreads all the way to the end of the verb, even though the last syllable of the verb is followed by a High toned syllable at the beginning of the noun. If it were the case that High Tone Spread is restricted so that it cannot spread onto a syllable followed by a High-toned syllable, then these data would be difficult to explain. Our proposal (namely, there is a *lexical* rule whereby a toneless syllable in front of a High projects a Left bracket to its Left) provides a solution. The last syllable of the verb [*vá-xavela* is, at the lexical level, not followed by a High-toned syllable (it stands in front of a High-toned syllable only at the post-lexical level), and thus the Pre-High Projection rule will not apply to it; the Pre-High Projection rule will also not apply to the object [*n'wá:ná* since it does not meet the structural description. At the post-lexical level, we will have the representation [*vá-xavela* [*n'wá:ná*; Syntactic Projection is irrelevant and the Bracket Matching Convention will yield [*vá-xavela*] [*n'wá:ná*]. High Tone Spread will extend the High of the prefix *vá* throughout its domain.

We have not yet addressed the fact that there is downstep in these examples between the two High-toned domains. We could simply assume that downstepping takes place between adjacent High tones as well as between two High tones separated by one or more toneless (Low) syllables. Schematically,

(9)   Downstepping

$H(L^*)H \Rightarrow H(L^*)!H$

(where L^*=any number of Low toned syllables and "!" indicates the occurrence of downstep, however one imagines downstep to be represented theoretically).

In a domain-based approach we could formalize this Downstepping as follows: the phonological representation is factored into what we will label !-domains by the following rule:

(10)   !-domain assignment

The leftmost syllable in a High-span projects a Left (!-domain) bracket to its Left. (A "High-span" refers to one or more successive syllables linked to a single High tone.)

Downstepping then is a rule whereby the pitch register of successive !-domains is lowered.

High-toned verb stems in the present tense provide some additional data pertinent to the treatment of downstep in Xitsonga. Recall that when the present tense verb is used at the end of a sentence, the vowel /a/ intrudes between the subject prefix and the verb stem. This /a/ vowel is toneless. The /a/ coalesces with the subject prefix into a single syllable. This syllable is High-toned when the subject prefix is High, and toneless otherwise. When a toneless syllable appears before a High verb stem, nothing of note happens. However, when a High syllable appears in front of a High verb stem, the verb stem High tone is downstepped relative to the preceding syllable.

(11) ndz-a-háké:lá 'I am paying'
      v-á-h!áké:lá 'they are paying'

      ndz-a-lóvó:lá 'I am paying the brideprice'
      v-á-l!óvó:lá 'they are paying the brideprice'

      ndz-a-pfú:ná 'I am helping'
      v-á-pf!ú:ná 'they are helping'

      ndz-a-své:ká 'I am cooking'
      v-á-sv!é:ká 'they are cooking'

When the present tense verb has a complement object, the /a/ vowel does not appear. Notice that the subject prefix and the verb stem retain their High tones and there is no downstepping between the prefix High and the verb stem High.

(12) ndzi-lává xí-kó:mu 'I want the hoe'
      vá-lává xí-kó:mu 'they want the hoe'

      ndzi-vóná n-gúlú:ve 'I want the pig'
      vá-vóná n-gúlú:ve 'they want the pig'

If we are to maintain the downstepping analysis suggested above, we would need to assume that somehow the High-toned subject prefix and the High-toned verb stem do not constitute a *succession* of High-spans (otherwise they would be in different !-domains). We can do this by postulating a word-level rule of Fusion whereby two successive High tones are fused into a single High. Fusion does not occur in (11) due to the fact that there is a toneless syllable /a/ in between the High subject prefix and the High verb stem; in other words, Fusion is ordered *before* the merger of the subject prefix and the /a/ prefix. In (12), however, there is no toneless /a/ syllable between the subject prefix and the verb stem. Thus the H of the subject prefix and the H of the verb stem are fused into a single H; consequently, there will not be separate !-domains in the case of the words in (12).

3.3 Double Object Constructions

In this section we consider a *double object construction*. We consider first the case where both objects are toneless.

(13)   High in verb begins on the subject prefix

ndzi-xavela xi-phukuphuku fo:le 'I'm buying tobacco for a fool'
vá-xávélá xí-phúkúphúku fo:le 'they are...'

ndzi-xavela mu-nhu ti-n-gu:vu 'I am buying clothes for s.o.'
vá-xávélá mú-nhu ti-n-gu:vu 'they are...'

High in verb begins on the verb stem

ndzi-nyíká xí-kóxa nya:ma 'I am giving an old woman meat'
ndzi-nyíká mú-nhu nya:ma 'I am giving s.o. meat'
ndzi-nyíká n'ánga ti-n-gu:vu 'I am giving a doctor clothes'
ndzi-nyíká xí-phúkúphúku fo:le 'I am giving a fool tobacco'
ndzi-kómbélá mú-nhu ti-n-gu:vu 'I am asking s.o. for clothes'
ndzi-kómbélá xí-phúkúphúku n-gulu:ve 'I'm asking a fool for a pig'

From these data it is clear that a High tone from the verb spreads as far as the penultimate syllable of the *first* object noun. In other words, we want the last syllable of the first object to be excluded from the domain of the verb High. But the rule of Final Projection already predicts this.[5]

Let us review the derivation of *vá-xávélá xí-phúkúphúku fo:le*. At the lexical level, High Projection will assign the verb the structure [*vá-xavela*, and Final Projection will assign the nouns the D-structure *xi-phukuphu* [*ku* and *fo:*[*le*. The lexical rule of Pre-High Projection is not applicable to any of the words. At the sentence level, Syntactic Projection is vacuous: the representation [*vá-xavela xi-phukuphu* [*ku fo:*[*le* will be subject to the Bracket Matching Convention, resulting in the D-structure: [*vá-xavela phukuphu*] [*ku fo:*] [*le*]. High Tone Spread will spread the High tone throughout the first P-domain.

The two nouns in a double object construction can, of course, have any of the possible tone patterns that nouns exhibit. We will not here survey all the possible combinations. We just note that the interaction of the verb and the first object is exactly parallel to the interaction between a verb and a single object. What is critical for our present concerns is the case where the first noun ends in a High tone in its underlying structure and the second object noun is toneless.

---

[5] The rule of Syntactic Projection will turn out to also predict that the final syllable of the first object is set off into a separate domain. However, since the lexical rule of Final Projection will also predict these data, there is no necessity of invoking Syntactic Projection here.

(14) ndzi-xavela n'w-áná sví-yámbá:lo 'I am buying a child clothes'
ndzi-xavela mámáná tí-n-gú:vu 'I am buying mother clothes'
ndzi-nyíká xi-s!íwan!á xí-kó:mu 'I am giving the pauper a hoe'
ndzi-nyíká mu-nw!í tí-n-gú:vu 'I am giving the drinker clothes'
ndzi-xavela n-sátí tí-n-gú:vu 'I'm buying clothes for the wife'
ndzi-kómbélá h!ósí tí-ho:m!ú 'I am asking the chief for cattle'

Notice in (14) that the High tone from the first object can spread up to the penult of the second object. This demonstrates that there is a P-domain extending from the last syllable of the first object through the penultimate syllable of the second object. Clearly, P-domains are sometimes smaller than a word, but sometimes they extend across words as well.

Our analysis explains the data in (14) in a straightforward fashion. Consider *ndzi-nyíká mu-nw!í tí-n-gú:vu*. The underlying lexical items would receive the following D-structures: *ndzi-[nyíká, [mu-[nwí,* and *ti-n-gu:[vu.* When these words are combined into the post-lexical structure *ndzi-[nyíká [mu-[nwí ti-ngu:[vu,* Syntactic Projection will be vacuous and the Bracket Matching Convention will yield *ndzi [nyíká] [mu] [nwí ti-ngu:] [vu].* The only domain where there will be spreading is the one that begins at the end of the noun *mu-nwí* and extends into the second object *ti-n-guvu.* Each P-domain with a High tone will project a Left !-domain bracket; the second !-domain will be at a lower register than the first as a result of the Downstepping rule.

3.4 Postposing Constructions

In this section we return to the matter of Syntactic Projection. Consider the case of the juncture between a verb and its postposed subject. Some examples are cited in (15):

(15) v-á-tí:rha va:-nhu 'they are working, the people'
x-á-rí:la xi-hla:ngi 'it is crying, the baby'
x-á-hlé:ka xi-hla:ngi 'it is laughing, the baby'

There are a number of points to be made about these data. First, notice that even though the subject is postposed after the verb, the verb is still in agreement with the postposed noun phrase (i.e., the subject marker on the verb agrees with the noun class of the head of the postposed noun phrase). Second, the prefix /a/ appears after the subject prefix. Recall that the /a/ prefix is used in the present tense only when the verb is in some sense "final"; this indicates that the verb in (15) is "final". We take the syntactic distinction involved to be one that contrasts S' (the clause that contains the main verb) with S" (the syntactic unit which contains S' plus elements that have been extracted out of of S'). A present tense verb must contain /a/ when that verb stands at the end of S'.

Examination of the data in (15) shows that the High from the prefix cannot spread onto the final syllable of the verb (and since it cannot spread there, it also cannot spread into the postposed subject). We can account for the failure of the last syllable of the verb to be affected by appealing to Syntactic Projection. Specifically, in *v-á-tí:rha va:-nhu*, the final syllable of the verb is at the end of whatever syntactic domain it is that triggers Syntactic Projection. In other words, S' is an instance of the syntactic unit that is responsible for Syntactic Projection. This suggests two hypotheses about the formulation of Syntactic Projection. The first hypothesis is that the rule says: the last syllable in S' projects a Left bracket to its Left. The second hypothesis is that the rule says: the last syllable in a maximal projection (=NP, VP, S') projects a Left bracket to its Left. Since the latter formulation is the more general principle, we will adopt it. (Recall that non-verbal lexical categories trigger Final Projection at the lexical level; thus the application of Syntactic Projection is vacuous in many cases.)

Notice incidentally that the penultimate vowel of the verb is lengthened in (15). We assume that there is a domain, the L(engthening)-domain, which determines the assignment of length. It should be pointed out that an L-domain is not the same as a P-domain. For example, in *ndzi-nyíká xí-kóxa nya:ma* 'I am giving an old woman meat', the penultimate syllable of *xi-koxa* is at the end of a P-domain, but the first object does not define the edge of a L-domain. We do not pursue here an in-depth study of the L-domain, but the data examined so far, as well as subsequent data, would suggest a syntactic definition of the domain whereby each daughter node of S" is a L-domain.

The verbs in (15) ended in a toneless syllable. In (16) we illustrate verbs that end in a High tone. When the verb ends in a High tone, this High tone naturally spreads into the following postposed subject (since the last syllable of the verb is not in a separate P-domain from the subject).

(16)   x-á-f!á:mbá xí-hóntlóví:la 'he's going, the giant'
       v-á-f!á:mbá vá:-nhu 'they are going, the people'
       y-â:-j!á n-gúlú:ve 'it's eating, the pig'
       t-â:-j!á tí-n-gúlú:ve 'they are eating, the pigs'
       x-â:-nw!á xí-phúkúphú:ku 'he's drinking, the fool'
       x-á:-tá xí-kó:xa 'she's coming, the old woman'

Let us review briefly the derivation of *x-á-f!á:mbá xí-hóntlóví:la*. At the lexical level, High Projection and Final Projection will yield the D-structures [x-á [fámbá and xi-hontlovi:[la. Syntactic Projection is irrelevant, and the Bracket Matching Convention will yield [x-á] [fámbá xi-hontlovi:] [la]. This domain structure will correctly predict the extent of spreading. Notice from this example that a P-domain may be smaller than a maximal projection, but also crosses maximal projections. P-domains are formed on the basis of words and maximal projections, but they are formed in an indirect fashion and are in no hierarchical relationship to the actual morphological or syntactic domains themselves.

When the postposed subject is placed to the right of an object, we find what are by now expected results. In (17) we show that the final syllable of the object triggers Final Projection (Syntactic Projection is vacuous here), and in (18) we show that if the object ends in a H tone, this H tone spreads into the following toneless (postposed) subject.

(17) vá-lává tí-n-gú:vu va:-nhu 'they want clothes, the people'
      vá-rhándzá mú:-nti va:-nhu 'they like the village, the people do'
      xí-hléká ngó:pfu xi-hla:ngi 'it laughs a lot, the baby does'
      xí-xává nyá:ma xi-ko:xa 'she is buying meat, the old woman is'
      xí-lává tí-n-gú:vu xi-ko:xa 'she wants clothes, the old woman does'
      vá-rhándzá nyá:ma va-n!ú:ná 'they like meat, the husbands do'

(18) tí-nwá m-!á:tí tí-n-gúlú:ve 'they drink water, the pigs do'
      vá-xává tí-ho:m!ú vá:-nhu 'they are buying cattle, the people are'
      vá-rhándzá mu-nti w!á h:in!á vá:-nhu 'they love our village,
           the people do'

The derivation of vá-xává tí-ho:m!ú vá:-nhu will be as follows. At the lexical level, High Projection, Final Projection, and Pre-High Projection will yield the following domain structures: [vá-xava, ti [ho [mú, and va [nhu. At the post-lexical level, when these words have been grouped together in to a sentence, Syntactic Projection has no effect, and the Bracket Matching Convention will yield the final domain structure [vá-xava ti] [ho:] [mú va:] [nhu]. High Tone Spread will apply in the first and the third P-domain to yield the correct results.

There is another type of subject postposing in Xitsonga where the verb no longer agrees with the postposed subject; instead there is an impersonal subject prefix /kú/ on the verb. In some dialects (described by Beuchat) there is evidence that a new rule projecting P-domain brackets is required. (The asterisk in front of an example sentence is intended to remind the reader that the sentence is derived from Beuchat's works, which do not indicate downstep nor vowel lengthening and which describe several varieties of Xitsonga, not all of which we have personally studied.)

Examine the data in (19).

(19) *ndleleni kú-tsútsúmá ma-jaha [Beuchat 1962, p. 121]
'on the road there run young men'

*kú-tírhá tintombí [1959, p. 137]
'there work the girls, i.e., it is the girls who are working'

*kú-ta-fámbá valungu [1962, p. 121]
'there will leave the white people'

*kú-fámbá vanhu émútíni [1959, p. 137]
'there go people in the village,
i.e., there are people walking in the village'

Here the High toned "dummy" subject prefix /kú/ spreads to the very end of the toneless verb stem, e.g., /tsutsuma/. The last syllable of the verb does not trigger Syntactic Projection. This is clear evidence that the verb here is *not* located at the end of a maximal projection. The postposed subject is part of the verb phrase. However, the High of the verb *does not spread into the postposed subject*. In our analysis, this means that the postposed subject is not in the same P-domain as the verb. A rule is required that will guarantee the separation of the verb and the postposed subject into different P-domains. The data are insufficient to determine exactly how to formulate the principle. For example, if any material may occur between an impersonal verb and a postposed subject, we need to know whether this material is in a different P-domain from the impersonal verb or the same P-domain. We do not have relevant examples.

In other Xitsonga dialects, however, this phenomenon does not occur. Specifically, the impersonal verb still does not trigger Syntactic Projection (it is not at the end of a maximal projection) but High Tone Spread does cross from the impersonal verb into the postposed subject.

(20) *kú-étlélé xí-hlángi [1959, p. 137]
'there sleeps the baby, i.e., it is the baby who is sleeping'

*kú-fíké mu-bóhiwá [1959, p. 137]
'there arrived a prisoner, i.e., a prisoner arrived'

*kú-tírhá múcháyéri [1959, p. 137]
'there works the driver, i.e., it is the driver who is working'

3.5 Additional Cases Where P-domain Edges Are Inserted on the Basis of Syntax

In this section we examine some cases where more factoring into P-domains is required. First of all, High Tone Spread cannot cross the juncture between the subject NP and the VP. This point cannot be demonstrated with ease due to the fact that third person subject NP's require a High-toned subject prefix on the verb, thus third person subject NP's will not be followed by a verb that has initial toneless syllables. First and second person subject NP's *are* followed by toneless subject prefixes, but the only first or second person subject NP's are pronominal elements. Fortunately, these pronominal elements end in a High tone and we can demonstrate that these High tones *cannot spread into the verb*.

(21)   miná ndz-a-ti:rha 'as for me, I am working'
       hiná h-a-hle:ka 'as for us, we are laughing'

These examples establish that the subject and a following verb are in different P-domains. All of the projection rules we have formulated so far allow the final syllable of a word (if High-toned) to group with the following word, whatever the nature of the syntactic boundary being crossed. Here we have the first case (setting aside the one dialect mentioned above where impersonal verbs are not grouped with the postposed logical subject) where a P-domain bracket must be introduced between syntactic constituents. We consider later the issue of formulating a rule to project a P-domain boundary between the subject and the verb.

When a noun with a final toneless syllable occurs at the end of a subject noun phrase, the lexical rule of Final Projection will of course apply and create a P-domain internal to the subject noun phrase.

(22)   *voná vá-nhu a-vá-tírhí [Beuchat, 1959, p. 138]
       'as for them, the people, they are not working'

       *xoná xí-ámbálo xí-hándzúkíle [Beuchat, 1959, p. 138]
       'as for it, the garment, it is torn'

In these examples the subject noun phrase consists of an absolute pronoun followed by the noun to which the pronoun refers: *voná vánhu* and *xoná xí-ámbálo*. We see that the High tone from the absolute pronoun is able to spread into the noun, but the last syllable of the noun is not available for spreading. This is explicable since the last syllable of the noun triggers Final Projection and will be in a separate domain from the pronominal High tone.

Another example where High tones cannot spread across adjacent words involves the preposing of NP's into preverbal position. For example, an object preposed in front of a subject is in a different P-domain from the subject. This can be seen from the fact that a H at the end of the preposed object does not spread into a toneless subject noun.

(23)   ti-ho:mú xi-hontlovila x-!á-xá:va
'as for the cattle, the giant is buying'

ma-ta:ndzá mu-lungu w-!á-xá:va
'as for eggs, the white person is buying'

ma-ve:lé mu-nhu w-!â:-j!á
'as for maize, the person is eating'

It should be noted that the final syllable of these preposed objects do trigger Final Projection. This can be shown by putting a co-referential pronoun in front of the preposed object:

(24)   toná tí-ho:m!ú xi-hontlovila x-!á-xá:va
'as for them, the cattle, the giant is buying'

toná tí-n-gú:vu xi-hontlovila x-!á-xá:va
'as for them the clothes, the giant is buying'

The first example in (24) shows that when a preposed object noun phrase consists of a pronominal and a following co-referential noun, the H from the pronominal can spread into the following noun. The second example shows that this spreading can only go as far as the penult of the following noun. This establishes that the preposed object noun has triggered Final Projection as usual.

In the previous cases, the preposed object is located in front of the subject of the verb. It is also possible for a preposed object to be situated directly in front of the verb. In such a situation, the preposed object is in a different P-domain from the following verb; it is also in a separate P-domain from a preceding subject, if there is one. Consider first the case where there is no overt subject noun phrase.

(25)   ti-ho:mú ndz-a-xa:va 'as for the cattle, I am buying'
toná tí-ho:m!ú ndz-a-xa:va 'as for them the cattle, I am buying'
toná tí-ngú:vu ndz-a-xa:va 'as for them the clothes, I am buying'

In the first example in (25) we see that a High at the end of the preposed object must be in a different P-domain from the verb since the High from the object cannot spread into the verb. In the next examples, we see that the High from a preceding co-referential pronoun can spread into the noun, but the final syllable of the noun is in a separate domain (due of course to Final Projection).

In (26) below we show the case where the preposed object occurs between the subject and the verb. The first example shows that the subject and the preposed object are in different P-domains since a H at the end of the subject cannot spread into the preposed toneless object. The second sentence shows that the final syllable of the subject does trigger Final Projection as expected: a High from a pronominal in front of the subject noun spreads only to the penult of that noun. The third example shows that the final syllable of the preposed object also triggers Final Projection, since a preceding pronominal H spreads only to the penult of that noun.

(26) n-sá:tí ti-n-gu:vu w-!á-xá:va
'the wife, as for the clothes, she is buying'

voná vá:-nhu ti-n-gu:vu v-!á-xá:va
'them the people, as for the clothes, they are buying'

va:-nhu toná tí-n-gú:vu v-!á-xá:va
'the people, as for them the clothes, they are buying'

We have now seen that there are several instances where we must also assign additional P-domain brackets if we are to delimit the application of High Tone Spread properly. Specifically, a subject must be separated into a different P-domain from its following verb. A preposed object must be separated into a different P-domain no matter whether a subject noun phrase or the verb follows. A subject noun phrase must be in a different P-domain from a following preposed object.

The issue facing us is the following: what is the proper generalization that will cover all of these cases. The following treatment appears promising. Suppose that *all pre-verbal noun phrases are external to S'* and are daughters of S". We could then claim that every daughter of S" except S' projects a P-domain bracket. As a consequence, we would not get High Tone Spread crossing a subject to the verb, or from a preposed object to the verb, or from a subject to a preposed object, etc. Call this rule Daughter Projection.

There are two possible problems with Daughter Projection (assuming that the external nature of these pre-verbal noun phrases could be motivated syntactically). The first is that we have already observed a case where a High from one daughter of S" does spread onto another daughter. This was seen in examples such as *x-á-f!á:mbá xí-hóntlóví:la* 'they are going, the giants', where a High from the verb spreads into the following postposed subject. Recall that the present tense verb has the /a/ prefix, indicating that it is final in S'; also there is lengthening of the penult vowel of the verb, also indicating that the verb is final in some domain. We suggested that the verb is final in S'. This is a problem, however, only if Daughter Projection assigns a P-domain bracket *to the Left* of every daughter of S" (excluding S'); such a rule would make an incorrect prediction that the verb High could not spread into the postposed subject. However, proposing that Daughter Projection projects a P-domain bracket to the *right* of a daughter of S" (excluding S') will predict that there will be no domain edge between a verb and a postposed subject. Thus by specifying that a daughter of S" projects a bracket to its Right we will predict an asymmetry between pre-verbal daughters and a post-verbal daughter; the former will be in separate domains from what follows, while the latter will not be in a separate domain from the preceding S'. (If two daughters of S" could follow the verb, we predict that there would be a domain break between the two daughters. We have no relevant data bearing on this point.)

The second problem with Daughter Projection has to do with Lengthening. Notice the subject noun phrase immediately in front of its verb is *not* lengthened. A preposed object noun phrase *is* lengthened. A subject noun phrase that is followed by a preposed object noun phrase is also lengthened. There is thus some reason to believe that the domain of Lengthening may in fact be defined in terms of the daughters of S" (including S' in this case). This would correctly predict that Lengthening occurs on the penultimate syllable of S' (since S' is a daughter of S") in an example such as *x-á-f!á:mbá xí-hóntlóví:la* 'they are going, the giants'. Notice that the postposed subject in the preceding example would also be a daughter of S" and thus be subject to Lengthening. Assuming that a preposed object and a subject separated from its verb by a preposed object are also daughters of S" allows then the correct identification of a L-domain with a daughter of S". Such an account of Lengthening would however mean that a subject immediately in front of a verb *cannot* be external to S'. If it were, it would have to undergo Lengthening.

Since Daughter Projection seems to be the best available generalization with respect to P-domain construction, we will assume that it is the correct rule. There are different possible treatments of the case where a subject precedes its verb. If the subject is not external to S', then we would require

On Domains   157

yet another rule of P-domain construction to set off the subject from the
verb. If the subject is external to S', then there may simply be a kind of
restructuring rule affecting L-domains that brings the subject into the same
L-domain as the following verb. The ultimate resolution of the problem of
the pre-verbal subject is not particularly germane to the present discussion.
What is critical is that there must be a postlexical rule such as our Daughter
Projection to separate certain syntactic elements into distinct P-domains
from what follows them.

3.6 Modification and P-domains

In this section we explore one of the most interesting cases where P-domain
brackets are inserted on the basis of a syntactic property. Compare the
pairs of sentences in (27) below. In the first sentence of the pair, an object
following a verb is unmodified, while in the second sentence the object is
modified. We find that the extent of spreading is different in the two cases.

(27)   ndzi-vóná n-gúlú:ve 'I see a pig'
       ndzi-vóná n-guluve y!á we:n!á 'I see your pig'

       ndzi-vóná tí-n-gúlú:ve 'I see pigs'
       ndzi-vóná tí-n-guluve t!á we:n!á 'I see your pigs'

       vá-súsá n-gúlú:ve 'they are removing a pig'
       vá-súsá n-guluve y!á vo:n!á 'they are removing their pig'

       vá-súsá tí-n-gúlú:ve 'they are removing pigs'
       vá-súsá tí-n-guluve t!á vo:n!á 'they are removing their pigs'

       vá-xávísá n-gú:vu 'they are selling cloth'
       vá-xávísá n-guvu y!á vo:n!á 'they are selling their cloth'

       vá-xávísá tí-n-gú:vu 'they are selling clothes'
       vá-xávísá tí-n-gu:vu t!á von!á 'they are selling their clothes'

Notice that when there is no modifier present, the High of the verb spreads
as far as the penultimate syllable of the noun object. Clearly the verb High
and the object noun are gathered together in the same P-domain. However,
when there is a modifier on the object, the verb High *cannot* spread into
the stem of the following noun (although it can spread onto the syllable in
front of the stem, which is either the last syllable of the verb or else the
noun class prefix): *vá-xávísá tí-n-gu:vu t!á von!á*.

What these data demonstrate is that when an object noun is modified, the prefix of the noun object is inside a P-domain with the verb while the noun stem proper is in a different P-domain. In other words, a P-domain edge appears inside (what in the traditional Bantu linguistic literature has usually been considered to be) a phonological word. Recent theoretical work by Scott Myers (1987) has, however, suggested that from a syntactic point of view, a noun class prefix is a separate word from the noun stem. Xitsonga appears to support this view.

Notice that neither of our postlexical rules (Syntactic Projection and Daughter Projection) seem relevant to this case. Syntactic Projection says that the final syllable of a maximum projection projects a Left bracket to its Left. Obviously this has no potential for explaining why the High of the verb in *vá-xávísá tí-n-gu:vu t!á von!á* can spread onto the nominal prefix but not further. Daughter Projection could be relevant only if we assume that a modified noun is extracted from S'. But even assuming this, if daughters of S" project a bracket to their Right (as argued above), we would not expect a modified noun to be a barrier to spreading from the preceding verb.

Since there *is* a P-domain break between the modified noun and what precedes it, we have evidence for a third post-lexical projection rule. We assume a rule whereby the first syllable of a phrase consisting of a noun plus modifier projects a Left P-domain bracket to its Left. Call this Modifier Projection.

We should mention one piece of additional data relative to the domain structure of expressions with a modified noun. Consider the sentence *vá-rhándzá mu-nti w!á hi:n!á vá:-nhu* 'they love our village, the people do'. Notice that in this example the H of the verb *does not* extend onto the prefix of the noun *mu-nti*. From what we have seen above, we might have expected the prefix to be affected by High Tone Spread. We suggest that the failure of the prefix in *mu-nti* to be grouped into a separate P-domain from the stem may represent a *minimality* effect. Words in Xitsonga (with very few exceptions) consist minimally of two syllables. If the prefix is "removed" from bisyllabic nouns such as *mu-nti*, the result would be *a monosyllabic word and thus a violation of the minimality condition that requires two syllables in a word*. It seems then that the minimality condition requires the prefix to stay with the monosyllabic stem and thus escape being treated as a separated word. The P-domain bracket must therefore be inserted between the verb and *mu-nti* rather than in front of the noun stem.

So far we have seen that a noun object of a verb has a P-domain break in front of the noun when the noun is modified. When a noun-modifier construction is the second object in a double object construction, the noun is again segregated into a separate P-domain from the preceding object.

(28) *hi-nyíká mu-nwí tí-nguvu táyená [Beuchat 1959, p. 137]
'we give the drinker his clothes'

When a modified noun is used in conjunction with an absolute pronoun co-referential to it, we find that there is again a P-domain break between the noun and what precedes:

(29) *toná tí-n'anga létinéné tádyóndzísá [1959, p. 138]
'as for the good doctors they are teaching'

*híxoná xí-ambalalo xáminá [1959, p. 138]
'it is my garment, it is'

It is clear that it is the structure noun-modifier that projects a P-domain bracket to its Left, regardless of the nature of what precedes.

3.7 Negative Structures

Let us review our analysis of the complex Xitsonga data. We hypothesize that High Tone Spread operates internal to a P-domain. We construct these P-domains by projecting a Right (or Left) bracket to the Right (or Left) of a designated category (the category may be phonologically, morphologically, and/or syntactically defined). In most of the cases dealt with here, it is immaterial whether a Right or Left bracket is inserted, since either choice will in fact lead to the correct domain-structure.

We postulate three lexical rules projecting P-domain brackets. The first rule is High Projection: a High-toned syllable projects a Left bracket to its Left (i.e., it starts a domain). The second rule is Final Projection: a toneless syllable at the end of a non-verbal lexical category projects a Left bracket to its Left (i.e., a final toneless syllable in non-verbal categories cannot be gathered into the same domain as a preceding High). The third rule is Pre-High Projection: a toneless syllable in front of a H projects a Left bracket to its Left (i.e., such toneless syllables cannot receive spreading).

In addition to these lexical rules, there are post-lexical rules projecting P-domain brackets. Three of these are widespread in Xitsonga. Syntactic Projection says that a toneless syllable at the end of a maximal projection projects a Left bracket to its Left. Daughter Projection says that a syllable at the end of a daughter of S" (excluding S') projects a Right bracket to its Right. Modifier Projection inserts a Left bracket to the Left of the first syllable of a modified noun (where prefixes are considered not to be part of the noun unless minimality conditions force the inclusion of the prefix with the noun stem).

The critical feature of our analysis is simply this: whether or not a High tone spreads onto a following syllable is always and only a matter of whether the syllables are in the same P-domain. There are no other conditions on spreading. The reasons why two syllables are or are not in the same P-domain may vary, but the actual mechanism that accounts for the spreading of a High tone is unified. In this section, we attempt to provide evidence that this unification expresses a real generalization about Xitsonga tonology. The evidence derives from negative verbal structures.

In negative constructions in Xitsonga, the complement to the predicative element exhibits a different tonal pattern from what we have observed above. We illustrate this by examining complements to the negative copulative *ahí* 'it is not'. Let us first take the case of toneless nouns.

(30)   nyama   ahí nyá:má   'meat'
       n'anga   ahí n'á:ngá   'doctor'
       fole   ahí fó:lé   'tobacco'
       mu-nhu   ahí mú:nhú   'person'
       n-guvu   ahí ngú:vú   'clothes'
       nandza   ahí ná:ndzá   'servant'
       ndlopfu   ahí ndló:pfú   'elephant'

       gandlati   ahí gándlá:tí   'wave'
       papila   ahí pápí:lá   'paper'
       n-guluve   ahí ngúlú:vé   'pig'
       ma-landza   ahí má-lá:ndzá   'servants'
       ti-n-guluve   ahí tíngúlú:vé   'pigs'
       ma-gandlati   ahí má-gándlá:tí   'waves'

       xi-hlangi   ahí xí-hlá:ngí   'baby'
       xi-koxa   ahí xí-kó:xá   'old woman'
       ti-nguvu   ahí tí-ngú:vú   'clothes'
       xi-komu   ahí xí-kó:mú   'hoe'
       ti-manga   ahí tí-má:ngá   'groundnuts'
       ri-hlelo   ahí rí-hlé:ló   'winnowing tray'

       xi-phukuphuku   ahí xí-phúkúphúkú   'fool'
       xi-hontlovila   ahí xí-hóntlóvílá   'giant'
       xi-hlambetwana ahí xí-hlámbétwáná   'earthenware pot'
       ma-hungundlele ahí má-húngúndlélé   'rumors'

From these data, we see that the H tone of the negative copulative element *ahí* spreads throughout the noun. Notice that the High tone spreads onto the last syllable of the noun. In other words, the last syllable of the noun does not trigger the insertion of a P-domain bracket and thus the P-domain extends from the negative copulative element's High tone all the way through the noun. Before attempting to characterize what is going on here, consider next the case where the noun following the negative copulative has toneless syllables followed by a High syllable.

(31) homú   ahí hó:mú   'cow'
      tandzá   ahí tá:ndzá   'egg'
      mu-rhí   ahí mú:-rhí   'tree'
      yimpí   ahí yí:mpí   'army, war'
      yimbhú   ahí yí:mbhú   'ostrich'
      nyimpfú   ahí nyí:mpfú   'sheep'
      n-tlunyá   ahí ntlú:nyá   'timid person, coward'
      nalá   ahí ná:lá   'enemy'

      ti-homú   ahí tí-hó:mú   'cattle'
      va-lalá   ahí vá-lá:lá   'enemies'
      ma-tandzá   ahí má-tá:ndzá   'eggs'

      mu-fána   ahí mú-fá:ná   'boy'
      ti-búku   ahí tí-bú:kú   'books'
      ma-sócha   ahí má-só:chá   'soldiers'
      ma-hánci   ahí má-há:ncí   'horses'
      ma-kóti   ahí má-kó:tí   'vultures'
      keréke   ahí kéré:ké   'church'

      Xi-tsóngá   ahí Xí-tsó:ngá   'Xitsonga language'
      ri-sívá   ahí rí-sí:vá   'feather'
      mu-rísí   ahí mú-rí:sí   'herder'
      ti-hóngónyí ahí tí-hóngó:nyí   'blue wildebeests'

Notice that the syllable in front of the High in the noun *accepts* the spreading of the High from the negative, contrary to the cases discussed earlier where such syllables failed to be affected by High Tone Spread. In other words, the lexical rule of Pre-High Projection does not apply. Notice also that a toneless syllable at the end of a noun that is preceded by a High in the noun (e.g., *ma-kóti*) acquires a High tone in this context. In other word, the P-domain inserted by the Final Projection rule is not present. Notice also that there is no downstepping in these examples.

Let us now look at the cases where a noun begins with a High tone.

(32)

m-bútí	ahí mbú:tí	'goat'
nyóká	ahí nyó:ká	'snake'
húkú	ahí hú:kú	'chicken'
vúswá	ahí vú:swá	'porridge'
nyóxí	ahí nyó:xí	'bee'
hávi	ahí há:ví	'ox'
n'wáná	ahí n'wá:ná	'child'
hóngónyí	ahí hóngó:nyí	'blue wildebeest'
búku	ahí bú:kú	'book'
sócha	ahí só:chá	'soldier'
hánci	ahí há:ncí	'horse'
kóti	ahí kó:tí	'vulture'

From these data, it is clear that no downstepping is introduced between the negative element and the noun. Also, the final toneless syllable of the noun does not project a P-domain.

The preceding data would suggest that complements to a negative verb must be incorporated into the same P-domain as the verbal element (in other words, no projection rule can assign a P-domain internal to the complements of a negative verb). There is further evidence to support this generalization.

Consider next the case of a double object construction. For the sake of variation, we will use the negative present tense rather than the negative copulative. (Without going into details, the negative present tense involves a High-toned subject prefix as well as a "grammatical" High tone that is linked to the second syllable of the verb stem. The presence of this grammatical High tone is clear in the case of lexically toneless verbs; in the case of lexically High verbs, this grammatical tone fuses with the lexical tone.)

(33)   a-vá-xav!élí xí-kóxá nyá:má
        'they are buying meat for the old woman'
        a-ndzí-nyíkí mú-fáná tí-n-gú:vú
        'I am giving the boy clothes'

Notice in the first example that the High of the verb spreads through the toneless noun *xi-koxa* and also through the toneless noun *nyama*. In the second example, the H of the verb spreads onto the first syllable of *mu-fána*, while the H of the syllable *fá* spreads onto the last syllable of that noun and into the following toneless noun *ti-n-guluve*.

Next consider the case where a modified noun occurs as complement to a negative verb.

(34) a-ndzí-vóní n-gúvú yá mí:ná 'I do not see my cloth'
      a-ndzí-vóní tí-n-gúlúvé tá mí:ná 'I do not see my pigs'

Once again, we find that there is no P-domain break between the negative predicate and the nominal, even though it is modified. In other words, the rule whereby modified nominals project a P-domain bracket to their left does not operate.

We propose that all of the above facts involve a single constraint: no P-domain brackets (whether projected lexically or postlexically) can be inserted in the complement of a negative predicate. In other words, *the complement to a negative verb must form a single P-domain with the verb.* By bringing all of the complements of the negative verb into the same P-domain as the verb, we will for the first time have more than one High tone in the same P-domain. We cannot generate the correct output, however, if we allow all of these High tones to remain (as separate High tones). Specifically, recall that our rule of !-domain formation locates a !-break in front of each High-span. Since there is no downstepping in the complements of the negative verb, there must be a single High span. There are different means of securing this result. One alternative would be to allow each of the High tones in the negative structure to spread to the right in the domain, and then to invoke the Fusion rule. This would mean that Fusion would have to be permitted in certain post-lexical cases as well as lexically. A second alternative would be to claim that all Highs except the first H in a P-domain are deleted; the only remaining High could then spread throughout the domain. We leave this problem of implementation open.

Let us now consider some additional complications to the picture that we gave above concerning the affect of the negative verb on the domain structure of what follows it.

In section 3.4 we showed that a verb followed by a postposed subject triggers Syntactic Projection (since the verb is at the end of a maximal projection). However, we also saw that when the verb ended in a High tone, then the verb and (some subpart of) the following postposed subject could be united into the same P-domain. When the verb is a negative verb, some subpart of the postposed subject again can be in the same P-domain as the verb, but not all the syllables of the subject.

(35) a-rí-wángá rí-hlél:o 'it did not fall down, the winnowing basket'
      a-má-yángá má-lá:ndza 'they did not go, the servants'

It is immediately clear that the postposed subject *ri-hlelo* 'winnowing basket' is not behaving parallel to the object of a negative verb. The object of the negative verb would not have a final syllable unaffected by High Tone Spread; the postposed subject does have the final syllable outside the scope of High Tone Spread. Thus whereas a negative verb prevents an object from having an internal P-domain, it does not prevent a postposed subject from having such an internal P-domain. Thus the postposed subject does not count as a complement to a negative verb and thus the constraint requiring a single P-domain is not applicable.

The spreading from the negative verb onto the postposed subject is of course constrained by the usual considerations. If the postposed subject is a modified structure, then spreading will go only as far as the prefix of the noun.

(36) a-rí-wángá rí-hlelo r!á we:n!á
      'it did not fall, your winnowing basket'

The final H of the negative phrase is separated from an initial H in the postposed subject by downstep.

(37) a-vá-tángá v!á-va-s!á:tí 'they did not come, the women'

This demonstrates further that the postposed subject is *not* considered a complement to the negative verb for purposes of the constraint that says complements to a negative verb must be in the same P-domain as the verb.

4 Conclusion

There is no doubt but that the surface facts concerning High Tone Spread in Xitsognga are very complicated. In this paper, we have adopted the position that High Tone Spread itself is very simple: a High tone spreads iteratively to the right in a P-domain. The complexity of the data arises from the fact that there are several rules that project P-domain brackets, both lexically and post-lexically.

(38) Lexical rules:
   High Projection
   Final Projection
   Pre-High Projection

   Post-lexical rules:
   Syntactic Projection
   Daughter Projection
   Modifier Projection

One of the least obvious aspects of our analysis is the postulation of the lexical Pre-High Projection rule. This is the rule that accounts for the failure of a High to spread onto a toneless syllable in a word where the toneless syllable is followed by a High. At first it might seem as though there is little reason to *identify* the failure of High Tone Spread here with other instances of the failure of High Tone Spread, e.g., the lacking of spreading onto a modified noun. Pre-High projection seems to be accounting for a phonological limitation on spreading (avoidance of violations of the Obligatory Contour Principle) whereas Modifier Projection seems to reflect a syntactic limitation. The negative structures are critical in this respect: they demonstrate that when a more syntactic limitation on spreading is removed, the more phonological limitation is also removed. In other words, the negative structures provide evidence in favor of *equating* all cases of the failure to spread. We have done this by invoking only one means of limiting High Tone Spreading: specifically, a High tone can fail to spread onto a syllable only if that syllable is in a different P-domain. There is no other limitation on High Tone Spread. As a consequence, we can explain the tonology of the negative structure by claiming that it does not license the appearance of a P-domain bracket in its complements.

Our study of Xitsonga tonology and of the phonology-syntax interface in Xitsonga is still in progress. What we have attempted to do in this paper is to suggest that a fruitful line of research involves the factoring of phonological representations into domains, and allowing these domains to be constructed via appeal to a combination of phonological, morphological, and syntactic factors.

References

Beuchat, P. D. 1959. Tonomorphology of the Tsonga noun. *African Studies* 18:3, 133-145.

Beuchat, P. D. 1962. Additional notes on the tonomorphology of the Tsonga noun. *African Studies* 213-4:105-122.

Cassimjee, Farida. 1992. *An autosegmental analysis of Venda tonology.* Garland.

Cassimjee, Farida and Charles W. Kisseberth. 1992. Shingazidja metrical structure. To appear in the Proceedings of the 28th Regional Meeting of the Chicago Linguistic Society.

Cole, Jennifer and John Coleman. 1992. No need for cyclicity in generative phonology. To appear in the Proceedings of the 28th Regional Meeting of the Chicago Linguistic Society.

Halle, Morris and William Idsardi. 1992. General properties of stress and metrical structure. Paper presented at the DIMACS Workshop on Human Language.

Idsardi, William J. 1992. The computation of prosody. Ph.D. dissertation. MIT.

Myers, Scott. 1987. Tone and the structure of words in Shona. Ph.D. dissertation, University of Massachusetts.

Selkirk, Elisabeth. 1986. On derived domains in sentence phonology. *Phonology Yearbook*, 3:371-405.

Syntactic and Semantic Conditions in Kikongo Phrasal Phonology[1]

David Odden
Ohio State University

1 Introduction

This paper looks at tonal alternations in the Kimanyanga dialect of the Bantu language Kikongo, focusing on the question of how phonology, syntax, and semantics interact. One of the most controversial questions regarding the syntax—phonology interface is precisely how phonological rules can be made to refer to sentence structure. Kaisse (1985) and Odden (1987) argue that phonological rules may directly refer to properties of surface syntactic representations—these are the direct reference theories of the syntax-phonology interface. In contrast, Nespor and Vogel (1986), Hayes (1989), Inkelas (1990), Zec and Inkelas (1989), and Selkirk (1986) argue that phonological rules refer to various types of prosodic structures, which are themselves built by rules that refer directly to syntactic structures— these are the indirect reference theories of the interface.[2] The data to be discussed from Kikongo will be shown to pose a problem for the indirect reference theories of this interface. More importantly, besides bearing on the question of how directly phonology interacts with non-phonological aspects of a sentence, Kikongo provides new data regarding *what* aspects of a sentence can be referred to by the phonology.

The alternation in question is the deletion of the first stem H of nouns which stand in certain phrasal contexts. There are three problems to be considered. First, the rule Universal Effacement deletes H only if the noun is modified by a universal quantifier: this rule therefore requires access to aspects of the semantic representation. Second, the rule Argument Effacement deletes H in a general syntactic context, but is blocked when the noun head is modified by a non-universal quantifier: again, phonology must refer to the semantic representation. Finally, there is the problem of characterizing the rather broad range of syntactic contexts in the sentence where

---

[1] I would like to thank Kufimfutu Bakelana for the data on Kikongo, and Jill Beckman, Peter Culicover, David Dowty, Larry Hyman, Bob Levine, Shigeru Miyagawa, Carl Pollard, Craige Roberts, and Thilo Schadeberg for helpful suggestions and questions.

[2] Nespor and Vogel (1986) admit to the existence of phonological rules which refer directly to syntactic conditioning—their claims are more restricted, since that theory is addressed to phonological constituency as reflected in rules which have no non-phonological conditions. Selkirk (1986) also allows for the possibility that there are phonological rules which directly refer to syntactic structure.

Argument Effacement takes place. A major task of the paper is specifying what those contexts are, and characterizing those contexts in a natural way.

2 Phonological Background

We start with an overview of tone in nouns to facilitate understanding how sentence-level H deletion is manifested phonetically. Almost every noun stem in Kikongo is in one of three tone classes, seen in (1). Words of the first class have H on their final vowel. Words in the second class have one H on the initial stem mora and one on the penult (phonetically a level H on a long vowel, since there are no rising tones in the language—see (4)).[3] Words of the third class have a plateau of H tones stretching from the first stem mora to the final.

(1) **Final H**
    mu-teté 'box' mu-loongí 'teacher'
    kokotí 'coconut' bi-sanunú 'comb'
    ki-nwaanunú 'fighting tool'

    Stem Initial and Penult Mora
    bi-nyónya 'termites' mu-kúúnga 'song'
    mbééle 'knife' súkáádi 'sugar'
    ma-tábíísi 'gifts' ma-lémbelémbe 'bird (sp.)'
    dókotóólo 'doctor' mfúlutútu 'tortoise'

    H Plateau
    bi-kúní 'farmer' ma-gháálá 'branch'
    mu-táámbú 'trap' ki-kókílá 'herd'
    ki-kóómbóló 'broom' ma-fúngúnúnú 'bee (sp.)'

Underlyingly, nouns have one or two H tones, as in (2). If there is only one H it is final. If there are two Hs, the first links to the initial stem vowel. The second H may unpredictably appear on the final or the penult.

---

[3] Nouns in Kikongo are composed of a class prefix such as *ki*, *bi*, or *mu*, so the first H is on the first vowel of the word in *dókotóólo* but the second vowel of the word in *mukúúnga*. In both of these cases, though, the initial H is on the first *stem* syllable.

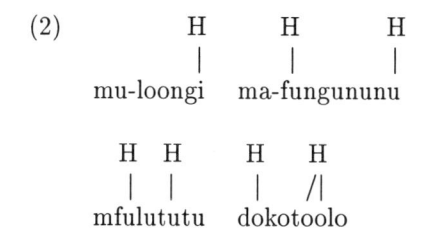

Syntactic and Semantic Conditions in Kikongo Phrasal Phonology 169

(2)
```
           H       H        H
           |       |        |
        mu-loongi  ma-fungununu

         H  H     H  H
         |  |     | /|
        mfulututu dokotoolo
```

In fact, the structures in (2) can be further analyzed, though this analysis is not crucial to the issue at hand. Nouns with a penultimate H will be treated as having a H prelinked to the penult in the lexicon. Nouns in the H plateauing set will have a floating H in their lexical representations. Every noun has a floating H, which stands to the left of any linked Hs, so the leftmost H in the examples above would actually be floating. The rightmost floating H links to the final vowel—thus the rightmost H of *muloongí* and *mafúngúnúnú* can actually be docked by rule. Finally, any remaining floating H, as one would find in *mfúlutútu* or *mafúngúnúnú*, links to the stem initial syllable. Furthermore, following Goldsmith (1987), nouns with penultimate H can be reduced to a subset of the floating H class, where the final syllable is lexically marked as extraprosodic.

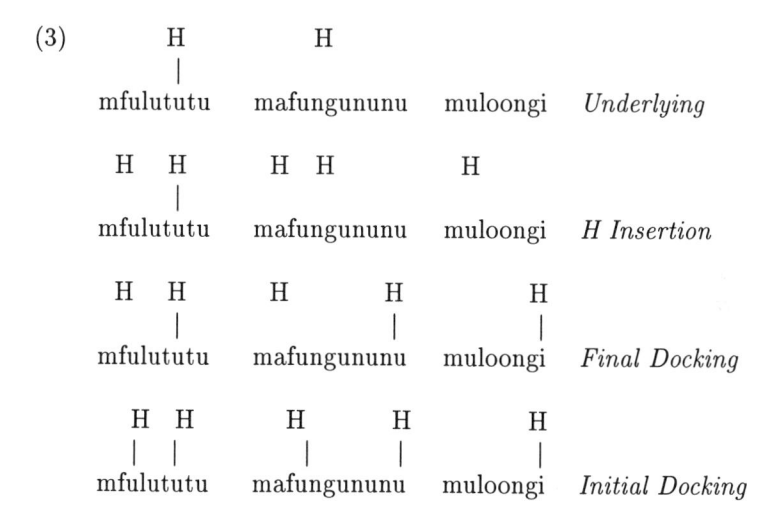

(3)
```
         H             H
         |
      mfulututu    mafungununu    muloongi      Underlying

       H  H        H  H
          |
      mfulututu    mafungununu    muloongi      H Insertion

       H  H        H     H          H
          |              |          |
      mfulututu    mafungununu    muloongi      Final Docking

       H  H        H     H          H
       |  |        |     |          |
      mfulututu    mafungununu    muloongi      Initial Docking
```

There are no surface rising tones in Kikongo, and we note that the penultimate syllable *dókotóólo* is level toned. Since in our analysis, *dókótóólo* has an H Lexically linked to its penultimate mora, we would expect *dókotoólo*. The rule Syllable Internal Spread in (4) will correct this problem.

(4) *Syllable Internal Spread*

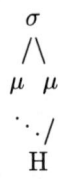

$$\begin{array}{c} \sigma \\ /\backslash \\ \mu\ \mu \\ \cdot\cdot/ \\ H \end{array}$$

Applying this rule then accounts for the surface form as in (5).

(5)
```
    H   H                              H    H
    |   |    Syllable Internal Spread  |   /\
    d o k o t o o l o        →         d o k o t o o l o
```

The iterative rule Plateauing (6) accounts for the surface realization of the H plateau nouns, which underlyingly only have H on the first and on the last syllables.

(6) *Plateauing*

```
    H            H
    |··          |
    V  V    X    V ω]
```

This rule spreads the stem initial H rightward, as long as the final vowel also has a H, as in (7).

(7)
```
       H              H                        H          H
       |              |      Plateauing       /\          |
    m a - f u n g u n u n u      ⟶         m a - f u n g u n u n u
```

Note that this rule does not apply to nouns like *mfúlutútu* or *dókotóólo* where the second H is not word final.

To further motivate the analysis of H plateauing nouns, consider the data of (8). Here, nouns undergo the rule Argument Effacement, which deletes the leftmost H of the stem. One of the contexts where that rule applies is when the noun is in subject position.

(8)

	Isolation	Subject	
Final H	ma-nkondé	ma-nkonde mabódidi	'the bananas rotted'
	mu-loongí	mu-loongi wufwíídí	'the teacher died'
	bi-sanunú	bi-sanunu bipásukidi	'the combs broke'
Initial and penult	ma-tábíísi	ma-tabíísi mabwíídi	'the gifts fell'
	mfúlutútu	mfulutútu yifwíídí	'the tortoise died'
Plateau	ma-láálá	ma-laalá mabódidi	'the oranges rotted'
	ki-kókílá	ki-kokilá kifwíídí	'the herd died'
	ki-kóómbóló	ki-koomboló kipásukidi	'the broom broke'
	ma-fúngúnúnú	ma-fungununú mantátíkídí	'the bees bit me'

Nouns like *mankondé* with a single final H simply lose their H in subject position. Nouns like *mfúlutútu* with initial and penultimate H lose the initial H, and keep the penultimate H. This is all as expected; in both cases, the first stem H deletes.

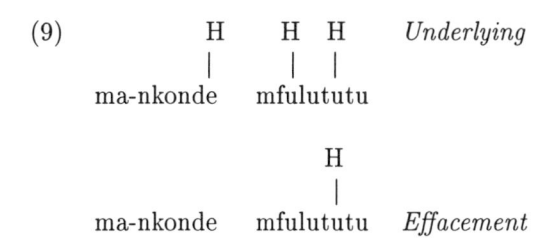

(9)   H   H H   *Underlying*
       | | |
    ma-nkonde mfulututu

              H
              |
    ma-nkonde mfulututu   *Effacement*

Nouns like *mafúngúnúnú*, though, appear to delete the initial string of H tones. In fact, there is nothing surprising about the derivations in (10) as long as we keep in mind the fact that the H plateauing nouns underlyingly have one H on the initial vowel and one on the final. Argument Effacement deletes the initial H, so that H is no longer around to spread rightward.

(10)   H   H
        | |
      ma-fungununu   *Underlying*

              H
              |
      ma-fungununu   *Effacement*

The hallmark of the H-plateauing class, then, is that in comparing the citation form with its subject form, these nouns seem to lower a whole string of Hs, leaving behind only the final H.

A further complication in these alternations is that the H plateauing class splits into two subclasses, namely the polymoraic stems, and the dimoraic stems. As shown in (11), disyllabic trimoraic nouns such as *maláálá* keep the final H, just as other H plateau nouns do. But dimoraic nouns like *bikúní* delete both stem Hs.

(11)   **Isolation**   **Subject**
        ma-láálá   ma-laalá mabódidi   'the oranges rotted'
        ma-gháálá   ma-ghaalá mabódidi   'the branches rotted'
        ki-kúúkú   ki-kuukú kibwíídi   'the cookhouse fell'

        bi-kúní   bi-kuni bifwíídí   'the farmers died'
        mu-lélé   mu-lele wubódidi   'the cloth rotted'
        ma-tádí   ma-tadi mabwíídi   'the stones fell'

The contrasting behavior of these two phonological classes can be explained on the basis of the fact that they have structurally different representations of their Hs at the point where H tone deletion applies. At the stage in the derivation where the H deletes, dimoraic nouns like *bikúní* have only one H tone linked to the two stem vowels, and polymoraic nouns like *maláálá* have two separate Hs.

(12)   H   H H
         /\ | |
       bi-kuni ma-laala

But all H plateauing nouns have two separate Hs in underlying representations, so the multiply attached H tone in *bikúní* derives from the underlying form in (13).

(13)   H H   H H
        | | | |
       bi-kuni ma-laala

The representation in (13) is converted into that in (12) by applying the Tone Fusion rule.

(14)   *Tone Fusion*
        H   H   → ∅
        |˙˙˙|
        •   •   TONE NODES

Since the two H tones of *bikúní* are adjacent, they are subject to fusion, but since a toneless mora stands between the two Hs of *maláálá*, the tones cannot fuse. Tone Fusion must apply prior to Plateauing, since Plateauing would bring the first and final H tones together, and therefore incorrectly render the entire surface string of H tones in *maláálá* subject to deletion.[4]

The divergent treatment of dimoraic and polymoraic stems as a result of tone fusion furthermore gives us evidence for treating this H ~ ∅ alternation as arising from a rule of H deletion in some environment, rather than H insertion in the complementary environment. We have noted that H-Plateau stems such as *maláálá* can be analyzed as having only one underlying H (which docks to the final vowel), where the second H can be inserted by rule—since all nouns have a H in the citation form. It might be tempting to eliminate the rules of H tone deletion, by putting appropriate restrictions on the insertion of the secondary H. Under this analysis, the form seen in subject position in (11) would in essence be the basic form. Similarly, stems like *mankondé* being underlyingly toneless show up as toneless in subject position. The surface H in the citation form would, again, result from insertion of H in the complementary environment.

We would still be faced with the problem of encoding the syntactic and semantic restrictions on this H tone—the conditions would simply have to be stated as the conditions where secondary H is not inserted. But there is a more fundamental problem with trying to explain these alternations by restricting the insertion of secondary H. Nouns like *bikúní* are toneless in subject position, and in the citation form they have H on the two stem

---

[4]In Odden 1990, it is also shown that stems of the structure CVVNCV such as *mazáángá* have underlying short vowels. The two H tones of this stem undergo Tone Fusion and act like surface dimoraic stems. This is shown by the form *nsábúkí mázaanga* 'I crossed the lakes', where all of the stem Hs delete in object position, analogous to *mwéní bíkuni* 'I saw the farmer'.

moras. An analysis where H insertion is constrained semantically and syntactically cannot predict this contrast in the citation form between *bikúní* and *mankondé*, since the subject position tone of these nouns is identical. So while the final H of *mankondé* and the initial H of *mfúlutútu* are indeed derived by rule, we nonetheless must insert that H in all contexts, let it undergo Tone Fusion as is appropriate, and later delete it in certain syntactically and semantically characterized positions.

The last complication to be considered is the insertion of H at the beginning of a word at the phrasal level. The examples in (15) show direct object nouns after the verb. Direct object position is another context where Argument Effacement applies, which is why the final H of *mankondé* or the initial string of Hs in *mafúngúnúnú* is missing. However, we also find a H on the word initial vowel of the noun. Furthermore, looking especially at nouns like *mankondé*, we note that this H may spread from the noun class prefix to the stem initial vowel.

(15) ma-nkondé   mboongidí má-nkónde   'I took bananas'
      bi-sanunú   mboongidí bí-sánunu   'I took combs'
      ki-nwaanunú   mboongidí kí-nwáanunu   'I took a fighting tool'
      kokotí   mboongidí kókoti   'I took a coconut'

      bi-nyónya   tuvoondidí bí-nyónya   'we killed termites'
      mu-kúúnga   yímbidi mú-kúunga[5]   'he sang a song'
      ma-tábíísi   numuveení má-tábíísi   'I gave him gifts'
      lémbelémbe   tuvoondidí lémbelémbe   'we killed a lembelembe'

      bi-kúní   tumweení bí-kuni   'we saw farmers'
      ma-záángá   mweení má-zaanga   'I saw lakes'
      ma-láálá   díídí má-laalá   'he ate oranges'
      ki-kóómbóló   mboongidí kí-koomboló   'I took the broom'
      ma-fúngúnúnú   mweení má-fungununú   'I saw the bees'

In general, a noun receives word initial H when it is at the left edge of its phrase and is preceded by some word. Except in the H-plateauing nouns, this H will spread from the prefix to the stem initial vowel by the rule of Doubling to Stem.[6]

---

[5] Whenever a CVVCV noun stem in the penult-and-initial tone class undergoes deletion of its leftmost stem H, the stem loses both of its H tones, since the initial and penultimate Hs are adjacent, so undergo tone fusion.

[6] At present, I have no explanation for why this rule does not apply to the stem initial vowel of H plateauing nouns, when it does apply to nouns of the initial and penult tone pattern.

(16) Doubling to Stem

$$\begin{array}{c} H \\ | \cdot \cdot \\ V \; [_{stem} V' \end{array}$$

What is crucial to understand about these H tones that appear at the left edge of the noun is that they constitute a further and later complication which renders the operation of H deletion opaque, since on the one hand H deletion should eliminate the first stem H, and on the other hand, this later rule puts back in a H. There are a number of other complications, especially those posed by nouns in Class 5 lacking noun class prefixes or by nouns whose stems are vowel initial; giving a complete account of those complexities would distract us significantly from the goal of understanding the syntactic and semantic conditions on the rules of H tone deletion. As an expository aid, each noun in the examples which undergoes one of the Effacement rules will be annotated with a small *e* subscript.[7]

3 Universal Effacement

Having covered the vital background material, we now turn to the focus of the paper, the conditions on the two processes of tone deletion. In the first case, nouns lose their tones in isolated noun phrases, providing there is a universal quantifier in the phrase. Consider the data in (17). Nouns generally have the same tone pattern in isolation as they have when followed by modifiers, including adjectives, possessives, wh-words, numerals and other non-universal quantifiers.

---

[7]For most stems of the initial-and-penult class, it is difficult to see directly that H deletion has applied when the noun is preceded by a word. This is because the prefix receives a H tone, and that H then spreads to the stem; this effectively reinstates the H which was deleted by the tone deletion rule. So, compare the citation for *ma-tábíísi* 'gifts' with the object form *má-tábíísi*: here we have no direct evidence that the first stem H has been deleted. However, disyllabic nouns with a long vowel, such as *mukúunga*, are useful in this respect since the post-verbal form (*múkúunga*) has a falling tone in the stem, as opposed to the citation form which has a level H.

(17) mankondé mankondé matááta   'father's bananas'
               mankondé mabóla   'rotten bananas'
               mankondé mamííngi   'many bananas'
               mankondé mátatú   'three bananas'

     bikúní   bikúní byabííngi   'many farmers'
               bikúní byándá   'tall farmers'
               bikúní byámbóte   'good farmers'
               bikúní byáBánduundu   'farmers of Banduundu'
               bikúní byabínéne   'large farmers'
               bikúní byoolé   'two farmers'
               bikúní bítatú   'three farmers'
               bikúní bííya   'four farmers'
               bikúní bíkwa   'how many farmers'
               bikúní byánáni   'whose farmers?'

     binyónya binyónya byabííngi   'many termites'
               binyónya byámbóte   'good termites'
               binyónya byamuloongí   'the teacher's termites'
               binyónya bitatú   'three termites'
               binyónya bíkwa   'how many termites'
               binyónya byánáni   'whose farmers?'

The examples of (17), which have the same tone in the modified form as in the citation form, are to be contrasted with those in (18). In (18) are nouns followed by one of the two lexical universal quantifiers. When followed by a universal quantifier, the first stem H is deleted.

(18) mankondé   mankonde$_e$ mámánsó   'all bananas'
     miloongí   miloongi$_e$ myámínsó   'all teachers'
     binwaanunú   binwaanunu$_e$ byáwóonsono   'all fighting tools'

     binyónya   binyonya$_e$ byábínsó   'all termites'
     mikúúnga   mikuunga$_e$ myámínsó   'all the songs'
     matábíísi   matabíísi$_e$ mámánsó   'all gifts'
     madókotóólo   madokotóólo$_e$ máwóonsono   'all doctors'

     bikúní   bikuni$_e$ byábínsó   'all the farmers'
     malaálá   malaalá$_e$ mámánsó   'all oranges'
     mafúngúnúnú   mafungununú$_e$ mámánsó   'all bees'

This can be accounted for by positing a rule to delete the first stem H if a universal quantifier follows. Additional data show that simply listing the lexical items which trigger the rule is not sufficient. There is a construction in Kikongo, illustrated in (19), used to express the notion 'All X things',[8] where X is any number. The construction is formed by prefixing what is known as the associative prefix to the appropriate numeral. So, for example, *bikuni byábítatú* is composed of the noun *bikúní*, the associative morpheme *byá*, and the number three, *bitatú*.

(19)   bikúní   bikuni$_e$ byáabyóóle   'all two farmers'
                        bikuni$_e$ byábítatú   'all three farmers'
                        bikuni$_e$ byábííya   'all four farmers'

          maláálá   malaalá$_e$ mánsámbwáádi   'all seven oranges'
                        malaalá$_e$ mákúumí   'all ten oranges'
                        malaalá$_e$ makumí ná matatú   'all 13 oranges'

What must be noticed in these examples, and in a literally infinite set of parallel examples, is that the stem initial H is deleted. As we can see in (20), deletion of H is not triggered simply by the presence of the associative morpheme *bya-*, nor it is triggered by the presence of a numeral.

(20)   bikúní byánáni   'whose farmers?'
            bikúní bítatú   'three farmers?'

The only property unifying (18) and (19) is the semantic one, namely that the meaning of the modifier includes a universal quantifier.

    A legitimate countermove would be to assume that universal quantifiers and nouns also happen to have a characteristic constituent relation, and that the rule of H tone effacement reacts to this constituency, not to the semantics. So far, we have only considered two-word phrases, so attributing this apparent sensitivity to semantics to different constituent structure is conceivable. For example, it might be that universal quantifiers group further from the noun, as in (21a) or they are closer to the noun, as in (21b).

---

[8]A conventional translation of *bikuni byábítatú* would be 'the three farmers'—the meaning of the expression is 'all individuals in the universe composed of a certain three farmers'.

(21) a.   NP   b.   NP
            / \   / \
          N'   Univ.   N'   Adj
          /\   /\
         N Adj   N Univ.

Such an approach would be plausible if the word order of universal quantifiers and other modifiers were somehow circumscribed, but the fact is that, as seen in (22), quantifiers and other modifiers co-mingle freely, and there is no difference in this respect between universal and non-universal quantifiers. And, just as crucially, the stem H is still deleted from the head noun whenever there is a universal quantifier, no matter where that quantifier stands.

(22)
bikúní	bikúní byabííngi byáBanduundu	'many farmers of Banduundu'
	bikúní byáBánduundu byabííngi	=
	bikúní bítatú byámbóte	'three good farmers'
	bikúní byámbóte bitatú	=
	bikuni$_e$ byábínsó byáBánduundu	'all farmers of Banduundu'
	bikuni$_e$ byáBánduundu byábínsó	=
	bikuni$_e$ byábítatú byámbóte	'all three good farmers'
	bikuni$_e$ byámbóte byábítatú	=

A flatter constituent structure than (21) is needed on syntactic grounds, hence we cannot consign this semantic reference to syntax. Therefore, we require a rule such as (23), which refers to a property of semantic representations.

(23)   *Universal Effacement*

$$H \rightarrow \emptyset\ /\ [_{NP}\ [_N\ \text{---}\ ]\ ...\ \forall\ ...\ ]$$

Of course, the rule formalism in (23) involves a bit of shorthand, since it represents the tone being deleted, the syntactic condition that the rule applies to the head noun of a phrase, and the semantic property that there is a universal quantifier, all on a single line, whereas these things are really properties of three separate representations.

4 Argument Effacement

We now turn to the second rule of H deletion, Argument Effacement, which deletes H from the head of a phrase in certain sentential positions. The examples in (24) provide examples of nouns and time adverbs (which can be treated as nouns) undergoing deletion of H. The left edge of the VP is marked with a bracket as an aid to parsing sentences.

(24)
bikúní	bikuni$_e$ [bifwíídí	'the farmers died'
	farmers died	
	[mweení bíkuni$_e$	'I saw the farmers'
	I-saw farmers	
	bikuni$_e$ [tubavoondidí	'we killed the farmers'
	farmers we-them-killed	
mazóónó	[wakatukidí mázoono$_e$	'he left yesterday'
	he-left yesterday	
lúmbúkí	[kátukidí lúmbukí$_e$	'he left today'
	he-left today	
	lumbukí$_e$ [tudiidí	'we ate today'
	today we-ate	
mankondé	mankonde$_e$ símátootwá	'the bananas will be harvested'
	bananas they-will-be harvested	
	kabadíídí mánkónde$_e$ kó	'they didn't eat bananas'
	not-they-ate bananas not	

Recall that when a noun is preceded by a word, H is added at the left, for instance in *kátukidí lúmbukí*. A comparison with the citation and sentence initial forms reveals that H effacement has applied, and in the postverbal forms as well we see evidence of effacement since the middle vowel of the word has lost its H.

4.1 The Syntactic Context

Below is a listing of various contexts where nouns can be shown to lose their initial H tone.

(25) Subject (before VP)

   Immediately postverbal object, indirect object or adverb.
   Any object, indirect object or adverb precededed
      by an object, indirect object or adverb.
   Preposed object, indirect object or adverb immediately before VP.
   Preposed object, indirect object or adverb separated from VP
      by subject or by another preposed object,
      indirect object or adverb.

We have seen examples of single preverbal adverbs, NP subjects, and NP objects in (24) where Argument Effacement applies. Additional examples, involving full pronouns and proper names, are given below.[9]

(26) móno   'I, me'
      mono$_e$ ndémbidiingí   'I slept'

      béétó   'we, us'
      beeto$_e$ tulémbidiingí   'we slept'

      Bángána   P.N.
      Bangana$_e$ wutumwééní   'Bangana saw us'

      Mayáángi   P.N.
      Bangana$_e$ zéébí Máyáangi$_e$ 'Bangana knows Mayaangi'

In (27) are examples of Effacement applying to both of the postverbal NPs in a double object construction.

---

[9]It appears from the data available to me that pronouns and proper names – and some adverbs – behave slightly differently with respect to tone classes. Specifically, any surface sequence of consecutive H tones is represented as a single multiply linked H. Hence, *béétó* will have a single H linked to every vowel in the word so that application of Argument Effacement to this word will render the word toneless; this is in contrast to the case with *maláálá*, where Argument Effacement only deletes the first H, resulting in *malaalá*.

(27)
[yanwiisa múúntu$_e$ máláfu$_e$ 'I made the person drink wine'
I-made-drink person   wine

(muuntú; malafú)
[ndaambídí kíkuni$_e$ mádéeso$_e$ 'I cooked the farmer beans'
I-cooked-for farmer beans

(madééso)
[ka kiláámbídí kíkuni$_e$ mádéeso$_e$ kó   'I didn't cook the farmer beans'
not I-cook-for farmer beans not

This shows that the rule applies to phrases which do not stand right next to the verb. Analogous examples can be seen in (28) where we have a direct object and an adverb: Argument Effacement applies to both the adverb and the direct object.

(28) [twatootidí mádéeso$_e$ mázoono$_e$
      we-harvested beans   yesterday
      'we harvested beans yesterday'

      mfumu$_e$ [wunámfíla mbóongo$_e$ lúmbukí$_e$
      chief   he-will-me-give money   today
      'the chief will give me money today'

      baana$_e$ [badíídí mádéeso$_e$ lúmbukí$_e$
      boys   they-ate beans   today
      'the boys ate beans today'

Argument Effacement can apply to three phrases in a row, as shown by the double object constructions with an adverb in (29). Here the rule applies to the beneficiary or causee, the direct object, and the adverb.

(29) [ndaambídí kíkuni$_e$ mádéeso$_e$ lúmbukí$_e$
      I-cook-for   farmer   beans   today
      'I cooked the farmer beans today'

      [twanywiisa bákeentó$_e$ máláfu$_e$ mázoono$_e$
      we-cause-drink women   wine   yesterday
      'we had the women drink wine yesterday'

In short, all postverbal phrases within the VP are subject to Argument Effacement.

In addition to applying to the preverbal subject, Argument Effacement will apply to preposed objects and adverbs, and will apply to these phrases across a full NP subject (which itself undergoes the rule). This can be seen in (30), where the preposed adverb *lúmbúkí* comes before the subject *bááná*, and still undergoes Argument Effacement.

(30) baana$_e$ [ka badíídi mádéeso$_e$ lúmbukí$_e$ kó
      children not they-ate beans today not
      'the children didn't eat beans today'

     lumbukí$_e$ báana$_e$ [ka badíídi mádéeso$_e$ kó
     today children not they-ate beans not
     id.

     mukeentó$_e$ [wunátéka mééki$_e$ mbási$_e$
     woman she-will-sell eggs tomorrow
     'tomorrow the woman will sell eggs'

     mbasi$_e$ múkeentó$_e$ [wunátéka mééki$_e$
     tomorrow woman she-will-sell eggs
     id.

     mfumu$_e$ [wunámfíla mbóongo$_e$ lúmbukí$_e$
     chief he-will-me-give money today
     'today the chief will give me money'

     lumbukí$_e$ mfumu$_e$ [wunámfíla mbóongo$_e$
     today chief he-will-me-give money
     id.

A case of multiple preverbal objects and adverbs can be seen in (31), where effacement applies to all of the preposed phrases.

(31) mazoono$_e$ málaalá$_e$ [twasuumbidí   'yesterday we bought oranges'
      yesterday oranges we-bought

Constructions with the copula as the verb also undergo Argument Effacement. Some samples of this are seen in (32), where a noun loses its H before the copula.

(32) kwé mánkónde$_e$ [mená   'where are the bananas?'
     where bananas   they-be
     kwé bíbulu$_e$ [byená   'where are the animals?'
     (bibúlú)
     kwé mághaalá$_e$ [mená   'where are the branches?'

A word order variant of this construction is illustrated in (33) where the noun appears after the copula. Here too Argument Effacement applies—interestingly, there is no H tone at the beginning of the noun, as there has been in all other examples of sentence medial structures. It may simply be that the copula is a lexical exception in not triggering the insertion of H tone, but at any rate we have another context where Argument Effacement applies.

(33) kwé [kwéna malaalá$_e$ 'where are the oranges?'
     kwé [kwéna muungwa$_e$ 'where is the salt?'
     [véna malaalá$_e$ 'where there are oranges?'
     [véna mbeele$_e$ 'where the knife is'
     [ká véna zimbeele$_e$ kó   'where there are no knives'
     banáni [béna bibuunda$_e$ 'who are the elders?'

At this stage, there seems to be only one context where Argument Effacement does *not* apply, and that is in the citation form. In fact, there are other contexts where the rule does not apply. This brings us to a consideration of the focus position for Kikongo, which is one context where nouns do not undergo the rule, and raises the question of the syntactic structure of the focus position within the sentence: we shall see that it is still within the VP.

The leftmost element in the VP is usually the verb, either the main verb or the auxiliary verb in periphrastic constructions, and this verb is the one that bears the subject inflection. Two things can come before the verb in the VP, as illustrated in (34). The first is the negative word *ka* which is always paired with VP-final *ko*, and the second is an object pronoun such as *ya*, which happens to be focused. When both *ka* and a pronoun are present, *ka* precedes the pronoun.

(34) (NEG.) (OBJ.PRO.) SUBJ.+VERB

[twéti tékísá   'we are selling'
we-be sell
[ka twéti tékísá kó   'we are not selling'
not we-be sell   not
[yá twéti tékísá   'we are selling it'
it we-be sell
[ka yá twéti tékísá kó 'we are not selling it'
not it we-be sell not

This construction leads to consideration of another morphosyntactic property of the language, namely the fact that the Class 1 subject prefix on verbs has a syntactically conditioned allomorph. When it is preceded by something within the VP, the prefix takes the form *ka* or phonetic variants thereof. Otherwise, when VP-initial, the prefix is *wu* or ∅ as is appropriate for the verb tense. So the 3 singular prefix is *wu* in the first example below, and *ka* in the other examples.

(35) ALTERNATION *ka* ~ *wu*
[wéti tékísá   'he is selling'
(wu-eti → weti)
[ka kéti tékísá kó   'he is not selling'
(ka-eti → keti)
[yá kéti tékísá   'he is selling *it*'
[ka yá kéti tékísá kó   'he is not selling *it*'

Data demonstrating that it is initiality in the VP, not initiality in the sentence, which determines the choice of *ka* versus *wu* are given in (36). Here we find *wu* when the verb is VP initial, even though the verb is not sentence initial.

(36) mwaana [wéti tékísá   'the child is selling'
     mwaana [ka kéti tékísá kó   'the child is not selling'
     mwaana [yá kéti tékísá   'the child is selling *it*'
     mwaana [ka yá kéti tékísá kó   'the child is not selling *it*'

In order to capture these generalizations regarding the allomorphy of the Class 1 verbal subject prefix, it is necessary for the negative and the slot for the focused object pronoun to have some special constituent relationship with the VP, to make it distinct from the subject NP, which also precedes the verb. There are many possible structures which could capture this relation: (37) is chosen somewhat arbitrarily, but seems one of the more natural and simple analyses.

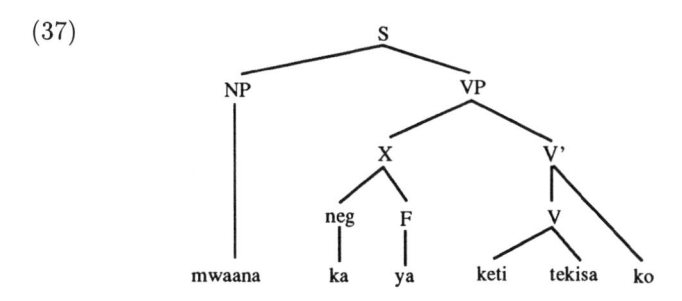

(37)

```
                    S
              ┌─────┴─────┐
             NP           VP
              │       ┌────┴────┐
              │       X         V'
              │     ┌─┴─┐    ┌──┴──┐
              │    neg  F    V
              │     │   │   ┌─┴─┐
           mwaana   ka  ya keti tekisa  ko
```

The interesting property of the slot marked F in (37) is that a full phrase can be put there if it is focused. Two other things are noteworthy, looking at the examples in (38). First, when the verb is VP initial in the perfective tense, the zero allomorph of the 3rd singular subject prefix is selected over the variant *wu*, whereas when the focus position is filled with a noun phrase, the verb takes the VP-medial variant with *ka-* (marked "med"), as predicted. Second – and this is the most important point – a phrase in the focus position does not undergo Argument Effacement. However, a noun phrase preceding the phrase in the focus position does undergo the rule, as the second and last examples below show.

(38)

mwaana_e [vóóndídí bíkuni_e   'the child killed the farmers'
child   he-killed   farmers
(mwááná)
mwaana_e [bikúní kavóóndídí   'the child killed the *farmers*'
       ↑_____|
child   farmers (med)he-killed

[ka kavóóndídí bíkuni_e kó   'he didn't kill the farmers'
not (med)he-killed farmers not
[ka bikúní kavóóndídí   kó   'he didn't kill *the farmers*'
  ↑_____|
not farmers (med)he-killed   not
mwaana_e [ka kavóóndídí bíkuni kó   'the child didn't kill the farmers'
child   not (med)he-kill farmers not

mwaana_e [ka bikúní kavóóndídí kó   'the child didn't kill *the farmers*'
child   not farmers (med)he-kill not

Why these phrases do not undergo Argument Effacement is the fundamental question regarding this rule.

A further illustration of the focus construction is in (39), which contains examples of the 'NP is NP' construction. The nominal predicate is focused, and stands before the copula. The subject undergoes Argument Effacement, but the noun in the focal position does not.

(39)   muloongi_e [kikúní kyéna   'the teacher is a *farmer*'
        kikuni_e [muloongí kéna   'the farmer is a *teacher*'

More examples of elements in the focus position can be seen in (40), with additional types of predicative structures involving demonstratives. In the first three examples, the NP is focused, so is moved into the focus position, and does not undergo Argument Effacement. The first example is a focused nominal which precedes the copula, and we note that the tones of the focused noun are unaffected, though the H of the preceding demonstrative which serves as the subject is deleted. The second example shows that the demonstrative is optional. The third example shows that the copula is also optional. The actual presence of a verb word is irrelevant in calculating the ability of the noun to be in the focus position. In the final example, the demonstrative is focused so it does not undergo Argument Effacement, but the subject NP is not focused so it loses its H tone.

(40) ema [maláálá ména   'these are *oranges*'
     [maláálá ména   =
     edi [kokotí   'this is *coconut*'
     edi [ka kokotí kó   'this is not a *coconut*'
     (cf. kokoti [edí   '*this* is coconut')

To summarize, we have seen that Argument Effacement applies to the noun which is the head of a phrase, if the phrase stands in any of the boxed positions in (41), but the rule does not apply when the phrase is in the focused slot, which is circled, and the rule does not apply to phrases in isolation.

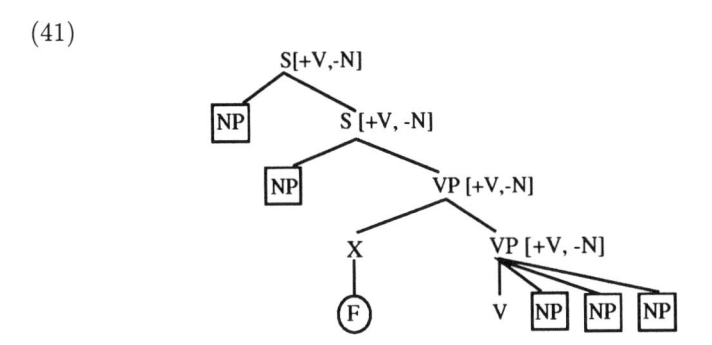

(41)

There is a generalization to be captured here, and that is that the head of an NP undergoes Argument Effacement if it is immediately dominated by S or VP. If we give a feature analysis of S and VP such that both are [+V,-N] and differ only in the feature [SUBJ], we can state the rule as applying to NPs immediately dominated by a maximal projection of [+V,-N].

(42) *Argument Effacement*
     H → ∅ / [$_{[+V,-N]}$max ... [$_{NP}$ [$_N$ ... __ ...] ...] ...]

Although it isn't clear what X is, it is clear that it *isn't* a VP or an S, so the reason why nouns in the focus position do not undergo Effacement is that they are not immediately dominated by the required category.

It is worthwhile to reflect for a moment on the issue of the conditioning factor for Argument Effacement. This rule seems to be the most extreme form of syntactic conditioning of phonological rules that one can imagine. The role of syntactic structure in conditioning certain rules of Kimatuumbi (Odden 1987) is quite significant—for example, Shortening applies to the head of X' followed by phonetic material with no regard for other properties of the following word. Nevertheless, it is crucial that some word actually follow the focus, in order for Shortening to apply. The situation is Kikongo is more extreme: it does not matter if any word precedes or follows the target of Argument Effacement. All that is important is that the word be dominated by the requisite syntactic node.

Examples from conjoined noun phrases show that the first conjunct undergoes Argument Effacement.[10]

(43)
nsuumbidí mbisi$_e$ ye méeki   'I bought meat and eggs'
I-bought   meat   and eggs

Bangana$_e$ tekisi másaangu$_e$ ye lóóso   'Bangana sold corn and rice'
Bangana   he-sold corn   and rice

mbisi$_e$ ye méeki bibódidi   'the meat and eggs rotted'
meat   and eggs they-rotted

mbeele$_e$ ye kííbi byáméeno byayíbúlú   'a sharp ax and knife were found'
knife   and axe sharp   they-were-found

Given the usual assumptions about the syntax of conjunctions, the first example of (43) should have something like the following structure.[11]

---

[10]It is impossible to tell whether the second conjunct undergoes Argument Effacement, since the conjunction *ye* itself has a tonal effect, adding a H to the following noun which makes it impossible to see if Argument Effacement applies.

[11]Rather than employing an autonomous conjunction analogous to 'and', Kikongo marks the second conjunct with the instrumental preposition *ye-*.

(44)

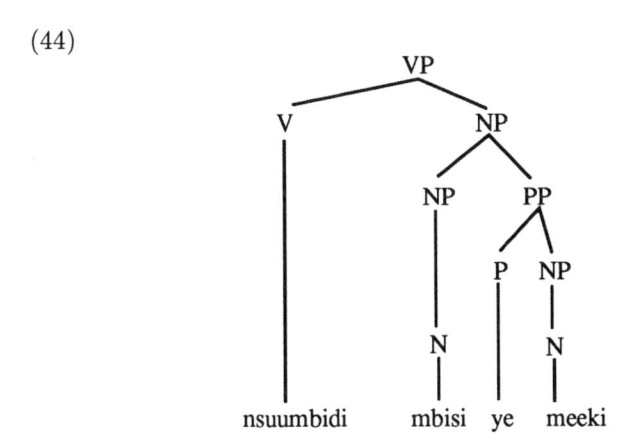

```
            VP
          /    \
         V      NP
         |    /    \
         |   NP    PP
         |   |    /  \
         |   |   P    NP
         |   |   |    |
         |   N   |    N
         |   |   |    |
      nsuumbidi mbisi ye meeki
```

The problem which this poses is that the N" immediately dominating the noun which undergoes the rule is not itself immediately dominated by a maximal projection of [+V,-N]—rather, it is immediately dominated by another N", which is itself immediately dominated by the relevant phrasal category. On those grounds, Argument Effacement might be blocked. We cannot dispose of the problem by positing an independent rule which deletes H from the first half of a conjunction, since conjunctions in isolation do not undergo Argument Effacement. Nor does a conjoined NP lose its H when it stands in the focus position.

(45) mbééle ye kííbi   'knife and axe'
     masáángú ye lóóso   'corn and rice'
     Bangana$_e$ [masáángú ye lóóso katékísí   'Bangana sold *corn
     and rice'

The reason why Argument Effacement applies in conjunctions is that the higher N" is transparent—there is an unbroken chain of projections of N between the noun and the projection of the verb.

Nouns which are the objects of prepositions are potentially interesting for understanding what syntactic contexts trigger Argument Effacement. First we consider noun phrases in isolation which contain possessor NPs. If the possessor noun is of the H-plateauing set, both Hs of dimoraic nouns or the initial H of polymoraic nouns is shifted to the noun class prefix (which then spreads to a following stem vowel).

(46) bikúní   'farmers'
      zimbééle zabíkúni   'knives of the farmers'

      matádí   'stones'
      kúlééri za-mátádi   'colors of the stones'

      malááló   'oranges'
      kipáánú kya-máláalá   'basket of oranges'

      kipáánú   'basket'
      musiimbulú wa-kípáanú   'handle of the basket'

      kikálúngúlú   'frying pan'
      mutí wa-kíkálungulú   'handle of the frying pan'

Otherwise there is no change in the tonal shape of the possessor noun.

(47) mankondé   'bananas'
      kipáánú kya-mankondé   'basket of bananas'

      mbééle   'knife'
      mutí wa-mbééle   'handle of the knife'

      mpoká   'animal horn'
      kúlééri ya-mpoká   'color of animal horn'

      mukúúnga   'song'
      máázú ma-mukúúnga   'sound of song'

      kinikunú   'grinding tool'
      yúlu dya-kinikunú   'top of grinding tool'

      kisakalá   'pile'
      yúlu dya-kisakalá   'top of pile'

      Mayáánsi   (PN)
      mwááná wa-Mayáánsi   'child of Mayansi'

If an NP containing a possessive phrase stands in a sentential context where Argument Effacement might be applicable, we find that while the head noun of the phrase undergoes the rule, Argument Effacement cannot apply to the noun within the possessive phrase.

(48) mwaana$_e$ waMayáánsi wufwíídí
 child   of-Mayansi   s/he died'
 'the child of Mayansi died'

 mbweení maghaayi$_e$ mamalémbelémbe
 I-saw   wings   of-lembelembe's
 'I saw the wings of the lembelembe's'

The syntactic structure of the second example would be as follows.

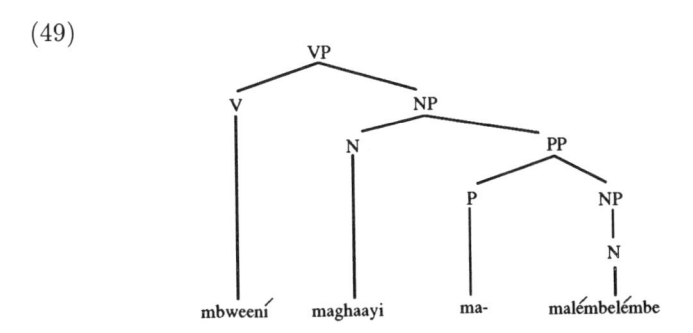

(49)

```
                    VP
              ┌──────┴──────┐
              V             NP
              │        ┌────┴────┐
              │        N         PP
              │        │    ┌────┴────┐
              │        │    P         NP
              │        │    │         │
              │        │    │         N
              │        │    │         │
           mbweení  maghaayi ma-   malémbelémbe
```

The NP immediately dominating *malembelembe* is itself dominated by PP (which has the features [-N,-V]), and that structure does not trigger the Argument Effacement rule.

A similar failure of Argument Effacement is seen in (50), where the noun *muuntú* within the PP does not undergo the rule, since PP intervenes between the NP containing *muuntú* and the VP which triggers the rule.

(50) yavaana mbwááta kwa-muuntú   'I gave the bottle to the person'
     I-gave   bottle   to-person

It should be pointed out, though, that this behavior could be attributed to a nonsyntactic fact. In each of these cases, the preposition is realized as a prefix which appears at the left of the lexical class prefix of the head noun. The behavior of these examples could be accounted for if deletion of H tone is constrained to apply only to nouns lacking such prefixes, in which case these examples have no bearing on the syntactic context where the rule applies.

4.2 The Semantic Restriction

So far we have only considered nouns which are the sole word in their phrase. It is now time to consider what effect the presence of other modifiers in the phrase has on Argument Effacement. As we see in (51), the rule generally applies if modifiers follow the noun within the phrase.

(51) bikuni$_e$ byámbóte bifwíídí   'good farmers died'
       farmers   good   they-died
       bikuni$_e$ byáBánduundu bifwíídí   'farmers of Bandundu died'
       farmers   of Bandundu   they-died

       mweení bíkuni$_e$ byámbóte   'I saw good farmers'
       I-saw   farmers   good
       mweení bíkuni$_e$ byáBánduundu   'I saw farmers of Bandundu'
       I-saw   farmers   of Bandundu

But if the phrase contains a non-universal quantifier, Argument Effacement is blocked. Consider first the postverbal examples in (52). Direct objects after the verb normally undergo Effacement. However, if the phrase contains quantifiers such as 'other', 'many' or numerals, there is no deletion of the H tone. Thus *bikúní* retains its H in all the forms in (52).

(52) tubweení bikúní bítaanú   'we saw five farmers'
       we-saw   farmers   five
       tubweení bikúní bítaanú byánúna   'we saw five old farmers'
       we-saw   farmers   five   old
       tubweení bikúní byánkáka   'we saw other farmers'
       we-saw   farmers   other
       ka tubwééní bikúní bítatú kó   'we didn't see three farmers'
       not we-saw   farmers   three   not
       ka tubwééní bikúní byabííngi kó   'we didn't see many farmers'
       not we-saw   farmers   many   not

The head noun of an object phrase containing a universal quantifier is not prevented from losing its H tone: this is because, as we have seen, aside from the blocking effect of quantifiers on Argument Effacement, universal quantifiers themselves independently trigger their own rule of H tone deletion.

(53) tubweení bíkuni byábínsó   'we met all the farmers'
       tubweení bíkuni byábítatú   'we met all 3 farmers'

Other examples, seen in (54), show that the blocking effect of a quantifier affects only the phrase containing the quantifier, and that blocking within the phrase holds no matter whether the quantifier immediately follows the head noun or is separated from the head by another modifier. In the first example, the noun *miloongí* does not lower when the quantifier immediately follows the noun, and in the second example *miloongí* does not lower when the quantifier is separated from the noun by another modifier. In either case, the presence of a quantifier in the first phrase does not prevent the rule from applying to *lúmbúkí*.

(54) tubweení miloongí myamííngi myáKínshasa lúmbukí$_e$
 we-saw teachers many of Kinshasa today
 'we saw many teachers of Kinshasa today'

 tubweení miloongí myáKínshasa myamííngi lúmbukí$_e$
 we-saw teachers of Kinshasa many today

In (55) are examples of preverbal subjects which contain quantifiers; these subjects are also immune to Effacement. The verb following a finitely quantified subject has the relative clause form, indicated in the examples as "RC."[12]

(55) bikúní bítatú bíkinini   'three farmers danced'
 farmers three they-danced(RC)
 bikúní byabííngi bíkinini   'many farmers danced'
 farmers many they-danced(RC)
 bikúní byafyóotí bíkinini   'some farmers danced'
 farmers few they-danced(RC)

Similarly, subject NPs containing quantifiers as well as other modifiers do not undergo Argument Effacement, regardless of the order of the blocking quantifier and other modifiers.

---

[12] In a number of other Bantu languages – e.g., Shona and Kenyang – a verb preceded by a WH-subject is in the relative clause form; we will see that this is true for Kikongo as well. The difference is that Kikongo has expanded the range of modifiers within the subject which trigger selection of the relative clause verb form. The relative clause form of the verb is distinguished from the main clause variant only by tone: the subject prefix in a relative clause verb is H-toned whereas in a main clause it is L-toned, and (roughly) in the relative clause form the initial H of the stem (found in main clause verbs) is deleted.

(56) bikúní bítatú byáBánduundu bíkinini
    farmers three of Bandundu they-danced(RC)
   'three farmers from Banduundu danced'

   bikúní byáBánduundu bítatú bíkinini
    farmers of Bandundu three they-danced(RC)
   id.

As (57) demonstrates, the blocking effect of a quantifier is limited to the phrase containing the quantifier. Any preposed adverb will undergo Argument Effacement, even if the following subject NP contains a quantifier.

(57) mazóónó   'yesterday'
     mazoono$_e$ bááná bátatú báyelé   kúlúkoolo
     yesterday children three they-went(RC) to school
     'yesterday three children went to school'

     lúmbúkí   'today'
     lumbukí$_e$ bikúní bítatú bífwiidi
     today   farmers three they-died(RC)
     'today three farmers died'

In addition to the obvious quantifiers, WH-words, which are classically treated as a kind of quantifier (Engdahl 1986), also prevent the application of Effacement to the noun. Examples of WH-words blocking application of Effacement to the subject can be seen in (58). This blocking effect even holds within a conjoined NP.

(58)
bikúní bíkwa   bíkinini   'how many farmers danced?'
 farmers how many they-danced(RC)
bikúní byánáni bíkinini   'whose farmers danced?'
 farmers of-who they-danced(RC)
mééki yé mbisi byá náni bíbódidi   'whose eggs and meat rotted?'
 eggs and meat of who they-rotted(RC)

Finally, we see examples of object NPs containing WH-words in (59). The blocking effect of WH-modifiers on objects can only be illustrated with sentence-initial objects, due to WH-movement. WH-marked object phrases move from postverbal position to the preverbal focus position, and then move to the front of the sentence, leaving a trace in the focus position which triggers the selection of the VP-medial subject marker *ka*. We see that objects with WH-words in them also do not undergo Argument Effacement.

(59) bikúní bíkwa kamwééní   'how many farmers did he see?'

   bikúní byánáni kamwééní   'whose farmers did he see?'

   bikúní bíkwa   mwaana$_e$[_t__ kamwééní__
   ↑_____↑_____|
   farmers how many   child   (med)he-saw

   'how many farmers did the child see?'

   bikúní yánáni mwaana$_e$ kamwééní
   farmers of-who child   (med)he-saw

   'whose farmers did the child see?'

   bikúní bíkwa   byáBánduundu múlóongi$_e$ kazóónsidí yébyó
   farmers how many of B.   teacher   (med)he-speak with-them
   'how many farmers of Bandundu did the teacher speak with?'

There is another line of evidence showing that presence of a quantifier in the semantic representation of the phrase blocks Argument Effacement. Examples of two kinds of associative construction are given in (60). In the first example in each pair, we find a partitive genitive, that is, a use of the associative construction to indicate a quantity of the substance in question. In these examples, Effacement is blocked. The second example of each pair is a possessive genitive, and here Effacement is not blocked.

(60)
nsuumbidí muteté wabyáási   'I bought a box of palm fruits'
ntekisí mútéte$_e$ wampángyáámí   'I sold my brother's box'
nwiini kóópó dyamíliki   'I drank a cup of milk'
mbwiisidí kóópo$_e$ dyampángyáámí 'I dropped my brother's cup'
katutwéédi mbííndá yamázá kó   'we didn't bring a gourd of water'
katutwéédi mbiinda$_e$ yamwáána kó 'we didn't bring the child's gourd'
mweeni mbwaatá yamalafú   'I found a bottle of wine'
nziimbisí mbwáata$_e$ yakíkúni   'I lost the farmer's bottle'

The verb has the relative clause form when the subject contains a partitive genitive, just as it does in general when the subject is a quantifier.

Furthermore, Argument Effacement does not apply to the subject.

(61) mbwaatá yamafutá yísamukiní   'the bottle of oil spilled'
      bottle   of-oil   it-spilled(RC)

      mbwaata$_e$ yatááta yisámukiní   'father's bottle spilled'
      bottle   of-father it-spilled

This distribution is as predicted, under the hypothesis that Argument Effacement is blocked by the presence of a quantifier in the phrase.

Therefore, Argument Effacement must be stated so the rule is blocked in case the phrase contains a quantifier in the semantic representation. Moreover, as the examples of partitive genitives have demonstrated, the head noun is not always followed by a word which is a quantifier—indeed, in such examples the syntactic head noun in the phrase arguably *is* the quantifier. As a small side issue, there is no standard symbol which conventionally represents quantifiers of all types, so the class of quantifiers will be referred to as Q.

(62) *Argument Effacement* (revised)

$$H \to \emptyset \;/\; [\; _{[+V,-N]}{}^{max} \;\ldots\; [_{NP}\; [_N \;\ldots\; \sim\; Q \;\ldots\;]\;\ldots\;]\;\ldots\;]$$

5 Further Problems

There remain a few problems which have not yet been integrated into the overall picture, and we turn to these problems here.

5.1 Relative Clause Verbs

As (63) shows, a noun which is the head of a relative clause (be it subject or object within the relative clause) also loses its first H tone, even when that NP does not stand in a complete sentence.

(63) zinzúúngu   'pots'
      zinzuungu$_e$ zábafyétikisi   'the pots that they squeezed'

      ngoombé   'cow'
      ngoombe$_e$ zíkavóóndídí   'the cows which he killed'
      ngoombe$_e$ zímúvoondidi   'the cows which killed him'
      ngoombe$_e$ zimuvóóndídí   'the cows killed him'

      mwííkú   'spoon'
      mwiiku$_e$ wúyikuvééní   'the spoon which I gave you'

Note also that if the noun is modified by a quantifier, it does not lose its H tone, either in isolation or in sentential contexts where Argument Effacement applies.

(64) díídí mankondé mamííngi mánimuvééní
      'he ate many bananas which I gave him'

      ntekisí bikálúngúlú byabííngi bíyídíkídí
      'I sold many frying pans that you fixed'

The problem which this poses is that in all other examples, nouns do not undergo Argument Effacement if they are in phrases not immediately dominated by VP or S. A relative clause should be simply another kind of modifier, so there is no structural reason why Argument Effacement should apply, given the present understanding of the conditions under which that rule applies. It is possible that there is another rule of tone deletion, which affects nouns modified by relative clauses—such a rule would also have to be blocked from applying if the phrase contains a quantifier.

5.2 Picture Phrases

As seen in (65a), the noun *fotó* 'picture' undergoes Argument Effacement even when modified by a possessor, and when *fotó* is the subject, the verb selects the usual main clause form. However, as (65b) shows, when the modifier of *fotó* is the person in the picture, *fotó* does not undergo Argument Effacement, and the verb has the relative clause form. In short, picture phrases behave as though they contain a quantifier.

(65) a. foto_e kibwíídi váméesa
    picture it-fell   on-table
    'the picture fell on the table'

    nzukudí fóto_e kyáándi
    'I found his picture' (=picture which he owns)

  b. fotó kyáámi kíbwíidi váméesa
    picture mine it-fell(RC) on-table
    'the picture of me fell on the table'

    nzukudí fotó kyáándi
    'I found a picture of him'

Why picture noun phrases should behave this way is unclear at present.

5.3 Demonstratives

Finally, there seems to be an extension of Universal Effacement, whereby nouns modified by demonstrative pronouns may also lose their H tone. It appears that this rule (or extension of Universal Effacement) is optional, whereas the application of the rule in the environment of a universal quantifier appears to be obligatory.[13]

(66) kyaandú   'chair'   kyaandu ékina 'that chair'
    byáási   'palm fruits'   byaasi ébyo 'those palm fruits'
    zisábúúni 'soaps'   zisábúúni ézo ∼
                               zisabúúni ézo 'those soaps'

It is unclear why this kind of extension of Universal Effacement should be found.

6 A Prosodic Account

This section briefly shows why a prosodic account of H deletion in Kikongo is simply impossible. This then supports the claim of Kaisse (1985) and Odden (1987) that phonological rules may have direct access to syntactic – and, as the evidence given here has shown, semantic – levels of representation. Even ignoring the issue of how semantic properties either trigger or

---

[13]In my data, the overwhelming majority of tokens of phrases containing a universal quantifier show loss of H tone, whereas with phrases containing a demonstrative there is a significant number of tokens where there is no loss of H.

block rules, just stating the conditions for Argument Effacement prosodically is impossible. Consider the fact that the nouns in the structures of (67a) do not undergo Argument Effacement, but those of (67b) do.

(67) a. kikálúngúlú   'frying pan'
       kikálúngúlú kyakínéne 'small frying pan'

    b. kikalungulú$_e$ kibwíídi   'the frying pan fell'
       nsuumbidí kikalungulú$_e$ 'I bought a frying pan'

Since the citation form stands at the end of every phonological domain, the triggering factor cannot be domain final position—similarly, since the citation form is also at the beginning of every phonological domain, the trigger cannot be merely domain initial position. Therefore, Argument Effacement must be a domain juncture rule (Nespor and Vogel 1986).

To represent the difference between *kikalungulú kibwíídi* where H is deleted, and *kikálúngúlú kyakínéne*, where H is not deleted, in prosodic terms, we must group these words into phonological constituents differently. We start with the natural assumption that sets of words within a syntactic phrase are parsed into a single lower level constituent of the prosodic hierarchy, and that groups of syntactic phrases which form higher level clauses are parsed into a higher level constituent of the prosodic hierarchy. Hence the following prosodic grouping would be needed.

(68) [kikálúngúlú kyakínéne]$_{Dn}$
      [[kikalungulú$_e$]$_{Dn}$ [kibwíídi]$_{Dn}$]$_{Dn+j}$
      [[nsuumbidí]$_{Dn}$ [kíkálúngúlú$_e$]$_{Dn}$]$_{Dn+j}$

We might then attempt to state the rule as deleting H from a noun at the beginning of domain D_n if preceded or followed by another D_n within domain D_{n+j}. Since the noun may precede or follow the verb and undergoes Argument Effacement in either case, the linear order of the two constituents is irrelevant. Furthermore, for this approach to have any effect, we must not allow the verb and a following object within the VP to group together in D_n, since doing so would not result in the required joined domains which trigger deletion of H.

Since multiple postverbal (or preverbal) constituents can undergo the rule, D_{n+j} must contain multiple occurrences of D_n.

(69) [[twatootidí]$_{Dn}$ [mádéeso$_e$]$_{Dn}$ [mázoono$_e$]$_{Dn}$]$_{Dn+j}$
      'we harvested beans yesterday'

Now we face the problem of excluding any element within the focus position from the rule. To handle the contrast between (70a) and (70b) we must assign different domains to these structures.

(70)   a.   kikalungulú$_e$ [$_{VP}$ kibwíídi]   'the frying pan fell'
       b.   [$_{VP}$ kikálúngúlú katékísí]   'he sold the frying pan'

The general rule for grouping domain D_n, which applies to syntactic phrases, will automatically place the focused NP in its own domain D_n. We do not want (70a) and (70b) to group together in the same way. Furthermore, recall that a subject NP which precedes a noun in the focus position does undergo Argument Effacement (cf. *mwaana$_e$* [$_{VP}$ *bikúní kavóóndídí* 'the child killed the farmer'). This can be handled if we adopt the following phonological constituency.

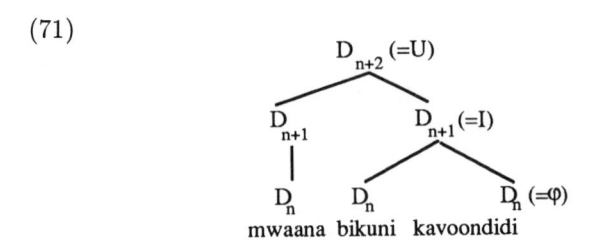

(71)

```
              D_{n+2} (=U)
             /          \
          D_{n+1}      D_{n+1} (=I)
            |          /       \
           D_n       D_n        D_n (=φ)
         mwaana    bikuni    kavoondidi
```

By assumption, D_{n+1} will generally be nonbranching, with the exception that a noun in the focus position groups with the following verb under D_{n+1}. At this point, we will decide what specific domains we are speaking of: D_n is φ, D_{n+1} is I, and D_{n+2} is U.

With this constituency, Argument Effacement might be stated as follows.

(72)   H → ∅ / [$_U$ ... [$_{I\alpha}$ _   ] [$_I$]...]   where I_α does not branch

The non-branching condition prohibits a noun in the focus position from undergoing the rule, since the only branching I-phrase dominates the focused noun and the following verb.

However, this does not suffice. Recall that nouns can be in the focus position and not be followed by a verb – for example *edi* [$_{VP}$ *kokotí* – and do not lose their H. The structure of this example must be as follows.

(73)
```
         U
        / \
       I   I
       |   |
       φ   φ
      edi_e kokotí
```

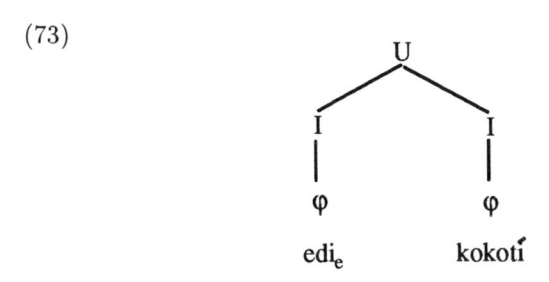

Since neither I-phrase branches, both nominals should undergo Argument Effacement: nothing in the prosodic account explains why only the first in fact does.

7 Conclusions

To conclude, we have seen that phonological rules of Kikongo can be sensitive to the feature representation of syntactic nodes, and also to semantic properties. This latter conclusion is no doubt the more startling one, and it raises the question of what the full range of semantic properties is that phonological rules might be sensitive to. It is obviously too early to speculate about what kinds of other cases there might be in language, so the answer to this question must be left to future research.

References

Engdahl, E. 1986. *Constituent questions: The syntax and semantics of questions with special reference to Swedish.* Dordrecht: Kluwer.

Goldsmith, D. 1987. Tone and accent and getting the two together. *BLS* 13:88–104.

Hayes, B. 1989. The prosodic hierarchy in meter. In P. Kiparsky and G. Youmans 1989.

Inkelas, S. 1989. *Prosodic constituency in the lexicon.* Ph.D. dissertation, Stanford University.

Kaisse, E. 1985. *Connected speech.* Orlando: Academic Press.

Kiparsky, P. and G. Youmans (eds.). 1989. *Rhythm and meter.* Orlando: Academic Press.

Nespor, M. and I. Vogel. 1986. *Prosodic phonology.* Dordrecht: Foris.

Odden, D. 1987. Kimatuumbi phrasal phonology. *Phonology yearbook* 4:13-26.

Odden, D. 1990. VVNC in Kimatuumbi and Kikongo. *South African Journal of African Languages* 10.4:159–165.

Selkirk, E. O. 1986. On derived domains in sentence phonology. *Phonology yearbook* 3:371-405.

Zec, D. and S. Inkelas. 1990. Prosodically constrained syntax. In Inkelas and Zec (eds.), *The phonology-syntax connection* (pp. 365-378). Chicago: University of Chicago Press.

Complex Onsets as Single Segments: The Mazateco Pattern

Donca Steriade
UCLA

1 Introduction[1]

1.1 Summary

In 1947, Kenneth and Eunice Pike (PP) published an analysis of syllable structure in Huautla Mazateco, an Otomanguean language of Oaxaca, Mexico. PP's study of Mazateco is the first systematic illustration of the idea that syllables have hierarchically arranged internal structure, or, as PP put it, "successive layers of immediate constituents" (1947:78). In this account, the onsets of Mazateco, in addition to the rimes, were analyzed in terms of headed subconstituents: each complex onset contained a principal and a subordinate constituent, and each principal constituent could in turn be divided into a principal and a subordinate member. I offer here a new analysis of PP's data, which eschews constituent structure in onsets, but does offer an understanding of the basic intuition that led PP to the principal/subordinate distinction.

The analysis I present will rely on the hypothesis that plosives (stops and affricates) have representations in which their closure and release appear as distinct positions, capable of independently anchoring distinctive features. The Mazateco data, along with similar patterns of onset formation from other Amerindian languages, will show that plosives have more clustering possibilities than continuants, because plosives are bipositional.

A distinct ingredient of our account will be the idea that the degree of markedness in onset clusters is at least in part determined by the degree of similarity between the cluster and a single consonant: the better the onset, the closer it is in structure and feature composition to a single segment.

Although most aspects of the onset inventory discussed here are independently attested in other American Indian languages, the overall system, shown below in (1), looks highly unusual when compared to the obstruent-

---

[1] The material presented here originates as lecture notes for a UCLA seminar in the Spring of 1991. I am grateful to the participants for their comments. I would also like to thank the members of the UCLA phonetics Laboratory, who made possible the completion of this work by providing help and companionship: Dani Byrd, Edward Flemming, Rob Hagiwara, Joyce McDonough and Michael Shalev.

liquid or obstruent-glide clusters found in the better-studied Indo-European or South-East Asian languages:

(1) The Mazateco onset inventory in outline

    a.   n-plosive   h-plosive   ʔ-plosive   consonant-h   consonant-ʔ
            n-plosive-h
            n-plosive-ʔ
            ʔ-n-plosive
            h-n-plosive

    b.   s-plosive
            s-plosive-ʔ

Some Mazateco dialects possess both the (1.a) and the (1.b) clusters, while others are limited to a subset of the clusters in (1.a). The suggestion made here is that onset systems like (1) are governed by the same organizing principles as standard onset inventories of the type {single C; or pr, tr, kr, pl, kl}. If anything, the more unusual cluster set in (1.a) will emerge as better, i.e., structurally closer to the optimal single C onset, than the standard collection of obstruent-liquid clusters.

1.2 Constituent Structure

The aspect of PP's study that I focus on here is their hierarchical analysis of Mazateco onsets. Their claim is that a complex onset divides between a principal and a subordinate constituent. An example is /ntsʔ/ which is analyzed into the subordinate /n/ and the principal unit /tsʔ/. The principal unit further subdivides into a principal (/ts/) and a subordinate (/ʔ/) member. In bracketed notation, the structure PP assigned to such strings would be [n[[ts]ʔ]].

More recent attempts to find hierarchical structure within the syllable – beyond the widely, though not universally, accepted division into rime and onset – have not met with considerable success. Kiparsky (1979, 1980) and Cairns and Feinstein (1982) have claimed that certain phonotactic properties of the onset can be expressed with the help of constituent structure. But neither proposal would be compatible with Pike and Pike's findings in Mazateco, as we shall see. Levin (1985) has used the X-bar notions of head, complement and specifier to distinguish subconstituents of the syllable. Levin's head/non-head distinction does correspond to PP's principal/subordinate distinction. But Levin did not find compelling reasons to extend this distinction to the onset. In general one expects all prosodic constituents – above and below the level of the syllable – to be the domain of phonological rule application. But the subconstituents of the onset, in all theories that postulate them, never play this role of prosodic domain.[2] Their only function is to facilitate some characterization of the notion possible onset in language L. This is, in part, why we view them with some doubt.

At the same time, PP were clearly justified in thinking that there are differences of status between the various components of a Mazateco onset. The central observation in this regards is that, while any Mazateco consonant can be the unique occupant of the onset position, larger onset clusters divide into members that are largely unrestricted and members drawn from a very small, systematically restricted set of non-primary articulations: the laryngeals, /h/ and /ʔ/, and nasality, transcribed as /n/. PP called the unrestricted members principal and the restricted ones subordinate. (Hockett (1955), who had adopted some of their ideas, referred to the subordinate members as *satellites*, a term I will occasionally use here.). Thus /ts/ is the principal member of the onset [n[[ts]ʔ]] because any plosive could occupy its position. /N/ and /ʔ/ are subordinate, or satellites, because one cannot randomly substitute segments for them and still obtain a well-formed Mazateco onset: in this particular cluster only /h/ could be substituted for /ʔ/ (yielding /ntsh/) and only /h/ could replace /n/ (yielding /hts/), though not both simultaneously (since all /hCh/ are disallowed). I will review below the grounds for this distinction between restricted and unrestricted members. But two fundamental points can be made immediately. First, any description of Mazateco must explain the restrictions on cluster composition which PP characterized by means of headed constituent structure: we must understand why it is that only /h/, /ʔ/ and /n/ are satellites in the Mazateco onset system and under what conditions they may co-occur with other features. Second, there is no intrinsic connection between the fact that the satellites belong to the small set of non-oral articulations and the hierarchical relations postulated by PP. Neither PP nor Hockett explained what exactly it was that the primary/subordinate distinction contributed to an explanation of the facts they recorded. Any other way of formally encoding the patterning differences would appear to do as well. The analysis proposed below will seek to give a non-arbitrary characterization of these properties.

1.3 Aperture Positions and Patterns of Association

One of the most striking facts about Mazateco complex onsets is that plosives differ from continuants in their clustering possibilities. Although the Mazateco consonant inventory is roughly evenly divided between plosives

---

[2]CF. Clements and Keyser (1983) and McCarthy and Prince (1986) for discussion.

and continuants, plosives give rise to significantly larger numbers of combinations. In particular, plosives may be followed or preceded by the laryngeal consonants /h/ and /ʔ/, while continuants can be, with minor surface exceptions, only followed by /h/ and /ʔ/. This has nothing to do with relative sonority: the stops /n/ and /t/ function in this respect alike, although their sonority status relative to fricatives like /s/ is quite different.

The observation that clustering possibilities are more extensive for plosives than for continuants is not an isolated one. Cluster patterns similar to those of Mazateco will be examined later in this paper. And I have argued elsewhere (Steriade 1992) that the cross-linguistic realization of nasality occasions a similar contrast between plosives and continuants: plosives can be oral, nasal, prenasal or postnasal whereas continuants can be either oral or fully nasal, displaying no true phonological instances of nasal contours. The suggested interpretation for this fact is that stops and affricates carry two positions – closure and release – whereas continuants carry only one. Nasality, a privative feature, can be realized on closure, on release, on both or on neither thus yielding, potentially, a four-way contrast, as in (2.a). Continuants, on the other hand, because they lack a second position, can display only a two-way contrast: [nasal] is either associated to their unique position or not associated at all, as shown in (2.b). (C= Closure; R=Release)

(2) Nasality and A-positions:

   a. nasal stop   prenasal stop   postnasal stop   oral stop

       [nas]   [nas]   [nas]
       / \ | |
       C R   C R   C R   C R

   b. nasal continuants   oral continuants

       [nas]
        |
        R   R

As can be inferred from (2), I view released stops as sequences of closure plus release, and continuants as positions identical in type to the release varieties attested on plosives. I refer to closure and release as Aperture (A) positions and assume that they are defined in terms of degree of oral aperture. The total inventory of consonant A positions assumed here is: closure (defined as minimal aperture; A_0), fricative (intermediate aperture,

Complex Onsets as Single Segments: The Mazateco Pattern   207

sufficient to create turbulent airflow; A_f), approximant (maximal aperture for a consonant; A_{max}). I leave open the question of how to represent, in terms of A positions, the distinction between approximants and vowels. Where needed for purposes of illustration, I will represent vowels as A_{vowel} positions, without however making a serious commitment to such a category. Also left open is the question of possible additional stricture distinctions within the approximant class.

(3)   Some frequent sound classes represented in terms of A-positions

    released stops: $A_0 A_{max}$ approximants: A_{max}

    affricates: $A_0 A_f$ fricatives: A_f

    unreleased stops: A_0

If the analysis of nasal contours sketched in (2) is on the right track, it suggests that features other than nasality can similarly contrast in their association mode to the A positions of a consonant. An analysis of the Mazateco data will allow us to investigate this possibility for the laryngeal features of aspiration and glottalization. We will encounter in Mazateco and in other North American Indian languages patterns of laryngeal association identical to those seen in (2) for nasality. The findings I anticipate are outlined below, using the feature of glottalization, [constricted (glottis)]:

(4)   Glottalization and A-positions

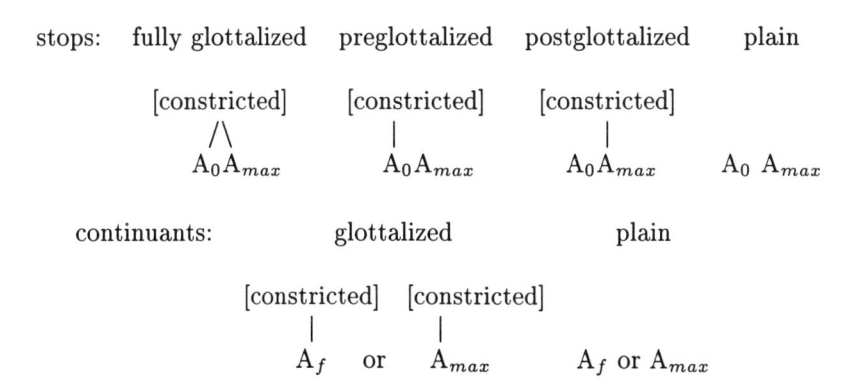

    stops: fully glottalized   preglottalized   postglottalized   plain

        [constricted]   [constricted]   [constricted]
           /\ | |
        $A_0 A_{max}$ $A_0 A_{max}$ $A_0 A_{max}$ $A_0\ A_{max}$

    continuants: glottalized   plain

        [constricted] [constricted]
           | |
        A_f or A_{max} A_f or A_{max}

The Mazateco data will show that plosives display three of the four patterns of association shown in (4) – plain, preglottalized and postglottalized – whereas continuants are systematically restricted to only a two-way contrast, which we shall identify as plain vs. glottalized. The full range of contrasts between plain, preglottalized, postglottalized and fully glottalized plosives is attested in Kashaya (Southwestern Pomo), a language whose laryngeal clusters have been recently analyzed by Buckley (1992), and which we shall discuss below. In Kashaya, as elsewhere, the continuants contrast with the stops in displaying no more than a binary contrast between plain and glottalized. This systematic difference in the anchoring possibilities offered by plosives and continuants is one of the central points of this study.

Since the presence of release is not distinctive for the plosives of any language,[3] I will assume that releases are projected from underlying representations in which the stops are mere closures:

(5) Release Projection

$A_0 \rightarrow A_0\ A_{max}$

Most languages disallow released stops in rime position. The result are unreleased stops, whose representation is that of simple closures: A_0. The prohibition against released rime stops could be expressed as below, using the moraic notation to refer to rimes (cf. Hyman (1985), Hayes (1989), Zec (1989) and others).

(6) No released stops in rime

$$* \begin{array}{c} A_0\ A_{max} \\ \backslash / \\ \mu \end{array}$$

An alternative account of the distribution of unreleased plosives is that stop releases are disallowed before A positions involving a greater degree of oral stricture: one possibility is the constraint below, inspired by Flemming (1991).

(7) No released stops before stops or fricatives

$*A_0\ A_{max}\ /\ \_\_A_n$, where A_n is more constricted than A_{max}

---

[3] On this point, see McCawley (1967), the first phonologist who has explicitly argued that stop releases are phonologically relevant.

It is possible that both (6) and (7) are operative, perhaps in different languages. An indication of this is the fact that the distribution of released stops varies somewhat from language to language. Korean, for instance, disallows any stop releases in word-medial as well as word-final rimes, regardless of what follows (McCawley 1967, Kim-Renaud 1986). This behavior points to (6). On the other hand, Italian and Marshallese (Byrd 1992) allow word-final but not word-medial released coda stops, a fact which is inconsistent with (6) and suggests (7).[4] This is clearly a subject that awaits fuller study. The derivational position of filters like (6) and (7) is also open to a variety of interpretations: one may assume that these filters operate to block the projection of releases in the positions they designate, or that they block only the surface occurrence of plosive releases in those positions, or that both functions are instantiated, in different languages.

Under circumstances discussed elsewhere (Steriade 1989, 1992), the approximant releases of normal stops turn into the distinctive fricative releases that characterize affricates: a plain stop ($A_0 A_{max}$) becomes an affricate ($A_0 A_f$). There are three claims being made: first, affricates are, like stops, sequences of closure plus release; second, affricates have releases consisting of positions identical to those carried by fricatives (A_f); third, stops and affricates are underlyingly distinguished not by the quality of their release but by their other specifications, primarily those involving place features. The simplest case illustrating the non-distinctive nature of fricated releases involves the most widespread affricate type, the palatoalveolar [tʃ] (Maddieson 1984). In the segment inventories of most languages – including English, Turkish, Sanskrit, Irish, Spanish, Farsi, Hindi, Bengali etc. – [tʃ] is the only affricate type as well as the only palatoalveolar plosive. It would be redundant to differentiate it underlyingly from other stops both in place of articulation and in stricture features. Further, in languages like English where the [tʃ]/[t] opposition is mirrored by that between [ʃ] and [s] it would be odd to claim that the underlying distinction between [tʃ] and [t] involves stricture (the contrast between a coronal stop and a coronal affricate), while at the same time admitting that the underlying contrast between [ʃ] and [s] involves place features ([+anterior] vs. [-anterior]). The optimal system is clearly one in which both the [s] : [ʃ] and the [t] : [tʃ] contrasts are identically described. The conclusion then is that, for such widespread cases at least, the affricate [tʃ] is nothing but an underlying palatoalveolar stop: its affricate nature is derivative from its place specifications.

I claim that this is the case not only in such transparent plosive systems as the ones mentioned above, but also across the board, for all affricates. This claim cannot be defended in detail here, but we can note two facts

---

[4]Byrd (1992) also demonstrates that the contrast between released word-final codas and unreleased medial ones cannot be attributed to extrametricality.

that bear on one of its aspects: the hypothesis that affricates are, like the stops, sequences of closure and release. Affricates and stops pattern alike in allowing nasal contours: affricates, unlike genuine continuants, can be pre- and postnasalized (cf. Poser (1979) and Steriade (1992)). They can be, because they carry two aperture positions, each of which is separately available for association to [nasal]. Affricates and stops are also identical in their ability to be pre- and postaspirated, or pre- and postglottalized. In this respect too, they are different from the continuants. Much of the present study documents this claim.

The notational framework sketched above is still being developed; many of the assumptions made here for the sake of explicitness may have to be abandoned later, when we gain a better understanding of the typology and phonetic realization of consonant clusters. For this reason, I would like to emphasize the essential element in my proposals: *released plosives – in contrast to all other sound classes – have two positions that can anchor distinctive features.* Their second position, the release, is identical in type to the unique position projected by continuant consonants, the approximants or the fricatives. The main reason these ideas seem worth exploring is that they promise to eliminate a long-standing question in modern phonology: why is it that the only reliably attested segmental contours – for nasality and continuancy – are found among released plosives? The emerging answer is simple. There are no true segmental contours. There are no intra-segmental sequences of the form $[\alpha\ F]\ [-\alpha\ F]$. The apparent contour segments involve two distinct positions – closure and release – each of which can be separately characterized by the relevant feature or stricture degree.[5]

1.4 Segmental Contours and Privative Features

The three satellite features involved in the composition of most Mazateco complex onsets are aspiration, glottalization and nasality. My analysis of the role they play in the formation of onsets will rely on the claim that they are privative, or single-valued features: that only [+spread glottis], [+constricted glottis] and [+nasal] are phonological values. This assumption is sufficient to explain why contours for these features – of the type illustrated in (2) and (4) – can be realized only on released plosives, that is, on bipositional segments. What we call contour segments emerge as segments possessing two aperture positions, of which only one is associated to a given feature. When the feature giving rise to contours is privative, as we claim [nasal], [constricted] and [spread] are, the only segments that can display contours will necessarily be those possessing two A positions.

---

[5]There is more discussion of this subject in San (1990) and Steriade (1992). San's view is that many instances of tonal contours can also be reanalyzed when a better understanding of syllable weight in the relevant languages is gained.

These are the released plosives. Since a significant amount will ride on the claim that nasality, aspiration and glottalization are privative, I sketch here some of the motivation behind it.

Some discussion of the privative nature of [nasal] is provided by Trigo (1992) and Steriade (1992). Lombardi (1991) argues that all laryngeal features are single-valued.[6] In the case of glottalization and aspiration, a simple argument for privative status can be based on the observation that all dissimilatory or assimilatory processes involving these features require reference to [+constricted] and [+spread] as the active value, never to [-constricted] or [-spread]. Thus root constraints involving aspiration[7] or glottalization[8] refer exclusively to the presence of [+constricted] or [+spread] segments, never to that of [-constricted] or [-spread] ones. The case has yet to be found in which a language disallows the occurrence, within a given domain, of more than one unaspirated or unglottalized segments. This should, by itself, be sufficient to suggest that such segments do not carry, in any language, any values for the relevant features.

A distinct consideration favoring privative status for laryngeal features is the fact that there exist segments – /h/ and /ʔ/ – which contain, on the surface, no more than one phonological specification, [+spread] for /h/ and [+constricted] for /ʔ/ (cf. Keating (1988) on the phonetic evidence to this effect, and Steriade (1987) on the phonological side of the argument). If [spread] and [constricted] were binary, we would have to ask why we are missing two other conceivable segments: the one containing nothing but [-spread] and the one containing just [-constricted].

Finally, we note that plain consonants – unaspirated and unglottalized – are always available as landing sites for the features of aspiration or glottalization, as long as the general co-occurrence constraints of the language are not being violated. If plain consonants were specified as [-spread, -constricted], we would expect that such specifications would block – at least occasionally – the linking of the conflicting values [+spread] or [+constricted]. An instance of this argument is provided by the behavior of aspiration in Ancient Greek, a language that contrasts $\{p^h, t^h, k^h\}$ and $\{p, t, k\}$. If [spread] is privative, we understand why a plain stop becomes aspirated in Greek when morpheme or word concatenation creates an in-

---

[6]The privative status of [voice] was earlier discussed by Mester and Ito (1989). I do not discuss [voice] here because the languages analyzed in this study make little reference to this feature and because the nature of the arguments bearing on this point is rather different from the evidence establishing that [constricted] and [spread] are single-valued. See Lombardi (1991).

[7]Examples are Grassmann's Law in Indo-European, on which see Collindge (1985) for references; the constraints holding within Harauti nominals, on which see Allen (1970); and the Kashaya aspiration and glottalization disharmony discussed by Oswalt (1976:3).

[8]On Yucatec glottalization disharmony, see Lombardi (1990).

termediate stop-h cluster. If, on the other hand, [spread] is binary and
{p, t, k} are [-spread], the aspiration process can perhaps be described —
by means of rules delinking [-spread] or assumptions about underspecification — but not explained, since no particular outcome is being predicted.
The examples below illustrate only two subcases of this phenomenon: (a)
plain stops directly followed by /h/; (b) plain stops followed by a vowel —
which elides — followed by /h/.

(8)   /h/ linking in Ancient Greek:

    (a) ouk ho:s → ouk^{h}o:s 'not thus'
    (b) kata horao: → kat^{h}orao: 'to look down'
        kai hiketeuete → k^{h}iketeuete 'and ye beseech'

Note that voiced stops do not become aspirated when followed by /h/.

(9)   No effect on voiced stops
    oude heis → oudeis 'not one', not *out^{h}eis.

The reason for this is that the [+voice] value of /d/ is incompatible with the
[+spread] specification of /h/: aspirated stops cannot be voiced in Greek.
What happens in such cases, as in all cases where an /h/ follows a consonant that cannot be linked to [spread], is that /h/ is simply lost. This
indicates that, in the process of associating [spread] to a consonant, it is
not possible to override the consonant's specifications for an incompatible
feature. This reasoning leads us once again to conclude that plain unaspirated stops do not contain a specification incompatible with [spread]. A
similar argument involving glottalization is provided by the behavior of underlying sequences of consonant plus glottal stop in Klamath (cf. Barker
1964), Kashaya (Buckley 1990) and elsewhere: in Klamath, for instance,
the plain consonants become glottalized when followed by an underlying
/ʔ/, whereas the underlying aspirated ones remain unchanged.

    One might attribute observations such as these to the effect of markedness: [-constricted] and [-spread] are widely considered the unmarked values, [+constricted] and [+spread] the marked ones. Perhaps marked values
can override specified unmarked ones. Perhaps, but there is no a priori
reason to expect this as one of the reflexes of markedness. The most restrictive view compatible with the data I am aware of is that [-constricted]
and [-spread] are permanently missing values, not just unmarked ones. I
will consequently assume here that the correct interpretation of statements

such as "α is the unmarked value of F" is that F is a privative feature and [α F] refers to its absence. The burden of proof is clearly on those who wish to draw a distinction between unmarked values and non-existent ones.

1.5 Onset Markedness, A Position and Merger Mechanism

The suggestion that released plosives contain two positions leads one to speculate that the distinction between single segments and segment clusters might not be as clear-cut as it is generally assumed. If a released stop /p/ consists of a closure and an approximant release then perhaps it bears some structural similarity to a cluster such as /pr/, which consists of a stop released into an approximant /r/. I will now outline in more detail this speculation, which ultimately bears on the analysis of Mazateco onsets.

My hypothesis is that the relative markedness of different types of onset clusters is determined by the structural and featural similarity between single consonants and consonant clusters. I suggest that the least marked onsets are identical in structure (i.e., sequence of A positions) and feature composition to single segments. The best onset cluster is one consonant.

An onset cluster is an underlying sequence of several distinct segments that end up in onset position. This cluster of distinct segments will produce an unmarked onset to the extent that the consonants of the cluster can acquire the structure of a single segment. Here is an example: an onset like /pr/ – one of the most frequently encountered onset types – consists underlyingly of two distinct segments, each of which will project its own aperture positions. The stop /p/ will carry a closure and project a release yielding a $A_0 A_{max}$ sequence; the approximant /r/ will carry an A_{max} slot. Once concatenated, the approximant releases of /p/ and /r/ can merge, given that they are identical in type, non-distinct in feature composition and adjacent.

(10)   Release merger in /pr/

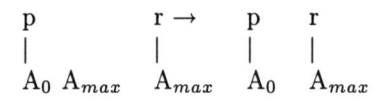

```
p         r  →   p      r
|         |      |      |
A₀ Amax   Amax   A₀    Amax
```

The result in (10) is a cluster of articulations which is structurally identical to a single stop – in that it contains the same sequence of aperture positions that /p/ would have generated by itself. It is not however, featurally identical to a single stop, given that it contains two distinct sets of place of articulation features. It follows then that /pr/ will be a more marked onset than either /p/ or /r/ by themselves. This is of course true. It also follows that /pr/ will be a less marked onset type than /pn/, since /pn/

is composed of two stops and cannot be straightforwardly reduced to a sequence that is even structurally, let alone featurally, identical to a single consonant.

One bonus of this type of analysis is that, in addition to explaining the markedness ranking p > pr > pn – without recourse to complex computations of sonority distance[9] – we explain why the stop in /pr/ onsets is released *into* the liquid rather than separately released. Notice that this is not a fact of phonetic realization that we can ignore in the phonology: this appears to be the invariant realization of onset clusters consisting of stop followed by approximant. As such it deserves an explanation, and the analysis sketched here provides it straightforwardly.

Consider now a different case: that of the underlying cluster /p + h/. From a cluster like this, an onset cluster can be derived by merging the two adjacent approximant releases. The mechanics will be identical to those generating a /pr/ onset but the output is different in one respect: we now have an onset that is both featurally and structurally identical to a single segment.

(11)   Release merger in /ph/ clusters

$$\begin{array}{cccc} p & h & \rightarrow & p \quad h \\ | & | & & | \quad | \\ A_0\ A_{max} & A_{max} & & A_0\ A_{max} \end{array}$$

The /ph/ sequence representing the output of (11) is featurally identical to a single segment because it contains a single set of place of articulation features and a single set of laryngeal features. It is structurally identical to one because it contains the same sequence of aperture positions that /p/ alone would have been entitled to. The prediction then is that the markedness ranking of onset clusters will be p > ph > pr > pn. (In this ranking /ph/ is ranked lower than /p/ simply because it is featurally a more complex single segment.)

Although we cannot investigate in detail all aspects of this predicted markedness scale, one observation that supports it is the fact that, in languages where /ph/ sequences are provably underlying clusters – rather than underlying aspirated stops – the /ph/ onsets are the least restricted in their distribution, because they are the least marked. An instance of this is Kammu (a Mon-Khmer language), whose phonology and morphology have been carefully analyzed by Svantesson (1983). Svantesson shows that /stop-h/ clusters are separable by various morphological processes in Kammu and

---

[9] On sonority distance and its putative role in determining onset systems, see Selkirk (1984), Steriade (1982), and Clements (1991).

concludes from this that they are underlying clusters. But, as Svantesson shows, the /stop-h/ onsets occupy a peculiar place in the complex onset inventory of Kammu: unlike the other onset clusters, which consist of stops followed by the approximants /r/, /l/, /w/, the stop-h clusters are allowed not only in major syllables (syllables with a full nuclear vowel) but also in minor syllables (reduced syllables whose nucleus is a consonant). I attribute this effect to the markedness rank of the two onset types: the more marked onset clusters (stop-liquid, stop-glide) are subject to additional distributional restrictions and thus disallowed in minor syllables. The least marked onsets, single segments and stop-h clusters, are distributionally free: they are least marked because they are indistinguishable from single segments.

According to the hypothesis advanced here, the only distinction between a single segment /p^h/ and an onset sequence /p-h/ is their underlying representation: on the surface, they are non-distinct. Indeed, no language displays contrasts such as the one shown below.

(12)   Unattested contrast

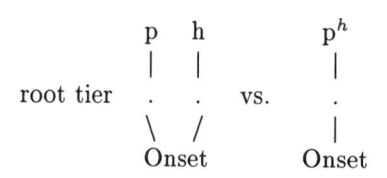

```
              p   h              pʰ
              |   |              |
root tier     .   .      vs.     .
              \  /               |
              Onset              Onset
```

The absence of surface contrast between /C-h/ onset clusters and aspirated stops is a fact left unexplained by standard views on feature geometry and cluster composition. (The point obviously carries over to the case of stop-? onsets.) Our explanation is that the contrast in (12) is unheard of because (a) syllable structure is defined on A positions and (b) the merger of non-distinct A-positions (such as the A_{max} release of /p/ and the A_{max} position carried by /h/) is obligatory, at least in the case of tautosyllabic sequences.

The cases considered so far involve clusters created through the merger of identical, adjacent, and featurally non-distinct A positions. I believe that several other cases of A position merger can be identified in the cross-linguistic study of consonant clusters. However, only one of these will be relevant for our present concerns: Mazateco will exemplify the possibility that any two adjacent A positions – distinct in type or not – may merge, provided that the features they carry are drawn from the complementary sets of nasality, place and laryngeal features and therefore represent, at least in principle, mutually compatible articulations. The general motivation for this type of merger is discussed in the next section.

1.6 Single Segments and Segment Clusters

It is standard in contemporary phonology to identify the notion of single segment with a position serving as anchor for distinctive features. The root node, introduced in Clements' (1985) and Mohanan's (1984) studies of feature organization, plays exactly this role.

The proposal central to this study – that closure and release in plosives are distinct phonological entities – is roughly equivalent to the claim that plosives have two root nodes, one for closure and one for release. One of these positions, the release, has clearly an auxiliary and disposable status: it is not distinctive and it is not necessarily present in all contexts. But in contexts where plosive releases are present, the following question arises: what identifies a released stop as a single segment?[10] The empirical interest of this question will become apparent below, in the discussion of Mazateco. For the moment I propose a general answer to it, outlined earlier in Steriade (1992), which can be used as a reference point in later discussion. In trying to characterize the structures that will count as single segments, we must define a number of terms:

(13)   Derived and basic A positions

    (a)   Derived A position: an aperture position attributable to the projection mechanisms (e.g. (5)).

    (b)   Basic A position: all other aperture positions.

(14)   Feature compatibility

Two autosegments F and G are compatible in some language L iff:

    (a)   the corresponding articulatory gestures can be realized simultaneously and

    (b)   there is no filter blocking the co-occurrence of F and G in the inventory of L.

We can now define what structures can be identified as single segments. Bear in mind that this definition is relevant for derived representations: in underlying representations, segments are trivially distinguishable from

---

[10] Thanks to Daniel Silverman for first raising this questions.

clusters, since, prior to the projection of stop releases, there is a one-to-one correspondence between segments and A positions.

(15) Single segments in derived representations
A string of adjacent A positions and associated autosegments is a single segment iff:

(a) It contains at most one basic A position.
(b) Any derived A positions it contains are attributable to projection by the basic A position.
(c) It contains at most one place node.
(d) For any pair of autosegments F and G that it contains, F and G are compatible.

The clauses (a-b) in (15) insure that released plosives (i.e., sequences such as $A_0 A_{max}$ or $A_0 A_f$) can count as monosegmental, in contrast to sequences such as $A_f A_{max}$, or $A_{max} A_f$, $A_f A_0$, $A_{max} A_0$, in which neither A position could have been projected by the other. The notion of structural similarity between a string of A positions and a single segment that I alluded to earlier in discussing onsets like /p-r/ is now defined by clauses (a-b). The notion of featural similarity between a cluster and a segment, also mentioned earlier, is defined by clauses (c-d) in (15) . These clauses are meant to guarantee the articulatory coherence of the cluster of features that represents a single segment. The claim I make in defining single derived segments in these terms, is that even features that are not simultaneous on the surface must pass a test of mutual compatibility in order for the structure encompassing them to count as monosegmental. The evidence for this claim is presented below.

The definition in (15) has a certain global derivational flavor, in that the ability of a surface structure to pass as monosegmental depends on whether it is attributable to the operation of a projection rule. But (15) is not a mechanism for reconstructing derivational origin. The aim of this definition is not to discover which sequences come from underlying single segments and which ones do not. Rather, we refer to the notion of (derived) single segment defined by (15) in order to explain why certain surface articulatory sequences are well-formed onsets and, as the saying goes, *pattern as single segments*, while others are not and do not. As we shall see below, many types of underlying clusters of distinct consonants can yield, through merger, surface sequences that will satisfy the criteria of single segmenthood.

To illustrate the notion of single segment defined by (15) I provide below an annotated list of representative structures:

(16)

	structure	example	mono-segmental?	comments

(a)	place place
	  | |
	  A_0 A_{max}
		pr	no	two place nodes

(b)	place [constricted]
	  | |
	  A_0 A_{max}
	  |
	  [nasal]
		^{n}t'	yes	

(c)	place [constricted]
	  | |
	  A_0 A_{max}
	  |
	  [spread]
		^{h}t'	no	incompatible: [spread] and [constricted]

I have not explored here the more challenging possibility that segments – and therefore the distinction between single segments and clusters – can be entirely dispensed with by using the syllable and its subconstituents as the minimal concatenative units. This hypothesis was originally suggested by Fujimura and Lovins (1978) and is currently being investigated by Fujimura (1992a,b). The fact that the dialect of Mazateco considered here contrasts onsets such as /ht/ and /th/ raises obvious difficulties for Fujimura's idea that features are predictably linearized within the demisyllable. This should not however obscure the similarity between Fujimura's approach and ours: both theories claim that it is impossible to identify surface segments as single anchoring positions.

The remainder of this study seeks to document two points: first, the existence of aspiration and glottalization patterns similar to those anticipated above in (4)—with a binary contrast among continuants and a ternary or quaternary one among plosives; second, the phonological relevance of the notion of derived single segment outlined in (15) in the analysis of an unusual type of onset inventory.

Complex Onsets as Single Segments: The Mazateco Pattern   219

2 Mazateco

2.1 Segments and Syllables

My source on Mazateco is PP's study (1947). The dialect described is that of Huautla de Jimenez. I have replaced PP's notation with the corresponding IPA symbols.

(17)   Mazateco consonants

		strident	post-			
labial	alveolar	alveolar	alveolar	retroflex	velar	laryngeal
	t	ts	tʃ	tʂ	k	
v						
m	n		ɲ			
	s		ʃ	ʂ		
	l			y		h ʔ

In addition to these segments, the stops /p/, /b/, /d/, /g/ appear in Spanish loans, as do the trill /rr/ and the tap /r/.

The native spirant written <v> is described as a "bilabial fricative with flat (i.e., not markedly rounded) lips" (1947:80). A more accurate phonetic transcription would then be [β]. This [β] occupies an odd position in the Mazateco consonant system: it is the only voiced fricative of a language in which an oral bilabial stop is strikingly absent. Very few languages lack a bilabial oral stop; and relatively few have, in their phonemic inventories, voiced bilabial fricatives. Mazateco seems to have reversed the markedness status of /b/ and /β/: this suggests that [β] is the surface realization of an underlying stop, /p/ or /b/. In the absence of other voicing contrasts among Mazateco stops, /p/ seems the logical choice for the underlying inventory. But, given that our interest here concerns only the input to the processes of onset-cluster formation, /b/, which is phonetically closest to the recorded [β], seems an equally good candidate.[11] The stop chart relevant here will then be the following:

(18)   Mazateco plosives

| b | t | ts | tʃ | tʂ | k | oral plosives |
| m | n | | ɲ | | | nasal stops |

---

[11] Languages with a surface inventory comparable to the one I attribute to Mazateco – comparable in that the bilabials stops are either invariably voiced or represent the only voiced plosives – include Arabic and Arapaho, an Algonquian language (Salzmann 1956).

The vowel inventory of Mazateco includes /a/, /e/, /o/, /i/ and the corresponding nasalized vowels. From PP's comments on vowel allophony one gathers that /o/ has high as well as non-high allophones. We shall see that it behaves somewhat ambiguously as a potential target of glide formation, a rule that affects high vowels.

According to PP, Mazateco syllables are always open. We can confirm this: words end invariably in vowels and medial clusters closely mirror those attested initially.[12] Onsets are obligatory: "every nucleus is preceded by its consonantal margin" (1947:83).

Nuclei may contain from one to three vowels. PP refer to the initial member in two- or three-member nuclei as weak or subordinate. The final vowel in three-member nuclei is also subordinate. There are restrictions on possible vowel combinations within a nucleus, but these will not be dealt with here. According to PP, the overall duration of the nucleus is constant, regardless of the number of vowels or tones it carries. It is unclear how to translate this observation into a proposal for phonological representation, since the facts are consistent with a number of divergent structures.

2.2 Complex Onsets: An Overview

The complete list of complex onsets attested in Mazateco is given below, using the principles of PP's sequential notation.

(19) Two member onsets:
    a.   ht hk hts htʃ htṣ hv hy hm hn hɲ
         ʔv ʔy ʔm ʔn ʔɲ
         nt nk nts ntʃ ntṣ
         tʔ kʔ tsʔ tʃʔ tṣʔ vʔ yʔ mʔ nʔ ɲʔ sʔ ṣʔ lʔ
         th kh tsh tʃh tṣh vh mh nh sh ṣh

    b.   sk ʃk ʃn

    Three members onsets:
    a'   hnt hnk hnts hntʃ hntṣ
         ʔnt ʔnk ʔnts ʔntʃ ʔntṣ
         ntʔ nkʔ ntsʔ ntʃʔ ntṣʔ
         nth nkh ntsh ntʃh ntṣh

    b'   htsʔ htʃʔ
         skʔ ʃkʔ ʃtʔ

---

[12] PP note that /ʔm/ and /ʔn/ sequences are found only intervocalically: but more complex clusters, like /ʔnt/ /ʔnts/, are attested initially, and this suggests that the gap is accidental.

A look at the list in (19) reveals two major subgroups:

(i) Sequences whose global feature composition is monosegmental, according to the definition in (15), in that the entire cluster contains at most one set of place specifications, at most one (distinctive) laryngeal feature and at most one [nasal] value. These sequences include the /hC/ and /Ch/, /ʔC/ and /Cʔ/ clusters as well as /(h)nC/, /ʔnC/ and /nC(ʔ)/ and /nCh/.

(ii) Sequences that must count as featurally bisegmental according to (15), in that they contain either two distinct sets of place features (as in /sk/, /ʃt/) or two distinct and incompatible laryngeal specifications (as in /htsʔ/). In section (2.6.) we will discover that the /hCʔ/ clusters originate as /sCʔ/. Anticipating this result, we may state now that the only featurally bisegmental clusters of Mazateco are fricative-stop-(ʔ) sequences.

Although PP don't formulate the monosegmental principle governing the clusters in (19.a′) in exactly the same terms, they are clearly aware of something akin to it. They state (1947:p.80) that the /h/, /ʔ/, and /n/ elements of the clusters in (19.a′) are subordinate elements "because the articulation of the subordinate one tends to be secondary [or] tertiary [...] in relation to the primary articulations of the other members of the clusters." (Primary articulations are defined as oral constrictions, secondary ones are nasal gestures and tertiary ones are laryngeal gestures.) In other words, the primary member of the cluster contributes the oral gesture, while the satellites – /h/, /ʔ/, /n/ – contribute the complementary featural components of nasality and aspiration/glottalization. Implicit in this analysis is the view that the whole cluster functions as *one coherent ensemble of features* rather than as a sequence of featurally independent elements. It is this idea that I will try to incorporate in my analysis.[13]

What is most striking about the clusters in (19) is that a large number of them violate the Sonority Law, whereby sonority must steadily increase from the beginning to the center of the syllable.[14] This observation may suggest that phonetic clusters like /ht/, /ʔnt/, /nt/, /ʃt/ represent underlying unit phonemes. PP reject this interpretation: they point out that a large subset of Mazateco consonants may be both preceded and followed by /ʔ/ and /h/. If /nʔ/ is interpreted as a glottalized /n'/ then how are we to interpret the contrasting sequence /ʔn/? The same question applies to clusters like /hk/ vs. /kh/ or /ʔnk/ vs. /nkʔ/. I would endorse this argument, with the following limitation: contrasts like /hk/ vs. /kh/ demonstrate that

---

[13] A related intuition was later expressed in work by Fujimura and Lovins (1978), Fujimura (1992a, b) and, under the name of *prosodic licensing*, by Goldsmith (1989:123ff). PP's notion that oral constrictions function as superordinate to nasal and laryngeal ones will also find its counterpart in this study, as we shall see. It should be noted, however, that PP do not consider the fricative-stop clusters or the /hCʔ/ sequences to have a distinct status from that of other Mazateco clusters, as I do.

[14] See Clements (1991) for references and recent discussion of the Sonority Law.

such sequences cannot both be *underlying* single segments. Their surface status as single segments or clusters remains to be established.

PP's own assumption is that the Mazateco consonantal sequences are surface clusters. This hypothesis runs into even greater difficulties. If the onsets in (19) are polysegmental, why do they violate the Sonority Law? Equally puzzling on the cluster analysis is the fact that /h/ and /ʔ/ do not co-occur within a Mazateco onset:[15] if /ht/ and /tʔ/ are clusters, we would expect the product of their concatenation – */htʔ/ – to be attested as well. Why isn't it? The same point can be raised in relation to the attested /ʔn/, /nh/ vs. the unattested */ʔnh/. Our reasoning in such cases is based on the principle that the overall wellformedness of a cluster is an exclusive function of the wellformedness of the segment sequences composing it (cf. Clements and Keyser 1983 for discussion). This principle, when applied to Mazateco, predicts that /ht/ and /tʔ/ jointly imply */htʔ/—in the same way that /pr/ and /sp/ in English jointly imply /spr/. Why is this prediction wrong for Mazateco? Similarly, given the joint presence of /hn/, /nh/ and /ht/ in Mazateco, we expect */hnht/ as well as a contrast between */nht/ and /hnt/ sequences. The cluster analysis has no meaningful ways of nullifying these wrong predictions.[16]

The analysis I will propose claims that all complex onsets in Mazateco are underlying clusters: they originate as underlying sequences of distinct feature matrices linked to distinct A positions. However, in the process of onset formation, these clusters merge into structures that correspond to single segments. Thus, /ht/ and /th/ are both segment sequences underlyingly. This is why they can be lexically distinct. But they are both monosegmental on the surface: one a preaspirated, the other a postaspirated stop, whose A-position structure and feature composition satisfies the requirements for single segmenthood spelled out in (15).

---

[15] The surface clusters /htsʔ/, /htʃʔ/ will emerge as surface realizations of /stsʔ/ and /stʃʔ/. Aside from these cases, /h/ cannot precede or follow /ʔ/ in a cluster.

[16] Could a sequential analysis of C clusters succeed in Mazateco, if it were to abandon the claim that wellformedness is always computed on *adjacent* pairs of C's? Perhaps, but it is by no means clear what principles can be employed in a sequential analysis in order to rule out onsets like /htʔ/, /nhk/, /Chn/. My claim is that even if such principles could be found, they would essentially import into a sequential analysis the basic claim to be made here: that this class of Mazateco onsets are not surface sequences but rather single segments.

(20) Surface structures for Mazateco /ht/ and /th/
(place component omitted)

$$\begin{array}{cc} [\text{spread}] & [\text{spread}] \\ | & | \\ A_0 \ A_{max} & A_0 \ A_{max} \\ \\ [\text{ht}] & [\text{th}] \end{array}$$

Only certain underlying clusters can yield, through A position merger, single segments: for instance, the merger of /h/ and /t/ can produce one monosegmental unit, whereas that of /h/ and /?/, or /h/ and /t/ and /?/, or /p/ and /y/ cannot, for reasons spelled out in (15). It is this factor that will explain the limitations on possible onsets in Mazateco. The observation made above, that aspiration and glottalization do not co-occur within a single Mazateco cluster, follows from the claim that the clusters become surface single segments: in virtue of (15), they cannot contain incompatible feature values, such as [spread] and [constricted], even in cases like /ht?/ where these values would be realized as temporally sequenced (cf. (16.c)).

I will suggest then that the group of clusters in (19.a) are generated by the merger of any sequence of adjacent aperture positions, subject to one constraint on the immediate output : the result of merger must be monosegmental.

2.3 Prenasal Onsets

The set of complex onsets which best illustrates the claim that Mazateco onsets are surface unit phonemes involves nasals followed by a plosive. We analyze first the clusters /nk/, /nt/, /nts/, /nʧ/, /nṭṣ./, leaving the laryngeally specified clusters like /nk?/, or /hnk/ for later consideration. The nasal is always homorganic to the following stop: this is explicitly mentioned by PP (1947:80) for /nk/ clusters and can be assumed to hold for /nts/, /nʧ/ and /nṭṣ./.[17] Thus the NC sequence contains a single set of place features. The plosive is voiced in these cases, although not recorded as such by PP: /nk/ stands for [ŋg], /nt/ for [nd], /nts/ for [ndz] etc. (PP 1947:79): the nasal and the plosive share one [+voice] specification.[18] Given

---

[17] Jamieson (1977), who analyzed the related dialect of Chiquihuitlan Mazateco, notes that all /nC/ cluters are homorganic in Chiquihuitlan, including /nʧ/.

[18] PP and Jamieson (1977) note that the plosive in /nCh/ onsets is not voiced. I suspect that what these writers are reporting is the delay in the onset of voicing on the following vowel – a delay made inevitable by the fact that the stop release is aspirated – rather than the absence of vocal cord vibration during the closure interval of the stop. For this reason, I continue to assume that the prenasal stops have voiced closures in

that the stricture, place and laryngeal features of the nasal and the stop are identical, we can identify these NC clusters as standard prenasal segments. The examples below are given in PP's notation.

(21) Prenasal onsets:

PP's notation (adapted)	Phonetic	Example	Gloss
<nt>	[nd]	nta	'good'
<nts>	[ndz]	ntsa	'my hand'
<nʧ>	[ɲdʒ]	nʧao	'tomorrow'
<ntṣ>	[n̠d̠ẓ]	ntṣati	'comb'
<nk>	[ŋg]	nkahao	'water hole'
loans: <mb>	[mb]	mba	'grandfather' (from /compadre/)

A comparison between the list of prenasal onsets and the larger list of Mazateco consonants reveals that all and only the surface plosives can form complex onsets with a preceding nasal. If we leave aside the less well entrenched loans (e.g., /ganʧo/, or /seda/), a second generalization emerges: of the plosives, all and only those with nasal closure are voiced in Mazateco.[19]

These observations lend themselves to a simple two-step analysis in the framework sketched above. The prenasal onsets are single plosives arising from the association of nasality to a closure. And the [+voice] value of prenasals is derived by the same redundancy rule that must in any case be responsible for the fact that nasals in general are voiced: an A_0 position associated to [nasal] is specified as [+voice].[20]

Mazateco, regardless of what follows.

[19]The voicing process affects certain loanwords, perhaps the earlier ones, though not all: contrast /mba/ 'grandfather', from Spanish /compadre/, displaying the effects of prenasal voicing, with /ganʧo/ 'crochet hook' in which /ʧ/ is – according to PP – voiceless.

[20]I assume, following Keating (1990), that the feature [voice] associates invariably to closure.

(22) Analysis of prenasalized onsets (preliminary):

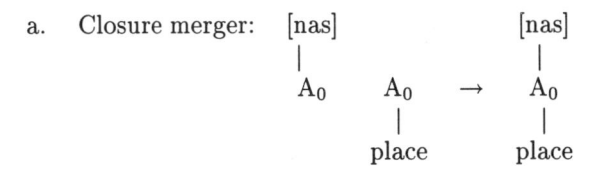

a. Closure merger:

$$\begin{array}{ccc} [\text{nas}] & & [\text{nas}] \\ | & & | \\ A_0 \quad A_0 & \rightarrow & A_0 \\ & | & | \\ & \text{place} & \text{place} \end{array}$$

b. Nasal voicing:

$$\begin{array}{c} [\text{nas}][\text{voice}] \\ |\,\cdot\cdot \\ A_0 \end{array}$$

The partial derivation of an onset like [nd] (spelled as <nt> in PP's materials) appears below:

(23) Derivation of [nd]

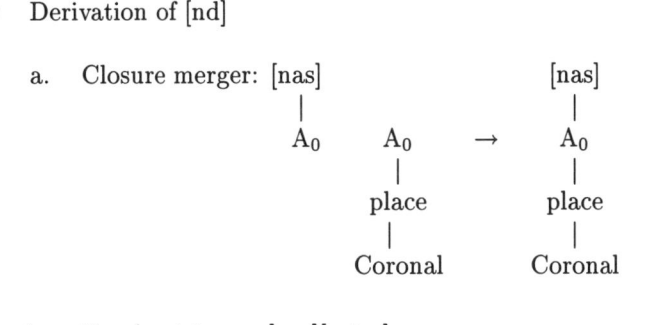

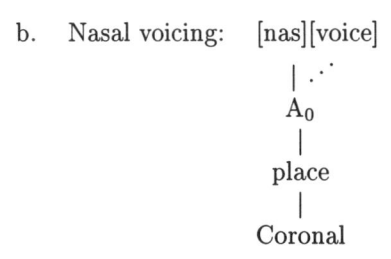

a. Closure merger:

$$\begin{array}{ccc} [\text{nas}] & & [\text{nas}] \\ | & & | \\ A_0 \quad A_0 & \rightarrow & A_0 \\ & | & | \\ & \text{place} & \text{place} \\ & | & | \\ & \text{Coronal} & \text{Coronal} \end{array}$$

b. Nasal voicing:

$$\begin{array}{c} [\text{nas}][\text{voice}] \\ |\,\cdot\cdot \\ A_0 \\ | \\ \text{place} \\ | \\ \text{Coronal} \end{array}$$

Two questions must be answered now. First, is this the right way to represent prenasal consonants, in Mazateco and elsewhere? PP perceived not only a nasal closure and an oral release, as represented in (23.b), but actually two distinct phases in the closure, a nasal and an oral one: does our analysis do justice to the facts they recorded? Second, where does the [nasal] closure in the input to (22-23.a) come from? If it's an underlying nasal stop, why does it lack release and place features?

The first question – which concerns the proper representation of prenasals in general – has been considered more carefully elsewhere, in Maddieson and Ladefoged (1993) and Steriade (1992). Notations like [nd] or [^{n}d] – the appropriate transcriptions for PP's <nt> – reflect the perception that only the first part of the closure phase is significantly nasalized. The velum raises before the oral release, yielding three different stages: oral closure first accompanied by nasal airflow, then accompanied by nasal closure, then oral release. This articulatory reality cannot be faithfully reflected in the phonological representation: given our decision that [nasal] is privative, the closure phase – like any other phonological anchoring point – can be represented as either associated to [nasal] or unassociated. It is phonologically either oral, or nasal, and cannot be part-nasal part-oral. But a phonological representation like (23.b) is compatible with three distinct phonetic realizations, representing three ways of synchronizing the actual articulatory gestures involved: (a) the velum may raise slightly before the oral release (yielding a brief oral interval of closure); (b) the oral release may strictly coincide with the lowering of the velum (yielding a fully nasal closure and a fully oral release); (c) the velum may raise slightly after the oral release (yielding a fully nasal closure and a release whose beginning is lightly nasalized). Option (c) is perhaps attested but it yields a barely distinct result from the realization of a fully nasal stop, whose closure and release are both nasalized, and for that reason it is probably avoided in languages like Mazateco where prenasals and nasals must contrast. Option (b) is indeed attested, as indicated by Maddieson and Ladefoged (1993), who call the relevant segments *post-stopped nasals* and transcribe them as [m^b], [n^d], etc. It is not widely attested, presumably because it requires a very precise synchronization between articulatory gestures. Option (a) is, as shown by Maddieson and Ladefoged (1993), the most widespread phonetic realization of prenasal plosives. The reason for its popularity is precisely the fact that it allows for the most secure contrast between prenasals and full nasal stops: only this class of prenasals has a fully and reliably oral release.

We may conclude then that transcripts like [nd] stand for the most common phonetic realization – option (a) – of a stop whose closure is nasal and whose release is oral: the output of (23.b). Supporting this conclusion is the observation that the three ways of realizing this phonological structure do not contrast in any language: in particular, the standard prenasals like [^{n}d] (option (a)) do not contrast with the corresponding poststopped nasals like [n^d] (option (b)), even though the two segment classes are perceptually quite distinct.[21] They do not contrast precisely because they represent the

---

[21] This point is made in Maddieson and Ladefoged (1993).

same phonological structure: a nasal closure and an oral release.

I turn now to the second question: what is the source of the unreleased nasal stop in (22-23.a)? If it's an ordinary nasal stop, why does it lack release?[22] The answer is that most preconsonantal stops will lack release if filter (7) is operative in Mazateco. The effect of (7) is to disallow stop releases before other stops or fricatives. Why then does this unreleased nasal stop lack point of articulation features? It is frequently the case that unreleased nasal stops cannot support perceptual point of articulation distinctions (Ohala and Ohala 1992), a process we can formalize as the removal of their place component. Let's assume that this happens in Mazateco: then any nasal-stop cluster will yield a sequence of two closures in which the first lacks any specifications other than [nasal] while the second is specified for place. Since the two closures carry complementary specifications, they can be viewed as subject to the same merger of identical, featurally non-distinct A positions which is responsible for the creation of /pr/ or /ph/ onsets discussed above. The result of merger in the case of structures like (22-23.a) is a sequence that passes the test of monosegmentality. In that sense, the prenasal onsets are maximally unmarked.

What happens with nasals preceding a fricative? We expect them to be unreleased and thus to lose place features. Why then do they fail to yield nasalized fricatives, through merger with the Af position of the following fricative ? The most plausible answer is that Mazateco, like many other languages, allows nasality on vowels and closures, but not on positions of intermediate stricture (approximants and fricatives).[23] This hypothesis will prove useful at other points in the analysis.

---

[22] Note that we cannot assume that the [nasal] feature yielding prenasals is underlyingly floating: it must be ordered in underlying representation relative to the oral segments of the string, as shown by pairs such as /ntsati/ 'comb' vs. /tsinka/ 'shirt'. If the nasality of prenasals was underlyingly floating, we could not devise a coherent linking algorithm that would generate such pairs.

[23] We would have to qualify this by stating that [nasality] on the A_{max} release of plain stops is licensed by its association to closure: this is what accounts for the presence of nasal stops in the language, where nasality extends from closure to release. However, the prohibition against nasalized A_f is absolute, as we see in the next section: all A_f positions must be oral, regardless of whether they represent the release of a nasal closure or not. This distinction fits what we know about the relative markedness of nasalized approximants vs. fricatives: many languages allow nasalized approximants, at least in their derived representations, but few permit nasalized fricatives.

2.3.1 Excursus: Merger of Oral Stop with Following C in Mataco

If nasal stops lack release when they precede segments involving a significant oral constriction, we expect oral stops to behave identically: hypothetical sequences like /k-s/ should contain an unreleased /k/. Although PP provide no information on the morphology and morphophonemics of Huautla Mazateco, we must still consider what would happen if such underlying sequences were to arise in the underlying representations of the language. One possibility is that the oral stops, just like their nasal counterparts, would lose their place component when they lack release. In such a case, the stop would be reduced to a bare A_0 position which cannot be realized in the absence of any associated features. If so, the /k-s/ sequence would surface as a simple /s/. But even if the unreleased oral stop maintains its place component, sequences like /k-s/ are not expected to survive as such in a language where surface onsets must be monosegmental: the only uncertainty we are left with is exactly how such clusters are eliminated.

One strategy for turning clusters of oral stop + C into monosegmental sequences is illustrated in Mataco, an Indian language of Argentina whose phonology was briefly described by Najlis (1971). Morpheme-internal clusters consisting of stop-C become monosegmental by place assimilation: "within morpheme boundaries the first member necessarily assimilates to the second in place of articulation and *the cluster becomes a single phone*. Under these circumstances, /t/ and /q/ irretrievably merge." (Najlis 1971:128; italics mine, D.S.). The following table, provided by Najlis, illustrates the fact that the stop's closure is maintained, although its place features disappear, while the following continuant becomes the release of the newly formed plosive. (A note on Najlis's notation: /q/ is probably a velar, /c/ a palatal stop; /x/ a 'frictionless continuant', i.e., a glottal fricative possessing both [x] and [h] allophones (Tovar 1979). On clusters with /p/ see below.)

(24) Mataco merger in /stop-C/ clusters:

{t, q} s → ts
        l   tl
        j   kj
        x   qx
        w   qw

The results of (24) are affricates (ts, qx), laterally released stops (tl), and plain stops like /kj/, /qw/, where palatality and rounding are phonetically present on the release, as well as the closure. I represent below the regressive assimilation process that yields the outcomes given in (24). As before, A_n stands for an A_f or A_{max} position:

(25) Merger via place assimilation:

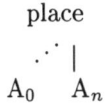

$$\begin{array}{cc} & \text{place} \\ & \overset{\cdot\cdot\cdot}{}\,| \\ A_0 & A_n \end{array}$$

The overall effect of the rule in (24) is to eliminate the bisegmental clusters in its input. What then of the /p-C/ clusters? Of these, only two are discussed by Najlis. The sequence /px/ is maintained intact because it contains, according to Najlis, an "orally neutral" /x/: I interpret this to mean that /x/ = [h] and /px/ = [p^h]. The sequence /pw/ is dissimilated to /fw/ - which Tovar (1979) identifies as a rounded bilabial fricative [ϕ^w], not a cluster. According to Najlis, /fw/ may optionally become /xw/, which I assume to be also the sequential transcription of a labiovelar spirant [x^w], also a unit phoneme. The source of the difference between the bilabial and the other stops remains unclear. But the overall picture is significant in any case: all stop-C clusters yield surface single segments, even though the treatment of labial stops diverges from that of other stops, in that the former maintains its place features.

The Mataco case illustrates what may be expected to happen to preconsonantal oral stops in languages like Mazateco where the occurrence of bisegmental sequences is either limited or entirely prohibited.

2.4 Onsets with Aspiration
2.4.1 Overview

I analyze next the class of complex onsets generated by a pre- or postposed /h/. The examples in (26) are given in PP's transcription. They are preceded by indications of what PP's transcriptions represent phonologically and what I reconstruct them to represent phonetically. Comments on the phonological representation and phonetic realization of these clusters follow in sections (2.3.2) and (2.3.3.).

(26) Preaspirated onsets

a. Two-member onsets

PP's	Phonological	Phonetic	Example	Gloss
\<hv\>	/hb/	[hβ]	/hva/	'watery'
\<ht\>	/ht/	[ʰt]	/hti/	'fish'
\<hts\>	/htŝ/	[ʰt̂s]	/htse/	'a sore'
\<htʃ\>	/htʃ/	[ʰt̂ʃ]	/htʃi/	'small'
\<hts̬\>	/hts̬/	[ʰt̠s̬]	/hahts̬o/	'in the opening'
\<hk\>	/hk/	[ʰk]	/hka/	'stubble'
\<hm\>	/hm/	[m̥m]	/hma/	'black'
\<hn\>	/hn/	[n̥n]	/hno/	'corn'
\<hɲ\>	/hɲ/	[ɲ̥ɲ]	/hɲa/	'woods'
\<hy\>	/hi/	[hy]	/hyona/	'I want'

b. Three-member onsets

PP's	Phonological	Phonetic	Example	Gloss
\<hnt\>	/hnt/	[n̥d]	/hnti/	'dirty'
\<hnk\>	/hnk/	[n̥g]	/hnka/	'wing'
\<hnts\>	/hnts/	[n̥d̂z]	/wihntsi/	'you look for'
\<hntʃ\>	/hntʃ/	[n̥d̂ẑ]	/hntʃa/	'salty'

I have omitted from this list the clusters /hts?/ and /htʃ?/, which Pike and Pike record as "tending to vary to /ts?/ and /tʃ?/" (1947:82). In a later section they will emerge as surface realizations of /sts?/ and /stʃ?/. Aside from these, preaspirated clusters cannot be either pre- or post-glottalized.

With the exception of /hy/ and /hβ/, the preaspirated clusters involve only surface plosives. There are no /hs/, /hʃ/, /hl/, or /hr/ preaspirated clusters. We therefore need to explain the place of /hy/ and /hβ/, the sole apparent preaspirated continuants in the Mazateco system.

2.4.2 Preaspirated Glides?

As it turns out, the contrast between /hyV/ and /hiV/ sequences is tenuous in Mazateco. I will show now that there is in fact little reason to analyze the string in /hyona/ – the unique example of a /hy/ cluster – as involving /hyo/ rather than /hio/. PP discuss a related issue at some length and thus provide some considerable evidence bearing on this point. Their concern is to establish that /y/ and /i/ are distinct phonemes, a fact that seems beyond dispute. But in the course of settling this issue, they note that "/y/ and weak /i/ as first of a vowel cluster are quite similar" (1947:86). Their evidence also reveals that /yV/ and /iV/ sequences do not contrast in all environments. I turn to this point next.

PP believe that Mazateco contrasts /hyV/ and /hiV/ sequences, but this opinion is based on one pair of items which, on closer analysis, turns out to be irrelevant: /hyona/ 'I am willing' vs. /-hĩõ/ 'not you (pl)'. The pair is irrelevant because the nucleus in /-hĩõ/ is nasalized. More generally, oral /hiV/ sequences (where /h/ is syllable initial) are not attested in Mazateco. The same restriction holds, as we shall see, of syllable initial /ʔiV/ sequences. The last piece in the puzzle is PP's observation (1947:79) that one clue they use for the distinction between /y/ and /i/ is that /i/ can be nasalized whereas /y/ may not be.

Taken together these facts suggest that underlying syllable initial /hiV/ and /ʔiV/ sequences are subject to a rule that turns nuclear /i/ into onset /y/. This rule applies (or is perceived to apply) to oral /i/ but not to nasalized /ĩ/.

The motivation for this process of glide formation is that /hiV/ and /ʔiV/ syllables lack a supralaryngeally articulated onset: by turning /i/ into /y/ they will acquire one. Mazateco is not unique in discounting /h/ and /ʔ/ as optimal onsets: Ancient Greek allows /h/ syllable-initially only in word-initial position. In other contexts, hV sequences behave as if they represent onsetless syllables. The laryngeal /h/ may be a segment, but cannot qualify as onset. In Mazateco, unlike in Greek, the laryngeals /h/ and /ʔ/ are allowed to stand alone in onset position, but their defective distribution – i.e., the absence of /hiV/:/hyV/ and /ʔiV/:/ʔyV/ contrasts – indicates that onsets lacking supralaryngeal articulations are allowed only as a last resort.

The Mazateco rule that turns /hiV/ to /hyV/ fails to apply to nasalized /ĩ/. We could explain this by noting that all nasalized continuant consonants are disallowed in this language: [nasal] in consonants must have an association to A_0. Alternatively, given PP's admission that they cannot easily distinguish between /y/ and weak /i/, we might think that the nasality of /i/ in sequences like <hĩo> led them to *assume* that they heard [hĩõ] rather than [hỹõ]: PP admit elsewhere that they use the nasality of vocoids as a clue to syllabicity.

I conclude then that the /hy/ cluster in /hyo-na/ represents a basic /hio-na/. More generally, my claim is that preaspirated /y/ is not created by the same cluster formation processes responsible for other pre- or postaspirated segments, and does not exist until a very late stage in the derivation. The process responsible for /hy/ is glide formation in syllables lacking supralaryngeally articulated onsets.

What then of the /hβ/ clusters? There are two possibilities here. The surface /β/ may originate as a bilabial stop. As mentioned above, there is good reason to believe that Mazateco does have an underlying oral bilabial stop. If at least some instances of /β/ represent an underlying stop, then we expect this stop to pattern like other plosives and allow preaspiration. We shall see below that /b/ permits preglottalization as well, as plosives do. If so, /hβ/ represents /hb/ or /hp/ rather than an underlying /hw/. Alternatively, /hβ/ represents phonological /hw/ and its derivation is parallel to that of /hy/: its /β/ originates as an underlying rounded vowel. The chief difficulty to overcome in this case is the apparent existence of surface contrasts between /hoV/ and /hβV/ sequences. The one relevant pair cited by PP is /hva/ 'watery' vs. /hoa/ 'we are two', where both nuclei are oral. Recall that /o/ is the only surface rounded vowel in Mazateco. If /hvV/ comes from underlying /hoV/ by glide formation, the contrast between /hoV/ and /hvV/ cannot be explained. Although there are possible ways around this problem, the account favored by the information PP provide appears to be the former: /hβ/ is /hb/.

This reasoning eliminates the only preaspirated continuants recorded by Pike and Pike and allows us to maintain that only plosives, or segments that originate as plosives, can be preaspirated.

2.4.3 Analysis of Preaspirated Clusters

One other striking restriction observable on preaspiration is that it does not co-occur with either preposed or postposed /ʔ/. We might expect clusters like /hkʔ/, /htʔ/, /hnʔ/, since their components (/hk/ and /kʔ/, etc.) are attested. But – with the apparent exception of /htʃʔ/, /htsʔ/ – such sequences are impossible in Mazateco.

The observations made so far on the Mazateco preaspirated onsets are summarized below:

(27)   Generalizations on preaspirated onsets
    a.   All simple plosives can be preaspirated.
    b.   All prenasals can be preaspirated.
    c.   Only (underlying) plosives can be preaspirated:
        /hy/ = /hi/ and /hβ/ = /hb/.
    d.   Preaspiration is incompatible with either pre- or postglottalization.
    e.   In sum, all and only plosives and plosive clusters can be preaspirated, provided they do not contain /ʔ/.

I suggest that these observations follow from an analysis in which preaspirated onsets are represented as plosives with aspiration associated to their closure. The general structure underlying the hC clusters is given below (A_n is a variable over release types, A_{max} and A_f):

(28) Representation of hC onsets

$$[\text{spread}]$$
$$|$$
$$A_0 \; A_n$$

The structure in (25) results from the merger of the A_{max} position of /h/ with the A_0 closure of a following plosive. A preliminary statement of the merger is given below:

(29) Merger deriving hC onsets (preliminary)
       Merge: $A_{max} \; A_0$
                      $|$
                  [spread]

The output of merger is always a single A-position, the one involving the greatest degree of stricture. All features of the input sequence are associated to it. This means that the merger of A_0 and A_{max} in (29) will yield a single A_0 to which are associated both the original features of the closure and the [spread] feature originally belonging to the approximant /h/.

My claim then is that /h/ in /hC/ clusters is not sequentially ordered before C but rather phonologically simultaneous with its closure. One bit of phonetic evidence supporting this is PP's observation that /h/ becomes "a voiceless nasal fricative" when it occurs before nasals (1947:80). In a different passage, PP note that /hn/ sometimes sounds like /nhn/, once again suggesting that the first half of the nasal stop is both aspirated and nasalized. In his description of the Chiquihuitlan Mazateco dialect, Jamieson (1977:94) makes a similar observation: "/h/ is the voiceless counterpart of a following ... sonorant", where sonorant turns out to mean nasal stop. Jamieson's transcriptions for /hma/, /hne/, /hɲa/ are [M̥mã], [N̥nẽ] [N̥ɲã]. I interpret digraphs like [M̥m] to indicate that aspiration is phonetically realized as simultaneous with at least the first half of the stop closure. The corresponding phonological representation for the /h-nasal/ onsets of Huautla and Chiquihuitlan is given below:

(30) The structure of /h-nasal/

[spread]
|
A_0 A_{max}
\ /
[nasal]

The representation proposed in (28) for the /hC/ onsets of Mazateco explains all but one of the generalizations listed earlier: the incompatibility between preaspiration and pre- or post-glottalization. Anticipating a bit, we note that /?C/ onsets have one of the essential properties of /hC/ onsets: they involve stops only. Preglottalization will accordingly be analyzed as association of [+constricted] to the closure of a stop. From this it follows that a preaspirated stop cannot be simultaneously preglottalized: and this explains the absence of /h?C/ or /?hC/ onsets. More challenging is the absence of postglottalized preaspirated stops /hC?/. Such sequences will emerge from the discussion of /C?/ onsets as having the following structure:

(31) Putative /hC?/

[spread]   [constricted]
| |
A_0 A_n

There is no absolute constraint against such structures, since the incompatible specifications [spread] and [constricted] are sequenced rather than simultaneous. Indeed such sequences are encountered in Mazateco as transforms of underlying fricative-postglottalized stop sequences (e.g., /sts?/ → /hts?/), a cluster type discussed below. Why is it then that the /h-stop-?/ sequences cannot be generated directly by the conjunction of preaspiration and postglottalization? Why can their *only* source be the underlying fricative prefix on a stop? The answer is that the onsets with aspiration or glottalization are generated by a merger process whose immediate output must be a monosegmental sequence of A positions: the structures outlined in (31) are not monosegmental, in virtue of (15.d). In contrast, the fricative-plosive-(?) clusters – the source of /hC?/ onsets – will be shown to have independently observable bisegmental properties: given this, the co-occurrence of aspiration and glottalization in such sequences is not surprising.

Complex Onsets as Single Segments: The Mazateco Pattern 235

2.4.4 Postaspirated Clusters

I turn next to the post-aspirated clusters. PP's list of examples is given below:

(32) Postaspirated clusters

Two-member onsets

PP's	Phonological	Phonetic	Example	Gloss
<vh>	/bh/	[ɸh]	/vhi/	'he goes'
<th>	/th/	[t^h]	/tha/	'light in weight'
<tsh>	/tsh/	[ts^h]	/tshe/	'clean'
<ʧh>	/ʧh/	[ʧ^h]	/ʧha/	'brother-in-law'
<tṣh>	/tṣh/	[tṣ^h]	/tṣhoa/	'skin'
<kh>	/kh/	[k^h]	/kha/	'bad smelling'
<mh>	/mh/	[m^h]	/vʔa.mhe/	'I walk'
<nh>	/nh/	[n^h]	/nhe.na/	'it is gained by me'
<sh>	/sh/	[s^h]	/sha/	'bitter'
<ʃh>	/ʃh/	[ʃ^h]	/ʃhao/	'dew'

Three-member clusters

PP's	Phonological	Phonetic	Example	Gloss
<nth>	/nth/	[^{n}d^h]	/nthao/	'wind'
<ntsh>	/ntsh/	[^{n}d̂s^h]	/ntshao/	'rust'
<nʧh>	/nʧh/	[^{n}d̂ʃ^h]	/nʧha/	'fat'
<ntṣh>	/ntṣh/	[^{n}d̂ṣ^h]	/yantṣhi/	'meat hook'
<nkh>	/nkh/	[^{ŋ}g^h]	/nkhi/	'many'

The most significant observation here is that continuants can be postaspirated in Mazateco. Not all are recorded with postaspiration: /yh/ and /lh/ are left unmentioned by PP. There are gaps among the stops as well: /ŋh/ is missing. We will seek to explain most of these gaps below.

PP do not discuss the phonetic realization of the postaspirated clusters except to note that /v/ in /vh/ is voiceless. The analysis I propose will claim that /h/ is phonologically simultaneous with the last A position of the onset: it is superimposed on the release of stops and on the unique A position of continuants.

(33)   Representation of postaspirated onsets

   a.   Plosives   b.   Continuants

   A_0 A_n A_n
        | |
    [spread]   [spread]

The representations in (33) explain why /β/ in /βh/ is voiceless: on the surface /β/ is a spirant and thus necessarily simultaneous with /h/. The same assumption may also explain the absence of /yh/: if /y^h/ is aspirated /Y/, rather than a sequence of /y/ plus /h/, then it may become indistinguishable from /ʃ^h/. The process that will neutralize the distinction between /y^h/ and /ʃ^h/ will look as follows:

(34)   Fricativization: /y^h/ → /ʃ^h/
       [spread]
          |
       A_{max} → A_f
          |
       Coronal
          |
       [-anterior]

The rule of Fricativization states that laminopalatal aspirated releases are realized with frication.[24] This process may also be assumed to turn the postaspirated stop /ɲh/ – whose absence was noted above – into the postaspirated affricate /ɲʧ^h/. I assume here that nasality is removed from the A_f position of /ɲʧ^h/ after (34) applies, since fricatives (i.e., A_f positions) cannot be nasal in Mazateco. Note that (34) takes crucial advantage of the assumption that intermediate /y^h/ and /ɲ^h/ are not true clusters on the surface, but rather aspiration associated to a pre-existing release.

I conclude then that postaspirated stops result from the association of /h/ to the last A position of an existing consonant. Preaspirated stops have been analyzed as the effect of the symmetric operation: the association

---

[24] Phenomena comparable to (34) are attested elsewhere: see, for instance, Trubetzkoy's (1939) discussion of Nama affricates as the realization of underlying Nama aspirated stops. In Nama, the aspirated A_{max} release of an underlying stop turns into a fricated release, A_f. This is exactly what (34) does, only to a more limited class of segments.

of /h/ to the first A position of a consonant. A process of bidirectional merger between an A position and /h/ will cover both cases. Bearing in mind that the number of A positions ranges between two (for plosives) and one (for all others), we note that this extension of our analysis will explain why plosives can be pre- or postaspirated whereas continuants can be only postaspirated. To see this, we examine the derivation of /hm/, /mh/ and /sh/. No direction is specified in (35.a) and no restrictions are imposed on the nature of the second A position: merger will take place in all /hC/ and /Ch/ clusters.

(35) a. Analysis of pre- and post-aspirated onsets

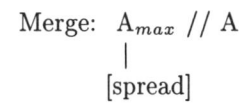

  Merge: A_{max} // A
  |
  [spread]

b. Derivations

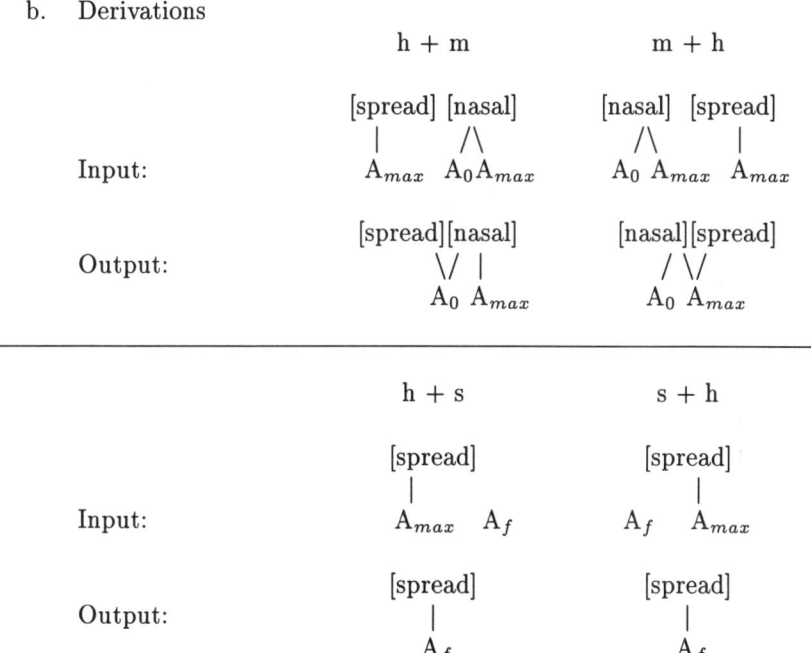

$$\begin{array}{ccc} & h+m & m+h \\ \text{Input:} & \begin{array}{c} \text{[spread] [nasal]} \\ | \quad /\backslash \\ A_{max} \quad A_0 A_{max} \end{array} & \begin{array}{c} \text{[nasal] [spread]} \\ /\backslash \quad | \\ A_0 \ A_{max} \quad A_{max} \end{array} \\ \text{Output:} & \begin{array}{c} \text{[spread][nasal]} \\ \backslash/ \ | \\ A_0 \ A_{max} \end{array} & \begin{array}{c} \text{[nasal][spread]} \\ | \ \backslash/ \\ A_0 \ A_{max} \end{array} \end{array}$$

$$\begin{array}{ccc} & h+s & s+h \\ \text{Input:} & \begin{array}{c} \text{[spread]} \\ | \\ A_{max} \quad A_f \end{array} & \begin{array}{c} \text{[spread]} \\ | \\ A_f \quad A_{max} \end{array} \\ \text{Output:} & \begin{array}{c} \text{[spread]} \\ | \\ A_f \end{array} & \begin{array}{c} \text{[spread]} \\ | \\ A_f \end{array} \end{array}$$

The derivations in (35.b) show that, under merger with /h/'s position, a stop can become preaspirated, if /h/ originates on its left, or postaspirated, if /h/ originates on its right. A continuant will become simply aspirated, whether /h/ came from its left or right, since merger will cause aspiration to become simultaneous with all other features of the continuant.[25] We explain in this way the differences in clustering possibilities between plosives and continuants.

2.4.5 Preaspirated Prenasalized Clusters

The assumption that /hC/ and /Ch/ onsets have surface structures in which aspiration is superimposed on one of C's aperture positions can explain another interesting fact about Mazateco onsets. There is no contrast between /hnC/ and /nhC/ onsets. The lack of contrast is predicted if nasality and aspiration are simultaneous on the closure of prenasals, as indicated below.

(36)   Representation of /hnC/ onsets

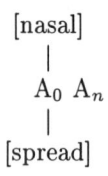

[nasal]
|
A_0 A_n
|
[spread]

The absence of /hnC/: /nhC/ contrasts is unexpected if the complex onsets are analyzed as true sequences of articulations: that is, if /hnC/ is analyzed as /h/ followed by /n/, followed by C. Given that /nh/, /hn/ and /hk/ are all possible onsets, a sequential analysis will lead one to expect that both /nhk/ and /hnk/ will be well-formed and distinct from each other. This expectation is informed, as noted above, by the observation that well-formedness conditions governing systems of complex onsets operate in general only on adjacent pairs of segments: this means that, if C_1C_2 and C_2C_3 are well-formed onsets, then $C_1C_2C_3$ is also expected to be well-formed. In light of this principle, the absence of a distinction like /hnk/ vs. /nhk/ is striking. This is not an accidental gap: none of the five surface plosives of Mazateco shows such a contrast, even though each one of them displays all conceivable combinations of prenasalization, pre- and postaspiration or pre- and postglottalization.

A sequential analysis of pre- and post-aspirated clusters must explain two other systematic gaps. First, the presence of /C-h/ and /h-n/ clusters predicts the unattested /C- h-n/. The logic of this prediction was outlined

---

[25] The assumption I am making throughout is that all autosegments linked to the same A position are phonologically simultaneous. Therefore A positions linked to [spread] and [nasal] in the output of (35) are understood to be simultaneously aspirated and nasalized, rather than first aspirated and then nasalized, or the other way around.

above: in sequential analyses, C_1C_2 and C_2C_3 jointly imply $C_1C_2C_3$. Second, the presence of /C-h/ and /h-stop/ predicts /C-h- stop/ sequences. Such clusters are also unattested, for any choice of C.

Our analysis rules out /C-h-n/ sequences by noting that their final member /n/ will be prevocalic and therefore, necessarily, a released nasal stop. Since the stop is released, it will have a full set of point of articulation features. The input sequence for putative /stop-h-n/ or /fricative-h-n/ clusters will have the representations shown in (37):

(37) Representation of putative /C-h-n/ sequences in Mazateco

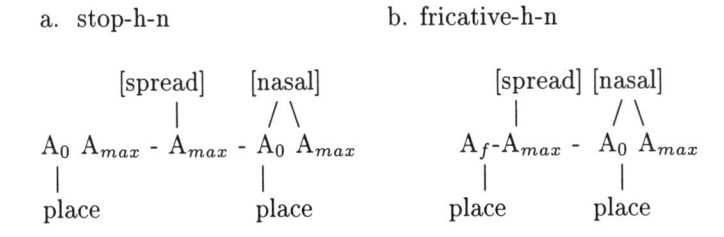

a. stop-h-n   b. fricative-h-n

$$
\begin{array}{cc}
\text{[spread]} \quad \text{[nasal]} & \text{[spread]} \quad \text{[nasal]} \\
| \quad\quad /\,\backslash & | \quad\quad /\,\backslash \\
A_0 \; A_{max} - A_{max} - A_0 \; A_{max} & A_f\text{-}A_{max} - A_0 \; A_{max} \\
| \quad\quad\quad\quad | & | \quad\quad\quad | \\
\text{place} \quad\quad \text{place} & \text{place} \quad \text{place}
\end{array}
$$

Merger with /h/ can take place in any one of the structures shown in (37) but its outcome is irrelevant: both the input and the output structures of merger differ substantially from all other onsets of this class, in that they will possess two place nodes. Our working assumption is that surface clusters with [nasal], /h/ and /?/ are well formed in Mazateco only to the extent that they are analyzable as monosegmental. The clusters shown in (37) are not and cannot become monosegmental.[26] The same assumptions explain the absence of /C-h-stop/ sequences: both C and the stop will have independent specifications for place and thus could not pass for single segments, even if subjected to merger.

The account sketched so far has explained several phonological properties of Mazateco aspirated onsets: the fact that pre- and postaspirated plosives are allowed, while only "postaspirated" (i.e., fully aspirated) continuants are permitted; the absence of contrast between /h-N-C/ and /N-h-

---

[26]There is an alternative explanation for the absence of /stop-h-n/ clusters. We may assume here, as we have assumed earlier for /n-h-stop/ sequences, that the stop will be unreleased. If so, it is conceivable that the process removing the place features of an unreleased nasal stop applies to oral stops as well. In that case the /stop-h-n/ cluster will reduce to a sequence consisting of a placeless A_0 (a remnant of the original stop, relieved of its release and place features), followed by /h/, followed by /n/. Such a sequence will turn into preaspirated /hn/, an attested Mazateco onset. The general point emerging from either this analysis or the one offered in the text is this: the clusters containing two underlying sets of place features will either lose one place component, in which case they will yield, through merger, a structure identifiable as a single consonant and hence well formed; or, if they don't, they will be eliminated as ill-formed.

C/; and the absence of /C-h-N/ and /C-h-stop/ clusters. The fundamental assumption made here, that the glottal feature of /h/ becomes phonologically simultaneous with a pre-existing A position, will be further confirmed in the analysis of ʔ-onsets, to which I turn next.

2.5 Onsets with Glottalization

The preglottalized onset clusters of Mazateco involve the nasals, the prenasals, the voiced fricative /v/ (= /β/) and the glide /y/.

(38) Onsets with preglottalization

b. Two-member onsets

PP's	Phonological	Phonetic	Example	Gloss
<ʔm>	/ʔm/	[ʔm]	/soʔma/	'earthen jar'
<ʔn>	/ʔn/	[ʔn]	/naʔni/	'brier'
<ʔɲ>	/ʔɲ/	[ʔɲ]	/niʔɲa/	'writing pen'
<ʔv>	/ʔb/ or /ʔo/	[ʔβ]	/ʔva/	'hook'
<ʔy>	/ʔi/	[ʔy]	/ʔya/	'rainbow'

b. Three member clusters

PP's	Phonological	Phonetic	Example	Gloss
<ʔnt>	/ʔnt/	[ʔⁿd]	/ʔnta/	'good'
<ʔnk>	/ʔnk/	[ʔⁿg]	/ʔnka.ha/	'water hole'
<ʔnts>	/ʔnts/	[ʔⁿd͡z]	/ʔntsa/	'my hand'
<ʔnʧ>	/ʔnʧ/	[ʔⁿd͡ʒ]	/ʔnʧiʔe/	'bee'
<ʔnts̪>	/ʔnts̪/	[ʔⁿɖ͡ʐ]	/ʔnts̪ati/	'comb'

With the exception of /ʔy/ and /ʔβ/, preglottalization is permitted with plosives only: there are no /ʔs/, /ʔʃ/, /ʔl/, /ʔr/ clusters in Mazateco. An additional restriction is that the closure of a preglottalized stop must be nasal.

The preglottalized /ʔy/ is clearly an underlying sequence /ʔi/, in which /i/ is the first member of a complex nucleus. There is no contrast between /ʔyV/ and /ʔiV/ syllables in Mazateco, as PP note: "The combinations /oV/ and /iV/ may follow /Cʔ/ but not /ʔ/ or /Vʔ/; this restriction does not apply to /õa/ or /ia/ etc., nor to simple /o/ and /i/. Thus one finds /ʧʔoa/ 'his mouth' /ntʔia/ 'house', /ʔõa/ 'we are five', /toncoʔo/ 'spider', /ʔivi/ 'here' but not */ʔoa/ or */ʔia/." (1947:87).

The suggestion was made earlier that onsets lacking supralaryngeal articulations are disfavored in Mazateco; and that syllables containing such onsets turn a high oral vowel into a glide, provided that this does not entirely eliminate the nucleus. This analysis explains every aspect of PP's observations. Glide formation is not needed in syllables beginning with /CʔV/ (or /ʔC/) since these onsets do contain a supralaryngeal gesture: this is why /tsʔoa/ does not become */tsʔwa/. Glide formation is needed in forms like /ʔi(-vi)/ but cannot apply without eliminating the nucleus of the initial syllable. On the other hand, glide formation, although needed in forms like /ʔõa/, cannot apply there because it would yield a nasalized continuant /w̃/ : *ʔw̃a/. Finally, glide formation does apply in underlying /ʔia/, /ʔoa/ and yields /ʔya/ and intermediate /ʔwa/ respectively, the latter spelled <ʔva> by PP.

PP's remarks indicate that at least some instances of [ʔβV] originate as /ʔoV/ and represent an intermediate sequence /ʔw/. Since /β/ represents not only a glide but also an underlying bilabial stop, I will assume that /ʔβ/ clusters have a diverse derivational source: some originate as /ʔb/ while others come from /ʔoV/, via glide formation. For instance, glide formation may have applied in /ʔva/ 'hook', in which case this item originates as /ʔoa/, to become intermediate /ʔwa/. The information provided by PP does not allow us to tell whether the two classes of surface [ʔβ] differ in their phonological behavior.[27]

Having eliminated the preglottalized continuants, we turn to the plosives. There is a predictable relation between preglottalization and nasality in Mazateco, which suggests that preposed /ʔ/ induces prenasalization in a plosive. The simplest statement of this relation will be based on the assumption that preglottalized plosives have /ʔ/ superimposed on their closure rather than linearly ordered before it:

(39)   Preglottal nasalization

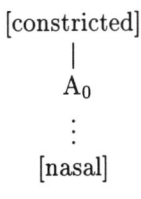

[constricted]
|
A₀
⋮
[nasal]

---

[27] One point that remains unclear is the fact that Glide Formation applies to /ʔoV/ sequences (since PP observe that /ʔoV/ does not surface as such) but not to /hoV/ sequences (given the surface contrast between [hβV] and [hoV]). Glide Formation applies to /i/ in both /ʔiV/ and /hiV/ sequences. Perhaps this difference between /i/ and /o/ is attributable to the fact that only /i/ is unambiguously a high vowel.

The rule in (39) allows us to assume that every Mazateco segment endowed with a closure can be preglottalized. The surface absence of /ʔt/, /ʔts/, /ʔk/ etc., is due to Preglottal Nasalization: /ʔt/ becomes /ʔnt/, and finally [ʔnd]. This simplifies considerably the analysis.[28]

(40) How /ʔt/ becomes [ʔnd]

    (i) Merger:

$$\begin{array}{c}[\text{constricted}] \\ | \\ A_{max} + A_0 \ A_{max} \\ | \\ \text{coronal}\end{array} \quad \rightarrow \quad \begin{array}{c}[\text{constricted}] \\ | \\ A_0 \ A_{max} \\ | \\ \text{coronal}\end{array}$$

    (ii) Preglottal nasalization:

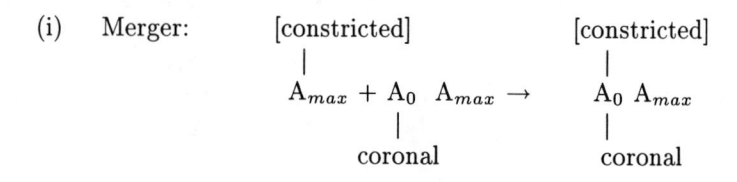

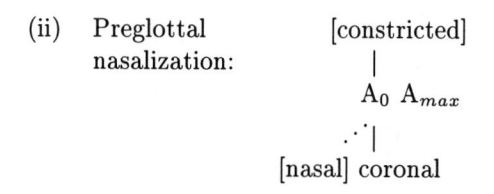

$$\begin{array}{c}[\text{constricted}] \\ | \\ A_0 \ A_{max} \\ \cdot\cdot\, | \\ [\text{nasal}] \ \text{coronal}\end{array}$$

    (ii) Prenasal voicing:

$$\begin{array}{c}[\text{constricted}] \ [\text{voice}] \\ |\cdot\cdot \\ A_0 \ A_{max} \\ /\backslash \\ [\text{nasal}] \ \text{coronal}\end{array}$$

The absence of surface contrast between preglottalized prenasals (e.g. underlying /ʔ-N-t/), prenasalized preglottals (e.g., underlying /N-ʔ-t/) and preglottalized stops subject to (39) (e.g., underlying /ʔ-t/ becoming prenasalized) is explained by the nature of the representations we propose: in all three cases nasality and glottalization will end up being simultaneously present on A_0. Such structures will be necessarily identical.

---

[28]Since we assume that some instances of /ʔβ/ originate as /ʔb/, we must explain why /ʔb/ does not become /ʔmb/. This appears to require the assumption that the spirantization of /b/ precedes and bleeds rule (39). A better explanation is that the primary step in the derivation of the prenasalized /ʔC/ onsets is the voicing rather than the nasalization of the closure. Prenasalization is simply an enhancement strategy for voicing, needed for stops with a relatively small supraglottal cavity, but not needed for bilabial stops, whose supraglottal cavity is sufficiently large to maintain vocal cord vibration.

Complex Onsets as Single Segments: The Mazateco Pattern 243

The list of Mazateco postglottalized onsets is given below. As before, I omit the /hCʔ/ clusters, whose status will be discussed separately.

(41) Postglottalized onsets

a. Two-member onsets

PP's	Phonological	Phonetic	Example	Gloss
<tʔ>	/tʔ/	[tʔ]	/tʔi/	'go' (imperative)
<tsʔ>	/tsʔ/	[tsʔ]	/tsʔe/	'lazy'
<ʧʔ>	/ʧʔ/	[ʧʔ]	/ʧʔoa/	'parrot'
<tṣ>	/tṣʔ/	[tṣʔ]	/tṣʔoale/	'pieces left over'
<kʔ>	/kʔ/	[kʔ]	/kʔia/	'then'
<mʔ>	/mʔ/	[mʔ]	/mʔẽ/	'he is sick'
<nʔ>	/nʔ/	[nʔ]	/nʔo/	'rope'
<ɲʔ>	/ɲʔ/	[ɲʔ]	/ɲʔãi/	'difficult'
<sʔ>	/sʔ/	[sˀ]	/sʔoi/	'fiesta'
<ʃʔ>	/ʃʔ/	[ʃˀ]	/ʃʔi/	'man'
<lʔ>	/lʔ/	[lˀ]	/lʔi/	'fire'
<vʔ>	/bʔ/	[βˀ]	/vʔe/	'I hit'
<yʔ>	/yʔ/	[yˀ]	/yʔa/	'I carry'

b. Three member onsets

PP's	Phonological	Phonetic	Example	Gloss
<ntʔ>	/ntʔ/	[ⁿdʔ]	/ntʔe/	'industrious'
<ntsʔ>	/ntsʔ/	[ⁿdzʔ]	/ntsʔe/	'his brother'
<nʧʔ>	/nʧʔ/	[ᶮdʒʔ]	/nʧʔã/	'cold'
<ntṣʔ>	/ntṣʔ/	[ⁿdẓʔ]	/ntṣʔoe/	'he hears'

For postglottalized clusters, PP's information about phonetic realization are limited to the following: "there is usually a very slight open transition between the stop and the /ʔ/ in the same syllable, so that the stops are not phonetically glottalized - i.e., they are not made with egressive pharynx air [...] and [...] this phonetic gap between the stop and the /ʔ/ in clusters is often further accentuated in that /ʔ/ may be actualized as the laryngealization of the following vowel rather than as a separate stop, while often there is a slight prearticulation of the vowel before the /ʔ/ (but after the glottal stop in the sequence of oral plus glottal stop)." (1947:81) . I interpret this statement about /stop-ʔ/ clusters to indicate that the glottal gesture is phonologically aligned with the stop release, as shown below, but phonetically realized at the boundary between the release interval and the following vowel. The "slight prearticulation of the vowel" occurring between the end of stop closure and the glottal is simply an indication that the phonetic transition between the oral constriction of the stop and that of the vowel takes place *simultaneously* with the glottal gesture. As in the case of postaspirated onsets, I will assume that the glottal gesture in /Cʔ/ onsets is phonologically simultaneous with the rightmost A position of the preceding consonant.

(42) Phonological representation of Cʔ onsets

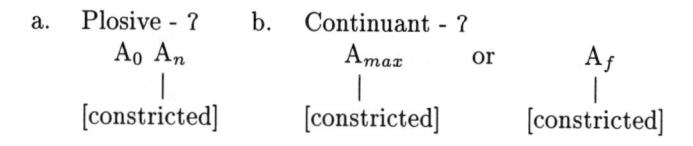

    a. Plosive - ʔ   b. Continuant - ʔ
        $A_0\ A_n$ A_{max} or A_f
           | | |
    [constricted]   [constricted]   [constricted]

The analysis of pre- and post-glottalized onsets emerging from this section is entirely parallel to that of pre- and postaspirated onsets. We may assume then that a single process is responsible for their formation: an extension of the merger in (35). But rather than complicate the statement of the rule by mentioning a disjunction of features (i.e., Merge A_{max} // A, iff the former dominates only [spread] or only [constricted]) we will assume that A-position merger takes place wherever its immediate output is a single segment. This formulation will cover both the merger with /h/ and /ʔ/ and the merger with unreleased placeless nasal A_0, the former (22.a).

(43) Merger (final)

Merge any adjacent pair of A-positions iff the immediate output is monosegmental according to (15).

The unique condition imposed on (43) – the monosegmental quality of the output – will ensure that only three elements will be able to freely merge with the Mazateco consonants: a placeless nasal closure and the placeless approximants /ʔ/ and /h/. All other segments carry a place component and will necessarily yield bisegmental outputs when in combination with another consonant.

2.6 S-stop Onsets

2.6.1 A Preliminary Analysis

A final class of Mazateco clusters consists of sequences in which the spirants /s/ and /ʃ/ (abbreviated below as S) precede a stop. We will observe in what follows that the /S-stop/ clusters fall under different generalizations from the other Mazateco onsets. They are not featurally monosegmental, insofar as the spirant and the stop contain each its own distinctive place specifications. Whether these onsets are structurally monosegmental is a harder point to settle. What I propose below is primarily a description of the relevant sequences in Mazateco, focussing on the source of /hC?/ clusters and, as an aside, a speculation about the phonological representation of the /S-stop/ clusters. Because several fundamental questions about the cross-linguistic properties of fricative-stop sequences remain unanswered, the main goal of this section is merely to verify that our analysis of the monosegmental onsets of Mazateco is compatible with the generalizations holding of the bisegmental /SC/ sequences.

The following are the transparent examples of the class of /S-stop/ clusters:

(44) Mazateco surface /S-C/ onsets

a. Two member onsets

sk: ska 'crazy'
ʃt: ʃti 'children'
ʃk: ʃka 'trousers'
(ʃn): nkaʃni 'Chiquihuitlan'

b. Three-member onsets:

sk?:   sk?ao 'It will break'
ʃt?:   haʃt?a lanka 'good bye'
ʃk?:   ʃk?e 'thin'

According to PP, the example of /ʃn/ is unique in the Huautla dialect. This, the fact that the example is a toponym, and the absence of /sn?/, /sm/, /sm?/, /ʃm/, /ʃm?/, /sɲ/, /sɲ?/ casts doubt on the presence of /S-nasal/ onsets in this dialect. The Chiquihuitlan dialect studied by Jamieson (1977) has a number of better attested /S-n/ onsets: the gloss makes it obvious that /nkaʃni/ 'Chiquihuitlan' represents an unassimilated loan.

2.6.2 An Outline of the Analysis

The most obvious gap in the paradigm of (44) are sequences in which the spirant and stop are either [α anterior] or else are both strident. The following clusters, although structurally identical to those in (44), remain unattested.

(45) Missing S-onsets: coronal clusters

st
sts   sʧ   sts̪
ʃts   ʃʧ   ʃts̪
stʔ
stsʔ   sʧʔ   sʧʔ
ʃtsʔ   ʃʧʔ   ʃts̪ʔ

We may now recall the clusters /htsʔ/ and /hʧʔ/, set aside earlier as unique and aberrant cases of coexistence between aspiration and glottalization. The complementary distribution between /S-C-ʔ/ and /h-C-ʔ/ clusters suggests strongly that the latter are surface realizations of the former.

(46) h-C-ʔclusters
/stsʔ/ = [htsʔ]   htsʔe 'sprout'
/sʧʔ/ = [hʧʔ]   ʔntihʧʔa 'orphan'

The process that replaces in these examples a spirant with preaspiration can be identified as dissimilation: two coronals may not remain adjacent if they are either homorganic ([α anterior]) or strident. When they do co-occur in intermediate representations, the spirant loses its place features but leaves behind its laryngeal component, which surfaces as preaspiration. This will explain the absence of the clusters in (45), most of which are attested as surface preaspirated onsets, indistinguishable from underlying /hC/ clusters. A distinct advantage of this idea is that it accounts for the complete absence of /ʔCh/ clusters in Mazateco: these could not have a debuccalized fricative as their underlying source, since /(ʔ)-stop-fricative/ clusters do not exist anywhere in the language. The process of debuccalization is formulated and explored in further detail in section 2.6.2.

Another gap attributable to dissimilation is that involving clusters consisting of a sibilant attached to a pre- or postaspirated stop: sequences like /shk/ or /skh/ are also systematically missing. I propose to explain this by noting that, although Mazateco fricatives are not distinctively aspirated, they are clearly phonetically aspirated, as indicated by the fact that they yield /h/ under debuccalization. A dissimilatory process comparable to debuccalization is probably responsible for the absence of clusters in which /h/ co-occurs with an /S-stop/ cluster. However, in the absence of information about the morphophonemics of Mazateco, we cannot tell whether underlying /skh/ becomes /kh/ or /sk/. This explanation for the

Complex Onsets as Single Segments: The Mazateco Pattern   247

absence of /sCh/ raises an interesting question for our analysis: if /s/ is phonetically aspirated, what explains the surface contrast between /s/ and post-aspirated /sh/? I address this issue in section (2.6.4).

Also systematically missing are the onsets listed below, in which the closure is nasalized. I omit from this list clusters in which the fricative and the stop are homorganic: the absence of /sn/ or /snts?/, for instance, need not be mentioned again, since it is parallel to the absence – discussed above – of /st/ or /sts?/.

(47)   More missing S-onsets: S-nasal

```
sm      sɲ              snk
sm?     sɲ?             snk?
s?m     s?ɲ             s?nk
ʃm              ʃnt     ʃnk
ʃm?             ʃnt?    ʃnk?
ʃ?m             ʃ?nt    ʃ?nk
```

A feature common to the missing /S-C/ clusters in (47) is the presence of nasality on closure: both //ʃnt/ and //ʃn/ are disallowed, in contrast to /ʃt/.

Preglottalization (i.e., glottalization linked to closure) also blocks the attachment of the sibilant: there are no /s?C/ clusters. This could be plausibly attributed to the fact that preglottalized stops are subject to prenasalization (rule (39)). There are no /s?C/ sequences because they would all surface as /s?nC/: whatever explains the absence of the clusters in (47) will explain the lack of /s?C/. I summarize now the observations made on the restrictions to which /S-stop/ clusters are subject in Mazateco:

(48)   Generalizations about S-stop onsets

(a) S is attached to a closure: */sl/, */sy/, */sr/ */sʃ/
    (the latter realizable as debuccalized *[hʃ]).
(b) S may not attach to a nasalized closure: *//ʃnt/, */s?m/
(c) S does not surface if attached to an aspirated stop:
    */skh/, */shk/.
(d) S and the stop may be heterorganic: cf. //ʃt/.
(e) S and the stop must be heterorganic on the surface:
    cf. /st/ → /ht/.

There are two types observations here: one class, (48.c and e), involves OCP-style dissimilatory conditions imposed on the surface feature composition of S-stop sequences. Such conditions appear to follow the attachment of the sibilant to the closure of the following stop. For instance, the constraint in (48.e) does not block the attachment of /s/ to /ts?/: it merely repairs the OCP violation resulting from this attachment, by removing the place component of /s/. The second class of conditions holding of the S-stop clusters of Mazateco involves the nature of the position to which a sibilant may be prefixed in the first place: this position is a closure, bare of any features other than [place].

We may briefly compare the Mazateco /S-C/ clusters to their counterparts observed elsewhere, in languages like English, Latin and in modern Romance. The Mazateco sequences are typical of this class in three respects: (a) they attach only to closures, (b) they attach to closures that are minimally specified, carrying place features but not nasality or voicing, and (c) they precede the closure. The Mazateco /S-C/ onsets are somewhat atypical – though not unique – in one respect: they display a place contrast between /ʃ-C/ and /s-C/, absent from many languages where /fricative-stop/ clusters coexist with place distinctions within the fricative series. Thus English allows /s-stop/ but not /ʃ-stop/, /f-stop/ or /θ-stop/ onsets. Sanskrit has numerous /s-stop/ clusters, as well as homorganic /ʃʧ/ and /ṣṭ/ but no heterorganic /ʃ-stop/, /ṣ-stop/ sequences.

Given the need to distinguish the place features of the fricative from those of the stop, we will assume that the /S-C/ clusters are linearly ordered sequences rather than phonologically simultaneous components. One possibility then is to analyze the /S-C/ clusters as $A_f A_0$ sequences. This structure leaves one important question unanswered: why are the /S-Stop/ clusters significantly more widespread than other structurally bisegmental sequences, such as $A_{max}Af$, $A_f A_{max}$, $A_{max} A_0$, $A_f A_f$ etc. A possible alternative analysis is that the fricative occupies not the expected A_f position but a segment-internal slot previously unidentified: that of Approach-to-Closure, or Approach.[29] On this hypothesis, the full structure of Closure would look as follows:

(49) Approach as a subconstituent of Closure

[[Approach [Closure Proper (A_0)]] Release (A_{max})]

---

[29]Ian Maddieson first suggested to me the idea of an Approach position. He is not to blame for its use in this context.

Like the release of the stop, the Approach position would not necessarily carry features distinct from those present on the closure proper: this would be the case, for instance, with plain stops, for which we might assume a featurally bare Approach position. The presence of Approach would manifest itself phonologically only in case a distinct set of point of articulation features would come to lodge there, as in the case of /S-stop/ clusters, which could be represented as follows:

(50)   S-stop clusters

      Approach A_0 A_{max}
          | |
        place   place

The principal merit of this type of analysis is that it helps explain why /S-stop/ clusters are widespread onsets and even more widespread intervocalic clusters: they are structurally monosegmental, in that the place features of the fricative occupy a position projected by the stop. In this respect, they are structurally parallel to the stop-liquid clusters, where the liquid occupies the release position of the plosive. If this idea is adopted, the derivational origin of the /S-Stop clusters/ could be the merger of a stop's approach with a preceding fricative's A_f position. A distinct consideration that favors the analysis in (50) is the fact that it will allow us to express what *all* Mazateco onset clusters have in common: they are structurally monosegmental.

Whether or not the Mazateco /S-Stop/ clusters are analyzed as in (50), they are clearly bisegmental in feature composition, as they contain two distinct place components. Another argument to the same effect is the joint presence of the two incompatible features of aspiration and glottalization in /hts?/, /htʃ?/, the outputs of debuccalization. The monosegmental onsets of Mazateco – resulting from prenasalization, pre- and postaspiration and pre- and postglottalization – do not allow aspiration and glottalization to co-occur, precisely because they must be monosegmental (cf (43) above). On the other hand, the /S-stop-?/ clusters, whose bisegmental feature composition has been established independently, are not constrained by any considerations of feature compatibility. There is therefore no reason to expect /h/ and /?/ to exclude each other in such structures. Note that the aspiration is present in the /S-stop-?/ sequences even before debuccalization applies: the effect of the latter is simply to eliminate all features of the sibilant other than its aspiration.

Before turning to the specifics of the analysis, we should address an important typological question. The overall view of Mazateco clusters emerging from the discussion is that the language possesses numerous underlying clusters but only one set of surface bisegmental clusters, the /S-stop/ sequences. The question that arises is whether this situation is attested elsewhere: are there other languages whose only bisegmental onsets are /fricative-stop/ sequences? I raise this issue because our exposure to the cluster systems of Indo-European languages – in which /S-stop/ is frequently not an allowable onset cluster – may create the impression that /S-stop/ is a very marked variety of onset, allowed only in the company of other, less marked, onset types, such as /obstruent-liquid/. Among the North American-Indian languages the onset inventory we attribute to Mazateco – single C's and /S-stop/ clusters – is in fact encountered elsewhere. Haida (Sapir 1922) possesses onset clusters which may consist only of /s/ followed by a stop or by /ł/ followed by a stop. Since /ł/ is the only spirant of the language other than /s/, the Haida inventory of surface onsets can be described in terms identical to that of Mazateco: single segments and fricative-plosive clusters. Similar onset inventories are attested in Havasupai (Kozlowsky 1976), Yuchi and Chiquihuitlan Mazateco, the latter two discussed below. What this indicates is that there is no implicational relation – and hence no markedness ranking – between /S-stop/ and /stop-liquid/ onsets: a language may possess one or the other type, both or neither. This lends further support to the Approach hypothesis, which succeeds in identifying the fact that onsets like /ʃt/ and /tr/ are structurally equivalent, and hence equivalent in degree of markedness.

2.6.3 Debuccalization

It was suggested above that the absence of the homorganic or nearly homorganic clusters in (45) stems from a process in which the sibilant loses its point of articulation features. I call this type of rule debuccalization, adopting McCarthy's (1988) term, and attribute its application in the Mazateco onsets to the requirements of the Obligatory Contour Principle.

(51)   Debuccalization (preliminary)

place tier   .   .
            ≠ |
            A   A

Trigger: OCP violation on [anterior] and/or [strident] tier
Condition: A-positions are adjacent.

Rule (51) will turn not only postglottalized /sts?/, etc. into /hts?/ but also plain /sts/, /st/ into /hts/, /ht/ etc. In this case however, the preaspirated output of the rule is inevitably identical to a basic preaspirated plosive. I indicate below the possible derivational sources of the Mazateco coronal preaspirates:

(52)   Surface   Underlying

      ht   s t
              h t

      hts   sts
              hts
              ʃts

      htʃ   stʃ
              htʃ
              ʃtʃ

      hts?   sts?
              ʃts?

      htʃ?   stʃ?
              ʃtʃ?

PP note (1947:82) that the /hts?/ and /htʃ?/ clusters they recorded are infrequent and that they "tend to vary to /ts?/ and /tʃ?/". This could be explained rather simply in the framework of our analysis. If the distributional restrictions on /hC?/ are the only indication as to their underlying source as /SC?/ clusters, the Mazateco speakers may misanalyze them as ill-formed outcomes of the merger process in (43), ill-formed because they contain the incompatible specifications of aspiration and glottalization. If so, the speakers will tend to eliminate either /h/ or /?/: and it is likely that /h/ is being eliminated because its association to closure makes it less salient perceptually.

The tendency to drop preaspiration in /hC?/ clusters may explain the absence of recorded /ht?/ and /hts̩?/, sequences predicted to occur as debuccalized outcomes of underlying /st?/ and /sts̩?/, /ʃts̩?/. The fact that they were not recorded as such could easily be attributed to the fact that the entire class of postglottalized preaspirates resulting from debuccalization is only occasionally distinguishable from underlying postglottalized coronals: /ht?/ and /hts̩?/ are probably there but PP may have recorded them only as /tʔ/, /tsʔ/, indistinguishable from underlying postglottalized /tʔ/, /tsʔ/. With this proviso, I conclude that debuccalization accounts for each one of the missing onsets listed above in (45).

It was mentioned earlier that the /S-stop/ clusters of Mazateco must be featurally bisegmental. The surface contrast between /sk(ʔ)/ and /ʃk(ʔ)/ and that between /ʃk(ʔ)/ and /ʃt(ʔ)/ are sufficient to indicate that both the stop and the spirant have their own distinctive place specification. The dissimilation rule in (51) makes the same point: dissimilation would be inapplicable in the absence of some [αF][αF] sequence. Such a sequence is, according to (15), the trademark of a bisegmental cluster.

2.6.4 Excursus on [strident]

The dissimilatory debuccalization in (51) appears unusual in that it is triggered by identity in either point of articulation or in one stricture feature, [strident]. The problem stems directly from our use of the feature [strident].

I suspect that in this and other cases where the sibilants (/s/, /ʃ/) and the coronal affricates (/ts/, /tʃ/, /ts̪/) act as a natural class they do so for one of two reasons: they are either all [laminal] in articulation (as in Yucatec Mayan: cf. Straight 1976) or they share [+strident]. We cannot tell whether the sibilants and affricates of Mazateco are laminal and, for this reason, we cannot pursue the first possibility.

In what follows I will suggest the possibility that the behavior of [strident] in the Mazateco debuccalization is due to the fact that this feature is always a dependent of the coronal node: in effect, a place feature. The general motivation for this is the fact that [strident] is, for all practical purposes, restricted to coronal consonants. This renders it suspect as a genuine stricture feature, since one expects stricture distinctions to be freely distributed across points of articulation. A more likely possibility is that [strident] – if it exists at all – is a coronal dependent, like [laminal] or [anterior]. The immediate consequence of this proposal for Mazateco is that we can eliminate the disjunction between [anterior] and [strident] as the tiers where OCP violations may trigger debuccalization: [anterior] and [strident] are the only terminal features present in the place component of Mazateco which may occasion an OCP violation inside an /S-C/ cluster. We may assume then that the debuccalizing dissimilation applies between adjacent consonants that dominate *any identical pair of terminal place feature specifications*.

(53) Debuccalization (final)

place tier . .
           ╪ |
           A A

Trigger: OCP violation on any terminal tier
Condition: A-positions are adjacent.

Let us clarify now the relation between the facts described and the reformulated rule (53). We note first that Coronal is not a terminal feature: it has either [anterior] or [strident] dependents or both. This allows the dissimilar coronals /ʃ/ and /t/ – distinct in both anteriority and stridency – to coexist in the clusters /ʃt/ and /ʃtʔ/. All other clusters that can be generated in Mazateco by prefixing /s/ or /ʃ/ to a coronal plosive will be identical with respect to the terminal feature [strident] or [anterior] or both: this will trigger (53). Because of the monosegmental nature of the Mazateco onsets other than the /s-C/ clusters, no other allowable consonant sequences will contain two sets of specifications – identical or not – for any feature F. Therefore no other obvious possibilities for the application of (53) exist. However, an extension of (53) to non-place features may explain the absence – noted above – of /S-Stop/ onsets involving pre- or postaspirated stops.

2.6.5 A Further Remark on the Aspiration of /s/

The co-occurrence restriction barring /s/ and /ʃ/ as prefixes on pre- and postaspirated plosives was explained above by postulating that Mazateco spirants are aspirated, a common phonetic characteristic in voiceless fricatives. The aspiration is clearly redundant in this case, but its phonological presence is also fairly clear: no other assumption will explain the absence of /S-stop-h/.

This fact must however be reconciled with our treatment of postaspirated continuants. Recall from section 2.4.4., that the analysis of aspirated continuants /sh/, /ʃh/, /lh/ is based on the hypothesis that aspiration becomes simultaneous with the features of the existing A-position. We claimed that the distinction between surface /s/ and /sh/ is not that between a single segment and a cluster but rather that between a plain unaspirated consonant and its aspirated counterpart. Since this requires that surface /s/ and /ʃ/ be unaspirated, we seem to have derived a contradiction.

The solution is this. Vowels are laryngealized after /ʔ/ and aspirated after /h/, as noted, in the case of laryngealization, by PP (1947:79-80) and demonstrated, for aspiration and laryngealization, by Kirk, Ladefoged and Ladefoged (1984). However, no amount of vocalic aspiration is reported after the plain spirants or affricates and the instrumental data reported by Kirk, Ladefoged and Ladefoged indicates that the plain, unaspirated, fricative and affricates (i.e., /s/, /ʃ/, /ts/, /tʃ/, /ts̪/) do not induce aspiration of the following vowel. This suggests that *only distinctive laryngeal features* spread onto following vowels. The redundant aspiration associated to A_f positions is not involved in this process. The rule ordering sketched below is one way of accomplishing this:

(54) Ordering of Mazateco processes involving aspiration

- (i) Formation of /C-h/ onsets through merger of A-positions (cf. (43) above).
- (ii) Spread glottal features onto adjacent A position of tautosyllabic vowel.
- (iii) A_f is redundantly aspirated: [+spread]
$$\vdots$$
$$A_f$$
- (iv) Delink [+spread] where OCP is violated.

The scenario sketched above will derive surface sequences such as [sʰA] and [sʰa] in which the spirants themselves are both aspirated but in which the following vowel is aspirated only after /sh/, the fricative with *distinctive* aspiration. The surface phonological representations of [sʰA] and [sʰa] are shown below.

(55) Derivation of /s^{h}A/ and /s^{h}a/ (post merger (43))

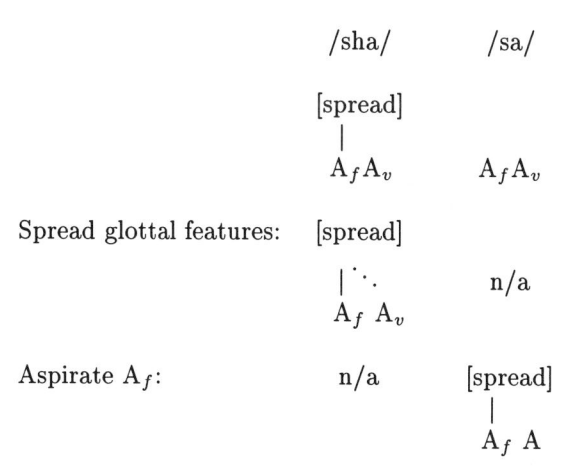

	/sha/	/sa/
	[spread] | A$_f$A$_v$	A$_f$A$_v$
Spread glottal features:	[spread] |∴ A$_f$ A$_v$	n/a
Aspirate A$_f$:	n/a	[spread] | A$_f$ A

This analysis, which Kirk, Ladefoged and Ladefoged's data support independently, reconciles our claim that /s/ and /ʃ/ have phonologically represented aspiration with the idea that "postaspirated" /sh/ onsets are monosegmental and possess a single A position. The contrast between what PP transcribed as /sh/ and /s/ exists, but resides in the vocalic context rather than the consonantal articulation.[30]

2.7 Summary of the Analysis

I conclude that PP were justified in deciding that the Mazateco onsets contain underlying sequences of distinct consonants: the only reasonable explanation for the surface contrast between pre- and postaspirated stops or pre- and postglottalized nasals is the existence of underlying /C-h/, /h-C/, /C-ʔ/, /ʔ-C/ sequences. I have suggested however that the vast majority of these underlying clusters – all those involving the satellites /h/, /ʔ/ and /n/ – are allowed to surface as onsets because the merger of A positions in (43) turns them into articulatory sequences that are analyzable as monosegmental.

Aside from these derived monosegmental onsets, Mazateco possesses true bisegmental clusters: the /S-Stop/ sequences. The major question left open is to understand why these are the only bisegmental onsets Mazateco tolerates. More concretely, if both /ʃt/ and /tr/ are bisegmental, then why does Mazateco allow one of these to surface but not the other? I have

---

[30] A final assumption is that glottalized /sʔ/ blocks the application of the redundancy rule introducing aspiration.

suggested above that it is not in fact predictable whether a language will allow bisegmental onset clusters consisting of only /S-Stop/ (as in Haida) or of only /Stop-Approximant/ (as in Latin and Romance) or of both /S-Stop/ and /Stop-Approximant/ (as in English). Thus the question raised now is not whether we can *explain* the choice made in Huautla Mazateco among possible types of bisegmental onsets: that choice is clearly arbitrary. Rather, the question is whether we can globally characterize which clusters are allowed to surface in Huautla, since, without such a characterization, we cannot *describe* the fact that /tr/ is absent from this language. A possible answer emerges if /S-stop/ sequences are analyzed as in (50), as resulting from the merger between an A_f position and the Approach of a following stop. If (50) is adopted, then we can assume that a minimal condition of well-formedness for all Huautla onsets is that they must be *structurally monosegmental*. The /S-Stop/ sequences, when analyzed as in (50), as well as the /nC/, /hC/, /ʔC/, /Ch/ and /Cʔ/ onsets, share this property. The answer to our earlier question – why /ʃt/ but not /tr/ – reduces in that case to this. Huautla allows the merger of A positions in only two circumstances, neither of which fits the case of /tr/: it allows the merger of A_f and Approach, regardless of whether the outcome of merger is featurally monosegmental, and it allows the merger of any two A positions, but only in case the result is featurally monosegmental.

3 Comparison with Pike and Pike's Account

The analysis presented here departs significantly from that proposed by PP. The principal point of difference between the two approaches is that PP take at face value the phonetic sequencing of articulatory gestures within a Mazateco onset and attribute segment status to almost every single consonantal gesture that could be temporally isolated in a sequence. Thus PP appear to have perceived two sequenced gestures in a Mazateco /ht/ cluster and they conclude from this that the cluster contains two segments . The present study, without denying the accuracy of the phonetic observations made by PP, has experimented with the idea that the phonetic sequencing of gestures is less important for the phonological analysis than the need to explain the properties of the overall cluster system. The system as a whole can be coherently described only if articulatory sequences like /ht/, /ʔnt/, /sʔ/ are viewed as phonologically simultaneous or overlapping. The theory of aperture positions presented at the beginning of this study has allowed us to maintain the claim that /h/ overlaps phonologically with /t/ both in /ht/ and in the distinct /th/ sequences.

A second point of difference revolves around PP's claim that that the onset clusters of Mazateco are hierarchically organized. There are two aspects to this claim. One is the principal/subordinate distinction – referred to below as headedness – and the other is the subconstituency involved in three-member onsets. PP claim that a tripartite onset like /nts?/ consists of the multiply embedded structure [n[ts?]]. The evidence cited in favor of this structure is the fact that occasionally, the first member of three-consonant onsets is syllabified with the preceding vowel, as a coda.

The analysis presented here does not employ constituent structure, for a very simple reason: we found no need for it and, besides, no structure *could* be defined within one segment. The occasional heterosyllabicity of /n/ in /nts?/ and perhaps other clusters may simply indicate that the closure – hence the nasal interval of the consonant – sometimes geminates, as appears to happen in Tlacoyalco Popoloca (Stark and Machin 1977), a language discussed below. (Some suggestions about the analysis of geminate consonants within our aperture position framework can be found in Steriade 1992.) Nor did we find any reason to define a head segment in either the cluster that represents the input to A position merger or in the structure resulting from merger.

But in several interesting respects, there is convergence between our analysis and PP's ideas. PP assume that the head of the onset is the consonant carrying the features of the oral constriction. It seems clear that PP relied here on the implicit assumption that bracketed structures may possess only one head, in order to explain why only one set of place features will exist within a Mazateco onset. The head consonant, according to their analysis, is the one carrying place and stricture specifications: if clusters are headed structures, then the limitation to one set of place features follows from the limitation to one head. We have attempted to capture this same intuition more directly, without the intermediary of a head-satellite distinction: our claim is that Mazateco onsets (other than the /S-stop/ clusters) contain only one set of place features because these onsets are single segments and single segments necessarily possess only one place node. The second point of convergence between the two analyses is this: PP's head consonants find a counterpart within our analysis as *the consonants which preserve their underlying A positions and features*: the satellites either lose their own A positions through merger (as in the case of /h/ in the derivations in (35.b)) or lose their underlying place components (as in the case of the unreleased nasals stops, which preserve only their nasality: cf. (22)). Finally, PP's characterization of the major components of Mazateco onsets – nasality, laryngeal features and oral constriction – indicates awareness of the featurally monosegmental character of these clusters.

The differences between PP's analysis and ours – differences which follow directly from the decision to incorporate a closure-release distinction in the phonological representations – were pointed out above. PP did not explain why plosives can head twice as many clusters – involving pre- and postglottalization, pre- and postaspiration – as continuants can. PP also failed to explain why prenasalized clusters combine in only two distinct ways with aspiration – as /nCh/ and /hnC/ – rather than in all three ways that seem compatible with the principles of their analysis: they did not explain the absence of /nhC/ as a third possibility. Finally, PP conflate the categories of monosegmental and bisegmental onsets into a single class: for them, /SC(ʔ)/ and /hCʔ/ are not distinct from the other onset types of Mazateco. This makes it impossible to understand, among other things, why the /hCʔ/ onsets are so few and unstable and why /ʔCh/ – the mirror image structures – remain completely unattested.

4 Other Mazatecan and Popolocan Onset Systems

A number of other dialects of Mazateco have been described briefly, along with dialects of the closely related Popolocan language. None of the descriptions available to me match in richness of detail PP's account of the Huautla de Jimenez dialect analyzed above. However, I will consider briefly three of these dialects, as a means to verify the main elements of the analysis of Huautla onsets. All the dialects of Mazateco-Popolocan I have encountered differ from Huautla in lacking a widespread and systematic contrast between pre- and postaspirated or pre- and postglottalized onsets. Consequently, most of their onsets can be analyzed as involving sequences that are monosegmental both on the surface and in underlying representations.

4.1 Western Popoloca

The phonology of this dialect of Popoloca has been described by Pierson (1953) and Williams and Pike (1968). Its consonant inventory (culled from Williams and Pike) is essentially identical to that of Huautla Mazateco:

(56)   Western Popoloca consonants   Notes

```
p   t   ts   tʃ   tʂ   k              - p: only in loans
    d   dz   dʐ                       - dz, dʐ: possibly
m   n        ɲ                          realizations of z, ʐ.
v       s    ʃ    ʂ    ɣ              - v: in free variation
    r                  y   h   ʔ        with w.
```

The Western Popoloca onsets are listed below. On the few points where Pierson's description differs from that of Williams and Pike, I followed the latter.[31]

(57) Western Popoloca onsets

    a. voiceless plosive + h: th, tsh, tʃh, tṣh, kh
    b. nasal + plosive   nd, ndz̹, nk, mp
    c. h + sonorant   hn, hm, hɲ, hv, hy
    d. h + nasal + stop   hnd, hnk
    e. ʔ + nasal   ʔn, ʔm, ʔɲ
    f. ʔ + nasal + plosive   ʔnt ʔntʃ
    g. ʔ + y   ʔy
    h. C + ʔ   tʔ, tsʔ, tʃʔ, kʔ, sʔ, ʃʔ, ṣʔ, nʔ, mʔ, ɲʔ, gʔ, rʔ, yʔ, hʔ
    i. voiceless plosive + h + ʔ   thʔ, tshʔ, khʔ
    j. h + nasal + ʔ   hmʔ, hnʔ, hɲʔ
    k. nasal + plosive + ʔ   nkʔ, ntʔ, ntʃʔ

Unlike Huautla Mazateco, Western Popoloca allows a coda segment: /ʔ/. Examples such as /tiʔ/ 'fresh corn', /riyeʔ/ 'a boil' illustrate the word-final coda /ʔ/. In forms like /tuʔtʃʔia/ 'my knee', /tuʔsʔi-na/ 'our (exclusive) necks', we must assume a coda /ʔ/ in the initial syllable, since /ʔts/, /ʔs/ onsets are not independently attested. The existence of coda /ʔ/ renders ambiguous all word-medial examples of /ʔ-nasal/ or /ʔ-nasal-plosive/ clusters.[32] I have listed them in (57.e-f) only because some instances of word-initial /ʔ-nasal-(plosive)/ are in fact encountered. Unattested initially remain the clusters /ʔ-nasal-(plosive)-ʔ/ which one might expect on the basis of the joint existence of /ʔ-nasal-(plosive)/ and /nasal-(plosive)-ʔ/ clusters: it is possible that such clusters are well-formed and only accidentally missing in initial position. Medially they are attested in forms such as /tʃaʔnkʔinaa/ 'my necklace'.

The prenasal stops have phonetically voiced closures, as in Huautla Mazateco: /nk/ is [ŋg]. The analysis given for Huautla prenasals appears

---

[31] In particular, Pierson records two clusters /pn/ and /py/ which Williams and Pike do not mention.

[32] Williams and Pike make no explicit statement about syllabic division in the ambiguous VʔN(C)V sequences but on page 375 they list them among the heterosyllabic clusters. On page 369, they mention that the first vowel in VʔCV' sequences, where C is voiced and the second syllable bears stress, fails to be laryngealized. Normally, coda ʔ laryngealizes slightly a preceding nucleus. This suggests that in the cases where VʔCV' contains a voiced consonant, the ambiguous clusters belong to the onset in their entirety.

to apply to Western Popoloca as well: the prenasals may arise from the merger between a placeless nasal closure – the remnant of an unreleased nasal stop – and a following A position. We will reconsider this possibility below.

We note next that the position of aspiration within the onset is not distinctive in Western Popoloca: among the aspirated plosives, those with voiceless closure are postaspirated, while those with voiced (i.e., nasal) closure are preaspirated. This distribution can be explained by assuming that /hC/ and /Ch/ are underlying single segments, containing [spread] in their matrix. In this respect, we must assume that Western Popoloca and Mazateco differ: there is no need to postulate underlying /hC/, /Ch/ clusters of distinct segments in Popolocan.

(58) Underlying /hn/ and /th/ in Western Popoloca

[spread]   [spread]
   | |
  A₀   A₀
   |
[nasal]

Once releases are projected, [spread] gravitates towards a [voiced] (or [nasal]) closure; and, in its absence, towards the plosive release. Note that the prenasals realize aspiration on the closure: we get /hnk/ rather than /nkh/. This confirms our hypothesis that it is nasal closures (rather than oral releases) which get first shot at anchoring aspiration. I leave open the question of explaining why [spread] seeks out [nasal] or [voiced] closures in this language.

(59) Realization of [spread] on Western Popoloca plosives

Associate [spread] to release, unless closure is [nasal].

The analysis suggested for Huautla Mazateco /hy/, /hv/ and /ʔy/ appears to carry over to a large extent to Western Popoloca. As in Huautla, /y/ and /v/ are the only preaspirated continuants, /y/ is the only attested preglottalized continuant. As in Huautla, there is no contrast between /hia/ and /hya/, /hua/ and /hva/, or /ʔia/ and /ʔya/ sequences. As in Huautla, onsets lacking supralaryngeal articulations are disfavored: in sequences where glide formation could not apply – because the high vowel is either nasalized or alone in its nucleus – Williams and Pike indicate (p.376) that /uʔi(V)/ sequences may be realized [uʔwi(V)], with an excrescent glide originating in the preceding syllable. We may assume then that the preaspirated or preglottalized continuants originate from glide formation: there are no underlying aspirated glides.

Preglottalization has the same properties as in Huautla: it surfaces on nasal closures only. I assume therefore that the process of preglottal nasalization is active in Western Popoloca as well. I defer a full analysis of the Western Popoloca onsets with glottalization until after the /CʔC/ sequences have been discussed.

We must consider now what is clearly the most striking property of Western Popoloca onsets: the fact that aspiration and glottalization are apparently allowed to co-occur within a cluster, in sequences such as /hʔ/, /hnʔ/, /thʔ/.[33] Less obvious but equally important is that /h/ and /ʔ/ may co-occur only if glottalization follows aspiration: clusters such as */ʔh/ or */ʔCh/ or */ʔhC/ are not recorded. The absence of contrast in the linear ordering of /h/ and /ʔ/ might suggest that the two are phonologically simultaneous in clusters transcribed with digraphs such as /hʔ/, /Chʔ/.

(60) An underlying structure for (C)h(C)ʔ clusters?

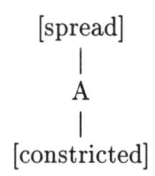

[spread]
|
A
|
[constricted]

This structure, however, incorporates an untenable claim: under any theory of phonological representations, incompatible features like [spread] and [constricted] may co-occur only if sequenced.[34] This alone explains facts like the universal absence of plosives that are underlyingly both aspirated and glottalized: although the two incompatible features can be phoneti-

---

[33]Note that Western Popoloca and Huautla Mazateco differ in the types of /h(C)ʔ/ they allow and in the relation between these clusters and other onsets present in the language. First, practically all conceivable /h(C)ʔ/ sequences are present in Western Popoloca, provided that the /hC/ subsequence is independently attested. In contrast, Huautla permits only two unstable instances of /hCʔ/, /htsʔ/ and /htʃʔ/. Second, the attested Huautla /hCʔ/ clusters occupy obvious gaps in the system of /S-stop-ʔ/ clusters, whereas the /h(C)ʔ/ sequences of Western Popoloca are not distributionally related to any other class of clusters. In particular, /S-stop/ onsets are completely absent in this dialect of Popoloca. Thus, despite the superficial similarity between Huautla /htsʔ/ and Western Popoloca /tshʔ/, the two clusters must be analyzed differently.

[34]See, however, Lombardi (1990) for a theory of affricate structures in which [+cont] and [-cont] are phonologically simultaneous values. Lombardi avoids facing the general question raised by such structures by claiming that [+cont] and [-cont] are distinct privative features, rather than different values of the same feature.

cally realized as sequenced, with one realized on the closure and the other on the release, their underlying representation would necessarily involve simultaneity of aspiration and glottalization. We must seek an alternative account for the fixed order between the /h/ and /ʔ/ elements.

My suggestion is that all sequences transcribed as /Cʔ/ – including those in which the stop is pre- or postaspirated – have glottalization associated not to the onset but to the following nucleus. If so, aspiration and glottalization do not co-occur within the onsets transcribed /hʔ/, /Chʔ/ etc. much less within a single A position. The fixed order between /h/ and /ʔ/ is explained by the fact that onsets necessarily precede nuclei.

(61) The structure of (C)h(C)ʔV sequences

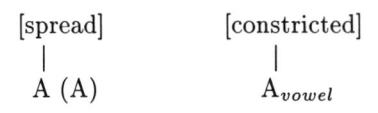

[spread]   [constricted]
  | |
A (A)   A$_{vowel}$

There is considerable evidence for such an analysis in Williams and Pike's study. These writers note that all Cʔ onsets are realized with a considerable lag between the release of stop and the /ʔ/ element. It is not just the case that the plosives are fully released before the glottal gesture in /ʔ/ is initiated: continuants are also followed by a vocoid transition when postglottalized, as indicated in transcriptions like [ruʔa] 'mouth' for /rʔua/. In this respect, the /Cʔ/ sequences differ from the /Ch/ clusters. Moreover, the transitional vocoid preceding a /ʔ/ has the vowel qualities of the first nuclear vowel and carries mid tone. If the nucleus contains two vowels, the /ʔ/ is heard between the first and the second: thus /ʧʔu/ is narrowly transcribed [ʧuʔu] whereas /tʔie/ and /nʔue/ are transcribed [tiʔe] and [nuʔe]. In contrast, a /Ch/ cluster such as /th/ is transcribed [th] (e.g. [thate] p.377), without any indication of a lag between the stop release and the glottal gesture. To further illustrate the difference in behavior between postaspiration and postglottalization, Williams and Pike state that in /ChʔV$_1$V$_2$(V)/ sequences with distinct V$_1$ and V$_2$, the aspiration affects completely the initial vowel, turning it into a voiceless vowel, which is followed by /ʔ/: /khʔuia/ is transcribed [kUʔiaa]. Given this, it appears that the glottal gesture is timed, at least in heterorganic nuclei, to coincide with the beginning of the second vowel: such timing would be incomprehensible if /ʔ/ belonged to the onset. A final argument for the analysis in (61) is the observation that postglottalized consonant clusters induce a tonal shift in nuclei that contain tone contours: "If the [CʔVV, D.S.] syllable has a tone cluster, the two tones are actualized as a glide on the last vowel: /rʔùá/ [ruʔă] 'your sing. mouth'" (p.373). We may explain this by assuming the phonological representation in (61) – in which glottalization occupies the first mora – plus a rightward shift of the tones in CʔVV(V) syllables: the tone of the first vowel migrates rightward whenever it co-occurs with glottalization. Phonetically, the glottal feature is realized not as laryngealization of the vowel but as a glottal stop at the boundary between the first and the second vocalic gesture. In monovocalic nuclei, it appears that the glottal stop occurs in the middle of the vocalic gesture. I leave open the question of representing such cases.

How then do we distinguish /CʔV/ from /CVʔ/ and /CʔVʔ/ sequences? We must assume that the coda /ʔ/ carries its own A_{max} position and, possibly, its own mora. Representations for all three cases are given below:

(62)   Syllables with nucleus and coda /ʔ/

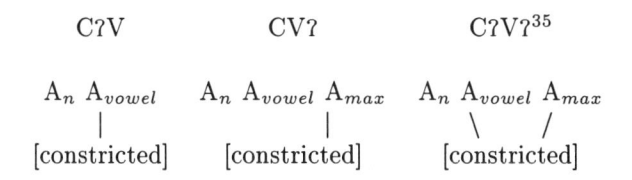

CʔV   CVʔ   CʔVʔ[35]

A_n A_{vowel} A_n A_{vowel} A_{max} A_n A_{vowel} A_{max}
   | | \   /
[constricted]   [constricted]   [constricted]

As Williams and Pike note (p.369-370), the vowel is more heavily laryngealized in the /CʔVʔ/ syllables, where the [constricted] feature spans the entire rime, than in /CVʔ/ cases, where [constricted] is not, according to our representations, phonologically associated to the nucleus. This observation is sufficient to exclude an interpretation which would identify /ʔ/ in /CVʔ/ as a phonological property of the nucleus.

Otomanguean languages in which vocalic glottalization is realized in a fashion similar to the one I attribute to Western Popoloca include Chiquihuitlan (discussed below), Choapan Zapotec (Lyman and Lyman 1977) and Guelavila Zapotec (Jones and Knudson 1977). Choapan provides the closer parallel: in this language a checked vowel – the term for the relevant structures – is realized prevocalically with the glottal gesture positioned between it and the following vowel (i.e., [V₁ʔV₂]) and otherwise with the glottal closure in its center, as [V₁ʔV₁]. This was exactly what the transcriptions indicated to be happening in Western Popoloca. But could one claim perhaps that, despite its odd timing relative to vowel gestures, the glottal stop of *both* Western Popoloca and Choapan [CVʔVX] syllables belongs structurally to the preceding onset? The Choapan data eliminate

---

[35] Nothing hinges on my decision to adopt representations in which /CʔVʔ/ contains a single [constricted] value rather than two. I am simply assuming that, in the absence of evidence to the contrary, the Obligatory Contour Principle obtains.

this possibility: any one of the three vowels in a Choapan nucleus may be distinctively checked. Thus /rue̱/ 'give' (with checked /u/; realized [ruʔe]) contrasts with /rdue̱/ 'be ashamed' (with checked /e/; realized [rdueʔe]). The glottal is clearly an individual vowel's property, with no connection to the onset.

Aside from explaining the distribution of tonal contours within /CʔVV/ and the timing of the glottal gesture in bivocalic nuclei (/CʔV$_1$V$_2$/), the analysis of postglottalization proposed in (61) allows us to understand the apparently odd co-occurrence of /h/ and /ʔ/ at the beginning of Western Popoloca syllables, as well as the source of the main difference between Popoloca and Mazateco syllables. The fact that /hʔ/ occurs as a tautosyllabic sequence in Popoloca, but not in Mazateco, reflects not a difference between the organizing principles of their onset structure but rather the fact that Popoloca has, and Mazateco lacks, glottalized nuclei. We can therefore maintain that /hʔ/ – as well as /ʔh/, /ʔCh/, /hCʔ/ etc. – are impossible onsets in any language that requires tautosyllabic clusters to be monosegmental.[36]

Having understood that Western Popoloca postglottalization is a feature of the nucleus, we may conclude that the only onsets containing glottalization are the preglottalized plosives with nasal closure /ʔn(C)/. This means that the position of glottalization is not distinctive within the onsets of this dialect: the /ʔn(C)/ onsets can be viewed as underlyingly glottalized plosives rather than as clusters of /ʔ/ plus plosive.

(63) Underlying /ʔn/ in Western Popoloca

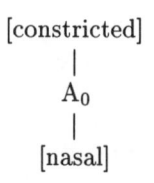

[constricted]
|
A$_0$
|
[nasal]

Western Popoloca emerges from this discussion as a language which essentially lacks underlying clusters. What our sources represent as sequences

---

[36]Note that heterosyllabic clusters, which at least in this language, are not subject to any constraint, may have co-occurring aspiration and glottalization. Williams and Pike (p.375) cite numerous examples of coda /ʔ/ followed by onsets with pre- or postaspiration: /kuntaʔtʃhee/ 'buzzard' , /kuʔhwaʔ/ 'egg', /kusiʔhna/ 'deer', /tinkʔihnʔa/ 'I help'. The absence of coda /ʔ/ followed by preglottalized onset is perhaps attributable to cross-syllabic dissimilation. Dissimilation of /ʔ/ applies between the adjacent positions of coda and following onset but not between the nonadjacent coda and following nucleus. This is why /ʔʔC/ is absent while /ʔCʔ/ clusters are attested: /tuʔtʔee/ 'his foot', /ʃoʔʃʔonaa/ 'my glass', /tinkiʔhnʔa/ 'I help'.

of distinct consonants turn out to be, for the most part, single consonants – aspirated or glottalized plosives – or, in the case of /C?/, single consonants followed by glottalized nuclei.

To complete the picture, we must consider the possibility that the prenasal onsets {/nC/, /hnC/, /?nC/} are also monosegmental. The difficulty we have to face here is that the underlying contrast between /t/, /d/, /n/, and /nt/ (i.e. [nd]) cannot be represented if we maintain that plosive releases are non-distinctive: /nt/ and /n/ differ only in the oral vs. nasal quality of their release, while /nt/ and /d/ differ only in the presence of nasality on closure. In Western Popoloca the solution to this problem is clearly tied to the limited occurrence of the voiced obstruents, which fail to cluster with anything and have, for the most part, spirant realizations. Additionally, plain /d/ without prenasalization is attested by only one example in Pierson's article and fails to appear at all in the better documented study by Williams and Pike. I suggest then that Pierson's /d/ can be disregarded in the analysis, either because it is a continuant or, more likely, because it is not there: if so, the contrast between /t/, /n/ and [nd] can be characterized underlyingly as that between a voiceless oral stop, a nasal stop and a voiced stop, realized with surface prenasalization. (This is also Jamieson's (1977) proposal for the remarkably similar system of Chiquihuitlan Mazateco). The contrast between /?n/ and /?nt/ is then that between a glottalized nasal and a glottalized oral stop, whose glottalized closure induces voicing and prenasalization, as in Huautla. Similarly, the contrast between /hn/, /hnt/ and /th/ is that between an aspirated nasal, an aspirated voiced oral stop – whose voicing triggers prenasalization – and an aspirated voiceless oral stop. The overall conclusion then is that there are no underlying or surface onset clusters in Western Popoloca.

4.2 Tlacoyalco Popoloca

Stark and Machin (1977) have provided a brief description of a different Popoloca dialect, spoken in the village of San Marcos Tlacoyalco, of Puebla, Mexico. The Tlacoyalco dialect differs from Western Popoloca in displaying underlying clusters. It differs from Huautla Mazateco in having a surface inventory of complex onsets that represents a proper subset of the one analyzed in section 2. We will see that the difference in onset clusters has two sources: the different segmental inventories of Huautla and Tlacoyalco and the restricted nature of A-position merger in Tlacoyalco.

(64)   Tlacoyalco Popoloca phonemes (after Stark and Machin 1977)

oral plosives	p	t	T		ts	tʃ	tṣ	k		
voiceless fricatives	f				s	ʃ	ṣ			
voiced fricatives	b		d		z	ʒ		g		
nasal stops	m	n				ɲ				
approximants			l			y	r, rr		h	ʔ
oral vowels				i	e	a	o			
nasal vowels				ĩ	ẽ	ã	õ			

Note: /T/ = interdental stop

The onset sequences of Tlacoyalco, as presented by Stark and Machin, include the following:

(65)   Tlacoyalco complex onsets

(a)   Nasal plus plosive: nt   nT   nts   ntʃ   ntṣ   nk
(b)   Plosive plus /h/:   th   Th   tsh   tʃh   tṣh   kh
(c)   Nasal plus plosive plus /h/:   nth   nTh   ntsh   nkh
(d)   /h/ plus nasal plus plosive: hnt   hnk
(e)   /h/ plus nasal: hm   hn   hɲ
(f)   /ʔ/ plus nasal: ʔn
(g)   /ʔ/ plus nasal plus plosive: ʔnt   ʔnk
(h)   /h/ plus glide: hy

If we leave aside the contrast between /hnC/ and /nCh/ in (65.c-d), the system appears identical to that of Western Popoloca. The prenasal plosives – whose closures are phonetically voiced – may well represent prenasal realizations of voiced stops. The postaspirated stops and preaspirated nasals should be analyzed as underlying aspirated closures—as in (58). If so, we must also assume the realization rule in (59), which insures that aspiration will surface on a nasal closure and, in its absence, on an oral release. The preglottalized plosives can be represented underlyingly as in (63). The unique /hy/ is an underlying /hi/ sequence, as in Huautla and Western Popoloca: onsets are obligatory in Tlacoyalco and /hiV/ sequences are absent. I summarize part of the analysis in the list of representations given in (66). The underlying representations proposed below are followed by several derivational steps: the projection of releases, the alignment of aspiration with release in oral plosives, the spreading of nasality onto the release of underlying nasals and the nasalization of underlying voiced closures.

Complex Onsets as Single Segments: The Mazateco Pattern   267

(66) Underlying monosegmental sources for (65.a,b,e,f)

complex onset	underlying	project releases	alignment

(a) /nC/	A₀
	|
	[voice]
		(→ A₀ Aₙ →
		        |
		      [voice]
			A₀ Aₙ)
			/ ⋰
			[voice] [nasal]

(b) /Ch/	A₀
	|
	[spread]
		(→ A₀ Aₙ →
		        |
		      [spread]
			A₀ Aₙ)
			    |
			[spread]

(e) /hn/	A₀ / \ [spread][nasal]	(→ A₀ Aₙ → / \ [spread][nasal]	A₀ Aₙ) / \ / [spread][nasal]
(f) /ʔn/	A₀ / \ [constr][nasal]	(→ A₀ Aₙ → / \ [constr][nasal]	A₀ Aₙ) / \ / [constr][nasal]

Let us return now to the contrast between /hnC/ and /nCh/. The merger analysis given for such sequences in Huautla Mazateco was based on the observation that all plosives – oral, nasal or half-nasal – could be pre- or postaspirated. This is clearly not the case in Tlacoyalco: only prenasal onsets have a contrast between pre- and postaspiration. Why?

Before addressing directly this question, we can observe that the onsets composed of prenasalization, a plosive and a laryngeal feature – the set {hnC, nCh and ʔnC} – can be analyzed as composites of any surface nasal closure, which may carry a laryngeal feature, as in (66.e-f), and any surface stop release, which may carry aspiration, as in (66.b). Such composites can be viewed as the result of the merger of adjacent closures, if we assume that this process is subject to the restriction observed in Huautla: its immediate output must be monosegmental. Note that, although only one of the cluster types {hnC, nCh, ʔnC} must be analyzed as an underlying sequence of consonants – since the others are analyzable as their monosegmental counterparts in Western Popoloca – the simplest analysis we can provide indicates that the other two types have may have bisegmental sources as well. The data provided by Stark and Machin does not help resolve this potential ambiguity as to derivational source. (The brackets in the input sequences below help identify the boundaries of the original segments entering merger.)

(67) Some underlying bisegmental sources for (51.c-d-g)

(c) /nth/ from /n/ + /th/:

$$\begin{array}{ccc} A_0 & [A_0 & A_n] \\ | & | & | \\ [\text{nas}] & [\text{place}] & [\text{spread}] \end{array} \quad \rightarrow \quad \begin{array}{cc} A_0 & A_n \\ /\backslash & | \\ [\text{nas}][\text{place}] & [\text{spread}] \end{array}$$

(d) /hnt/ from /hn/ + /t/:

$$\begin{array}{ccc} A_0 & [A_0 & A_n] \\ /\backslash & | & \\ [\text{spread}][\text{nas}] & [\text{place}] \end{array} \quad \rightarrow \quad \begin{array}{cc} A_0 & A_n \\ /\,|\,\backslash & \\ [\text{spread}][\text{nas}][\text{place}] \end{array}$$

(g) /ʔnt/ from /ʔn/ + /t/:

$$\begin{array}{ccc} A_0 & [A_0 & A_n] \\ /\backslash & | & \\ [\text{constr}][\text{nas}] & [\text{place}] \end{array} \quad \rightarrow \quad \begin{array}{cc} A_0 & A_n \\ /\,|\,\backslash & \\ [\text{constr}][\text{nas}][\text{place}] \end{array}$$

The derivations sketched in (67) imply that the closure merger which yields the surface contrast between /nth/ and /hnt/ takes place after the linearization process (equivalent to (59)) which associates aspiration to the release of oral stops: otherwise the contrast between /hnt/ and /nth/, derived through closure merger, will be neutralized.

As in the analysis of Huautla prenasals, I assume that underlying stop_1-stop_2 sequences in Tlacoyalco will contain a necessarily unreleased instance of stop_1; and further, that an unreleased nasal stop will lose place features. What then will be left of the original closure? Anything other than place features: nasality, voicing, aspiration, glottalization or any licit combination of these. Closure merger will be able to combine the nasality and/or laryngeal features of the first A_0 with the place component (as well as, possibly, other features) of the second A_0.

(68) Closure merger

Merge $A_0\ A_0$ iff output structure is monosegmental (cf. (15)).
(Ordering: after Tlacoyalco equivalent of (59).)

The monosegmental condition explains the fact that only one set of place features emerges from the combination of two closures, as well as the fact that certain combinations of laryngeal features are not amenable to merger. I list some of these below:

(69) Merger blocked: immediate output is not monosegmental

(a) /ʔn/ + /hn/ or /hn/ + /ʔn/
(e.g. */ʔhn/, */hʔn/):
[spread] and [constricted] are incompatible

(b) /ʔn/ + /th/ (e.g. */ʔnth/):
[spread] and [constricted] are incompatible

(c) /hn/ + /th/ (e.g. */hnth/): two distinct [spread] values.

A further point explained by this analysis is the absence of /nCʔ/ clusters in Tlacoyalco. We have assumed that only closures merge in this dialect: therefore the only source of the unattested /nCʔ/ would have to be postglottalized oral stops, which do not exist in Tlacoyalco.

As far as onset clusters go, then, Tlacoyalco = Western Popoloca + A_0 merger.

4.3 Chiquihuitlan Mazatec

The syllable structure of Chiquihuitlan Mazatec was described by Jamieson (1977). This dialect shares with Huautla the presence of /S-stop/ onsets and with Western Popoloca the absence of A position mergers of any other type.

(70) Chiquihuitlan Mazatec phonemes (after Jamieson 1977)

oral plosives:			t	ts	tʃ	ṭ	k		
nasal stops:		m	n		ɲ				
fricatives:		β		s	ʃ				
approximants:			r		y			h	ʔ

vowels:	i	u	ĩ	ũ
	e	o	ẽ	õ
	æ	a	æ̃	ã

Chiquihuitlan syllables are open. Nuclei may contain distinctive aspiration or glottalization, indicated orthographically by Jamieson as syllable-final /h/ and /ʔ/: thus /suiʔ/ 'holiday' represents a glottalized nucleus, /ntoh/ 'soap' an aspirated one. In monovocalic nuclei, the aspiration or glottalization is realized in the center of the vowel and perceived as an interruption in the vocalic gesture: [VhV], [VʔV]. In complex nuclei, glottalization appears to be realized on the last vocalic element, although Jamieson provides no explicit statements on this score: /sĩũʔ/ 'we in grind' is realized as [sĩũʔũ]. Vowel glottalization and onset preglottalization contrast, as we shall see below.

Most of the complex onsets of Chiquihuitlan can be identified as monosegmental. The full list appears below, with annotations regarding the underlying source of the sequence. The orthography is Jamieson's: some comments on phonetic realization follow.

(71)   Chiquihuitlan Mazatec complex onsets

a.   /plosive+h/ =   aspirated plosive: th, ch, ch, ṭh, kh
b.   /h+sonorant/ =   aspirated sonorant: hm, hn, hɲ, hβ, hy
c.   /ʔ+ sonorant/ =   glottalized sonorant: ʔm, ʔn, ʔɲ, ʔy, ʔb
d.   /n + plosive/ =   voiced plosive realized with
                            prenasalization: nt, nts, nʧ, nṭ, nk
e.   /ʔ+n + plosive/ =   voiced glottalized plosive realized with
                            prenasalization: ʔn, ʔnṭ, ʔnts, ʔn, ʔnk
f.   /s + plosive/ =   st, sk, sm, sn
g.   /ʃ + plosive/ =   ʃt, ʃk, ʃn
h.   /r + plosive/ =   rk, (rn)

The aspirated onsets are realized, in the case of plosives, as in Western Popoloca: aspiration stays on a nasal closure, and otherwise migrates to an oral release. The aspirated continuants, although written sequentially, are realized simultaneously with the oral articulation: /hβ/ = [f] and /hy/ = [ç]. Similarly, Jamieson's narrow transcriptions for the glottalized continuants /ʔβ/, /ʔy/ indicate that laryngealization persists throughout the period of oral constriction: there is therefore no reason to analyze these as involving underlying or surface clusters.

The absence of distinctively aspirated or glottalized fricatives can be recorded as a constraint against laryngeal features linked to A_f, rooted in the phonetic aspiration of the voiceless fricatives. The remarks made in section 1.3 about affricates representing underlying stops apply rather strikingly to this case: /ʧ/ can be aspirated, but homorganic /ʃ/ cannot. The reason is that /ʧ/ starts out as a plain stop, lacking underlying frication, whereas /ʃ/ is an underlying A_f: what they have in common is point of articulation, not stricture. The same will have to hold for the pair /s/ vs. /ts/, whatever turns out to be the proper point of articulation distinction between /ts/ and /t/. The absence of /hnC/ or /nCh/ onsets – i.e., a voiced plosive accompanied by aspiration – can be attributed to a constraint against the co-occurrence of these two laryngeal features within one segment. This means that in /h-nasal/ onsets the nasality is primary, and voicing non-distinctive.

No plausible monosegmental sources can be offered for the clusters listed in (71.f-h). The main lines of the analysis suggested for Huautla /S-plosive/ onsets can be extended to Chiquihuitlan: there are obvious differences only regarding the possibility of [nasal] on the stop closure following /S/ and the limited scope of debuccalization in Chiquihuitlan. The absence of /S-nC/ onsets in Chiquihuitlan can be attributed to the fact that aspiration - including the redundant aspiration of /s/ - is incompatible with the distinctive voicing instantiated as prenasalization. The /r-C/ onsets seem too limited in occurrence and too isolated typologically to speculate about: only /rk/ is attested in more than one lexical item and at least /rn/ clearly originates in the syncope of rVC sequences.

The Chiquihuitlan onset system represents the combination of possibilities already encountered in languages analyzed above. The onsets with prenasalization, /h/ or /ʔ/ are monosegmental at all levels of phonological representation, as in Western Popoloca. Those consisting of a sibilant attached to a closure instantiate the possibility of generating structurally monosegmental onsets by placing the features of a fricative on the approach position of a stop. The global characterization of possible surface onsets is identical to that of Huautla: surface onsets clusters are all structurally monosegmental, whether or not they are featurally monosegmental.

4.4 A Summary of the Parameters Observed

All Mazateco-Popolocan languages considered here allow on the surface only onset clusters that can count as structurally monosegmental. The observed differences between the four languages can be summarized as corresponding to the following parameters.

(72) Some onset parameters in Mazateco-Popolocan:

    a. Are there *underlying* bisegmental clusters in onset?
       (Yes: Huautla, Chiquihuitlan, Tlacoyalco.
       No: Western Popoloca)

    b. Are there *surface* bisegmental clusters in onset?
       (Yes: the Huautla, Chiquihuitlan /SC/ clusters are featurally bisegmental;
       No: Tlacoyalco, Western Popoloca)

    c. Is there merger of A_f with Approach?
       (Yes: Mazateco (Huautla and Chiquihuitlan);
       No: Popoloca (Western and Tlacoyalco))

    d. Is there generalized merger (cf. (43))?
       (Yes: Huautla.
       No: Tlacoyalco, Western Popoloca, Chiquihuitlan)

    e. Is there closure merger (cf. (68))?
       (Yes: Tlacoyalco, possibly Huautla (subsumed by (43)).
       No: Western Popoloca, Chiquihuitlan)

The differences outlined above bear on three fundamental points: the allowable degree of complexity of underlying representations (72.a), the degree of complexity of surface structures (72.b) and the choice of mapping mechanisms between underlying and surface sequences, or, differently put, the choice of relevant optimization mechanisms (72.c-e).[37]

It is premature to conclude that all dialectal differences between the onsets of this language family can be reduced to those enumerated in (72). But the possibility of characterizing succinctly the differences observed between these four dialects – the only ones for which we had reliable descriptions – clearly supports the general framework of the analysis.

---

[37] On the concept of optimization, see, among many others, Yip (1988), Goldsmith (1989), Prince and Smolensky (1992), Kirchner (1992). It is clear that all instances of merger listed in (71) qualify as optimization strategies, since they promote the creation of clusters that are at least structurally monosegmental and hence closer to the optimal cluster: one segment.

5 Beyond Mazateco: Other Instances of Multiple Contrast in the Association of /h/ and /ʔ/ to Plosives

At least two other Amerindian languages display clear contrasts between pre- and post-aspirated or glottalized plosives. They are analyzed below. It is anticipated that the study of Otomi dialects, in particular Tenango (Blight and Pike 1976) and Temoayan (Andrews 1949), will yield further instances of such patterns of laryngeal association. The more complex cluster structure of Otomi is not discussed here.

5.1 Yuchi

A contrast between pre and post-glottalized plosives has been documented by Wolff (1948) in Yuchi, a language of Oklahoma distantly related to Siouan. Yuchi syllables are invariably open. Consonant clusters found intervocalically are also, for the most part, present initially. Words end in vowels. The consonant inventory of Yuchi is given below, in Wolff's notation.

(73) Yuchi consonants

```
p t  ts  tʃ  k
b d      dʒ  g
  ɗ
f    s   ʃ
w n  y
  l         h  ʔ
```

This list reflects Wolff's decision to phonemicize all Yuchi consonant sequences, including items such as /th/, /tʔ/, /sʔ/, as clusters rather than as unit phonemes. The clusters he reports fall into several classes: (a) distinctively pre- and post-glottalized plosives; (b) glottalized continuants, realized with preglottalization in the case of the sonorants /ʔy/ and /ʔl/ and with postglottalization otherwise (/sʔ/, /ʃʔ/, /fʔ/); (c) postaspirated stops; (d) obstruent-glide sequences, which include both Cw and Cy sequences; and (e) sibilant-stop clusters. I focus here on the clusters containing a laryngeal.

(74) a. Onsets with glottalization:
Plosives + ʔ: pʔ, tʔ, tsʔ, tʃʔ, kʔ, bʔ, dʔ, gʔ, tlʔ
ʔ+ voiceless plosives: ʔp, ʔt, ʔts, ʔk
Voiceless continuants + ʔ: fʔ, sʔ, ʃʔ
ʔ+ voiced continuants: ʔl, ʔy

b. Onsets with aspiration:
Voiceless stops + h: ph, th, kh

Most of these phonetic sequences could be analyzed as monosegmental at all levels of the derivation. The /Ch/ sequences may be aspirated stops, while the /Cʔ/ and /ʔC/ clusters involving a continuant C may be viewed as glottalized, since the linear order between cluster members in /sʔ/ and /ʔy/ is clearly non-distinctive. For continuants, the glottal gesture is produced before the oral constriction in sonorants (or A_{max} segments) and after it in obstruents (i.e., A_f).

We may now consider the contrast between pre- and postglottalized stops: /pʔ/, /tʔ/, /tsʔ/, /kʔ/ vs. /ʔp/, /ʔt/, /ʔts, /ʔk/. While one of these two series may instantiate an underlying series of glottalized plosives, the other cannot. Wolff notes that the /ʔ-stop/ clusters are frequently realized as preaspirated rather than pre-glottalized. Thus, /bʔaʔte/ 'horse' is alternately realized as [bʔaʔte] and as [bʔaxte] – where [x] stands for a fricated realization of [h]. Wolff gives no compelling reason for considering glottalization – rather than aspiration – as the basic allophone in this case. The point being developed here – that the contrast between pre- and postposition of laryngeal features is available only in plosives – goes through either way. I will assume in what follows that the plosive series with preposed laryngeal features represents basic preglottalized stops and affricates.

Since either the pre- or the postglottalized plosives result from underlying clusters, the simplest analysis will be to assume that all onsets with glottalization may originate as underlying clusters, via bidirectional merger.

(75) Yuchi merger with /ʔ/

   Merge A_{max} with adjacent A position
   |
   [constricted]

(76) a. Merger applied to plosives:

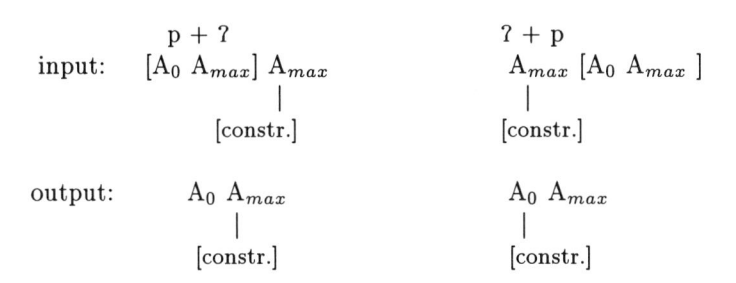

$$\begin{array}{ll}
& p + ʔ \qquad\qquad\qquad ʔ + p \\
\text{input:} & [A_0\ A_{max}]\ A_{max} \qquad A_{max}\ [A_0\ A_{max}] \\
& \qquad\quad |\qquad\qquad\qquad\qquad | \\
& \quad\text{[constr.]}\qquad\qquad\quad\text{[constr.]} \\
\\
\text{output:} & A_0\ A_{max} \qquad\qquad A_0\ A_{max} \\
& \quad\ \ | \qquad\qquad\qquad\quad\ \ | \\
& \text{[constr.]}\qquad\qquad\quad \text{[constr.]}
\end{array}$$

b. Merger applied to continuants:

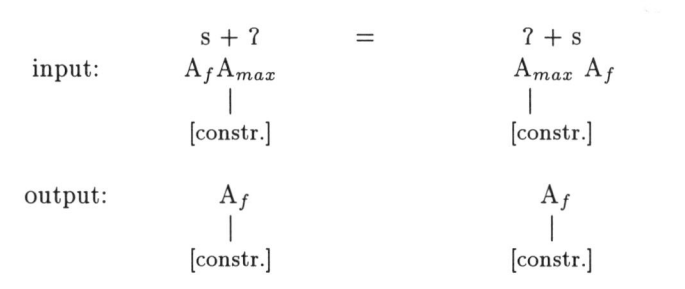

$$\begin{array}{ll}
& s + ʔ \qquad = \qquad ʔ + s \\
\text{input:} & A_f A_{max} \qquad\qquad\quad A_{max}\ A_f \\
& \quad | \qquad\qquad\qquad\qquad | \\
& \text{[constr.]}\qquad\qquad\quad \text{[constr.]} \\
\\
\text{output:} & A_f \qquad\qquad\qquad\quad A_f \\
& \ | \qquad\qquad\qquad\qquad\ | \\
& \text{[constr.]}\qquad\qquad\quad \text{[constr.]}
\end{array}$$

The remainder of the Yuchi complex onset system involves bisegmental sequences consisting of s-plosive. The analysis of Mazateco /S-plosive/ onsets appears to carry over to Yuchi. Since there are numerous gaps in this class of Yuchi onsets, we cannot tell if the absence of /S-C-h/ is significant or not. There are also palatalized and labialized obstruents in the list of clusters given by Wolff, but their status as clusts, rather than complex unit segments, is by no means clear.

In the typology defined by the parameters in (72), Yuchi is a language that allows both underlying clusters of distinct consonants (at least /ʔ/ + C, C + /ʔ/, /s+C/) and surface bisegmental onsets (/s-Stop/).

5.2 Kashaya

Further support for the idea that laryngeal features can associate to either the closure or to the release of plosives is provided by Kashaya, a Pomoan language spoken on the coast of Northern California. The consonant system of Kashaya has been analyzed in a series of recent publications by Buckley (1990, 1992). Kashaya is a language with simple CV(V)(C) syllable structure. Its consonant inventory is given below, following Oswalt's (1964) and McLendon's (1973) analyses:

(77) Kashaya consonantal phonemes
(after Oswalt 1964, McLendon 1973)

p	t	ṭ	č	k	q
p^h	t^h	$ṭ^h$	$č^h$	k^h	q^h
p'	t'	ṭ'	č'	k'	q'
b	d				
(f)	s		š		
	s'				
m	n				
w	l	(r)	y		h, ʔ

Notes: /f/ and /r/ attested in loanwords only.

Buckley (1990) shows that the surface voiced stops of Kashaya [b] and [d] are realizations of the glottalized nasals /n'/ and /m'/, which belong to a class of sequences we discuss below. According to Buckley, syllable-final /n'/ and /m'/ are preserved as such, while the syllable-initial variants become oral, non-glottalized [b] and [d]. Some of the evidence supporting this analysis will appear below.

5.2.1 Laryngeal Increments

In addition to the sounds listed in (77), Kashaya possesses *laryngeally incremented consonants*, clusters involving a consonant and a laryngeal, /h/ or /ʔ/. The incremented consonants function as tautosyllabic clusters – and, hence, pattern as single C's – in the deeper stages of the phonology. They surface, when word-medial, as heterosyllabic sequences of /h.C/ and /ʔ.C/. The laryngeally incremented clusters I have encountered in the sources cited above are listed in (78) in a notation that is similar to Oswalt's and McLendon, in that it transcribes the laryngeal increment *before* the consonant.[38]

(78) Some Kashaya laryngeally incremented clusters:

hp	ht		hť	hk	hq		hm	hn	hl	hy	hw
hph	hth	hṭh	hťh	hkh	hqh						
ʔp	ʔt	ʔṭ	ʔť		ʔq			m'	n'	ʔl	ʔy	ʔw
ʔp'	ʔt'	ʔṭ'		ʔk'	ʔq'	ʔs'	ʔm'	ʔn'			

The intermediate clusters /ʔm'/ and /ʔn'/ surface as [ʔb] and [ʔd]: this is exactly what Buckley's analysis predicts, given that the /ʔC'/ incremented clusters occur, as far as one can tell, only in onset position. A further point about phonetic realization is that the glottalized /s'/ is realized with affrication (E. Buckley, personal communication). Thus the incremented /ʔs'/ could be identified as a pre- and postglottalized affricate. Some of the contrasts listed in (78) are exemplified below:

---

[38] Buckley does not provide in his papers a full list of the attested incremented clusters. However, it is possible to form a clear picture of the permissible patterns of incrementation by simply reading through the materials published in Oswalt (1964): the laryngeal increments have a very high text frequency and this allows one to tell apart accidental from systematic gaps.

(79) Contrasts between incremented and non-incremented consonants
(data from Buckley 1990, 1992; unglossed forms from Oswalt 1973)

a.

	plain	aspirated	h-incremented	h-C^h
tʃ	-tʃa- 'sit-sg.'	-tʃ^{h}it- 'fall out'	-htʃa- 'fly'	-htʃ^{h}a:- 'knock over'
k	kolo: 'hollow'	nayak^{h}ulu:lu 'thrasher'	hku 'one'	-hk^{h}it' 'choke'
q	ʃaqa: 'valley quail'	q^{h}aʔaylo 'ogre'	hqowe (unglossed)	hq^{h}a 'water'
n	t' an		ʔp' ahn	

b.

	plain	glottalized	ʔ-incremented	ʔ-C'
tʃ	-tʃa- 'sit-sg.'	-tʃ' o:q- 'stab'	-ʔtʃoq- 'shoot'	
k	kolo: 'hollow'	-k' i:- 'scratch'		-ʔk' ol^h 'spill'
s	si:totto 'robin'	s' uʔnuʔnu 'huckleberry'		ʔs' ohn 'dent'
m	mayaltow 'by you (pl)'		dolom' 'wild cat' - m' a 'after'	ʔm' ahl 'turn'

The last two forms listed, /m' a/ and /ʔm' ahl/ contain glottally incremented nasals in onset position and surface, in accordance with Buckley's law, as [ba] and [ʔbahl] respectively.

The incremented clusters differ from other Kashaya consonant sequences in forming tautosyllabic clusters in the first stages of the phonology. This point is carefully established by Buckley (1992), who shows that this assumption sheds light on both the phonotactics of Kashaya and its reduplicative processes. We will note here only two significant facts: the incremented consonants are the only clusters attested word-initially and, for some of them, word-finally. They are also the only ones copied in toto by a process of CV reduplication. The contrast between the effect of reduplication on genuine clusters vs. laryngeally incremented ones is illustrated below:

(80) CV reduplication and cluster types:

    a. single C's and true clusters
       /biye:/ → biye:ye 'flower'
       /hisimta/ → hisimtata 'myth creature'   (*hisimtamta)
       /q^{h}aʔaylo/ → q^{h}aʔaylolo 'ogre'   (*q^{h}aʔayloylo)

    b. incremented consonants
       /hihla/ → hihlahla 'gossip'
       /suhmi/ → suhmihmi 'glimmer'
       /ht^{h}e/ → ht^{h}eht^{h}e 'spread out'

The incremented clusters also differ from other consonant sequences in their segmental composition: as can be seen from inspecting (78), the laryngeal elements must be compatible with the laryngeal features of the consonant they increment. Thus aspirated stops may be incremented by /h/ but not by /ʔ/: sequences like /ʔkh/ do occur in Kashaya but are systematically heterosyllabic and thus pattern differently from the laryngeally harmonic clusters /ʔk'/ or /hk^h/. Nor can glottalized stops be incremented by /h/: sequences like /ht'/ may be attested but, according to Buckley, do not pattern as a tautosyllabic cluster. Oswalt (1976) and McLendon (1973:54) are aware of this generalization about the synchronic situation in Kashaya; McLendon attributes a similar pattern of clustering to Proto-Pomo.

The laryngeally incremented clusters recorded by Oswalt and Buckley are interestingly restricted to certain consonant classes. Of the continuants, only /s/ displays more than a two-way contrast between plain and incremented: /s/ can be glottalized /s'/, as well as glottalized and incremented /ʔs'/. There is no clear data on h-incremented clusters with /s/ or /ʃ/: but we can safely assume that at least /hs^h/ and /hʃ^h/ are impossible onsets. Also, there appear to be no plain, unglottalized /s/'s that occur incremented with /ʔ/: no /ʔs/ onsets distinct from glottalized /s'/ . The other continuants do not display any contrast between postaspiration (C^h), preaspiration (hC) and pre-cum-postaspiration (hC^h) or between the same three options involving the feature of glottalization. Rather, the liquid /l/ and the glides /y/ and /w/ contrast plain and aspirated or plain and glottalized variants, with no further options.[39] On the other fricative, /ʃ/, see below.

The analysis of laryngeally incremented consonants in Kashaya requires only two assumptions: that plosives have closure and release and that, in Kashaya, the glottalized fricatives, /s'/ and /ʃ'/, are realized with affrication, as [ts'] and [tʃ']. Granted this, we can identify Kashaya as the language which displays the full range of contrasts between modes of laryngeal association anticipated in (4). Plosives have four options in the association of /h/ and /ʔ/ (to closure, to release, to both, to neither), while continuants have only two (associate or not). The representations in (81) illustrate this analysis of incremented consonants of Kashaya: /k/, /w/ and /n/ stand for oral stops, approximants and nasals. The fricatives are discussed separately.

---

[39] As indicated above, these generalizations were not expressed by any of the Pomoists whose work on Kashaya I have consulted. They derive entirely from my observations on the material presented by Buckley and from reading Oswalt's (1973) texts. However, Buckley has confirmed (personal communication, 1991) that /hCh/ and /ʔC'/ onsets are allowed only with the plosives and, in the case of /ʔC'/, with /s/.

Complex Onsets as Single Segments: The Mazateco Pattern

(81) Representations for Kashaya incremented consonants

a. h-increments

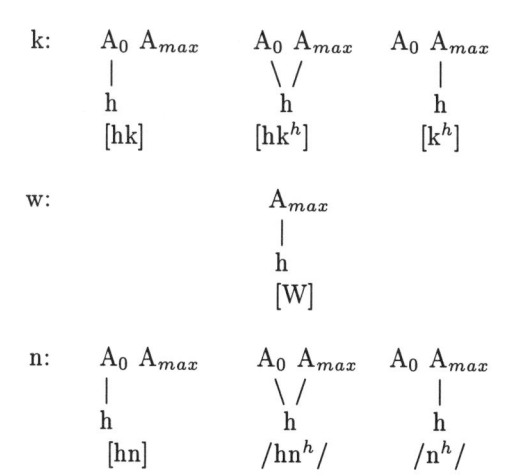

k: $\quad$ A_0 A_{max} $\qquad$ A_0 A_{max} $\qquad$ A_0 A_{max}
    $\qquad\;\;$ | $\qquad\qquad\quad$ \ / $\qquad\qquad\quad$ |
    $\qquad\;\;$ h $\qquad\qquad\quad$ h $\qquad\qquad\quad\;\,$ h
    $\qquad\;\,$ [hk] $\qquad\qquad\;\,$ [hk^h] $\qquad\qquad\;\,$ [k^h]

w: $\qquad\qquad\qquad\;\;$ A_{max}
    $\qquad\qquad\qquad\qquad$ |
    $\qquad\qquad\qquad\qquad$ h
    $\qquad\qquad\qquad\;\;$ [W]

n: $\quad$ A_0 A_{max} $\qquad$ A_0 A_{max} $\qquad$ A_0 A_{max}
    $\qquad\;\;$ | $\qquad\qquad\quad$ \ / $\qquad\qquad\quad$ |
    $\qquad\;\;$ h $\qquad\qquad\quad$ h $\qquad\qquad\quad\;\,$ h
    $\qquad\;\,$ [hn] $\qquad\qquad\;\,$ /hn^h/ $\qquad\qquad\;\,$ /n^h/

b. ʔ-increments

k: $\quad$ A_0 A_{max} $\qquad$ A_0 A_{max} $\qquad$ A_0 A_{max}
    $\qquad\;\;$ | $\qquad\qquad\quad$ \ / $\qquad\qquad\quad$ |
    $\qquad\;\;$ ʔ $\qquad\qquad\quad$ ʔ $\qquad\qquad\quad\;\,$ ʔ
    $\qquad\;\,$ [ʔk] $\qquad\qquad\;\,$ [ʔk'] $\qquad\qquad\;\,$ [k']

w: $\qquad\qquad\qquad\;\;$ A_{max}
    $\qquad\qquad\qquad\qquad$ |
    $\qquad\qquad\qquad\qquad$ ʔ
    $\qquad\qquad\qquad\;\;$ [w']

n: $\quad$ A_0 A_{max} $\qquad$ A_0A_{max} $\qquad$ A_0 A_{max}
    $\qquad\;\;$ | $\qquad\qquad\quad$ \ / $\qquad\qquad\quad$ |
    $\qquad\;\;$ ʔ $\qquad\qquad\quad$ ʔ $\qquad\qquad\quad\;\,$ ʔ
    $\qquad\;\,$ /ʔn/ $\qquad\qquad\;\,$ /ʔn'/ $\qquad\qquad\;\,$ /n'/
    $\qquad\;\,$ [ʔn] $\qquad\qquad\;\,$ [ʔb] $\qquad\qquad\;\,$ [b]

The postaspirated nasals, as well as the pre-and-postaspirated ones (/hn^h/), remain unattested, or at least, appear non-distinct from the preaspirated ones: this is probably a systematic gap, though I will not attempt to explain it. Aside from this, all and only the linking possibilities predicted by the theory of A positions presented here are instantiated in Kashaya.

As in Mazateco and Popoloca, Kashaya onsets must be monosegmental, not only structurally but featurally as well. The absence of incremented onsets like */hk'/ or */ʔp^h/ is explained as a direct consequence of their monosegmental nature: /h/ and /ʔ/ would be incompatible within one segment.

5.2.2 Excursus: Affrication of Glottalized Fricatives, a Proto-Pomo Sound Law

The patterning of fricatives with glottalization lends further support to the analysis sketched above. Based on the presence in Kashaya of affricated allophones of /s'/, I assume that, when glottalization associates to any fricative, /s/ or /ʃ/, the segment acquires closure and becomes a postglottalized affricate:[40]

(82)   Affrication of glottalized fricatives:

$$\begin{array}{ccc} A_f & \rightarrow & A_0\ A_f \\ | & & | \\ ʔ & & ʔ \end{array}$$

Several considerations support (82), quite aside from the need to characterize the affricated allophones of glottalized /s'/. This rule will neutralize the distinction between the glottalized fricative /ʃ'/ – which should exist but is not attested as such – and the postglottalized affricate /ʧ'/, which is amply documented. It will therefore account for an otherwise inexplicable contrast between /s/ and /ʃ/: the fact that /s/ is attested with glottalization, while /ʃ/ is not. Rule (82) will not have neutralizing effects in the case of /s'/, since Kashaya lacks an anterior affricate /ts/ or its underlying glottalized variant.

Suppose now that (82) is a pan-Pomo process. Then its effects should be recorded differently, depending on the phonemic inventory of affricates of each dialect: Pomo dialects which possess, unlike Kashaya, both underlying /ts/ and underlying /ʧ/ are predicted to be recorded as lacking surface glottalized /s'/ or /ʃ'/, since (82) will render these sounds indistinguishable

---

[40]More precisely, I am assuming that the glottalized fricatives are always phonologically represented as having the representations given in the output of (82), regardless of whether the affricated realization of /s'/ is invariant or not.

from the underlying glottalized affricates /ts'/ and /tʃ'/. For such dialects, it will appear that no fricatives can have glottalized variants. Glottalized fricatives should be recorded only in dialects where homorganic affricates do not exist.

A look at the comparative Pomo data gathered by McLendon (1973) indicates that this prediction is correct in every one of its aspects. First, all Pomo dialects which have the underlying palatoalveolar fricative /ʃ/ – i.e. all Pomo dialects except Central Pomo – also have the homorganic affricate /tʃ/, the latter appearing in plain, aspirated and glottalized form: as a result of (82), no dialect possesses a distinctive glottalized /ʃ'/. Wherever /ʃ/ occurs, /tʃ/ occurs as well: for glottalized /ʃ'/, (82) will neutralize the /ʃ/:/tʃ/ distinction in every relevant dialect. This explains the complete absence of surface /ʃ'/. Second, Southern, Northern and Eastern Pomo, dialects which possess plain as well as glottalized /ts/, are recorded by McLendon as lacking glottalized variants of /s/: this is, again, due to the effects of (82), which merges underlying /s'/ with the independently occurring /ts'/. In contrast, Southwestern Pomo (Kashaya) and Central Pomo, dialects which lack /ts/, are recorded as possessing glottalized /s'/: the affricated realization of /s'/ is not recorded as such, because, in these dialects, it is necessarily allophonic. The general conclusion then is that (82) applies across the board, in all Pomo dialects and explains the defective distribution of the glottalized fricatives.

The effect of (82) on underlying Kashaya /s'/ and /ʃ'/ is to create an additional aperture position, the A_0: this position may serve as anchor for a second /ʔ/. This will explain two additional facts: the absence of incremented /ʔs/ distinct from /s'/ and the possibility of glottalized and incremented /ʔs'/. Kashaya lacks /ʔs/ because /s/ – like all other continuants – can be only plain or glottalized: hence /ʔs/ is, under the present analysis of laryngeal incrementation, indistinguishable from /s'/. However, Kashaya possesses something which Buckley transcribes as /ʔs'/: our analysis identifies this as a pre-and-postglottalized affricate /ʔts'/, the result of applying (82**) to underlying /s'/ and then associating the increment /ʔ/ to its newly available closure. The synchronic genesis of this /ʔts'/ is outlined below: I make the assumption that all laryngeal increments originate as floating laryngeal features, lacking associated A positions.

(83) Deriving /ʔts'/ from floating /ʔ/ + /s'/

```
                                                      OCP-triggered
   underlying         (82)           associate ʔ        merger
      A_f       →    A₀  A_f    →    A₀  A_f     →    A₀  A_f
      |             |   |           |   |             \ /
      ʔ  ʔ         ʔ   ʔ           ʔ   ʔ               ʔ
```

In addition to explaining why /s'/ and /ʔs/ are non-distinct, despite the apparent existence of /ʔs'/, this analysis explains why glottalization and aspiration function differently when incrementing fricatives: /ʔs'/ is possible but /hsʰ/ is not, because /sʰ/, whether or not it exists as distinct from /s/, does not trigger (82).

5.2.3 Conclusion on Kashaya and Comparison with Buckley's (1992) Analysis

We noted earlier that the /hCʰ/ and /ʔC'/ incremented onsets are found only in onset position: this follows from the assumption that these segments possess both closure and release, and that release is unavailable in coda. Coda glottalized plosives are attested and transcribed as postglottalized, in forms such as /yahmot'/ 'it's a cougar' and /tʃahnotʃ' ba/ 'after speaking' but, given the lack of contrast between coda /C'/ and coda /ʔC/ or /ʔC'/, we may assume that these notations stand for structures in which the unreleased closure is associated to /ʔ/. The absence of release in coda explains the collapse of the four-way contrast into a binary one.

(84) Glottalized plosives in coda

```
A₀
|
ʔ
```

A last point to settle is the source of the difference between Kashaya and Huautla Mazateco. We observed only three-way contrasts among the Huautla plosives (/C/ vs. /Cʰ/ vs. /hC/ and /C/ vs. /C'/ vs. /ʔC/): the additional options of pre-and-postaspiration, pre-and-postglottalization, seen in Kashaya, are absent in Mazateco-Popolocan. A possible source for this difference is the strictness of OCP effects: Kashaya appears to tolerate intermediate OCP violations segment-internally (as in the next-to-last-step of the derivation in (83)). Mazateco does not: a second laryngeal feature, identical or not to one already linked, cannot associate to the A positions of the same segment.

Buckley (1992), whose work on Kashaya has inspired this section, presents a very different analysis of the laryngeal increments. According to Buckley, the incremented consonants represent two distinct root nodes associated to a mora. (L = laryngeal node)

(85) Incremented consonants in Kashaya (after Buckley 1992)

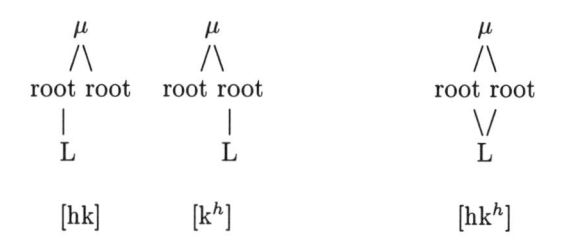

$$
\begin{array}{ccc}
\mu & \mu & \mu \\
/\backslash & /\backslash & /\backslash \\
\text{root root} & \text{root root} & \text{root root} \\
| & | & \backslash / \\
\text{L} & \text{L} & \text{L} \\
\\
\text{[hk]} & \text{[k}^h\text{]} & \text{[hk}^h\text{]}
\end{array}
$$

As Buckley points out, such structures require a morification algorithm akin to Zec's (1989), in which an underlying sequence of consonantal mora plus vowel becomes a single light syllable, with the consonant in onset position.

To account for the impossibility of /h/ co-occurring with /ʔ/ within an incremented onset – i.e., the impossibility of two distinct laryngeal nodes within the mora – Buckley assumes that an OCP effect on feature geometry requires that "only one node of each type be permitted per segment". This is clearly the right idea, but Buckley's representations do not allow it to be correctly implemented. The problem is that the structures in (85) do not contain one segment each, but rather two: there are two root nodes in every one of the moras of (85). We are left then with a fundamental unanswered question: what counts as one segment? Surely moras *can* be polysegmental, if not in Kashaya, whose syllable structure is too constrained to illustrate this point, then at least in languages where CVCC(C) syllables are allowed. Moreover, if the structures in (85) are monosegmental simply by virtue of being linked to the same mora, what prevents structures like those in (86) from being associated to one mora and thus counting as monosegmental onsets in some other language?

(86)   khk   s?s   yỹY

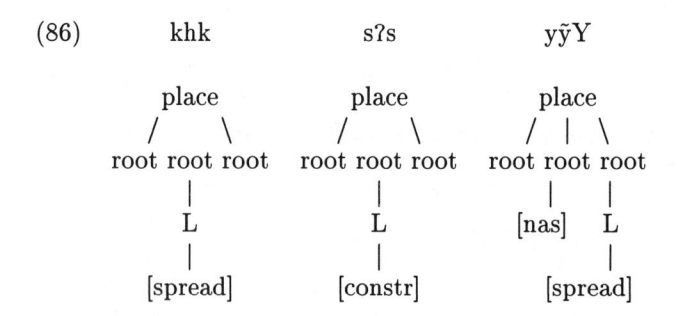

        place   place   place
       /   \   /   \   / | \
  root root root   root root root   root root root
       | | | |
       L   L   [nas]   L
       | | |
     [spread]   [constr]   [spread]

The non-segments in (86) do obey the conditions invoked by Buckley: they are homorganic and thus contain, at most, one place node, one laryngeal node and one nasal value. What is then the reason why Kashaya /hk^h/ counts as a possible single segment, while the very similar /khk/ cannot? This question is answered in the framework of our analysis by the notion of single segment defined in (15): the sequence of A positions contained within one segment must be reducible – by reference to the release projection mechanisms – to one basic A node. The clusters in (86) cannot be so analyzed.

Buckley does not discuss explicitly the restrictions observed on the type of consonants allowing the interesting /C^h/, /hC/, /hC^h/ contrasts. I submit that the representations he employs are in principle unable to explain why such contrasts are attested in their full expansion with plosives but not with continuants.

6 Brief Conclusion

This study set out to support the idea that closure and release are formally represented in the phonology, by documenting the existence of the patterns of laryngeal association in (4). A second goal was to motivate the notion that single segments cannot be simply defined as bundles of features linked to one anchor, whether this anchor is a root node or a weight unit. Rather, monosegmental status is a function of two distinct criteria: the sequence of A positions contained within the segment and their global feature contents.

References

Allen, W. S. 1970. "Aspiration in the Harauti nominals", in F. Palmer (ed.) *Prosodic Analysis*, London, Oxford University Press.

Andrews, H. 1949. "Phonemes and morphophonemes of Temoayan Otomi," *International Journal of American Linguistics* 15:213–222.

Barker, M. A. R. 1964. *Klamath Grammar*, University of California Publications in Linguistics vol. 32, University of California, Berkeley and Los Angeles.

Blight, R. and Pike, E. 1976. "The Phonology of Tenango Otomi", *International Journal of American Linguistics* 42:51–57

Buckley, E. 1990. "Glottalized and aspirated sonorants in Kashaya", in James E. Redden (ed.) *Occasional Papers in Linguistics* (papers from the 1990 Hokan-Penutian Languages Workshop), Department of Linguistics, Southern Illinois University, Carbondale, IL.

Buckley, E. 1992. "Kashaya laryngeal increments, contour segments and the moraic tier," *Linguistic Inquiry* 23:487–496.

Byrd, D. 1992. "Marshallese Suffixal Reduplication," to appear in J. Mead and M. Wessels (eds.) *Papers from WCCFL 10*.

Cairns, C. and Feinstein, M. 1982. "Markedness and the theory of syllable structure," *Linguistic Inquiry* 13:193–226.

Clements, G. N. 1985. "The geometry of phonological features," *Phonology Yearbook* 2:225–252.

Clements, G. N. 1991. "The role of the sonority hierarchy in core syllabification" in J. Kingston and M. Beckman (eds.) *First Conference in Laboratory Phonology*, Cambridge University Press.

Clements, G. N. and Keyser, S. J. 1983. *CV Phonology*, MIT Press.

Collindge, N. 1985. *The Laws of Indo-European*, John Benjamins, Amsterdam.

Flemming, E. 1991."Aperture positions and merger," ms. UCLA.

Fujimura, O. 1992a. "CD Model: a computational model of phonetic implementation," ms. of talk presented at the Princeton DIMACS Workshop, Ohio State University, Dept. of Speech and Hearing Science.

Fujimura, O. 1992b. "Phonology and phonetics: a syllable-based model of articulatory organization," *Journal of the Acoustical Society of Japan* (English Series) 13:39–48.

Fujimura, O and Lovins, J. 1978. "Syllables as concatenative units", in A. Bell and J. Hooper (eds.) *Syllables and Segments*, North Holland Publishing Company, Amsterdam.

Goldsmith, J. 1989. *Metrical and Autosegmental Phonology*, Basil Blackwell.

Hayes, B. 1989. "Compensatory lengthening in moraic phonology" *Linguistic Inquiry* 20:253–306

Hockett, C. 1955. *A Manual of Phonology*, Memoir 11 of the International Journal of American Linguistics, Baltimore.

Hyman, L. 1985. *A Theory of Phonological Weight*, Foris Publications.

Jamieson, A. 1977. "Chiquihuitlan Mazatec Phonology" in W. Merrifield (ed.) *Studies in Otomanguean Phonology*, Summer Institute of Linguistics, Dallas.

Jones, T. and Knudson, L. M. 1977. "Guelavia Zapotec Phonemes," in W. Merrifield (ed.) *Studies in Otomanguean Phonology*, Summer Institute of Linguistics, Dallas.

Keating, P. 1988. "Underspecification in the phonetics", in *Phonology* 5:2, 275–292.

Keating, P. 1990. Phonetic representations in generative grammar. *Journal of Phonetics*, 18:321–334.

Kim-Renaud, Y.-K. 1986. "Syllable boundary phenomena in Korean", in Y.-K. Kim-Renaud *Studies in Korean Linguistics*, Hanshin Publishing Company, Seoul.

Kiparsky, P. 1979. "Metrical structure assignment is cyclic", *Linguistic Inquiry* 10:421–442.

Kiparsky, P. 1980. "Remarks on the metrical structure of the syllable" in W. Dressler (ed.) *Phonologica*. Innsbruck: INS.

Kirchner, R. 1992. "An optimization approach to Yidiny phonology", University of Maryland MA Thesis.

Kirk, P., Ladefoged, P., and Ladefoged, J. 1984. "Using a spectrograph for measuring phonation types in a natural language," *UCLA Working Papers in Phonetics* 59:102–113.

Kozlowski, E. 1976. "Remarks on Havasupai Phonology", *International Journal of American Linguistics* 42:2, 140–149.

Levin, J. 1985. A Metrical Theory of Syllabicity, MIT Ph.D. Dissertation.

Lombardi, L. 1989. "The non-linear organization of the affricate", *Natural Language and Linguistic Theory* 8:375–425

Lombardi, L. 1991. *Laryngeal features and Laryngeal Neutralization*, Ph.D. Dissertation, University of Massachusetts, Amherst.

Lyman, L. and Lyman, R. 1977. "Choapan Zapotec Phonology", in W. Merrifield (ed.) *Studies in Otomanguean Phonology*, Summer Institute of Linguistics, Dallas.

Maddieson, I. 1984. *Patterns of Sounds*, Cambridge Studies in Speech Science and Communication, Cambridge.

Maddieson, I. and Ladefoged, P. 1993. "Phonetics of partially nasal consonants". In M. Huffman and R. Krakow (eds.) *Nasality: Phonological and Phonetic Properties*, Academic Press.

McCarthy, J. J. and Prince, A. 1986. *Prosodic Morphology*, ms., University of Massachusetts and Brandeis University.

McCarthy, J. J. 1988. "Feature geometry and dependency: a review", *Phonetica* 43:84–108.

McCawley, J. 1967. "The role of a phonological feature system in a theory of language," *Languages* 8:112–123.

McLendon, S. 1973. *Proto-Pomo*, University of California Press, Berkeley, London, Los Angeles.

Mester, A. and Ito, J. 1989. "Feature predictability and underspecification: palatal prosody in Japanese mimetics". *Language* 65:258–293.

Mohanan, K. P. 1984. "The structure of the melody," ms., MIT.

Najlis, E. 1971. "Premataco Phonology," *International Journal of American Linguistics*, 37:2, 128–130.

Ohala, J. and Ohala, M. 1992. article to appear in M. Huffman and R. Krakow (eds.) *Nasality: Phonological and Phonetic Properties*, Academic Press.

Oswalt, R. 1964. *Kashaya texts*, University of California Press, Berkeley, London, Los Angeles.

Oswalt, R. 1976. "Baby talk and some basic Pomo words ", *International Journal of American Linguistics* 42:1–13.

Pierson, E. 1953. "Phonemic Statement of Popoloca", *Lingua*, 2:426–429.

Pike, K. and Pike, E. 1947. "Immediate constituents of Mazateco syllables," *International Journal of American Linguistics* 13:2, 78–91

Poser, W. 1979. *Nasal Contour Consonants and the Concept of the Segment in Phonological Theory*, Harvard BA thesis

Prince, A. and Smolensky, P. 1992. "Optimality" to appear in J. Mead and M. Wessels (eds.) *Papers from WCCFL 10*.

Salzmann, Z. 1956. "Arapaho I: Phonology", *International Journal of American Linguistics* 22:1, 49–56.

San, D.-M. 1990. *A Formal Study of Syllables, Tone, Stress and Domain in Chinese Languages*, MIT Ph.D. Dissertation.

Sapir, E. 1922. "Haida Phonemes," *International Journal Of American Linguistics* 3–4, 151.

Selkirk, E. 1984. "Major class features" in M. Aronoff and R. Oehrle (eds.) *Language Sound Structure*, MIT Press.

Stark, S. and Machin, P. 1977. "Stress and Tone in Tlacoyalco Popoloca" in W. Merrifield (ed.) *Studies in Otomanguean Phonology*, Summer Institute of Linguistics, Dallas.

Steriade, D. 1982. *Greek Prosodies and the Nature of Syllabification*, MIT Ph.D. Dissertation.

Steriade, D. 1987. "Locality conditions and feature geometry" in B.Plunkett and J.McDonough (eds.) *Proceedings of NELS 17* 595–617.

Steriade, D. 1989. "Affricates are stops" paper presented at ESCOL 1989 and the *MIT Conference on Features and Underspecification*.

Steriade, D. 1992. "Closure, release and nasal contours" to appear in M. Huffman and R. Krakow (eds.) *Nasality: Phonological and Phonetic Properties*, Academic Press.

Straight, H. S. 1976. *The Acquisition of Mayan Phonology: variation in Yucatec child language*. Garland Press, New York.

Svantesson, J.-O. 1983. *Kammu Phonology and Morphology*, CWK Gleerup, Lund.

Tovar, A. 1979. Review of Lengua Mataca by M. T. Vines Urquiza, *International Journal of American Linguistics* 179, 45:3, 285–287.

Trigo, L. 1992. article to appear in M. Huffman and R. Krakow (eds.) *Nasality: Phonological and Phonetic Properties*, Academic Press.

Trubetzkoy, N. 1939. (published 1949) *Principes de phonologie*, translated by J. Cantineau, Paris, Klincksieck.

Williams, A. and Pike, E. 1968. "The phonology of Western Popoloca", *Lingua*, 20:368–380.

Wolff, H. 1948. Yuchi phonemes and morphemes", *International Journal of American Linguistics* 14:3, 24–243

Yip, M. 1988. "The Obligatory Contour Principle and phonological rules: a loss of identity, *Linguistic Inquiry* 19:1, 65–100.

Zec, D. 1989. *Sonority Constraints in Syllabification*, Stanford Ph.D. Dissertation.

Isolated Uses of Prosodic Categories

Moira Yip

Brandeis University

The general question I am interested in is how much evidence, and of what kind, do language learners need in order to posit the notions mora, syllable, and foot. I shall conclude that they don't need much, if any. A single phenomenon is, in and of itself, sufficient, and no external or independent evidence is needed. Consider what one might suppose would be "primary" or "essential" cues for particular prosodic entities.

For the mora, such cues might include a quantity sensitive stress system, or compensatory lengthening. For the syllable, such cues might include resyllabification, resulting in a mismatch between the morphological and syllable-based parsings, or syllabicity alternations. For the foot, such cues might include alternating stress systems or other rhythmic effects. In the cases I shall examine, such cues are either absent or restricted to the single phenomenon under discussion.

Focussing on Chinese now, Chinese dialects tend to show little traditional evidence for prosodic units below the level of the phonological phrase. They are not quantity sensitive, so the mora does not play an obvious role. The syllable is largely co-extensive with the morpheme, and resyllabification is extremely limited, so any generalization that makes reference to the syllable can be rephrased in terms of the morpheme. Many dialects lack noticeable stress, especially alternating stress, so the metrical foot is well-concealed. This is a markedly different situation from that of many languages whose prosodic phonology and morphology has been studied by many phonologists, most notably John McCarthy and Alan Prince in various papers, but also Junko Itô, Armin Mester, Bruce Hayes, Larry Hyman, and others. Frequently multiple sources of evidence, including stress, minimal word effects, quantity alternations, and the morphology, provide convergent evidence that a particular language has, say, an iambic foot structure (as in Lombardi and McCarthy's (1991) analysis of Choctaw, Spring 1989 for Axininca Campa), or a moraic trochee (as in McCarthy and Prince (1990) for Arabic, Itô (1990) on Japanese).

This paper argues that despite the extreme paucity of evidence for their existence in Chinese, the notions of mora, syllable, and foot play a crucial role in the phonology and morphology of some dialects. If the native speaker has little or no independent evidence for their existence, it seems necessary to conclude that these units are part of the inventory made available by universal grammar and are waiting in the wings, so to speak, to be made use of by the grammar. As Michael Kenstowicz puts it "the metrical constituents are known in advance." These results thus offer strong support for the theory of prosodic morphology laid out in various works by McCarthy and Prince.

I'd like to expand on this point a little with respect to the syllable. Chinese is often called a "mono-syllabic language," by which is meant that each morpheme is a single syllable and vice-versa. As Mester (1991) has noted for Sino-Japanese, each syllable retains its autonomy, so that there is essentially no resyllabification and the identity thus holds at the surface as well as in underlying representation. It might thus seem self-evident that the native speaker uses the notion syllable, but I would like to suggest that the reverse is the case.

Suppose we assume, as seems inevitable, that morphemes are identified as such by the language learner. In Mandarin, for example, we find *che* 'vehicle' in *huoche* 'train', *mache* 'cart', *dianche* 'tram', *zixingche* 'bicycle', *qiche* 'car', *chezi* 'small car', *chefei* 'fare', and *chezhan* 'station', among many others. Now suppose we encounter a generalization that apparently involves reference to the syllable, such as "syllables must end in [+son]" or "stress the final syllable." Because of the syllable/morpheme identity such generalizations can always be re-couched in terms of the morpheme, and the Chinese speaker can function very well without reference to the syllable at all.

It is therefore of some interest to look for incontrovertible use of the notion "syllable" in these languages, and I offer such evidence in this paper.

The shape of the paper is as follows. After some background, I discuss three cases in which the syllable plays a role, including one in which the mora also takes part since the language imposes a bi-moraic syllable requirement. Then I discuss Cantonese, in which the iambic foot plays a role in the native morphology and also in the loan-word phonology. The details of the analyses also support some of the principles which have been argued elsewhere to operate in prosodic phonology. The Maximality Condition on syllabification explains the shift of high nuclear vowels to onset position in Anxiang. We find an instance of truncation to a single syllable in Yuanyang, parallel to similar phenomena in Japanese. The bi-moraic syllable template, interacting with the Onset Principle, explains the treatment of intervocalic consonants in English loanwords into Cantonese. Investigation of familiar name formation in Cantonese reveals that it is the result of conformity to an iambic output template, again familiar from Japanese hypocoristics. Finally, Mandarin syllable-count restrictions in compounding are attributed to avoidance of a conflict between weight and prominence, extending our understanding of weight from mora count to syllable count.

Isolated Uses of Prosodic Categories 295

First, some background on Chinese, and some theoretical assumptions. The prosodic hierarchy of Chinese includes the familiar entities mora (μ), syllable (σ), foot (Φ). In many languages the notion minimal Word (Wd$_{min}$) also plays a role, and typically can be equated with the foot. In Chinese languages it is more usually to be equated with the syllable, which is generally bi-moraic (Duanmu 1990). The full picture is shown below:

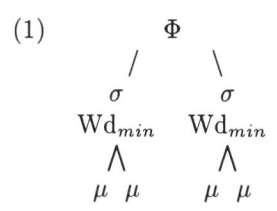

(1)
```
            Φ
          /   \
         σ     σ
      Wdmin  Wdmin
       / \    / \
       μ μ    μ μ
```

The affixation processes investigated in this paper require reference to the iambic/trochaic foot as a target for affixation (McCarthy and Prince 1990, Mester 1990). Neither of these can be identified with the Minimal Word, providing evidence in favor of the need to distinguish between foot and minimal word.

I assume the following principles operate universally. For a fuller explication, see the works cited below:

(2) *Onset Principle*: (Itô 1989:223)
     Avoid $_\sigma$[V

(3) *Maximality Principle* (Prince 1985, Itô 1989):
     "units are of maximal size, within the other constraints on their form"

(4) *Prosodic Licensing*: (Itô 1989):
     "all phonological units belong to higher prosodic structure"
     where "units" = segment, mora, syllable, foot etc.

     Unlicensed units delete by Stray Erasure, unless some process (for example, epenthesis) intervenes to license them.

(5) Mapping is continuous. (No skipping; McCarthy and Prince 1986)

(6) Directionality: L>R or R>L

The paper is organized into three sections. Section 1 deals with Cantonese loanwords, where both mora and syllable play a role. Sections 2 and

3 deal with two more cases where the syllable plays a role: Anxiang and Yuanyang. Section 4 deals with the role of the foot in Cantonese familiar name formation. Section 5 deals with weight and prominence in Mandarin compounding and shows that, just as two moras make a heavy syllable, two syllables can make a heavy foot.

1 The Mora and the Syllable in Cantonese

Hong Kong Cantonese shows evidence of crucial reference to the bi-moraic syllable in its loanword phonology. One simple argument that Cantonese syllables are minimally bi-moraic comes from the distribution of long and short vowels in Cantonese. If the vowel is followed by a stop, nasal, or glide, both long and short vowels are found. In vowel-final syllables, however, the vowel must be long: there are no short open syllables (and for this reason from henceforth length in open syllables will not be shown, as it is predictable). Note that short /a/ is phonetically [ɐ], long /aː/ is [a].

(7) fat55   'to remove (dirt,etc)'   faːt33   'set forth'
    fay22   'to bark'   faːy33   'fast'
    fan35   'rice noodle   faːn22   'rice'
    *fa   faː55   'flower'

Now consider the loanword vocabulary. English too has long and short vowels (although phonetically the long vowels are of course diphthongs). Word medially, these are both found in open syllables: short in *letter*, long in *soda*. It turns out that when these words are adapted into Cantonese, the short vowels are too short to fill the syllable, and the following consonant is geminated so as to function simultaneously as a coda of the first syllable (thus making that syllable bi-moraic) and an onset of the second syllable. No such gemination occurs after long vowels. This gemination after short vowels occurs no matter where the stress falls in the English input, incidentally, showing that it has nothing to do with the difference in syllabification in English associated with the difference in stress placement. The data below give examples of short vowels with stress before and after and of long vowels. Data are drawn from Cheung (1986), Chan and Kwok (1982), and Bauer (1985).

(8) *English VCV → Cantonese VC.CV*

  a. cópy k^hap55 p^hi35   shútter   sat55 ta35
      létter   let55 t^ha35
  b. guitár   kit33 t^ha55   commíssion k^ham33 mi55 sön35

(9)   *English VVCV → Cantonese V.CV*, phonetically [V:CV]

market	ma55 k̠ʰet35	porter	pʰo t̠ʰa
soda	so55 t̠a35	yoga	yü21 k̠a55
motor	mo55 t̠a35	major	me55 t̠sa35
foreman	fo55 m̠an35		

The details of the analysis[1] are as follows:

(i)   all Cantonese syllables are bimoraic;
(ii) English short vowels have one mora and English long vowels have two moras;
(iii) short vowels do not fill the bimoraic Cantonese syllable template, so the following consonant fills the empty mora;
(iv) the Onset Principle also syllabifies this consonant to the following syllable, causing gemination.

This is shown schematically below, abstracting away from segmental adjustments (such as English voiced /d/ becoming Cantonese voiceless unaspirated /t/).

(10)

Note that both stops and nasals count as moras in this process, supporting Duanmu's claim that even Ru Sheng (stop-final) syllables are bi-moraic.

This analysis requires reference to both syllable and mora. It is not the case that a bi-moraic output of the form $\sigma_\mu\sigma_\mu$ is sufficient, since the non-geminated forms [lɛ t'a] would meet this requirement. Rather it is specifically the syllable which must have two moras. McCarthy and Prince (1991) suggested that the Minimal Word always has either two syllables, or two moras. Since the Cantonese speaker is surrounded by evidence that the Minimal Word is smaller than two syllables, it must be two moras in Cantonese. If this is right, then the bi-moraic syllable requirement can be viewed as a requirement that each syllable in the language must be a Minimal Word, and since syllable and morpheme coincide this means that morphemes must be Minimal Words, an unsurprising result given the

---
[1] This solution is the result of a conversation with Duanmu San.

"isolating" morphology of the language. In fact, we have in a sense arrived at a partial explanation for the independence of morphemes and their phonological inertness: since each is already a Minimal Word, there is no phonological pressure to incorporate material from neighboring morphemes to achieve a Minimal Word target.

2 The Syllable as Suffix Template in Anxiang

Anxiang is of interest because it too makes crucial use of the syllable, here as a suffix template in reduplication, and also because of the role played by the Maximality Principle, (3), in syllabification. I argue that this principle alone suffices to explain the facts of Anxiang. (See Yip 1992 for arguments that alternatives involving rhyme substitution (Bao 1990) or rhyme substitution plus feature recycling (Duanmu 1990) are problematic.)

Anxiang is spoken in Hunan province, and described in two papers by Ying (1988, 1990). Diminutive ǝr suffixation in Anxiang is accompanied by reduplication. The reduplicated (that is, second) syllable replaces the rhyme by [ǝr], with the particular characteristic that high vowel nuclei are preserved in the form of pre-nuclear glides. Similar facts are found in Haimen "reverse talk" (Yin 1989:102). The data is given below; tones are not shown.

(11)
a.	tie	tie tiǝr	'small dish, plate'
	mian	mian miǝr	'face'
	tai	tai tǝr	'belt'
	pau	pau pǝr	'bud'
	ke	ke kǝr	'check, chequer'
	fa	fa fǝr	'law, way'
	o	o ǝr	'bird's nest'
b.	ti	ti tier	'bamboo flute'
	tin	tin tier	'nail'
	p^hu	p^hu p^huer	'spread'
	tçü	tçü tçüǝr	'pearl'

2.1 Analysis[2]

The analysis goes as follows. I assume a theory of syllabification along the lines of Itô (1989). The suffix is a syllable template. The base reduplicates. The melody -ər overwrites the base, from right-to-left, delinking base material as it goes under phonotactic pressure (cf McCarthy and Prince (1990) on melodic over-writing). Syllabification obeys the principles of Maximality, (3), and the Onset Principle, (2), which require that the largest possible syllable be constructed, and that all syllables have onsets. The maximal syllable in Anxiang has room for no other rhymal material beyond the /-ər/, but the onset has room for a CG sequence, as can be seen from words like /tie/, /mian/. Assuming obligatory syllabification of [ər], the derivation for [tin tiər] looks like this:

(12)
$$\begin{array}{cc} \sigma & \sigma \\ /|\backslash & /|\backslash \\ t\ i\ n & t\ i\ n \end{array} \rightarrow \begin{array}{ccc} \sigma & \sigma \\ /|\backslash & /|\backslash \\ t\ i\ n & t\ i\ n & \text{ər} \end{array} \rightarrow \begin{array}{cc} \sigma & \sigma \\ /|\backslash & //|\backslash\backslash \\ t\ i\ n & t\ i\ n\ \text{ər} \end{array}$$

The original syllabic position of the input high vowel or glide is totally irrelevant: it is simply that syllabification demands the maximal onset, and thus takes in any high vocalic material around. In this view, the survival of the high nuclear vowel in the form of an onset glide is simply a consequence of the fact that [+high] melodic elements can occur in either nuclear or onset position in a syllable, whereas [-high] elements are restricted to nuclei. Note that a high vowel coda will be delinked by right-to-left melodic overwriting, because the rhyme sequences /air/, /əir/, /aur/, /əur/ are ill-formed.

The output is a total of two syllables—a first syllable identical to the input, and a second syllable which must include the suffix, and thus has room only for an onset made up of material from the base syllable. Although I have couched the analysis in terms of suffixation of a syllable template, it is also possible to think of this as an bi-syllabic output template in the sense of McCarthy and Prince (1990) and Mester (1990). Ying's description suggests that it is a prosodic foot, specifically a syllabic trochee, with the second syllable unstressed and toneless.

---

[2]In Yip (1991) I give a somewhat different analysis, and in fact argue against melodic overwriting. I have since realized that melodic overwriting is not only tenable, but even avoids some technical problems associated with my earlier analysis. For present purposes, what matters is that both analyses share the essential insight that the reason high vowels survive under affixation of -ər is that the maximal syllable must be constructed, and that only high vowels can surface in pre-nuclear position as glides.

My conclusion, then, is that a straightforward syllabification analysis in which melodic overwriting forces delinking under phonotactic pressure, subject only to the Maximality Principle, derives the Anxiang data without problem. Many (but not all) Fanqie languages succumb to a similar treatment.

There is an interesting difference between Anxiang and English in their treatment of an almost identical suffix. English has several -*er* suffixes, very similar to Anxiang [ər]. In Anxiang, this suffix never surfaces as an independent syllable, but merges with the base material. In English, however, the suffix simply stays separate. Contrast Anxiang /pai-ər/ > [pər] and English *fly-er* /flay -ər/ > [flayər]. Anxiang shows the Chinese tendency towards monosyllabicity in its compression of base and suffix into this one syllable; this is typical of this kind of non-concatenative morphology, a point first made by Steriade (1988).[3]

3 Yuanyang Zi-suffixation: Syllable as Target for Truncation

Yuanyang is a N. Mandarin dialect related to Chengzhou. My data comes from Lin (1989:147), who took it from Li (1963). This dialect also seems to aim for a monosyllabic output in syllabification, but it turns out that simple appeal to a monosyllabic template will not suffice here. Instead monosyllabicity is the result of truncation to a single syllable, after both affixation and syllabification are over.

Typical data are given below.

(13) a. sua   suau   'brush'
        tɕie   tɕiau   'eggplant'
        pi   piou   'nose'
     b. pʰan   pʰa   'plate'
        kuan   kua   'container'

All available data is either -V# or -n#. Mandarin dialects normally allow -G#, and -ŋ#.

I suggest that the suffix is indeed /u/, and that affixation is immediately followed by syllabification. Assuming that syllabification is subject to Maximality and the Onset Principle, it will produce the following results:

---

[3]The picture is somewhat confused by the reduplication in Anxiang, but the general point is, I hope, clear.

Isolated Uses of Prosodic Categories

(14)   σ   σ   σ
      /:\\   //: /:
  sua-u → suau   kuan-u → kua nu

For /sua-u/, since syllables can obviously end in glides (viz. the final outputs in (13a)), the suffix can be fitted into a single syllable with the root. In /kuan-u/ this is impossible, for sonority reasons, so two syllables are formed, with /n/ as the onset of the second syllable.

The final step is one of truncation, keeping just the initial syllable. In the case of /suau/, truncation's effects will be null, but in the case of /kua.nu/ truncation will remove the final syllable, leaving simply [kua]. (cf. Mester 1990, Itô 1990)[4]

The first comment one can make about this is that again it seems to show the pull of the monosyllable in Chinese. Both here and in Anxiang root and suffix are not allowed to surface as more than one syllable, and this end is achieved by different means in the two languages. The second comment one can make has to do with an interesting parallel with Japanese. Poser (1990), Mester (1990), and Itô (1990) have all demonstrated the importance of a different prosodic unit, the bi-moraic foot, in Japanese. This foot manifests itself in a variety of ways, including as an output template and as the residue of truncation. We may now see that Chinese uses its favorite prosodic unit, the syllable, in exactly the same two ways. This is not chance, because it correlates with another difference between the two languages. In Japanese, the Minimal Word is any bi-moraic unit, whereas in Chinese it is bi-moraic, but also mono-syllabic. In other words, both languages may in fact use the same prosodic unit, the Minimal Word, but it is defined differently in the two languages.

In Sections 1-3 I have looked at three processes that seem to make crucial reference to the syllable in Chinese dialects. In no case is the syllable co-extensive with the morpheme. In Anxiang and Yuanyang suffixation a single syllable may be bi-morphemic. In Cantonese loanwords the syllable is sub-morphemic. I now move on to cases of the use of a larger prosodic unit, the foot, in Chinese.

4 The Iambic Foot: Cantonese Familiar Names

I now turn to a very different kind of affixation. It earns its place in this paper by virtue of the fact that the affix takes the form of a prosodic output template, specifically an iambic foot. Since Cantonese is a language with no

---

[4]Lombardi and McCarthy (1991) propose that truncation processes delete prosodic structure, and resyllabification may then salvage some melodic material. Such an approach fails here, as it would wrongly predict [kuan], not [kua].

noticeable stress distinctions (other than in the data to be discussed here), there is no evidence to lead the native speaker to posit the existence of a foot of any kind. The role of the foot in familiar name formation thus lends support to the notion that it is a universally available primitive which does not need to be learned.[5]

Cantonese forms a familiar form of address by prefacing [a^{33}] to the family name, and suffixing a high tone which is realized on the name itself. The result is a bi-syllabic form with a more prominent second syllable. The relative prominence of the second syllable is shown in three ways. First, the first syllable bears less stress than the second, the only place in the language where we find a stress distinction. Second, the second syllable ends on high pitch, being either high throughout if its base tone begins high, or rising to high pitch if the base tone begins non-high (for details see Yip 1980). Third, the second syllable is somewhat lengthened (Chao 1947), and this is particularly noticeable if it is obstruent final (and thus usually rather short). The first syllable, on the other hand, is noticeably short, in fact mono-moraic. Some typical examples follow. 5 denotes high pitch, 1 denotes low pitch, and so on. Cantonese has seven tones on sonorant-final syllables: 55, 33, 22, 21, 53, 35, 24. Obstruent-final syllables may be 55, 33 or 22 only.

(15) yip^{22} a^{33} yíp^{25}
      tshan^{21} a^{33} ts^{h}án^{25}
      tsoeŋ^{53} a^{33} tsoéŋ^{55}

The usual description of these facts involves a prefix and a high tone suffix (for example, see Yip 1980), but I argue that we are dealing with an output template that is an iambic foot and that all else follows from the attempt to fill this template with a monosyllable.[6] In Cantonese, fulfilling the iambic foot target requires two things: the addition of a syllable and establishment of the appropriate relative prominence relationship. Addition of a syllable can be accomplished by using the base melodic material (for example, by reduplication, or by spreading) or by default, and the latter tack is taken here. A minimal syllable is added, the single vowel /a/.[7]

---

[5] For a somewhat different view of the foot in Cantonese, see Silverman (1990) on loanword phonology.

[6] It is beyond the scope of this paper to discuss the full range of morphological circumstances in which a high toned suffix appears; I do not wish to claim that an iambic template is necessarily responsible for all these cases. For a very interesting discussion of output templates see McCarthy and Prince (1990), Poser (1990), Mester (1990), and Itô (1990).

[7] For discussion of minimal syllables in Chinese, see Chiang and Lin (1990).

An epenthetic syllable like this would be expected to use unmarked featural material, since it is presumably inserted by default. Evidence for the claim that /a/ is unmarked comes from two sources. First, /a/ and /a:/ are the only vowels that are not subject to any co-occurrence restrictions with particular onsets and codas, suggesting that they may lack most or all Place features (Cheng 1990). Second, if an utterance lacks a final particle there is a strong tendency to add the vowel [a] to the end for euphonic purposes (Law 1990). The remaining features of the epenthetic syllable are those of tone, and /a/ has the higher mid 33 tone, plausibly the default tone. This minimal epenthetic syllable /a/ is minimal in two other respects. It is one of a very small class of truly onsetless morphemes (the others are all interjections or particles), in that it cannot be pronounced with a velar nasal onset, [ŋa], unlike the majority of 'onsetless' morphemes (Chao 1947:21). Second, it appears to be mono-moraic in normal speech, unlike all the other open syllables in the language. The fact that it is usually transcribed with a long vowel, [a:], may be attributed to the fact that vowels are long in all other open syllables.

/a/ is prefixed, rather than suffixed, because mapping to the iambic template first fills the head position (the second position) with the available syllable, then supplies an epenthetic syllable for the rest of the template. Finally, the second syllable is made more prominent by the addition of high pitch and somewhat lengthened.[8] The initial syllable is correspondingly less stressed (almost the only situation in Cantonese where stress can be detected).

If it is correct to view this as adaptation to an iambic template, the prediction must be that bi-syllabic inputs will not receive the additional syllable /a/, although they should still get the prominent H on the final syllable. This prediction is borne out. Consider the following facts from Whitaker (1955:56), which illustrate the clear generalization: /a/ is only added to monosyllables, since bi-syllables are already long enough to fill the template.[9]

---

[8]Other dialects show somewhat similar facts. Yin (1989:117, 184) discusses a form of addressing children in Taiwanese Mandarin in which the tone pattern is fixed as L-LH, and the forms are mostly reduplicated. Kinship terms (Yin 1989:192) have the second syllable in H tone and stressed.

[9]In the case of bi-syllabic forms, the first syllable retains some stress, but the second syllable gains increased prominence by the addition of the high pitch. The same is true for an alternative familiar form created by prefixation of lou[24] 'old', to mono-syllabic names.

(16) a. Surnames
/tsʰan²²/   a³³ tsʰan²⁵
/yip²²/   a³³ yip²⁵
/au⁵⁵ tsoeŋ¹¹/   au⁵⁵ tsoeŋ¹⁵
/si⁵⁵ tʰou¹¹/   si⁵⁵ tʰou¹⁵

b. Family Relations
a³³ kuŋ⁵⁵   'grandfather (mother's side)'
a³³ yi⁵⁵   'mother's younger sister'
pʰo21 pho²⁵   'grandmother (mother's side)'
ku⁵⁵ tse⁵⁵   'father's younger sister'

c. Names based on birth order
/yi²²/   a³³ yi²⁵   'No. 2'
/ŋ²⁴/   a³³ ŋ²⁵   'No. 5'
/sap²² sei³³/   sap²² sei³⁵   'No. 14'
/sap²² ŋ²⁴/   sap²² ŋ²⁵   'No. 15'

d. Nicknames
/pai⁵³/   a³³ pai⁵⁵   'the lame'
/fei²⁴/   a³³ fei²⁵   'the fat'
/woŋ²¹ mou²¹/   woŋ²¹ mou²⁵   'the yellow-haired one'[10]
/maaŋ²¹ pei²²/   maaŋ²¹ pei²⁵   'deformed nose'

These Cantonese data, then, can be analyzed as the result of matching a monosyllabic input to a bisyllabic iambic output template, forcing the provision of an extra syllable, and a H-tone prominence marker at the boundary of the foot.[11] The iambic template here is a prosodic target. Note also that the foot is not co-extensive with the minimal word in Cantonese, since the minimal word is clearly the syllable.

---

[10] Whitaker's notation is unclear here; it looks as though he may have *mou*⁵⁵, which would be somewhat unexpected (although still in line with the iambic pattern).

[11] A number of sources agree that /a33/ is added only to monosyllabic family names. In addition to Whitaker, see Chao (1968) (p. 216), Hashimoto (1972). I have checked this data with three informants, all speakers of Hong Kong Cantonese of around 30 years old. Two of them agree with the description of the facts as presented here, but the other one cannot use the prefix in this way at all. For her, its only use is as a prefix to the second syllable of the personal name *meng*. According to one of the first two informants, who can use the prefix in either way, before a personal name there is less connotation of familiarity and more a simple vocative usage. Used in this way, the prefix is phonologically different too: the tone on the second syllable does not change, and /a33/ can be prefixed even to bi-syllabic names in the context of Cantonese opera (although it is only obligatory on monosyllables). I shall not discuss this usage here.

Isolated Uses of Prosodic Categories   305

Derivations for a bi-syllabic and a polysyllabic form are given below, using nicknames as examples:

(17)   [$\sigma[\mu\mu]_\sigma$]$_\Phi$ [$\sigma\ [\mu\mu]_\sigma$]$_\Phi$
    Mapping: [σ [fei^{21}]$_\sigma$]$_\Phi$ [[woŋ^{21}]$_\sigma$ [mou^{21}]$_\sigma$]$_\Phi$
    Default σ: [[a^{33}]$_\sigma$ [fei^{21}]$_\sigma$]$_\Phi$ [[woŋ^{21}]$_\sigma$ [mou^{21}]$_\sigma$]$_\Phi$
    Prominence: [[a^{33}]$_\sigma$ [fei^{21}]$^5_\sigma$]$_\Phi$ [[woŋ^{21}]$_\sigma$ [mou^{21}]$_\sigma$]$^5_\Phi$
              [a^{33} fei^{25}]   [woŋ^{21} mou^{25}]

Since the first syllable may be a full bi-moraic syllable like /woŋ/, the template cannot specify the weight of the first syllable, and the template is thus not strictly iambic, since an iamb requires a light first syllable. I view this template as a quasi-iamb striving for true iambicity, but thwarted by the need to preserve the melody (and thus usually both the moras) of the first syllable. In the case of a monosyllabic base, a true iamb is the outcome, because the epenthetic syllable is minimal, that is, a single mora, thus achieving an iambic pattern.

Cantonese offers an interesting example of the use of prosodic template as output target, the minimal realization of that template by epenthesis, and the reinforcement of prominence by tonal means. It provides an instance of extension of a base to fit an output template, alongside the more common cases of truncation to fit a template outlined in McCarthy and Prince (1990:257), Poser (1990), and Mester (1990), which discuss hypocoristics and vocatives in a variety of languages.

5 Mandarin Compounds: Avoidance of Weight/prominence Conflicts

This final section differs from the others in that it does not provide evidence for any of the well-understood prosodic units μ, σ, and foot, but rather proposes an extension of the theory. I argue that the notion of weight, traditionally μ vs. $\mu\mu$, may also exist at higher prosodic levels, specifically that σ vs. $\sigma\sigma$ also counts as a weight distinction. Indirectly this also provides evidence for the syllable as a unit, since stress is cross-linguistically not assigned to morphemes, but to metrical units such as mora and syllable.

Duanmu and Lu (1990) discuss constraints in Mandarin that limit the distribution of bi-syllabic and mono-syllabic variants of certain words. They observe that the distribution is stress-related and give an analysis within the framework of Halle and Vergnaud. I argue that the real reason for the restrictions has to do with an avoidance of conflict between metrical prominence and relative weight: the metrically prominent element cannot be lighter than the less prominent element. The notion of weight here is a new one: bisyllabic words are considered heavier than monosyllabic words, by analogy to bi-moraic syllables being heavier than mono-moraic syllables.

Some Mandarin words have two allomorphs, one bisyllabic and one monosyllabic. The choice between these is free in most contexts. Some examples are given below.

(18) xue-xi   xue   'to study'
      hui-hua   hua   'painting'
      ji-shu   ji   'skilled'
      gong-ren   gong   'worker'

In a left-headed verb phrase, V NP, like the following, only three of the four possibilities are allowed, with [σσ σ] not possible.

(19) xue-xi hui-hua   'to study painting'
      xue hua
      xue hui-hua
      *xue-xi hua

In a right-headed noun phrase or compound, modifier- N, again three possibilities are allowed, but it is a different one which is outlawed, [σ σσ].

(20) ji-shu gong-ren   'skilled worker'
      ji gong
      ji-shu gong
      *ji gong-ren

Duanmu and Lu then point out that stress is assigned to non-heads in Mandarin; since the notion "non-head" has no formal status in current theory I restate this as "Stress maximal projections." The stress contrast can be seen in the following.

(21) *Non-Head Stress*
              *   *
      mai shu   'to buy books'   hong shu   'red books'

Re-inspection of the data in (19-20) now reveals that the illicit combinations are ones in which the stressed constituent has fewer syllables than the unstressed constituent.

(22) xue-xi hui-hua: [. *] so xue-xi hua [σσ σ] is disallowed.
      ji-shu gong-ren: [* .] so ji gong-ren [σ σσ] is disallowed.

Isolated Uses of Prosodic Categories 307

This correlation suggests the following principle:

(23) A conflict between prosodic prominence and relative weight is avoided.

The prohibition is not absolute: if the lexical items involved have only mono-syllabic or bi-syllabic variants, such sequences are fine:

(24)
```
         *
xihuan gou    'to like dogs'
*
lao zuoye     'old exercise'
```

If correct, this analysis extends our notion of weight contrasts from the mora to the syllable level. Just as assignment of stress to syllables may access the μ vs. $\mu\mu$ distinction, so stressing of higher-order constituents may access the σ vs. $\sigma\sigma$ distinction, when checking against a well-formedness template. Note that the stress assignment does not change: rather the representation is thrown out as ill-formed and not used if an alternative exists.[12]

I conclude this section with some speculation on Chinese stress. Duanmu's claim that all syllables are bi-moraic, if true, correctly predicts that we will never observe quantity-sensitive stress in Chinese, because all syllables will be heavy and therefore stressed. In Cantonese, for example, this is exactly what we find: equal stress on every syllable. Some dialects of course have stress distinctions at the word level, singling out initial or final syllables as prominent (for example, Shanghai, Taiwanese), but these are not quantity sensitive, and the occasional alternating stress system (such as in Mandarin phonological phrases, see Hoa 1983) is not quantity sensitive either. The conjunction of no evidence for quantity sensitivity at the moraic level with apparent quantity sensitivity at the syllabic level suggests that quantity sensitivity itself is a very deep and universal notion.

6 Conclusions

This paper has argued that despite the extreme paucity of evidence for their existence in Chinese, the notions of mora, syllable and foot play a crucial role in the phonology and morphology of some dialects. If the native speaker has little or no independent evidence for their existence, it seems necessary to conclude that these units are part of the inventory made available by

---

[12]Note that English compound stress has no comparable sensitivity to syllable-count. We get initial stress in all possible combinations of one and two syllables in compounds: bluebird, bluebottle, yellowtail, yellowjacket.

universal grammar and are waiting in the wings, so to speak, to be made use of by the grammar.

The argument here is actually quite tricky. Suppose one finds just one phenomenon that uses the iambic foot in the language (as is the case in native Cantonese). "Ah!," you say, the native speaker therefore has positive evidence for the existence of the iamb, and we can deduce nothing about the iamb as a unit of Universal Grammar. I think, however, that one has to consider how this iambic process could have arisen in the first place. There is no reason that I know of to conclude that it is the remnant of a previously pervasively iambic language. Rather it appears to be the first use of the iamb in a possibly incipient full iambic system (extrapolating unjustifiably into the future!). It may have developed from simple suffixation of a H tone, which is found independently in other contexts in Cantonese. The question must then be reformulated: why should native speakers have re-analyzed this as the imposition of an iambic template, unless the notion "iamb" was already freely available from Universal Grammar? Put this way, the cases in this paper argue strongly for the universality of the units mora, syllable and foot.

Acknowledgements

Much of this material previously appeared in Yip (1992). I am grateful to Kluwer Academic Publishers for permission to re-use some of the contents of that paper here. My interest in this topic was sparked by reading Lin (1989). Comments from audiences at MIT, McGill, University of Ottawa, UC/Irvine, Ohio State, Brandeis, and this conference helped me greatly improve this paper. I would also like to thank an anonymous reviewer of the JEAL version of this paper, Matthew Chen, Harry van der Hulst, Michael Kenstowicz, Armin Mester, Glyne Piggott, Alan Prince, Doug Pulleyblank, and Duanmu San for useful discussion, and Lisa Cheng and Sam-po Law for data and helpful suggestions. All errors and omissions are of course mine.

References

Bao, Z. 1990. Fanqie languages and reduplication. *Linguistic Inquiry* 21.3.317-350.

Bauer, R. 1985. The expanding syllabary of Hong Kong Cantonese. *Cahiers de Linguistique - Asie Orientale* XIV:1.99-111.

Chan, M. and H. Kwok. 1982. *A study of lexical borrowing from English in Hong Kong Chinese.* Hong Kong: University of Hong Kong.

Chao, Y-R. 1947. *Cantonese primer.* Cambridge, MA: Harvard University Press.

Chao, Y-R. 1968. *A grammar of spoken Chinese.* Berkeley: University of California Press.

Cheng, l. 1990. Feature geometry of vowels and co-occurence restrictions in Cantonese. In A. Halpern (ed.), *Proceedings of the West Coast Conference on Formal Linguistics 9*, pp. 107-124. Palo Alto, CA: CSLI.

Cheung, Y-S. 1986. Xianggang Guangzhouhua Yingyu yinyi jieci de shengdiao guize. (On the tone system of loanwords from English in Hong Kong Cantonese.) *Zhongguo Yuwen* 1:42-50.

Chiang, W-Y. and Y-H. Lin. 1990. *Degenerate syllables and prosodic licensing in Chinese.* ms., University of Delaware.

Duanmu, S. 1990. *A formal study of syllable, tone, stress, and domain in Chinese languages.* Ph.D. dissertation, Massachusetts Institute of Technology.

Duanmu, S. and B. Lu. 1990. *Word-length variations in Chinese two-word constructions.* ms., Massachusetts Institute of Technology and University of Connecticut.

Hashimoto, A. 1972. *Studies in Yue dialects 1: Phonology of Cantonese.* Cambridge: Cambridge University Press.

Hoa, M. 1983. *L'accentuation en pekinois.* Editions Langages Croisés. Paris: Centre de Recherches Linguistiques sur l'Asie Orientale.

Itô, J. 1989. A prosodic theory of epenthesis. *Natural Language and Linguistic Theory* 7:2.217-260.

Itô, J. 1990. Prosodic minimality in Japanese. To appear in K. Deaton, M. Noske, and M. Ziolkowski (eds.), *Papers from the Parasession on the Syllable in Phonetics and Phonology, Chicago Linguistic Society 26-II*.

Law, S. 1990. *The syntax and phonology of Cantonese sentence-final particles*. Ph.D. dissertation, Boston University.

Li, R. 1963. *Hanyu fangyan diaocha shouce*. (Manual of survey of Chinese dialects.) Beijing: Kexue Press.

Lin, Y-H. 1989. *Autosegmental treatment of segmental processes in Chinese phonology*. Ph.D. dissertation, University of Texas, Austin.

Lombardi, L. and J. McCarthy. 1991. Prosodic circumspection in Choctaw morphology. *Phonology* 8:1.37-72.

McCarthy, J. and A. Prince. 1986. *Prosodic morphology*. ms., University of Massachusetts at Amherst and Brandeis University. Forthcoming, MIT Press.

McCarthy, J. and A. Prince 1990. Foot and word in prosodic morphology: The Arabic broken plural. *Natural Language and Linguistic Theory* 8:2.209-284.

McCarthy, J. and A. Prince 1991. Minimality. Paper presented at "The Organization of Phonology: Features and Domains" conference, University of Illinois at Urbana-Champaign.

Mester, A. 1990. Patterns of truncation. *Linguistic Inquiry* 21:3.478-484.

Mester, A. 1991. Metrical Optimization. Paper presented at "The Organization of Phonology: Features and Domains" conference, University of Illinois at Urbana-Champaign.

Poser, W. 1990. Evidence for foot structure in Japanese. *Language* 66:78-105.

Prince, A. 1985. Improving tree theory. *Proceedings of the Berkeley Linguistics Society* 11:471-490.

Silverman, D. 1990. *English loanwords in Cantonese: The rites of passage*. ms., University of California, Los Angeles.

Spring, C. 1989. *Reduplication without affixes: The prosodic word base in Axininca Campa*. ms., University of Arizona.

Steriade, D. 1988. Reduplication and syllable structure. *Phonology* 5:73-155.

Whitaker, K. P. K. 1955-6. A study of the modified tones in spoken Cantonese. *Asia Major* 5:9-36, 6:184-207.

Yin, Y-M. 1989. *Phonological aspects of word formation in Mandarin Chinese.* Ph.D. dissertation, University of Texas.

Ying, Y-T. 1988. Huan anxiang fangyan jilüe. (A sketch of the Anxiang dialect, Hunan province.) *Fangyan* 1:52-67.

Ying, Y-T. 1990. Hunan anxiang fangyan de erhua. (The suffix *er* in the Anxiang dialect.) *Fangyan* 1:52-59.

Yip, M. 1980. *The tonal phonology of Chinese.* Ph.D. dissertation, Massachusetts Institute of Technology. Published 1991 by Garland, New York.

Yip M. 1992. Prosodic morphology in four Chinese dialects. *Journal of East Asian Linguistics* 1:1.

CSLI Publications

CSLI Publications are distributed world-wide by Cambridge University Press unless otherwise noted.

Lecture Notes

A Manual of Intensional Logic. van Benthem, 2nd edition. No. 1. 0-937073-29-6 (paper), 0-937073-30-X

Lectures on Contemporary Syntactic Theories. Sells. No. 3. 0-937073-14-8 (paper), 0-937073-13-X

The Semantics of Destructive Lisp. Mason. No. 5. 0-937073-06-7 (paper), 0-937073-05-9

An Essay on Facts. Olson. No. 6. 0-937073-08-3 (paper), 0-937073-05-9

Logics of Time and Computation. Goldblatt, 2nd edition. No. 7. 0-937073-94-6 (paper), 0-937073-93-8

Word Order and Constituent Structure in German. Uszkoreit. No. 8. 0-937073-10-5 (paper), 0-937073-09-1

Color and Color Perception: A Study in Anthropocentric Realism. Hilbert. No. 9. 0-937073-16-4 (paper), 0-937073-15-6

Prolog and Natural-Language Analysis. Pereira and Shieber. No. 10. 0-937073-18-0 (paper), 0-937073-17-2

Working Papers in Grammatical Theory and Discourse Structure: Interactions of Morphology, Syntax, and Discourse. Iida, Wechsler, and Zec (Eds.). No. 11. 0-937073-04-0 (paper), 0-937073-25-3

Natural Language Processing in the 1980s: A Bibliography. Gazdar, Franz, Osborne, and Evans. No. 12. 0-937073-28-8 (paper), 0-937073-26-1

Information-Based Syntax and Semantics. Pollard and Sag. No. 13. 0-937073-24-5 (paper), 0-937073-23-7

Non-Well-Founded Sets. Aczel. No. 14. 0-937073-22-9 (paper), 0-937073-21-0

Partiality, Truth and Persistence. Langholm. No. 15. 0-937073-34-2 (paper), 0-937073-35-0

Attribute-Value Logic and the Theory of Grammar. Johnson. No. 16. 0-937073-36-9 (paper), 0-937073-37-7

The Situation in Logic. Barwise. No. 17. 0-937073-32-6 (paper), 0-937073-33-4

The Linguistics of Punctuation. Nunberg. No. 18. 0-937073-46-6 (paper), 0-937073-47-4

Anaphora and Quantification in Situation Semantics. Gawron and Peters. No. 19. 0-937073-48-4 (paper), 0-937073-49-0

Propositional Attitudes: The Role of Content in Logic, Language, and Mind. Anderson and Owens. No. 20. 0-937073-50-4 (paper), 0-937073-51-2

Literature and Cognition. Hobbs. No. 21. 0-937073-52-0 (paper), 0-937073-53-9

Situation Theory and Its Applications, Vol. 1. Cooper, Mukai, and Perry (Eds.). No. 22. 0-937073-54-7 (paper), 0-937073-55-5

The Language of First-Order Logic (including the Macintosh program, Tarski's World 4.0). Barwise and Etchemendy, 3rd Edition. No. 23. 0-937073-99-7 (paper)

Lexical Matters. Sag and Szabolcsi (Eds.). No. 24. 0-937073-66-0 (paper), 0-937073-65-2

Tarski's World: Macintosh Version 4.0. Barwise and Etchemendy. No. 25. 1-881526-27-5 (paper)

Situation Theory and Its Applications, Vol. 2. Barwise, Gawron, Plotkin, and Tutiya (Eds.). No. 26. 0-937073-70-9 (paper), 0-937073-71-7

Literate Programming. Knuth. No. 27. 0-937073-80-6 (paper), 0-937073-81-4

Normalization, Cut-Elimination and the Theory of Proofs. Ungar. No. 28. 0-937073-82-2 (paper), 0-937073-83-0

Lectures on Linear Logic. Troelstra. No. 29. 0-937073-77-6 (paper), 0-937073-78-4

A Short Introduction to Modal Logic. Mints. No. 30. 0-937073-75-X (paper), 0-937073-76-8

Linguistic Individuals. Ojeda. No. 31. 0-937073-84-9 (paper), 0-937073-85-7

Computational Models of American Speech. Withgott and Chen. No. 32. 0-937073-98-9 (paper), 0-937073-97-0

Verbmobil: A Translation System for Face-to-Face Dialog. Kay, Gawron, and Norvig. No. 33. 0-937073-95-4 (paper), 0-937073-96-2

The Language of First-Order Logic (including the Windows program, Tarski's World 4.0). Barwise and Etchemendy, 3rd edition. No. 34. 0-937073-90-3 (paper)

Turing's World. Barwise and Etchemendy. No. 35. 1-881526-10-0 (paper)

The Syntax of Anaphoric Binding. Dalrymple. No. 36. 1-881526-06-2 (paper), 1-881526-07-0

Situation Theory and Its Applications, Vol. 3. Aczel, Israel, Katagiri, and Peters (Eds.). No. 37. 1-881526-08-9 (paper), 1-881526-09-7

Theoretical Aspects of Bantu Grammar. Mchombo (Ed.). No. 38. 0-937073-72-5 (paper), 0-937073-73-3

Logic and Representation. Moore. No. 39. 1-881526-15-1 (paper), 1-881526-16-X

Words and the Grammar of Context. Kay. No. 40. 1-881526-17-8 (paper), 1-881526-18-6

Language and Learning for Robots. Crangle and Suppes. No. 41. 1-881526-19-4 (paper), 1-881526-20-8

Hyperproof. Barwise and Etchemendy. No. 42. 1-881526-11-9 (paper)

Mathematics of Modality. Goldblatt. No. 43. 1-881526-23-2 (paper), 1-881526-24-0

Feature Logics, Infinitary Descriptions, and Grammar. Keller. No. 44. 1-881526-25-9 (paper), 1-881526-26-7

Tarski's World: Windows Version 4.0. Barwise and Etchemendy. No. 45. 1-881526-28-3 (paper)

German in Head-Driven Phrase Structure Grammar. Pollard, Nerbonne, and Netter. No. 46. 1-881526-29-1 (paper), 1-881526-30-5

Formal Issues in Lexical-Functional Grammar. Dalrymple and Zaenen. No. 47. 1-881526-36-4 (paper), 1-881526-37-2

Dynamics, Polarity, and Quantification. Kanazawa and Piñón. No. 48. 1-881526-41-0 (paper), 1-881526-42-9

Defending AI Research: A Collection of Essays and Reviews. McCarthy. No. 49. 1-57586-018-X (paper), 1-57586-019-8

Theoretical Perspectives on Word Order in South Asian Languages. Butt, King, and Ramchand. No. 50. 1-881526-49-6 (paper), 1-881526-50-X

Perspectives in Phonology. Cole and Kisseberth. No. 51. 1-881526-54-2 (paper), 1-881526-55-0

Linguistics and Computation. Cole, Green, and Morgan. No. 52. 1-881526-81-X (paper), 1-881526-82-8

Modal Logic and Process Algebra: A Bisimulation Approach. Ponse, de Rijke, and Venema. No. 53. 1-881526-96-8 (paper), 1-881526-95-X

Quantifiers, Logic, and Language. van der Does and van Eijck. No. 54. 1-57586-000-7 (paper), 1-57586-001-5

Semantic Ambiguity and Underspecification. van Deemter and Peters. No. 55. 1-57586-028-7 (paper), 1-57586-029-5

Necessity or Contingency. Vuillemin. No. 56. 1-881526-85-2 (paper), 1-881526-86-0

Quantifiers, Deduction, and Context. Kanazawa, Piñón, & de Swart. No. 57. 1-57586-005-8 (paper), 1-57586-004-X

Logic, Language and Computation. Seligman & Westerståhl. No. 58. 1-881526-89-5 (paper), 1-881526-90-9

Selected Papers on Computer Science. Knuth. No. 59. 1-881526-917 (paper), 1-881526-925

Vicious Circles. Barwise & Moss. No. 60. 1-57586-008-2 (paper), 1-57586-009-0

Approaching Second. Halpern & Zwicky. No. 61. 1-57586-014-7 (paper), 1-57586-015-5

The Role of Argument Structure in Grammar. Alsina. No. 62. 1-57586-034-1 (paper), 1-57586-035-X

Complex Predicates. Alsina, Bresnan, & Sells. No. 64. 1-57586-046-5 (paper), 1-57586-047-3

Lectures on Deixis. Fillmore. No. 65. 1-57586-046-5 (paper), 1-57586-047-3

Language at Work. Devlin & Rosenberg. No. 66. 1-57586-051-1 (paper), 1-57586-050-3

Practical Guide to Syntactic Analysis.
Green & Morgan. No. 67.
1-57586-016-3 (paper), 1-57586-017-1

Direct Reference, Indexicality, and Propositional Attitudes. Künne, Newen, and Anduschus. No. 70.
1-57586-070-8 (paper), 1-57586-071-6

Ambiguity Resolution in Language Learning. Schütze. No. 71.
1-57586-074-0 (paper), 1-57586-075-9

Nonmonotonic Reasoning: An Overview. Brewka, Dix, & Konolige. No. 73.
1-881526-83-6 (paper), 1-881526-84-4

Dissertations in Linguistics Series

Phrase Structure and Grammatical Relations in Tagalog. Kroeger.
0-937073-86-5 (paper), 0-937073-87-3

Theoretical Aspects of Kashaya Phonology and Morphology. Buckley.
1-881526-02-X (paper), 1-881526-03-8

Argument Structure in Hindi. Mohanan.
1-881526-43-7 (paper), 1-881526-44-5

On the Placement and Morphology of Clitics. Halpern. 1-881526-60-7 (paper), 1-881526-61-5

The Structure of Complex Predicates in Urdu. Butt. 1-881526-59-3 (paper), 1-881526-58-5

Configuring Topic and Focus in Russian. King. 1-881526-63-1 (paper), 1-881562-62-3

The Semantic Basis of Argument Structure. Wechsler. 1-881526-68-2 (paper), 1-881562-69-0

Stricture in Feature Geometry. Padgett.
1-881526-66-6 (paper), 1-881562-67-4

Possessive Descriptions. Barker.
1-881526-72-0 (paper), 1-881562-73-9

Context and Binding in Japanese. Iida.
1-881526-74-7 (paper), 1-881526-75-5

Ergativity. Manning. 1-57586-036-8 (paper), 1-57586-037-6

The Geometry of Visual Phonology. Uyechi. 1-57586-012-0 (paper), 1-57586-013-9

Studies in Logic, Language and Information

Logic Colloquium '92. Csirmaz, Gabbay, and de Rijke (Eds.). 1-881526-98-4 (paper), 1-881526-97-6

Meaning and Partiality. Muskens.
1-881526-79-8 (paper), 1-881526-80-1

Logic and Visual Information. Hammer.
1-881526-99-2 (paper), 1-881526-87-9

Partiality, Modality and Nonmonotonicity. Doherty.
1-57586-030-9 (paper), 1-57586-031-7

Basic Model Theory. Doets.
1-57586-048-1 (paper), 1-57586-049-X

Principles of Knowledge Representation. Brewka. 1-57586-057-0 (paper), 1-57586-056-2

An Essay on Contraction. Fuhrmann.
1-57586-054-6 (paper), 1-57586-055-4

Arrow Logic and Multi-Modal Logic. Marx, Pólos, and Masuch.
1-57586-025-2 (paper), 1-57586-024-4

Exploring Logical Dynamics. van Benthem. 1-57586-059-7 (paper), 1-57586-058-9

Specifying Syntactic Structures. Blackburn and de Rijke. 1-57586-085-6 (paper), 1-57586-084-8

Studies in Japanese Linguistics

The Syntax of Subjects. Tateishi.
1-881526-45-3 (paper), 1-881526-46-1

Theory of Projection in Syntax. Fukui.
1-881526-34-8 (paper), 1-881526-35-6

A Study of Japanese Clause Linkage: The Connective TE in Japanese. Hasegawa. 1-57586-026-0 (paper), 1-57586-027-9

Complex Predicates in Japanese: A Syntactic and Semantic Study of the Notion 'Word'. Matsumoto.
1-57586-060-0 (paper), 1-57586-061-9

Stanford Monographs in African Languages

The Structure of Dagaare. Bodomo.
1-57586-076-7 (paper),

A Paradigmatic Grammar of Gĩkũyũ. Mugane. 1-57586-077-5 (paper),

Other CSLI Titles Distributed by Cambridge University Press

The Proceedings of the Twenty-Fourth Annual Child Language Research Forum. Clark (Ed.). 1-881526-05-4 (paper), 1-881526-04-6

The Proceedings of the Twenty-Fifth Annual Child Language Research Forum. Clark (Ed.). 1-881526-31-3 (paper), 1-881526-33-X

The Proceedings of the Twenty-Sixth Annual Child Language Research Forum. Clark (Ed.). 1-881526-31-3 (paper), 1-881526-33-X

Japanese/Korean Linguistics. Hoji (Ed.). 0-937073-57-1 (paper), 0-937073-56-3

Japanese/Korean Linguistics, Vol. 2. Clancy (Ed.). 1-881526-13-5 (paper), 1-881526-14-3

Japanese/Korean Linguistics, Vol. 3. Choi (Ed.). 1-881526-21-6 (paper), 1-881526-22-4

Japanese/Korean Linguistics, Vol. 4. Akatsuka (Ed.). 1-881526-64-X (paper), 1-881526-65-8

Japanese/Korean Linguistics, Vol. 5. Akatasuka, Iwasaki, & Strauss (Eds.). 1-57586-044-9 (paper), 1-57586-045-7

The Proceedings of the Fourth West Coast Conference on Formal Linguistics (WCCFL 4). 0-937073-43-1 (paper)

The Proceedings of the Fifth West Coast Conference on Formal Linguistics (WCCFL 5). 0-937073-42-3 (paper)

The Proceedings of the Sixth West Coast Conference on Formal Linguistics (WCCFL 6). 0-937073-31-8 (paper)

The Proceedings of the Seventh West Coast Conference on Formal Linguistics (WCCFL 7). 0-937073-40-7 (paper)

The Proceedings of the Eighth West Coast Conference on Formal Linguistics (WCCFL 8). 0-937073-45-8 (paper)

The Proceedings of the Ninth West Coast Conference on Formal Linguistics (WCCFL 9). 0-937073-64-4 (paper)

The Proceedings of the Tenth West Coast Conference on Formal Linguistics (WCCFL 10). 0-937073-79-2 (paper)

The Proceedings of the Eleventh West Coast Conference on Formal Linguistics (WCCFL 11). Mead (Ed.). 1-881526-12-7 (paper),

The Proceedings of the Twelfth West Coast Conference on Formal Linguistics (WCCFL 12). Duncan, Farkas, Spaelti (Eds.). 1-881526-33-X (paper),

The Proceedings of the Thirteenth West Coast Conference on Formal Linguistics (WCCFL 13). Aranovich, Byrne, Preuss, Senturia (Eds.). 1-881526-76-3 (paper),

The Proceedings of the Fourteenth West Coast Conference on Formal Linguistics (WCCFL 14). Camacho, Choueri, & Watanabe (Eds.). 1-57586-042-2 (paper), 1-57586-043-0

The Proceedings of the Fifteenth West Coast Conference on Formal Linguistics (WCCFL 15). Agbayani & Tang (Eds.). 1-57586-078-3 (paper), 1-57586-079-1

European Review of Philosophy: Philosophy of Mind. Soldati (Ed.). 1-881526-38-0 (paper), 1-881526-53-4

European Review of Philosophy vol. 2: Cognitive Dynamics. Dokic (Ed.). 1-57586-072-4 (paper), 1-57586-073-2

Experiencer Subjects in South Asian Languages. Verma and Mohanan (Eds.). 0-937073-60-1 (paper), 0-937073-61-X

Grammatical Relations: A Cross-Theoretical Perspective. Dziwirek, Farrell, Bikandi (Eds.). 0-937073-63-6 (paper), 0-937073-62-8

Grammatical Relations: Theoretical Approaches to Empirical Questions. Burgess, Dziwirek, Gerdts, (Eds.). 1-57586-002-3 (paper), 1-57586-003-1

Theoretical Issues in Korean Linguistics. Kim-Renaud (Ed.). 1-881526-51-8 (paper), 1-881526-52-6

Agreement in Natural Language: Approaches, Theories, Descriptions. Barlow and Ferguson (Eds.). 0-937073-02-4

Papers from the Second International Workshop on Japanese Syntax. Poser (Ed.). 0-937073-38-5 (paper), 0-937073-39-3

Conceptual Structure, Discourse and Language. Goldberg, (Ed.).
1-57586-040-6 (paper), 1-57586-041-4

Sociolinguistic Variation. Arnold et al. (Eds.). 1-57586-038-4 (paper), 1-57586-039-2

The Media Equation. Reeves & Nass. 1-57586-052-7 (paper),

Ordering Titles from Cambridge University Press

Titles distributed by Cambridge University Press may be ordered directly from the distributor at 110 Midland Avenue, Port Chester, NY 10573-4930 (USA), or by phone: 914-937-9600, 1-800-872-7423 (US and Canada), 95-800-010-0200 (Mexico). You may also order by fax at 914-937-4712.

Overseas Orders

Cambridge University Press has offices worldwide which serve the international community.

Australia: Cambridge University Press, 120 Stamford Road, Oakleigh, Victoria 31266, Australia. phone: (613) 563-1517. fax: 613 563 1517.

UK, Europe, Asia, Africa, South America: Cambridge University Press, Publishing Division, The Edinburgh Building, Shaftesbury Road, Cambridge CB2 2RU, UK.
Inquiries: (phone) 44 1223 312393 (fax) 44 1223 315052
Orders: (phone) 44 1223 325970 (fax) 44 1223 325959

CSLI Titles Distributed by The University of Chicago Press

The Phonology-Syntax Connection. Inkelas and Zec. 0-226-38100-5 (paper), 0-226-38101-3

On What We Know We Don't Know. Bromberger. 0-226-07540-0 (paper), 0-226-07539-7

Arenas of Language Use. Clark. 0-226-10782-5 (paper), 0-226-10781-7

Head-Driven Phrase Structure Grammar. Pollard and Sag. 0-226-67447-9 (paper)

Titles distributed by The University of Chicago Press may be ordered directly from UCP. Phone 1-800-621-2736. Fax (800) 621-8471.

Titles distributed by The University of Chicago Press may be ordered directly from UCP. Phone 1-800-621-2736. Fax (800) 621-8471.

Overseas Orders

The University of Chicago Press has offices worldwide which serve the international community.

Mexico, Central America, South America, and the Caribbean (including Puerto Rico): EDIREP, 5500 Ridge Oak Drive, Austin, Texas 78731 U. S. A. Telephone: (512) 451-4464. Facsimile: (512) 451-4464.

United Kingdom and Europe: (VAT is added where applicable.) International Book Distributors, Ltd., Campus 400, Maylands Avenue, Hemel Hempstead HP2 7EZ, England. Telephone: 0442 881900/Telex: 82445. Facsimile: 0442 882099. Internet: 536-2875@MCIMAIL.COM

Australia, New Zealand, South Pacific, Africa, Middle East, China (PRC), Southeast Asia, and India: The University of Chicago Press, International Sales Manager, 5801 South Ellis Avenue, Chicago, Illinois 60637 U.S.A. Telephone: (312)702-7706. Facsimile: (312)702-9756.
Internet: dblobaum@press.uchicago.edu

Japan: Libraries and individuals should place their orders with local booksellers. Booksellers should place orders with our agent: United Publishers Services, Ltd., Kenkyu-sha Building, 9 Kanda Surugadai 2-chome, Chiyoda-ku, Tokyo, Japan. Telephone: (03)3291-4541. Facsimile: (03)3293-8610. Telex: J33331 (answerback UPSTOKYO). Cable: UNITEDBOOKS TOKYO.

Korea, Hong Kong, and Taiwan, R.O.C.: The America University Press Group, 3-21-18-206 Higashi-Shinagawa, Shinagawa-ku, Tokyo 140, Japan. Telephone: (03)3450-2857. Facsimile: (03)3472-9706.

CSLI Titles Distributed by CSLI Publications

Hausar Yau Da Kullum: Intermediate and Advanced Lessons in Hausa Language and Culture. Leben, Zaria, Maikafi, and Yalwa. 0-937073-68-7 (paper)

Hausar Yau Da Kullum Workbook. Leben, Zaria, Maikafi, and Yalwa. 0-93703-69-5 (paper)

Ordering Titles Distributed by CSLI

Titles distributed by CSLI may be ordered directly from CSLI Publications, Ventura Hall, Stanford, CA 94305-4115. Orders can also be placed by FAX (415)723-0758 or e-mail (pubs@csli.stanford.edu).

All orders must be prepaid by check or Visa or MasterCard (include card name, number, and expiration date). California residents add 8.25% sales tax. For shipping and handling, add $2.50 for first book and $0.75 for each additional book; $1.75 for first report and $0.25 for each additional report.

For overseas shipping, add $4.50 for first book and $2.25 for each additional book; $2.25 for first report and $0.75 for each additional report. All payments must be made in U.S. currency.

CSLI Publications on the World-Wide Web

Please visit CSLI Publications' World-Wide Web page at: http://csli-www.stanford.edu/publications/ for a complete and updated list of publications.

Internet Gopher Access: University of Chicago Press catalogs can be searched on-line by connecting to the University of Chicago Press gopher:

   press-gopher.uchicago.edu